T0323862

Social Enterprise in Latin America

In the absence of a widely accepted and common definition of social enterprise (SE), a large research project, the "International Comparative Social Enterprise Models" (ICSEM) Project, was carried out over a five-year period; it involved more than 200 researchers from 55 countries and relied on bottom-up approaches to capture the SE phenomenon. This strategy made it possible to take into account and give legitimacy to locally embedded approaches, thus resulting in an analysis encompassing a wide diversity of social enterprises, while simultaneously allowing for the identification of major SE models to delineate the field on common grounds at the international level.

These SE models reveal or confirm an overall trend towards new ways of sharing the responsibility for the common good in today's economies and societies. We tend to consider as good news the fact that social enterprises actually stem from all parts of the economy. Indeed, societies are facing many complex challenges at all levels, from the local to the global level. The diversity and internal variety of SE models are a sign of a broadly shared willingness to develop appropriate—although sometimes embryonic—responses to these challenges, on the basis of innovative economic/business models driven by a social mission. In spite of their weaknesses, social enterprises may be seen as advocates for and vehicles of the general interest across the whole economy. Of course, the debate about privatisation, deregulation and globalised market competition—all factors that may hinder efforts in the search for the common good—has to be addressed as well.

The second of a series of four ICSEM books, *Social Enterprise in Latin America* will serve as a key reference and resource for teachers, researchers, students, experts, policymakers, journalists and other categories of people who want to acquire a broad understanding of the phenomena of social enterprise and social entrepreneurship as they emerge and develop across the world.

Luiz Inácio Gaiger is a full professor at Universidade do Vale do Rio dos Sinos (Unisinos, Brazil). He holds a Master of Science and a PhD in Sociology from the Catholic University of Louvain (Belgium).

Marthe Nyssens is a full professor at the School of Economics of the Catholic University of Louvain (UCLouvain, Belgium) and a member of the Interdisciplinary Research Centre on Work, State and Society (CIRTES, UCLouvain).

Fernanda Wanderley obtained her PhD in Sociology from Columbia University in the City of New York (US). She is the director of the Institute of Socio-Economic Research (IISEC) of the Bolivian Catholic University "San Pablo".

Routledge Studies in Social Enterprise & Social Innovation
Series Editors: Jacques Defourny, Lars Hulgård, and Rocio Nogales

Social enterprises seek to combine an entrepreneurial spirit and behaviour with the primacy of social or societal aims. To various extents, their production of goods or services generates market income, which they usually combine with other types of resources. A social innovation consists in the implementation of a new idea or initiative to change society in a fairer and more sustainable direction.

Routledge Studies in Social Enterprise & Social Innovation seeks to examine and promote these increasingly important research themes. It particularly looks at participatory governance and social-innovation dynamics in social enterprises and more widely in partnerships involving third-sector and civil-society organisations, conventional businesses and public authorities. In such perspective, this series aims to publish both breakthrough contributions exploring the new frontiers of the field as well as books defining the state of the art and paving the way to advance the field.

For a full list of titles in this series, please visit www.routledge.com

Social Enterprise in Latin America

Theory, Models and Practice

Edited by Luiz Inácio Gaiger, Marthe Nyssens and Fernanda Wanderley

Routledge
Taylor & Francis Group

NEW YORK AND LONDON

First published 2019
by Routledge
605 Third Avenue, New York, NY 10017

and by Routledge
2 Park Square, Milton Park, Abingdon, Oxon, OX14 4RN

First issued in paperback 2021

Routledge is an imprint of the Taylor & Francis Group, an informa business

© 2019 Taylor & Francis

The right of Luiz Inácio Gaiger, Marthe Nyssens and Fernanda Wanderley to be identified as the authors of the editorial material, and of the authors for their individual chapters, has been asserted in accordance with sections 77 and 78 of the Copyright, Designs and Patents Act 1988.

Library of Congress Cataloging-in-Publication Data
Names: Gaiger, Luiz Inâacio Germany, editor. | Nyssens, Marthe, editor. | Wanderley, Fernanda, editor.
Title: Social enterprise in Latin America : theory, models and practice / edited by Luiz Inâacio Gaiger, Marthe Nyssens and Fernanda Wanderley.
Description: New York : Routledge, 2019. | Series: Routledge studies in social enterprise & social innovation | Includes index.
Identifiers: LCCN 2019008369 | ISBN 9780367151195 (hardback) | ISBN 9780429055164 (ebook)
Subjects: LCSH: Social entrepreneurship—Latin America—Case studies.
Classification: LCC HD60.5.L29 S623 2019 | DDC 658.4/08098—dc23
LC record available at https://lccn.loc.gov/2019008369

ISBN 13: 978-0-367-67571-4 (pbk)
ISBN 13: 978-0-367-15119-5 (hbk)

DOI: 10.4324/9780429055164

Contents

Tables

Figures

Preface and Acknowledgements

This book is part of a series of four volumes produced under the International Comparative Social-Enterprise Models (ICSEM) Project and focusing respectively on Asia, Latin America, Western Europe and Eastern Europe. Various countries not belonging to these major regions were also covered by the Project; the contributions linked to these countries have been published in a special issue of the *Social Enterprise Journal*.[1]

Launched in July 2013, the ICSEM Project[2] is the result of a partnership between an "Interuniversity Attraction Pole on Social Enterprise" (IAP-SOCENT), funded by the Belgian Science Policy (BELSPO), and the EMES International Research Network. Over five years, it gathered around 230 researchers from some 55 countries across the world to document and analyse the diversity of social-enterprise models and their ecosystems.

First and foremost, the production of these volumes relied on the efforts and commitment of local ICSEM Research Partners. It was also enriched through discussion in the framework of Local ICSEM Talks in various countries, Regional ICSEM Symposiums and Global ICSEM Meetings held alongside EMES International Conferences on Social Enterprise. We are grateful to all those who contributed, in one way or another, to these various events and achievements of the Project.

All ICSEM-related publications also owe much to the outstanding editorial work of Sophie Adam, Coordination Assistant, to whom we express special thanks. We are also grateful to Elisabetta Severi, who provided a

---

1 Defourny, J. and Nyssens, M. (eds) (2017) "Mapping Social Enterprise Models: an International Perspective", *Social Enterprise Journal*, Vol. 13, No. 4. The following countries were covered in this issue: Australia, New Zealand, Israel, the United Arab Emirates, Rwanda and South Africa. A contribution about the United States was published, together with contributions about work-integration social enterprises in Japan, Ireland and Switzerland, in a special issue of another journal (Cooney, K. and Nyssens, M. [eds] [2016] "Work Integration Social Enterprises", *Nonprofit Policy Forum*, Vol. 7, No. 4).

2 www.iap-socent.be/icsem-project

valuable assistance in the cleaning of the data collected through a common questionnaire in most countries.

We also want to express warm thanks to BELSPO and to our Supporting Partners, the "Fondation Crédit Coopératif" and the "Groupe Caisse des Dépôts" (France) as well as the "Baillet Latour Fund" (Belgium), for their crucial financial support.

Jacques Defourny and Marthe Nyssens
Scientific Coordinators of the ICSEM Project

Editors and Contributors

Editors

Luiz Inácio Gaiger

Luiz Inácio Gaiger is a full professor at Universidade do Vale do Rio dos Sinos (Unisinos, Brazil). He holds a Master of Science and a PhD in Sociology from the Catholic University of Louvain (Belgium). Since 2000, he has been a researcher for the Brazilian National Research Council (CNPq). At Unisinos, he has been the General Research Director (1998–2003) and coordinator of the UNESCO Chair Work and Solidary Society (2005–2014). He has also been a member of the board of directors of the Brazilian Society of Sociology (2009–2011). He has research experience in citizen participation, social movements, solidarity economy and social entrepreneurship. He coordinated the first national Brazilian research project on the solidarity economy, supported by the Interuniversity Network UNITRABALHO, where he was also involved in the coordination of the Solidarity Economy Programme. He coordinates, with José Luis Coraggio (UNGS, Argentina), the Network of Latin American Researchers on the Social and Solidarity Economy (RILESS), and he is co-director of the *Otra Economía* journal.

Marthe Nyssens

Marthe Nyssens is a full professor at the School of Economics of the Catholic University of Louvain (UCLouvain, Belgium) and a member of the Interdisciplinary Research Centre on Work, State and Society (CIRTES, UCLouvain). She acts as the scientific coordinator, together with Jacques Defourny, of the "International Comparative Social Enterprise Models (ICSEM) Project". She was a founding member and is currently the president of the EMES International Research Network and the chair of the COST action "Empowering the next generation of SE scholars". She holds a Master in Economics (University of California at San Diego, US) and a PhD in Economics (UCLouvain). Her research work focuses on conceptual approaches to the third sector, both in developed and developing countries, as well as on the links between third-sector organisations and public policies. Her research deals with socio-economic logics of "not-for-profit organisations"; she analyses the role of these organisations and their relations with public policies, the market and civil society in fields such as work integration, care or the commons.

Fernanda Wanderley

Fernanda Wanderley obtained her PhD in Sociology from Columbia University in the City of New York (US). She is the director of the Institute of Socio-Economic Research (IISEC) of the Bolivian Catholic University "San Pablo". She has been a visiting professor at the University of Pádua (Italy) and at the University of Gothemburg (Sweden), and a consultant for the International Labour Organisation (ILO) and the United Nations Development Programme (UNDP). Her areas of interest are inclusive and sustainable development, public policies, labour market and inequalities and poverty. Her research themes are the care economy; the plural, social and solidarity economy; and feminist economy. She has published books, book chapters, refereed academic articles and working documents on these topics.

Contributors

Olivier Brolis

Olivier Brolis holds a PhD in Economics and Management Science; he is a lecturer and researcher affiliated with the CIRTES, Catholic University of Louvain, and the CES, University of Liege (Belgium). His research focuses *inter alia* on the impact of organisations' mission on job quality, organisational performance, discrimination and motivation at work, on the digitalisation process of social enterprises, on modelling social enterprises, and on public policies evaluation regarding quality of jobs and services in the proximity services industry.

Susy Caballero

Susy Caballero holds a Master of Science in International Development Studies of University of Amsterdam (UvA, the Netherlands) and a Bachelor of Business Administration of Universidad del Pacifico (UP, Peru). She has founded two social enterprises, did research about the topic in Peru and lecture courses about it at UP and at Pontificia Universidad Católica del Perú (PUCP). Her areas of interest are sustainable development, climate change, education and social entrepreneurship, and her research topics are social enterprise and CSR.

Genauto Carvalho de França Filho

Genauto Carvalho de França Filho is a full professor at Universidade Federal da Bahia (UFBA, Brazil), where he coordinates an incubator programme for solidarity economy and territorial development (ITES). He holds a MSc in Administration from the UFBA and a PhD in Sociology from the Université Paris VII (France). Since 2009, he has been a researcher for the Brazilian National Research Council

(CNPq). He has research experience in solidarity economy, social management, local development, social innovation, solidarity finance and social currencies.

Carola Conde Bonfil

Carola Conde Bonfil is a full-time researcher at the Universidad Autónoma Metropolitana Xochimilco (Mexico). She obtained her Master's degree in Public Administration from the Centro de Investigación y Docencia Económicas (CIDE, Mexico) and her PhD in Economic Sciences from the Universidad Autónoma Metropolitana Iztapalapa (Mexico). She is the author of six books and (co-)editor of four others; she has also published twenty-eight book chapters and twenty peer-reviewed articles on microfinance, public policy, social economy and gender issues.

Paulo Cruz Filho

Paulo R. A. Cruz Filho obtained his PhD in Strategic Management of Social Enterprises from the Université du Québec à Montréal (UQAM, Canada). He is a professor of strategy, leadership and social impact at FAE Business School (Brazil). He is involved in the development of individuals and organisations for a more conscious, inclusive and integral society. He is the co-leader of the B Corps Community of Curitiba and a member of the Network of Latin American Researchers on the Social and Solidarity Economy (RILESS).

Jacques Defourny

Jacques Defourny is a professor of non-profit and cooperative economics and comparative economic systems at HEC Liege—Management School of the University of Liège. He is the founder and director of the Centre for Social Economy (ULiège). He was also the founding coordinator and the first president of the EMES Network, and he is one of the scientific coordinators of the ICSEM Project. His research interests focus on conceptual and theoretical approaches of the social economy in industrialised and developing countries.

Philippe Eynaud

Philippe Eynaud is currently a professor at Sorbonne business school, University Paris 1 Panthéon Sorbonne (France) and a researcher in GREGOR (IAE Paris, France). He has experience in non-profit management sciences. His research focuses on civil-society organisations, social innovation, democratic governance, the commons, platform cooperatives and the solidarity-based economy. He has participated in different collective books and has been co-editor for special issues in academic journals.

Adriane Ferrarini

Adriane Vieira Ferrarini is a full professor at Universidade do Vale do Rio dos Sinos (Unisinos, Brazil). She holds a PhD in Sociology from the

Federal University of Rio Grande do Sul (Brazil) and a doctoral intern-
ship at the Centre for Social Studies of the University of Coimbra (Portugal). She is a researcher for the Brazilian National Research Council
(CNPq) and the head of the research group on the Solidarity and Cooperative Economy. Her main research topics are solidarity economy,
social innovation, social policy and epistemologies of the South.

Sebastián Gatica

Sebastián Gatica is a commercial engineer from the Pontificia Universidad Católica de Chile (UC). He holds an MSc and a PhD from University College London (UK). He has worked throughout Latin America
on projects involving social enterprises and social innovation. He is an
Ashoka fellow *qua* co-founder of Travolution.org, a global network of
community-based tourism. He works as an academic at UC's School of
Management, where he has founded CoLab UC, a laboratory focused
on hybrid enterprises, social innovation and systemic change.

Michela Giovannini

Michela Giovannini is a Marie Sklodowska Curie fellow at the Centre
for Social Studies (CES) at the University of Coimbra (Portugal). She
holds a PhD in Local Development and Global Dynamics from the
University of Trento (Italy, 2014). Her research work and research
interests focus on social and solidarity-economy organisations in Latin
America and Europe, the political dimension of solidarity-economy
organisations in Spain and Portugal, indigenous socio-economic initiatives, social movements and community development.

Jean-Louis Laville

Jean-Louis Laville is a professor at the Conservatoire national des arts et
métiers (Cnam, Paris) and the head of the Chair of Solidarity Econ-
omy. He is involved in many international research networks. He is
the European coordinator for the *Karl Polanyi Institute of Political
Economy*, and a founding member of the EMES Network and of the
Network of Latin American Researchers on the Social and Solidarity
Economy (RILESS). He has written books that have been translated in
Italian, Portuguese, English, Spanish and Japanese.

Andreia Lemaître

Andreia Lemaître, PhD, is a socio-economist and a professor in development studies at UCLouvain (Belgium). She is a member of the Centre
for Development Studies and of the Interdisciplinary Research Centre
on Work, State and Society (UCLouvain). She coordinates the Interdisciplinary Research Group on Latin America and the Chair of Social
and Solidarity Economy in the South at UCLouvain. Her research
focuses on the popular and solidarity-based economy, on its institutional paths and on substantive approaches to the economy.

Luciane Lucas dos Santos

Luciane Lucas dos Santos is a senior researcher at the Centre for Social Studies of the University of Coimbra (Portugal), where she co-coordinates the Research Group on Democracy, Citizenship and Law. She holds a PhD in Communication and Culture from the Federal University of Rio de Janeiro (Brazil, 2004). She has worked as a senior lecturer for almost twenty years in various universities. Her research interests are postcolonial studies on consumption and economics, feminist economics and the social and solidarity economy.

Pablo Nachar-Calderón

Pablo Nachar-Calderón is a professor in the Department of Business Management at the University Diego Portales (Chile). He holds a PhD in Economy and Management of Organisations from the University of Zaragoza (Spain, 2013). His research focuses on governance structures, cooperatives and viable systems, individual behaviour in economic decision-making processes, social-impact measurement and CSR. His teaching focuses on economic theory of the firm, strategic formulation and management control systems.

Leïla Oulhaj

Leïla Oulhaj graduated as an economist (UCL, Belgium, 1993); she obtained a Postgraduate degree in Development Studies (UCL, 1994) and a Master's degree in Population, Environment and Development Studies (UCL, 1995). She is finishing her PhD in Latin American studies at the UNAM (Mexico, 2019). She has been a full-time researcher at the Universidad Iberoamericana (Mexico) since 2014. Her main fields of research are the social and solidarity economy (SSE) in Mexico, SSE and migration in a gender perspective and financial inclusion.

Sergio Páramo-Ortiz

Sergio Páramo-Ortiz is a PhD candidate from the University of York (UK). His research focuses on the different models of social enterprise in Mexico and the different forms of social innovation that these generate. His studies are fully funded by the National Council of Science and Technology of Mexico. He holds a Master's degree in Corporate Social Responsibility with Environmental Management from the University of York and a Bachelor's degree in Business Management from the National Autonomous University of Mexico.

María Angela Prialé

María Angela Prialé is an associate full-time professor and researcher at Universidad del Pacífico (UP, Peru); she lectures on strategic social responsibility, social entrepreneurship and inclusive business. She holds a Master in Developing and International Aid (Universidad Complutense—UCM, Spain), a degree in Business Administration

(UP) and a PhD in Government and Public Management (UCM). Her main research topics are social enterprise, sustainability, corporate responsibility, pedagogy in higher education and corruption.

María-José Ruiz-Rivera

María-José Ruiz-Rivera is a PhD candidate in development studies at the Interdisciplinary Research Centre on Work, State and Society at UCLouvain (Belgium). She holds a grant from the Chair of Social and Solidarity Economy in the South at UCLouvain. She previously worked in development and research projects of the governmental sector in Ecuador. Her research focuses on popular and solidarity economy in Latin America, especially on organisations' discourses and practices, institutionalisation, public policy and political embeddedness.

Gonzalo Vázquez

Gonzalo Vázquez obtained his Bachelor in Economics from the University of Buenos Aires (UBA) and his Master's degree in Social Economy from the Universidad Nacional de General Sarmiento (UNGS, Argentina). He is a researcher and professor of the Instituto del Conurbano (UNGS). His main areas of interest are related to the economic development of Latin American countries and to the experiences and theories of alternative economics, and his main research topics focus on worker cooperatives and popular-economy initiatives.

Marília Veríssimo Veronese

Marilia Verissimo Veronese obtained her a PhD in Social Psychology from the Pontifícia Universidade Católica do Rio Grande do Sul (PUCRS) in 2004. She is currently an associate researcher in the Research Group on Solidarity and Cooperative Economics (Grupo ECOSOL) at the Universidade do Vale do Rio dos Sinos (Unisinos, Brazil). She has experience in the areas of sociology and social psychology, and she is also active in the area of collective health.

Introduction

Social Enterprise in Latin America: Context and Concepts

Marthe Nyssens, Fernanda Wanderley and Luiz Inácio Gaiger

Numerous works have been carried out since the 1970s to grasp and describe the reality and the scope of so-called non-conventional economic initiatives and organisations in Latin American countries (Cattani *et al.* 2009; Gaiger 2009, 2017; Wanderley 2015, 2017). Most of the historical sources of these initiatives are to be found in the experiences of cooperativism and associativism in the region, while the most recent sources have been located, since the 1980s, in the expansion of new initiatives promoted, mainly, by marginalised popular groups in a context of high informality, such as income-generation groups, "soup kitchens" (*comedores populares*), organisations of the worker-cooperative or user-cooperative type, exchange networks, ecological production groups, indigenous and peasant production communities, and short and solidarity marketing circuits. More recently, SMEs driven by economic and social goals and promoted by professionals have started emerging in the landscape. A main challenge in this field of research is to better grasp the diversity of these "alternative" economic types.

Different generic terms have also been used to qualify these initiatives: informal economy, popular economy, solidarity economy, social economy, community economy, "labour economy", solidarity enterprises, social enterprises, etc. Faced with the variety of terms and concepts used within and across regions all over the world, the "International Comparative Social Enterprise Models (ICSEM) Project" adopted the generic concept of "social enterprise" (SE) to encompass the wide spectrum of organisations that combine an entrepreneurial dynamic to provide services or goods with the primacy of their social aims. This book presents the results of this worldwide research project for Latin America.

In this introductive chapter, we first present the objectives of the ICSEM Project. Then, we briefly describe the Latin American context that shapes the SE landscape, before describing the main concepts used in Latin America to analyse this kind of initiative. In the following section, we present the different SE schools of thought. Finally, the general structure of the book is presented.

DOI: 10.4324/9780429055164-1

1. The "ICSEM" Project

ICSEM was designed and undertaken with one main objective, namely to document the diversity of SE models as a way: (1) to overcome most problems related to the quest for a unifying and encompassing conceptualisation of social enterprise; (2) to show that it was feasible to theoretically and empirically build typologies of SE models; and, consequently, (3) to pave the way for a better understanding of SE dynamics and ecosystems. The ICSEM Project was based on the assumption that a solid and scientific comparative knowledge of social enterprise worldwide implied to analyse these organisations through a multilevel approach, combining the micro, macro and meso levels, and relying on empirical studies using a common methodological approach and common tools.

After a year devoted to preparing the basis for this worldwide comparative research project, under the auspices of the EMES International Research Network and within an "Interuniversity Attraction Pole on Social Enterprise" funded by the Belgian Science Policy Office (BELSPO), the ICSEM Project was officially presented and launched in early July 2013, just after the 4th EMES International Research Conference on Social Enterprise, held at the University of Liege (Belgium). From the outset, some 100 researchers from 25 countries decided to get involved and committed themselves to carrying out the proposed work over at least four years. Over the following twelve months, many other researchers joined the Project; in total, some 230 research partners from 55 countries and all regions of the world became part of the ICSEM research community. In Latin America, seven countries took part in this ambitious project, namely Argentina, Bolivia, Brazil, Chile, Ecuador, Mexico and Peru.

All the researchers involved in the project were first asked to provide a "country contribution" about the SE "phenomenon" or "landscape" in their respective countries. Each contribution had a threefold aim:

- First, it should help to understand concepts and contexts and to appreciate the use and the relevance of the notion of social enterprise in each country, the existence of alternative concepts, the interest of public authorities for social enterprise and the specific schemes that these authorities set up for their promotion and support.
- Secondly, it also aimed to map SE models, i.e. to identify and characterise the main categories of social enterprise as well as their fields of activity, social mission and target groups; the public or private supports from which they benefit; their operational and governance models; their stakeholders, etc.
- Finally, it should propose an analysis of "institutional trajectories" through the identification and description of the main "institutions" (at large) shaping the profile of social enterprises: legal frameworks

used by social enterprises, public policies and programmes, major financial supports or other tools such as norms or accreditations, federations of which social enterprises are members, private charters to which they subscribe, etc.

In order to make up for the lack of reliable datasets at enterprise level and to allow undertaking international comparative works, the second phase of the ICSEM Project aimed to collect in-depth information on social enterprises deemed emblematic of the different SE categories or models identified in the country contributions. In such a perspective, a common questionnaire was co-produced with all research partners and used by them to interview social-enterprise managers in their country. Although the actual number of interviews differed across countries, detailed data were collected in a rather homogenous way for 721 social enterprises from 43 countries. Needless to say, the database which resulted from this survey represents a key achievement of the ICSEM Project.

2. Understanding the Latin American Context Surrounding Social Enterprise

As social enterprises are often regarded as new strategies to tackle social and societal problems, in order to analyse social enterprise in Latin America countries, we have to better understand the main challenges these countries are facing as well as the contexts in which social enterprises operate. Social, economic and political differences between countries in Latin America are significant. However, given the territorial continuity, common historical roots, similarity of patterns and convergence of challenges that can be observed in the region, it appears to make sense to talk about a Latin American context. We present here the most important features for the development of social enterprise.

2.1. Economic Context

Latin America has an exceptional natural wealth, with extremely diverse biozones. The great potential of this natural wealth transcends the exploitation of minerals, hydrocarbons and food that has characterised Latin American economies from colonial times to the present. The gap between the abundance of natural resources and the low degree of diversification of production (such diversification, despite differences among countries, is overall only incipient) is a sign that the region has not yet achieved its full productive potential. The still enormous availability of natural resources (water, land, abundant fauna and flora) is thus a great opportunity to move towards sustainable development and social justice (Bovarnick *et al.* 2010). Social enterprises have an important role to play in facing this challenge.

At the beginning of the 21st century, in a global context of increased demand for renewable and non-renewable natural resources, the region's growth pattern, based on the export of raw materials with low added value, was strengthened. In this period, countries rich in natural resources—such as Latin American countries—positioned themselves at the centre of the dispute about access to and control over strategic raw materials (Rojas 2015). The "re-primarisation" of the economies in the recent boom period has made possible significant economic growth and improvements in social indicators. However, this pattern of growth resulted in the acceleration of depredation of environmental heritage and strong social conflicts. With the slowdown in the global economy since 2014, it has shown its fragility to maintain stable levels of growth and social achievements. Under these conditions, this pattern of growth cannot be envisaged as a long-term option.

Although, in general, Latin American countries took advantage of the external bonanza to promote economic growth and social welfare, development strategies and policies of appropriation and distribution of revenues derived from the exploitation of natural resources were not homogeneous. While the governments of Bolivia, Ecuador, Argentina and Brazil opted for more state control over the exploitation and commercialisation of natural resources by private foreign companies and implemented some redistribution of income with a view to reducing poverty, the governments of Chile, Peru and Mexico adopted a policy of liberalisation to attract direct foreign investment, especially in the extractive and agribusiness sectors. However, it is interesting to note that, despite these differences in terms of strategies and policies, all Latin American countries followed the dynamics of accumulation based on the extraction and export of primary goods (Carbonnier *et al.* 2017).

In Latin America, the challenge of productive diversification has been on the public-policy agenda for the past 70 years. The policies of import substitution ("import substitution industrialisation", or ISI) implemented in the region in the 20th century and the subsequent efforts have had different outcomes. Some countries progressed towards productive diversification while others lagged behind, but overall, Latin American countries' role as raw material suppliers in the global economy did not change (Meller 2013; CAF 2006). Mexico and Brazil are the most industrialised countries, and they are exporters of manufactured goods in the region; in addition, they have a large domestic market. At the other extreme, Bolivia and Ecuador are the least industrialised countries, with a less diversified export basket; they have also significantly smaller national markets. An interesting indicator to measure the divergences between countries in terms of productive diversification is the Economic Complexity Index (ECI), developed by the Centre for International Development at Harvard University:[1] based on this index, in 2016, Mexico ranked 21st; Brazil, 53rd; Chile, 64th; Argentina, 83rd; Peru, 94th; Bolivia, 109th and

Ecuador, 113th among 127 countries. For these countries to overcome their position as net suppliers of raw materials and their high reliance on short-term earnings, institutional transformations aiming at increased sustainability, solidarity and equity would have to be implemented. In this context, social enterprises are key actors to promote alternative trajectories of development.

2.2. Social and Labour Context

Since 1990, significant improvements in social indicators have been achieved by the majority of Latin American countries. Infant mortality fell, access to safe water increased, primary education became almost universal and life expectancy rose. In the beginning of the 21st century, all countries except Mexico also experienced a significant reduction of monetary poverty and inequality and an expansion of the middle class (Duryea and Robles 2016).

The literature points to three factors that can account for these improvements in the last decade. The most important factor was the increase of the labour income of the poorest workers, which was mainly due to favourable external conditions (high commodities prices and ample access to external financing that altered labour-market dynamics). The second factor was a set of improvements in social policies (income transfers to households, targeted social programmes and social security system's expansion). Demographic changes (fewer children and a higher share of working-age people in the overall population) constituted the third factor (UNDP 2016).

Despite these advances, Latin America remains the region with the highest level of inequality in the world. In fact, the region's Gini index is 4% higher than that of Africa, and 16% higher than the indices for Europe and Central Asia. Moreover, eleven of the twenty most unequal countries in the world are located in the region (Duryea and Robles 2016). There is much to be done; disparities in the quality of private and public education and health services (schools and hospitals) are still a major problem in a majority of countries in the region. Significant social inequalities by gender, ethnicity and class also persist (ECLAC 2017). Among the main barriers to overcome poverty and inequality, the regressive tax and transfer systems stand out in most countries (Lusting 2017).

Ocampo and Gómez-Arteaga (2017) identify three ideal-typical systems of social protection in the region. The first one is the strict universal system, with public-sector organisation, different degrees of decentralisation and variable levels of private provision, mainly in education and health services. The second one is the segmented and corporatist social security system in its broader sense (health, pensions and professional risks). The third one is the system based mainly on targeted schemes,

Table 0.1 Key economic and social indicators

Countries	TOTAL POPULATION (million of persons) 2018	GDP PER CAPITA, PPP (current international)* 2017	GDP PER CAPITA, PPP (constant 2011 international $)** 2017	GDP, PPP (constant 2011 international $)*** 2017	GROWTH RATE (annual %)**** 2017	UNEMPLOYMENT(%) 2017	HDI INDEX***** 2017	HDI RANK (189 countries) 2017	GINI COEFICIENT	POVERTY (less than 1.9 US per day in % of population) 2016	POVERTY (less than 3.2 US per day, in % of population) 2016	ECI (Economic Complexity Index; 127 countries) 2016
Argentina	[B] 44,522	[C] 20,786.7	[C] 18,934	[C] 838,223.78	[C] 2.86	[C] 8.5	[E] 0.825	47	[C] 0.424(2016)	[C] 0.58	[D] 2.4	[F] 83
Bolivia	[B] 11,235	[C] 7,559.6	[C] 6,886	[C] 76,099.42	[C] 4.2	[C] 3.1	[E] 0.693	118	[C] 0.446(2016)	[C] 7.07	[D1] 12.63	[F] 109
Brazil	[B] 212,814	[C] 15,483.5	[C] 14,103	[C] 2,951,687.08	[C] 0.98	[C] 13.3	[E] 0.759	79	[C] 0.513(2016)	[C] 3.4(2015)		[F] 53
Chile	[B] 18,349	[C] 24,635.0	[C] 22,767	[C] 411,052.62	[C] 1.49	[C] 7.0	[E] 0.843	44	[C] 0.477(2015)	[C] 2.5		[F] 64
Ecuador	[B] 16,863	[C] 11,617.4	[C] 10,582	[C] 175,923.19	[C] 2.3	[C] 3.8	[E] 0.752	86	[D] 0.452(2014)	[C] 3.58	[D] 9.4	[F] 113
Mexico	[B] 129,499	[C] 18,258.1	[C] 17,336	[C] 2,239,235.14	[C] 2.04	[C] 3.4	[E] 0.774	74	[C] 0.434(2015)	[C] 2.17	[D] 7.88	[F] 21
Peru	[B] 32,554	[C] 13,434.1	[C] 12,237	[C] 393,599.59	[C] 2.53	[C] 3.6	[E] 0.75	89	[C] 0.438(2016)	[C] 3.49	[D] 10.05	[F] 94
Latin America and the Caribbean	[A] 652,012	[C] 15,776.9	[C] 14,532	[C] 9,360,513.51	[C] 1.72	[C] 8.3	[E] 0.758		[D] 0.491(2014)	[C] 4.1 (2015)	[D] 10.05	

Sources:

[A] United Nations, Panorama de la Poblacion Mundial, 2017. Available HTTP: http://esa.un.org/unpd/wpp/index.htm
[B] Economic Commission for Latin America and the Caribbean (ECLAC), Database on population, 2017. Available HTTP: www.cepal.org/es
[C] World Bank. Available HTTP: https://data.worldbank.org
[D] Economic Commission for Latin America and the Caribbean (ECLAC), Countries' Household Surveys (BADEHOG).
[E] United Nations Development Programme (UNDP), Statistical Update Team, Human Development Indicators and Indices, 2018.
[F] Center for International Development (CID), Harvard University. Available HTTP: atlas.cid.harvard.edu/rankings/

Notes:

* GDP per capita based on purchasing power parity (PPP). Data are in current international dollars based on the 2011 1CP round.
** GDP per capita based on purchasing power parity (PPP). Data are in constant 2011 international dollars.
*** PPP GDP is the gross domestic product converted into international dollars based on purchasing-power-parity rates. Data are in constant 2011 international dollars.
**** Annual percentage growth rate of GDP at market prices based on constant local currency. Aggregates are based on constant 2010 US dollars.
***** HDI Index is a composite index measuring average achievement in three basic dimensions of human development: a long and healthy life, knowledge and a decent standard of living.

such as conditional transfer programmes. The most important common characteristic of these three systems is their lack of clearly designed social rights and citizenship entitlements, such as those usually associated to the old conceptions of the welfare state.[2] In fact, the development of a welfare state in Latin America has remained incomplete, even in the countries that have moved furthest in this direction, such as Argentina, Chile, Uruguay and Brazil. In other countries, the education, health and security systems developed later, in the second half of the 20th century, and they followed the model of formal employment (labour-capital relation), leading to the emergence of segmented and incomplete welfare states, with high levels of exclusion.

Within the paradigm of universalism in social policy linked to the concepts of social rights and social citizenship, Ocampo and Gómez-Arteaga (2017) built a "social-protection index" based on three dimensions: universality, solidarity and social spending. More specifically, the index measures the degree of coverage achieved by the health care and pensions protection systems, the coverage gap between wage-earners and non-wage-earners, and social spending and/or efficiency of social assistance. On the basis of this social-protection index, three groups were identified in terms of comprehensiveness and universality. Chile, Argentina and Brazil were identified as having comprehensive systems of social protection; Peru, Mexico and Ecuador, as countries with intermediate systems; and Bolivia, as having a relatively limited system. These authors also found that, between 2002 and 2012, Peru and Bolivia were among the countries that registered the strongest improvements in the social-protection-index score; they were followed by Argentina, Ecuador, Mexico, Brazil and Chile (in this order).

However, in the majority of countries, significant inequalities still remain in terms of access to and benefits offered by the social-protection system. Such inequalities are linked to the type of labour relation (salaried or non-salaried workers), gender and income level. This is particularly true in the countries belonging to the second and third groups. In general, the share of people benefiting from a protection system in the fields of health care and pensions is lower among non-salaried workers. This has great implications for social and solidarity enterprises. Indeed, they operate in contexts of limited systemic solidarity, materialised in non-universal social-protection systems. The high level of insecurity in terms of reproduction of life in contexts of strong social inequalities negatively affects social cohesion and puts great pressure on interpersonal solidarity.

It is important to notice that, in Latin America and the Caribbean, in 2016, non-salaried workers represented 29.3% of the urban workforce, whereas employees accounted for 63.4% of this workforce and domestic salaried workers, for 6.5%. The remaining 0.8% were classified under the "others" category (ILO 2017). The total of non-salaried workers

(29.3%) was distributed among employers (4.1%), own-account workers (23.6%) and contributing family workers (1.6%) (ILO 2017). These data concern, as specified above, the urban workforce; if non-salaried rural workers were taken into account, the proportion of non-salaried workers would be higher than 30%. Significant differences can be observed among countries, but these data show that, overall, the labour structure in Latin America is characterised by a significant proportion of non-salaried workers. Moreover, they are indicators of the importance of the diverse types of labour relations and economic units in Latin America.

Although a significant share of workers in the region work outside formal capital-labour relation, a model of social protection based on employment still dominates. This is one of the reasons accounting for the limited coverage of the social-protection system. The other reason is the high proportion of salaried workers whose employers do not comply with the legal obligations imposed by labour and social legislation. In the region, in 2016, only 63.5% of urban employed workers and 39.1% of rural employed workers were covered by health insurance (ILO 2017). In Latin America, the dominant public-policy approach to the problem of informality is still based on the view of homogeneous economic landscapes, populated by enterprises that only differ in size. However, this view has been questioned by academics, and it is refuted by abundant empirical evidence, presented in the present book, of the plurality of types of economic organisation operating in national economies. Therefore, informality should not be understood as a simple breach of legislation by a "general and flat informal economy". On the contrary, informality hides a universe of diverse economic organisations and dynamics, which would require legal and regulatory frameworks adapted to their specificities. The fact that this economic diversity is not sufficiently recognised and incorporated in the national institutional frameworks and public policies does not only result in these economic organisations' inability to comply with formal requirements and to cover the costs linked hereto; it also impedes their development and limits their social and economic contribution.

2.3. *Political Context*

From the 1980s onward, Latin America returned to political democracy after a period of military dictatorships. Although most countries supported the consolidation of formal democracies with competitive electoral regimes and guarantees of political rights, this transition hitherto remains an incomplete process, subject to setbacks. Indeed, citizen dissatisfaction with democracy has increased in recent years, as shown by Latinobarómetro (2018). While, in 1997, 63% of Latin Americans supported the democratic regime, this figure fell to 48% in 2018. The escalation of corruption scandals in several countries and the growing knowledge of public management problems are important factors that explain the loss of credibility of democracy in recent years. No less important in some countries is the presence of (both left-wing and right-wing) governments that threaten democratic principles and values such as transparent elections, press freedom and independence of the executive, legislative and judicial branches.

Such estrangement between citizens and public institutions has been observed for a few years in the majority of Latin American countries. Although this phenomenon is not specific to the region, some factors that explain it are. The social improvements registered in recent decades and the expansion of the middle class are consolidating societies that demand better public services and more efficient, reliable and innovative institutions. When these expectations are not met, they generate feelings of frustration and disenchantment. In effect, the region faces persistent problems, such as significant social inequalities by class, gender and ethnicity; continuity of pockets of poverty; high levels of informality and exclusion from social-protection systems; and an increase in crime rates and citizen insecurity.

The great challenge in Latin America is the strengthening of both formal democracy and substantive democracy. Due to their close articulation, one cannot exist without the other. SE initiatives and their proposals for political, social and economic reordering are very important to face this challenge. As can be seen from the various chapters of this book, the aspirations of social actors, the new entrepreneurial logics that integrate both social and economic objectives and the initiatives to build new legal and regulatory frameworks mobilise an important social energy and, consequently, strengthen political citizenship in its struggle to create paths towards inclusive and sustainable development.

3. Understanding the Plurality of Concepts Surrounding Latin American Social Enterprise

As explained in the introduction, several generic concepts and terms are used to identify what has been referred to within the ICSEM Project as "social enterprise". Moreover, the interpretative frameworks used to apprehend these alternative forms of economic units in Latin America changed over time and according to the place and to the type of actors using these terms: informal economy, popular economy, "labour economy", popular and solidarity economy, community economy or social economy (Cattani *et al.* 2009). One of the most important differences between these theoretical frameworks lies in the role given to these initiatives and organisations in society and economy.

3.1. From the Informal Economy to the Popular Economy

As the data above show, informality remains an important phenomenon in Latin America. An abundant literature and a broad debate on the causes and consequences of informality have developed in the last five decades. Different approaches and concepts—such as the "informal sector" and "informal economy"—were developed to cover heterogeneous forms of economic strategies and labour relations in a variety of situations, from that of informal salaried workers to that of non-salaried workers in family and small economic units. In the 1970s, beginning with the first study on Africa (ILO 1972), autonomous workers' units in Latin America were considered as resulting from the inability of capitalist development to generate wage employment for a fast-growing urban population. This population was considered to be particularly at risk of poverty and stagnation, due to their supposed inability to produce surpluses. An almost direct association between poverty and the informal sector was established; the concept of informal sector came to be understood in a sense that was very close to that of "marginality" proposed by Quijano (1974) and to the concept of "marginal mass" put forward by Nun (1969), under the Marxist paradigm of uneven capitalist development. In this perspective, the informal sector was considered as the generator of an army of reserve labour, consisting of workers who could not be absorbed by the modern sector of the economy. In the Latin American case, the marginalised would be the urban poor, mostly migrants, precapitalist artisans and domestic workers.

In the1980s and 1990s, other theories were developed. De Soto (1989) interpreted informality as the response of marginalised social groups which, due to legal and economic barriers, generate productive and commercial activities outside of state regulation. Portes and Castells (1989) and Portes and Schauffler (1993) developed the perspective of structural articulation, which characterises informality as a universe of income-generation activities not regulated by the state and integrated into unified systems composed of networks of dense relations between formal and informal enterprises, mainly through subcontracting. In such perspective, informal economic units fulfil functions of support to formal enterprises, *inter alia* thanks to the fact that they escape labour regulations.

One of the main criticisms levelled at literature about informality points at its inability to understand the activities carried out by workers on their own terms, making invisible the types of work organisation, management modalities, and motivations and expectations of the actors. Such criticisms built the basis for the concept of "popular economy", which emerged in the 1980s. The popular economy is composed of a diversity of initiatives promoted by the popular classes and constituting alternatives to salaried work. Family relationships and primary solidarities, which fulfil reproductive functions of life, are central characteristics of these activities. The change of focus brought about by the popular-economy perspective is radical and allows for a deeper understanding of the broader economic, social and political dynamics and implications of informality and the popular economy (Wanderley 1999; Gaiger 2018).

The concept of popular economy evolved to reinterpret the set of economic activities and social practices developed by subjects belonging to the working class through the use of their own labour force and mobilisation of scarce resources. It came to define a way of producing, distributing and consuming goods and services that transcends the goal of obtaining monetary gains. The popular economy is associated to the logic of reproduction of life (and not of capital) in the sense of the satisfaction of values of use and the valorisation of work and of human beings (Icaza and Tiriba 2009: 150).

A set of adjectives often accompany the concept of popular economy. The notion of "popular economy of solidarity", or "popular solidarity economy", accounts for the collective forms of organisation whose political project is supporting the implementation of the principle of solidarity. One of the first to refer to the concept of popular solidarity economy was Luis Razeto. This author found that, in scenarios of precariousness and systemic insecurity, autonomous work organisation experiences, associative and community-work initiatives, workers' cooperatives, as well as initiatives that pursue common benefits or benefits for third parties emerge. The situation of deprivation, according to Razeto (1988), favours the association, complementation and active and direct cooperation among people who have scarce resources, generating bonds of solidarity. A solidary economic rationality and a transforming energy emerge from their ways of being and acting. It is in this context that the concept of popular economy was born, in association with the concept of solidarity economy.

Self-managed workers units were reinterpreted in light of these new approaches as non-capitalist experiences whose development is not only possible but also contains an emancipating and counter-hegemonic potential. These experiences would point at a possible other mode of production—an alternative to capitalism. Its specific rationality (subsistence, production of use value, simple or extended reproduction)[3] ceases to be understood as "pre-capitalist" to become regarded as "anti-capitalist". This interpretive change is observed in Quijano (2011), who points out that these actors stop being victims of development and become the new protagonists of a social-emancipation process.

3.2. The Solidarity Economy

In Latin America, "solidarity economy" is the concept most commonly used to refer to collective economic organisations oriented to income generation for their members as well as to broader social benefits. While, in Europe, the debate around the solidarity economy has its main roots in the historical experience of cooperatives and associations (the "social economy", see section 3.5), in a context characterised by the presence of strong welfare states, in Latin America, the historical roots of the solidarity economy are to be found in the popular economy, within a context marked by insufficient systems of social protection (Laville and Gaiger 2009). In Latin America, the solidarity economy offers a critical discourse about the capitalist economic system; it is understood as another way of producing and circulating goods and services, which articulates the state and the market to ensure the material survival of a large number of people. It is an approach that demands new regulating principles in the economy, oriented to a change of structural dimensions of inequalities (Gaiger 2017). In Europe, the solidarity economy has been defined as "all the economic activities that are subject to a will to act democratically, in which social relations of solidarity have priority over individual interest or material profit" (Laville 2005: 253–259; our translation).

Both approaches underline that solidarity-economy activities have economic and political dimensions that determine their originality. Economic rationality cannot be reduced to the market logic. Reciprocity and mutual commitment among the people who have given birth to the initiatives are key elements which underpin these initiatives. The political dimension of the solidarity economy is expressed by the contribution of these movements to public spaces.

3.3. The "Labour Economy"

Another important approach was developed by Coraggio (2009). With a view to analysing these alternative organisations, he proposes the concept of "labour economy" (*economía del trabajo*), which he defines as an economic order based on principles contrary to the "economy of capital": he opposes the logic of reproduction of life (in the labour economy) to the logic of accumulation of capital (in the economy of capital). In an alternative systemic logic, the labour economy would be oriented towards the expanded reproduction of the capacities of all people and the improvement of the quality of life in society. The principles of integration of this new system are: subsistence, intra- and inter-community reciprocity, redistribution at different levels of society, exchange in regulated or free markets and "complexity planning".[4]

With a view to building another, counter-hegemonic economy, there is a Latin American research agenda aimed at finding alternative forms to the capitalist enterprise and the state. This agenda aims to promote the potential of these alternative forms with a view to supporting in turn a gradual transformation or a radical reform of capitalism. As Coraggio puts it, the labour economy aims to "recognise, recover, empower, invent and develop other forms of motivation and coordination of human activities, so that other products and desirable results are achieved and so that [one] can fully enjoy daily life, which includes work as an experience of fraternity and pleasure" (*ibid*.: 122).

3.4. *The Community Economy*

The "community economy" is a more recent concept in Latin American literature. It is associated with systems of production and reproduction of social life based on the principles and practices of territorially delimited communities. Its historical roots go back to the native populations that inhabited the continent before the European colonisation and to the groups that have immigrated in the region since the 19th century. The community economy is present in several countries of the region, such as Bolivia, Mexico, Chile, Ecuador and Brazil. The fact of belonging to a community is determined by kinship and ethnic ties. Communities are constituted mainly by indigenous people, peasants, *quilombolas* (an Afro-Brazilian resident of the *quilombo* settlements, first established by escaped slaves and still present today in Brazil) and fishermen groups. The main features of the community economy are the collective governance of common goods and the management of economic and social activities based on solidarity practices. The levels of institutionalisation vary between countries but, in general, the degree of social recognition and the presence of norms and public policies to protect community-economy initiatives and support their development are very deficient (Hillenkamp and Wanderley 2015).

3.5. *The Social Economy and the Third Sector*

Other different terms and concepts, rooted in other contexts, such as the "social economy" or the "third sector", have been used to qualify (some) of these initiatives. In Latin America, these concepts are not commonly used. However, the European tradition of the social economy has been an important source of inspiration in some countries, like Argentina.

Although there is no single definition of the social economy, it is almost always presented as having two key aspects. On the one hand, the term is used to describe private, non-capitalist types of organisation, with special status and rules: cooperatives, associations, mutual societies and, with increasing frequency, foundations. On the other hand, the social economy refers to principles and values: social-economy organisations are characterised by independent management; they are set up with the aim of serving their members or the community rather than maximising profit (hence, the distribution of profits is limited in these organisations, and they have joint reserves that cannot be shared); and they are characterised by the equality of members and a democratic decision-making process. Despite social, cultural, political and epistemological differences between the social-economy approach and the solidarity-economy approach, debates in the North and in the South have been connected, giving rise to hybrid designations, like the "social and solidarity economy" in some national contexts and even in international settings, as testified by the name of the Intercontinental Network for the Promotion of Social Solidarity Economy (RIPESS).

Another significant influence can be found in the American concept of the "third sector", which reached Latin America *inter alia* through the Johns Hopkins Comparative Non-Profit Sector Project (CNP). The latter indeed included Argentina, Brazil, Chile, Colombia, Mexico and Peru. The CNP developed a structural operational definition, according to which non-profit organisations share five main features: they are organised, private, non-profit-distributing, self-governing and voluntary (Salamon and Anheier 1997).

More recently, the concepts of "social enterprise" and "social entrepreneurship" have also entered the debate in several Latin American countries, as they did in most regions of the world.

4. Different Schools of Thought in the Field of Social Enterprise

As explained at the beginning of this chapter, faced with the variety of terminologies and concepts, the "International Comparative Social Enterprise Models (ICSEM) Project" chose to adopt the generic concept of "social enterprise" (SE) as a heuristic tool, with a view to better understanding these "alternative" economic types of organisation.

It is now well documented that the concept of social enterprise has emerged simultaneously in the US and in Europe, in the 1990s, in reference to a set of new entrepreneurial initiatives seeking social goals. Defourny and Nyssens (2010) distinguish between three main "schools of thought": the earned-income school, the social-innovation school and the approach adopted by the EMES International Research Network.

4.1. The Earned-Income School of Thought

For the earned-income school of thought, social enterprise can be defined as any type of earned-income business or strategy undertaken by a non-profit to generate revenue in support of its social mission. Defourny and Nyssens (2010) distinguish a first stream, within this school, which they name the "commercial non-profit" approach, with a view to underlining a key difference (namely the fact that the organisations considered as social enterprises by scholars belonging to this first stream were all non-profits) with a later development, referred to as the "mission-driven business" approach, and which embraced all types of organisation, be they non-profit or for-profit, launching business activities to address social problems. Over the last years, when some networks (like the Social Enterprise Knowledge Network), linked to business schools,[5] started to embrace the concept of social enterprise in Latin America, it was most often used along the lines of this "earned-income" school of thought, as they define social enterprises as "private (and formal) organisations that employ market strategies to obtain financial resources, in order to achieve social value for [their] members and/or for groups or communities" (Márquez *et al.* 2010: 97).

To a large extent, the concept of social business as promoted by Muhammad Yunus (2010) can also be related to the "mission-driven business" approach, although it also involves stronger conditions: "A social business is a non-loss, non-dividend company designed to address a social objective" (Yunus 2010). This concept was mainly developed to describe a business model that focuses on the provision of goods or services to (very) poor customers, which constitute a new market segment (often called the "bottom of the pyramid") in developing countries. Such a social business is supposed to cover all its costs through market resources. It is owned by (often large) investors who, at least in Yunus's version, do not receive any dividend, as profits are being fully reinvested to support the social mission.

4.2. The Social-Innovation School of Thought

The social-innovation school of thought focuses on the very specific nature of the social entrepreneur and on his/her creativity, dynamism and leadership in coming up with new responses to social needs (Dees 1998). The emphasis here is on the systemic nature of innovation and the scope of its social or societal impact, rather than on the types of resources mobilised. The Ashoka organisation has played a pioneering role in promoting this way of thinking; since the early 1980s, it has supported entrepreneurs of this kind, even though the term "social entrepreneur" was only adopted at a later stage.

Some authors (such as Emerson 2006) emphasise the need to combine these different approaches into a common characterisation of social entrepreneurship based on four key criteria: the pursuit of social impacts; social innovation; the mobilisation of commercial revenues; and the adoption of managerial methods, whatever the legal status of the organisation (for-profit or not-for-profit, private or public). These authors emphasise the double, or even triple, bottom line of these organisations, and the creation of mixed or economic and social added value ("blended value"), with closely linked economic and social dimensions.

4.3. The EMES Approach

In Europe, the EMES International Research Network developed the first theoretical and empirical milestones of SE analysis (Borzaga and Defourny 2001). The EMES approach derives from extensive dialogue among several disciplines (economics, sociology, political science and management) as well as among the various national traditions and sensitivities present in the European Union. Moreover, guided by a project that was both theoretical and empirical, it preferred from the outset the identification of three subsets of indicators (relating respectively to the economic and entrepreneurial dimension, the social dimension and the governance of social enterprise) over a concise and elegant definition. These indicators are the following:

- *Economic and entrepreneurial dimension of social enterprise*

  a) *A continuous activity producing goods and/or selling services*

     Social enterprises, unlike some traditional non-profit organisations, do not normally have advocacy activities or the redistribution of financial flows (as, for example, many foundations) as their major activity, but they are directly involved in the production of goods or the provision of services to people on a continuous basis. The productive activity thus represents the reason, or one of the main reasons, for the existence of social enterprises.

  b) *A significant level of economic risk*

     Those who establish a social enterprise assume totally or partly the risk inherent in the initiative. Unlike most public institutions, social enterprises' financial viability depends on the efforts of their members and workers to secure adequate resources. These resources can have a hybrid character: they may come from trading activities, from public subsidies or from voluntary contributions.

  c) *A minimum amount of paid work*

     As in the case of most traditional non-profit organisations, social enterprises may also combine monetary and non-monetary resources, and voluntary and paid workers. However, the activity carried out in social enterprises requires a minimum level of paid work.

- *Social dimension of social enterprise*

  d) *An explicit aim to benefit the community*

     One of the major aims of social enterprises is to serve the community or a specific group of people. In the same perspective, a feature of social enterprises is their desire to promote a sense of social responsibility at the local level.

  e) *An initiative launched by a group of citizens or civil-society organisations*

     Social enterprises are the result of collective dynamics involving people belonging to a community or to a group that shares a well-defined need or aim; this collective dimension must be maintained over time in one way or another, even though the importance of leadership (by an individual or a small group of leaders) must not be neglected.

f) *A limited profit distribution*

The primacy of the social aim is reflected in a constraint on the distribution of profits. However, social enterprises do not only include organisations that are characterised by a total non-distribution constraint, but also organisations that—like cooperatives in many countries—may distribute profits, but only to a limited extent, thus allowing to avoid a profit-maximising behaviour.

• *Governance-related dimension of social enterprise*

g) *A high degree of autonomy*

Social enterprises are created by a group of people on the basis of an autonomous project and they are governed by these people. They may depend on public subsidies but they are not managed, be it directly or indirectly, by public authorities or other organisations (federations, private firms, etc.). They have both the right to take up their own position ("voice") and to terminate their activity ("exit").

h) *A decision-making power not based on capital ownership*

This criterion generally refers to the principle of "one member, one vote", or at least to a decision-making process in which the voting power is not distributed according to capital shares in the governing body which has the ultimate decision-making rights.

i) *A participatory nature, which involves various parties affected by the activity*

Representation and participation of users or customers, influence of various stakeholders on decision-making and a participative management often constitute important characteristics of social enterprises. In many cases, one of the aims of social enterprises is to further democracy at the local level through economic activity.

Such indicators were never intended to represent the set of conditions that an organisation should meet in order to qualify as a social enterprise. Rather than constituting prescriptive criteria, they describe an "ideal-type" in Weber's terms, i.e. an abstract construction that enables researchers to position themselves within the "galaxy" of social enterprises. In other words, they constitute a tool, somewhat analogous to a compass, which helps analysts locate the position of the observed entities relative to one another and eventually identify subsets of social enterprises they want to study more deeply. Those indicators allow for the identification of brand new social enterprises, but they can also lead to designate as social enterprises older organisations being reshaped by new internal dynamics.

These nine indicators are focused on the internal governance of social enterprises, but the EMES approach is not restricted to this aspect. Indeed, according to EMES, social enterprises also have a special place in society. They pursue simultaneously economic, social and political goals (Defourny and Nyssens 2006). They are economic actors, but they do not rely exclusively on the rationality of the market. Indeed, as the EMES indicators state, the financial viability of social enterprises depends on their members' efforts to secure adequate resources to support the enterprise's social mission, but these resources can have a hybrid character: they may come from trading activities, but also—to borrow concepts from Polanyi's substantive approach—from redistribution and reciprocity (Defourny and Nyssens 2006). Social enterprises pursue social goals connected to their social mission; their political goals refer to their "political embeddedness", which sheds light on the fact that SEs have a role in the constitution of a democratic framework for economic activity (Laville *et al.* 2006).

The EMES approach proved to be empirically fertile; it has constituted the conceptual basis for several EMES research projects, in different industries, such as personal services or local development (Borzaga and Defourny 2001) or work integration (Nyssens 2006), sometimes enlarged to Central and Eastern Europe (Borzaga *et al.* 2008) or Eastern Asia (Defourny and Kuan 2011).

5. Contents and Structure of the Book

The first part of the present volume gathers contributions that were drawn up in the framework of the ICSEM Project about seven Latin American countries:[6] Argentina, Bolivia, Brazil, Chile, Ecuador, Mexico and Peru. As explained above, these chapters, which are derived from contributions produced in the first phase of the Project, focus on the various national contexts and on the concepts used therein to capture the SE phenomenon or landscape.

In the framework of the ICSEM Project, no *a priori* definition of social enterprise was imposed for the national contributions. We just delineated the field of analysis as "made of organisations that combine an entrepreneurial dynamic to provide services or goods with the primacy of their social aims". Instead, the emphasis was put on the embeddedness of the SE phenomenon in local contexts. This methodological strategy was adopted in a perspective favouring a bottom-up approach, with a view to capturing the dynamics and initiatives that can be understood as social enterprises or SE-like organisations. All the national chapters describe the diversity of SE models in the light of their historical and institutional background as well as in their current ecosystem. However, the authors used the EMES indicators to analyse these models. Indeed, the ICSEM methodology relied on the hypothesis that the three dimensions of the EMES ideal type—namely the nature of the social mission or social aims, the type of economic model and the governance structure—were particularly well suited inform the diversity of social enterprises.

The second part of the book contains three chapters, which present comparative analyses of social enterprise in Latin American countries. We present here the main objectives of these chapters as well as some of their main conclusions in a transversal perspective.

Even though we observe a wide diversity of SE models within and across the different countries, shaped by the respective national contexts, Gaiger and Wanderley draw (in chapter 9) some supranational SE *patterns*, so as to offer a panoramic and integrated view of social enterprise in Latin America. The main criterion used to identify these patterns is the identity of the collective social agents that act as the main protagonists and determine the onset and trajectory of each pattern—a class, a social category, a group of individuals linked to a territory or a certain type of institution that promotes social enterprises to meet needs or respond to common aspirations. In order to lay down the main characteristics of these SE patterns, the authors compare them from the point of view of their degree of correspondence with each of the three dimensions of the ideal-typical EMES concept of social enterprise.

In chapter 10, based on the "sociology of absences and emergences" (Santos 2001, 2011), Laville, Carvalho de França Filho, Eynaud and Lucas dos Santos underline, in a historical perspective, the processes of "invisibilisation" that occur around the experiences in which most of the SE patterns are embedded. The "sociology of emergences" refers to "the procedure through which what does not exist, or that whose existence is socially ungraspable or inexpressible, is conceived as the active result of a given social process" (Santos 2001: 191). The sociology of emergences proposes a process of enlargement of knowledge, practices and agents in order to identify "plural and concrete possibilities, which are both utopian and realistic" (Santos 2011: 36). In the SE field, this approach highlights the importance of making visible the "hidden" SE patterns as well as their specificities.

Gaiger and Wanderley, through their transversal analysis, identify seven SE patterns: (1) ethnic and community-based organisations; (2) traditional social-economy organisations; (3) organisations based on the popular economy; (4) self-managed class-related organisations; (5) organisations for socio-economic inclusion; (6) philanthropic-solidarity organisations; and (7) social-purpose organisations oriented by market logic. Most of these patterns are driven by grassroots actors, operating on the margins of capitalist dynamics and excluded from institutionalised systems of solidarity. As underlined by Laville and his co-authors in chapter 10, these SE patterns are deeply historically rooted in popular practices that have been marginalised over time through processes dominated by the "hegemonic globalisation" movement which has shaped Latin America's conflicting history.

In order to make these SE patterns visible, the authors of both chapters underline the importance of enlarging the representation of the economy, analysing it through Polanyi's lenses. Following Polanyi (1944) in his historical and anthropological approach of the economy, we can say that, even though these social enterprises operate on the market, their rationality is not oriented towards the accumulation of profit. Indeed, without denying the importance of the profit motive that characterises the capitalist economy, Polanyi also highlights other economic practices, not oriented towards the accumulation of profit: redistribution, reciprocity and household administration. Social enterprises are characterised by the use of resources originating not only in the market (through the sale of products and services) or in the state (through redistribution via subsidies and tax advantages, among others), but also in reciprocity and domesticity. In reciprocity relationships, actors are voluntarily complementary and interdependent. Reciprocity is based on the gift as a basic social fact; it calls for a socially acceptable counter-gift, regulated by social norms (Polanyi *et al.* 1957). A special form of reciprocity is practiced within autarchic groups (such as the household units); Polanyi calls it "household administration". The economic logics of domesticity and reciprocity deeply shape some of the Latin American SE patterns embedded in the universe of the popular economy.

However, SEs are not just "hybrid" organisations, which combine different types of economic resources. They also shape new institutions and norms in society. As economic actors, they try to promote different types of market, not driven by the capitalist logic of private accumulation. From the point of view of governance, their autonomous collective management is a practical exercise and a fundamental institutional learning experience for the strengthening of participatory and deliberative democratic cultures. In the public sphere, the struggle for the legal recognition of the diversity of economic organisations and the leadership assumed by these organisations in proposing appropriate public policies and normative frameworks contribute to building alternative development routes, which take economic plurality into account. Therefore, political, social and economic processes cannot be dissociated in the analysis of the SE landscape.

Social enterprises also actually experience tensions, resulting in what various authors call the "blurring boundaries" between sectors, as they have to deal with contradictory pressures from multiple institutional referents (Battilana *et al.* 2014). A first type of tension lies in the conflict between the instrumental rationality of the market, which tends to be oriented to the maximisation and distribution of profit, on the one hand, and the primacy of the social mission and democratic values in social enterprises, on the other hand. Traditional social-economy organisations and social-purpose organisations oriented by market logic appear especially prone to this type of tension. A second type of tension could be identified in SE patterns where household administration and reciprocity have an important place. Relations based on power and subordination are deeply rooted in the region's patriarchal culture and can be reproduced in some ethnic and community-based organisations as well as in organisations rooted in the popular economy. In other cases, when social enterprises receive significant support from redistribution or philanthropy, especially when they are promoted by the state or NGOs' programmes, their strict regulation and supervision may hamper their autonomy and the emancipation of their main beneficiaries. A last type of tension can come from the type of discourse underpinning the SE field. Laville and his co-authors contrast two radically different types of societal projects: what they call the "solidarity-enterprise" project, shaped by a double—economic and political—dimension and embedded in a plural economy, and the discourse around "social business", considered as a new form of capitalism, driven by market and philanthropic logics.

One of the main goals of the ICSEM Project was to show that it was feasible to theoretically and empirically build typologies of SE models at the international level. The last chapter, by Defourny, Nyssens and Brolis, addresses the lack of a scientifically robust typology of SE. With a view to overcoming this gap, they propose a theoretical framework relying on two building blocks: on the one hand, "principles of interest", as key driving forces at work in various parts of the economy and as matrices from which social enterprise dynamics can emerge; on the other hand, "resource mixes", as a key dimension of social enterprise. On this basis, they identify four major SE models. The "entrepreneurial non-profit model" gathers all non-profit organisations (most often general-interest associations) that are developing any type of earned-income activities in support of their social mission. The "public-sector social-enterprise model" results from a movement of public services towards marketisation, which embraces *inter alia* "public-sector spin-offs". The "social-cooperative model" differs from traditional mutual-interest organisations—i.e. cooperatives and mutual-interest associations—in that it combines the pursuit of its members' interests (mutual interest) with the pursuit of the interests of the whole community or of a specific group targeted by the social mission (general interest). The "social-business model" is rooted in a business model driven by shareholders' (capital) interest, but social businesses mix this logic with a "social entrepreneurial" drive aimed at the creation of a "blended value", in an effort to balance and better integrate economic and social purposes.

This typology is tested through the statistical exploitation of the large international dataset resulting from the ICSEM survey. The main finding is that three of the four models are strongly supported by the empirical analysis, as it was also the case at the worldwide level: the existence of a cooperative-type SE model, a social-business model and an entrepreneurial non-profit model is fully confirmed at the Latin American level. Latin American SEs—be they cooperatives, non-profit organisations or social businesses—are much smaller than their world-level counterparts, though. These results also show that, although SEs are influenced by institutional factors at the macro and the meso level (which contribute to shaping various patterns, as we explained above), they stem from all parts of the economy and can be related to different organisational backgrounds—namely, the non-profit, cooperative and traditional business sectors.

It is not surprising that the cooperative type—and especially worker cooperatives—constitutes the dominant form of SE in Latin America. The pursued mutual interest refers to the jobs provided to workers under their own control. But the workers are generally poor people, living at the margins of the society. Therefore, members' mutual interest includes a true social mission from at least three points of view: first, providing workers with a job, and making it stable through these workers' control; secondly, improving members' income and living conditions as well as those of their families; and thirdly, pursuing a broader goal of empowerment of the poor and promotion of economic democracy in the workplace and beyond. Cooperative values are the crucible from which an important share of Latin American SEs emerge. However, this does not mean that all registered cooperatives in Latin America can be considered as SE as, in many cases, these organisations turn away from the cooperative ideals and, *a fortiori*, from the universe of social enterprise.

The organisations belonging to the entrepreneurial non-profit model display a diversity of resources, with less than one third of their income coming from the market; this contrasts with the view conveyed by some influential voices that highlight SE as "a market solution to a social problem". However, it also appears that the resource mix of Latin American SEs includes much fewer public resources than the resource mix of their counterparts at worldwide level; this feature reflects the weakness of state support to the SE field. We do not observe either an involvement of public authorities in the governance of SEs.

What is at stake with the quest for a typology of SE models at the international level is not just a wide, although simplified, view of the various SE types. It is not either a "struggle" against too much diversity. It is first and foremost a question of uncovering and acknowledging the fact that today, a wide range of initiatives, primarily driven by social aims, address social or societal challenges. This book provides an insight into the diversity and complexity of these SE models in Latin America; it likely represents one of the most extensive descriptions so far of the reality of social enterprise in large parts of this region.

Notes

1 The Economic Complexity Index measures the level of sophistication of productive structures based on information on the diversification of the export basket and its ubiquity, that is, the ability to export goods that very few countries export (Hausmann 2018).

2 The idea of state provision of basic services and protection under the concepts of social rights and social citizenship is rooted in the late 19th century, and it developed in industrial economies in the first half of the 20th century.

3 For an explanation of these notions, see Bottomore (2001).

4 "Complexity planning" (*planificación de la complejidad*) refers to a new analytical and planning framework which includes multiple interdependent factors that shape changing and unstable economic, social and environmental settings, whose future evolution is difficult to foresee. In particular, we refer here to foreseeing the non-intentional effects of particular actions.

5 This network brings together representatives from leading schools of business administration in Latin America (see www.sekn.org/en/publication-en/).

6 Earlier versions of most chapters have been published in the *ICSEM Working Papers Series*, which constituted the output of the Project's first phase (see www.iap-socent.be/icsem-working-papers).

References

Battilana, J. & Lee, M. (2014) "Advancing research on hybrid organizing—insights from the study of social enterprises", *The Academy of Management Annals*, Vol. 8, No. 1, pp. 397–441.

Borzaga, C. & Defourny, J. (eds) (2001) *The Emergence of Social Enterprise*, London and New York: Routledge (paperback edition: 2004).

Borzaga, C., Galera, G. & Nogales, R. (eds) (2008) *Social Enterprise: A New Model for Poverty Reduction and Employment Generation*, Bratislava: United Nations Development Programme.

Bottomore, T. (ed.) (2001) *A Dictionary of Marxist Thought*, Cambridge, MA: Blackwell Plublishers.

Bovarnick, A., Alpizar, F. & Schnell, C. (eds) (2010) *Latin America and the Caribean: A Biodiversity Super Power*, New York: UNDP.

CAF (2006) *Camino a la transformación productiva en América Latina. Reporte de Economía y Desarrollo*, Caracas: Unidad de Publicaciones de CAF.

Carbonnier, G., Campodónico, H. & Tezanos Vázquez, S. (2017) *Alternative Pathways to Sustainable Development: Lessons from Latin America*, Leiden: Brill Nijhoff.

Cattani, A. D., Laville, J-L., Gaiger, L. I. & Hespanha, P. (eds) (2009) *Dicionário internacional da outra economia*, Coimbra: Edições Almedina, AS.

Coraggio, J. L. (2009) "Economia do Trabalho", in Cattani, A. D., Laville, J-L., Gaiger, L. I. & Hespanha, P. (eds) *Diccionario Internacional de Outra Economia*, Coimbra: Edições Almedina, AS.

Dees, J. G. (1998) *The Meaning of Social Entrepreneurship*, Stanford: Stanford University, Mimeo.

Defourny, J. & Kuan, Y. Y. (eds) (2011) "Social enterprise in Eastern Asia", *Social Enterprise Journal*, Vol. 7, No. 1, pp. 85–109.

Defourny, J. & Nyssens, M. (2006) "Defining social enterprise", in Nyssens, M. (ed.) *Social Enterprise: Between Market, Public Policies and Civil Society*, London and New York: Routledge, pp. 3–26.

Defourny, J. & Nyssens, M. (2010) "Conceptions of social enterprise and social entrepreneurship in Europe and the United States: Convergences and differences", *Journal of Social Entrepreneurship*, Vol. 1, No. 1, pp. 32–53.

De Soto, H. (1989) *The Other Path*, New York: Harper & Row.

Duryea, S. & Robles, M. (2016) *Social Pulse in Latin America and the Caribbean: Realities and Perspectives*, Washington, DC: Inter-American Development Bank.

ECLAC (2017) *Social Panorama of Latin America*, Santiago: United Nations.

Emerson, J. (2006) "Moving ahead together: Implications of a blended value framework for the future of social entrepreneurship", in Nicholls, A. (ed.) *Social Entrepreneurship, New Models of Sustainable Social Change*, New York: Oxford University Press, pp. 391–406.

Gaiger, L. I. (2009) "Workers' economic solidarism in context: An overview in a Latin-American perspective", in Defourny, J., Hulgard, L. & Pestoff, V. (eds) *Social Enterprise, Social Entrepreneurship, Social Economy, Solidarity Economy: An EMES Reader on the 'SE Field'*, (e-book ed.) European Research Network, pp. 305–319.

Gaiger, L. I. (2017) "The solidarity economy in South and North America: Converging experiences", *Brazilian Political Science Review*, Vol. 11, No. 3, pp. 1–27.

Gaiger, L. I. (2018) "From informality to the solidarity economy: Enlarging the canon of knowledge", paper presented at the 3rd EMES-Polanyi International Seminar, Welfare Societies in Transition, April, Roskilde University.

Hausmann, R. (2018) "Complejidad económica en síntesis", in Wanderley, F. & Peres-Cajías, J. (eds) *Los desafíos del desarrollo productivo en el siglo XXI. Diversificación, justicia social y sostenibilidad ambiental*, La Paz: UCB, Plural Editores & FES.

Hillenkamp, I. & Wanderley, F. (2015) "Genèse et logiques de justification de l'économie communautaire et solidaire en Bolivie", *RECMA—Revue internationale de l'économie sociale*, Dossier 337.

Icaza, A. M. S. & Tiriba, L. (2009) "Economía popular", in Cattani, A. D., Laville, J-L., Gaiger, L. I. & Hespanha, P. (eds) *Diccionario Internacional de Outra Economia*, Coimbra: Edições Almedina, AS.

ILO (1972) *Employment, Income and Equality: A Strategy for Increasing Productive Employment*, Geneva: ILO.

ILO (2017) *Labour Overview: Employment, Unemployment, Labour Market, Wage, Minimum Wage, Gender Gap, Labour Statistics, Working Conditions, Latin America, Central America, the Caribbean*, Lima: ILO, Regional Office for Latin America and the Caribbean.

Latinobarómetro. (2018) *Informe 2018*, Banco de datos en línea. Available HTTP: www.latinobarómetro.org.

Laville, J-L. (2005) "Economie solidaire", in Laville, J-L. & Cattani, A. D. (eds) *Dictionnaire de l'Autre Economie*, Paris: Desclée de Brouwer, pp. 253–260.

Laville, J-L. & Gaiger, L. I. (2009) "Economía Solidaria", in Cattani, A. D., Laville, J-L., Gaiger, L. I. & Hespanha, P. (eds) *Diccionario Internacional de Outra Economia*, Coimbra: Edições Almedina, AS, pp. 169–178.

Laville, J-L., Lemaître, A. & Nyssens, M. (2006) "Public policies and social enterprises in Europe: The challenge of institutionalisation", in Nyssens, M. (ed.) *Social Enterprise: At the Crossroads of Market, Public Policies and Civil Society*, London and New York: Routledge, pp. 272–295.

Lusting, N. (2017) "El impacto del sistema tributario y el gasto social en la distribución del ingreso y la pobreza en América Latina. Una aplicación del marco metodológico del Proyecto Compromiso con la Igualdad (CEQ)", *El trimester Económico*, Vol. LXXXIV (3), No. 335.

Márquez, P., Reficco, E. & Berger, G. (2010) *Socially Inclusive Business, Engaging the Poor through Market Initiatives in Iberoamerica*, Cambridge and London: Harvard University.

Meller, P. (2013) *Recursos Naturales y Diversificación exportadora. Una mirada de futuro para América Latina*, Santiago: CIEPLAN-CAF.

Nun, J. (1969) "Superpoblación relativa, ejército industrial de reserva y masa marginal", *Revista Latinoamericana de Sociología*, Vol. 5, No. 2, pp. 178–236.

Nyssens, M. (ed.) (2006) *Social Enterprise: At the Crossroads of Market, Public Policies and Civil Society*, London and New York: Routledge.

Ocampo, J. A. & Gómez-Arteaga, N. (2017) "Protection system in Latin America: Toward universalism and redistribution", Centre for Studies on Inequality and Development (CEDE), *Working Paper*, No. 122.

Polanyi, K. (1944) *The Great Transformation: The Political and Economic Origins of Our Time*, Boston: Beacon Press.

Polanyi, K., Arensberg, C. & Pearson, H. (eds) (1957) *Trade and Market in Early Empires, Economies in History and Theory*, New York: Free Press.

Portes, A. & Castells, M. (1989) *The Informal Economy: Studies in Advanced and Less Developed Countries*, Baltimore: The John Hopkins University Press.

Portes, A. & Schauffler, R. (1993) "Competing perspectives on the Latin American informal sector", *Population and Development Review*, Vol. 19, No. 1, pp. 33–60.

Quijano, O. A. (1974) "The marginal pole of the Economy and the marginalized labour force", *Economy and Society*, Vol. 3, No. 4, pp. 393–428.

Quijano, O. A. (2011) "¿Sistemas alternativos de producción?" in de Souza Santos, B. (ed.) *Producir para vivir. Los caminos de la producción no capitalista*, Mexico: Fondo de Cultura Económica.

Razeto, L. (1988) *Economía de solidaridad y mercado democrático, Libro tercero, Fundamentos de una teoría económica comprensiva*, Santiago: P.E.T.

Rojas, D. M. (2015) "La región andina en la geopolítica de los recursos estratégicos", *Análisis político*, Vol. 28, No. 30, pp. 88–107.

Salamon, L. M. & Anheier, H. K. (eds) (1997) *Defining the Nonprofit Sector: A Cross-National Analysis*, Manchester: Manchester University Press.

Santos, B. de S. (2001) "Nuestra America: Reinventing a subaltern paradigm of recognition and redistribution", *Theory, Culture & Society*, Vol. 18, No. 2–3, pp. 185–217.

Santos, B. de S. (2011) "Épistémologies du Sud", *Études rurales* [online], p. 187. Available HTTP: https://journals.openedition.org/etudesrurales/9351 (published online on September 12, 2018).

UNDP (2016) *Informe Regional sobre Desarrollo Humano para América Latina y el Caribe*, New York: PNUD.

Wanderley, F. (1999) "Pequenos Negócios, Industrializaçao Local e Redes de Relaçoes Econômicas: Uma Revisao Bibliográfica em Sociologia Econômica", *Revista Brasileira de Informaçao Bibliográfica em Ciências Sociais (BIB)*, No. 48, pp. 15–50.

Wanderley, F. (2015) *Desafíos Teóricos y Políticos de la Economía Social y Solidaria. Lecturas desde América Latina*, País Vasco: HEGOA.

Wanderley, F. (2017) "Entre el concepto minimalista y el concepto maximalista de economía social y solidaria. Tensiones teóricas y agenda future", *Revista Economía*, Vol. 69, No. 109, ISIP, UCE.

Yunus, M. (2010) *Building Social Business: Capitalism That Can Serve Humanity's Most Pressing Needs*, New York: Public Affairs.

Part I

National Overviews of Social Enterprise

1 Social- and Solidarity-Economy Organisations in Argentina

Diversity, Models and Perspectives[1]

Gonzalo Vázquez

Introduction

The ICSEM Project aims to carry out a comparative identification and characterisation of the different social-enterprise models in a variety of national contexts. In Argentina, the concept of "social enterprise" (*empresa social*) is limited to one type of initiatives, namely organisational experiences that focus on the work integration of people with disabilities or mental health problems. Consequently, and in order to cover a greater number and diversity of initiatives existing in the country, we decided to use the more comprehensive concept of "social- and solidarity-economy organisations" (SSEO).

The *comprehensive concept of SSEO* adopted in this study intends to include a great variety of organisations that can be considered to be part of the field of the social and solidarity economy in Argentina, and which share, to a greater or lesser extent, the following characteristics: *they are associative experiences engaged in a given kind of economic activity (productive, financial, commercial or consumer activity), organised according to the principles of self-management, participation and internal democracy, and which pursue social and political objectives directed towards satisfying the needs of their members and communities, through social integration and transformation.*

Nevertheless, the concept of SSEO that we are proposing relates without major problems with that of "social enterprise" proposed by the ICSEM Project. For the ICSEM Project, a broad definition has been proposed to delineate what can be called "social enterprises" as "organisations that combine an entrepreneurial dynamic to provide services or goods with the primacy of their social aims". Moreover, a hypothesis was central to the project: three major dimensions would particularly inform the diversity of SE models: the nature of the social mission or social aims, the type of economic model and the governance structure. This hypothesis is embedded in the EMES approach to social enterprise, which proposes nine indicators: social enterprises (a) develop production activities and/or sell goods or services, (b) on the basis of a minimum amount of

DOI: 10.4324/9780429055164-3

paid labour, and (c) they face a significant amount of economic risk (economic dimension); they are (d) collective initiatives fostered by groups of people and organisations, (e) with explicit social objectives, and (f) they limit and direct the distribution of their income and surpluses (social dimension); lastly, the governance of these organisations (g) is based on the autonomy and self-management of their members, through (h) democratic mechanisms of decision-making, based on member equality and on (i) the active participation of the different stakeholders interested in the project (governance dimension) (Defourny and Nyssens 2012).

These nine indicators are focused on the internal governance of social enterprises, but the EMES approach is not restricted to this aspect. Indeed, according to EMES, social enterprises also have a special place in society. They pursue simultaneously economic, social and political goals (Defourny and Nyssens 2006). They are economic actors but they do not rely exclusively on the market. As the EMES indicators state, the financial viability of social enterprises depends on their members' efforts to secure adequate resources to support the enterprise's social mission, but these resources can have a hybrid character: they may come from trading activities, but also—to borrow concepts from Polanyi's substantive approach—from redistribution and reciprocity (Defourny and Nyssens 2006; Gardin 2006). Social enterprises pursue social goals connected to their social mission; their political goals refer to their "political embeddedness", which sheds light on the fact that SEs have a role in the constitution of a democratic framework for economic activity (Laville *et al.* 2006).

The main purpose of this chapter is to elaborate a proposal of identification and characterisation of the different types of SSEOs in the Argentinian context by classifying them into five main models. Before that, we present a brief historical framework of the Argentinian economy and an account of the emergence of the concepts and experiences that make up the field of the social and solidarity economy in the country. The chapter ends with some considerations regarding the particularities of Argentinian SSEOs in an international perspective, and their prospects in the current national and Latin American context.

1. Brief Historical Framework

In schematic terms, we can state that three different development models can be distinguished in Argentina throughout the country's economic history, up to the beginning of the 21st century: the "agro-export model" (from 1880 to 1930), the "industrialisation model" (between 1930 and 1976) and the "neoliberal model" (from 1976 to 2001). So as to gain a better understanding of the experiences and organisations of the SSE in their historical national context, it is useful to provide a brief characterisation of these models and stages of the Argentinian development.

As regards the *agro-export model*, it was systematically promoted by the dominant sectors of Argentinian capitalism (landowners) since the beginning of the modern organisation of the nation, in the second half of the 19th century. This model was based on the productive specialisation of the agricultural and livestock sector, taking advantage of the temperate climate and fertile soil of the vast humid *pampas*. The production (mostly cereals and beef) was to be exported to the European markets, and especially to Great Britain—the world's leading power at the time. At the same time, Argentina was a growing market for the core countries' industrial goods and to carry out profitable capital investments in sectors related to agro-export activities (railways, ports, cold storage, banks, etc.). This economic model—which constituted a typical form of integration of a periphery-capitalism country in the world market[2]—generated a significant GDP growth and huge profits. But these benefits were exclusively appropriated by and concentrated in the hands of the dominant local class (large estate owners) and their foreign allies. The government, dominated by this "landowning oligarchy", directed its policies and resources towards consolidating this model and did not pursue redistribution policies towards the less advantaged sectors. While the native indigenous peoples were either killed or expelled from their lands, the population of the country increased fourfold with a massive arrival of European (especially Spanish and Italian) immigrants, who were welcomed by the Argentinian state with openness, but without any major resources other than a public and free education of relatively good quality.

It was precisely from the knowledge, experiences and cultural traditions of the workers belonging to this immigrant European population that the first experiences of the social economy developed in Argentina: the first unions, mutuals and cooperatives emerged with the purpose of addressing the basic needs of their native communities and of the working class as a whole. Other cooperatives were fostered by small- and medium-scale businessmen, as a way to carry out their activities while confronting big monopolies and a financial sector which did not take them into consideration. Furthermore, many other cooperatives emerged to provide basic public services in small- and medium-sized towns. All these organisations, which can be considered as the "founders" of the social economy in Argentina, were created without the support of the state, which, in general, did not consider them to be within its purview (Plotinsky 2017).

The agro-export model was hit by a crisis in the 1930s, as the international commercial scheme within which it was inserted started to weaken, due to the new protectionist policies that the core countries were adopting in the face of the severe worldwide crisis of capitalism of the time. In this context, in particular during Juan D. Perón's government (1946–1955), a new development model was launched. It was based on the increase of industrial production for domestic consumption. Due to Keynesian state policies of market regulation and income redistribution, there was an increase and growth in the sector of national capital enterprises, especially of the small- and medium-sized businesses. Fostered by this *industrialisation model*, full employment was attained and maintained for three decades, and salaries enabled the workers to sustain increasing levels of consumption and welfare. At the same time, universal social policies were introduced. They guaranteed the satisfaction of different needs (education, health care, housing, culture, leisure, etc.) for a big majority of the Argentinian population.

This context of a growing domestic market saw the emergence of many production, consumer and credit cooperatives (Levin and Verbeke 1997). The state also began to promote these initiatives: for example, in its first five-year plan, Perón's government promoted agricultural cooperatives in rural areas and consumer cooperatives in the cities; its second five-year plan proposed the creation of a "large national cooperative system", but this plan could not be implemented due to the coup that overthrew the Peronist government in 1955. The national institutions and laws that still regulate cooperatives and mutuals in Argentina were designed at the end of the industrialisation period, at the beginning of the 1970s (Plotinsky 2017).

Despite the social improvements described above, the industrialisation model could not be permanently consolidated in Argentina. This was so, in part, because of structural economic problems (the dependency on foreign goods, technologies and capitals; a national rentier and short-term-oriented bourgeoisie; etc.), and also because of the permanent political opposition exerted by the most powerful economic sectors (landowners who exported agricultural goods, big transnational companies and their representatives in the governments of the core countries and in international institutions), who never accepted the policies of market regulation and resource redistribution from the capital owners towards the workers that were advocated by the industrialisation scheme. This is why, in the context of a major internal political conflict, a change in the economic model was forcibly imposed by another coup on March 24, 1976. Any intention of popular resistance was eliminated by an extremely violent repressive policy, which included kidnapping, torturing and the disappearance and death of thousands of workers, students and political and social activists. This civil-military dictatorship, which lasted from 1976 to 1983, marked a point of inflection in the Argentinian history, and it heralded a period of profound economic, social and cultural degradation for the majority of the population.

The *neoliberal model* introduced by this dictatorship was subsequently reinforced during the democratically elected governments (mainly in the 1990s), which gave in to the pressures of the International Monetary Fund to adopt the policies of the so-called Washington Consensus, in the context of a new period of capitalist globalisation. The policies carried out during this period promoted the liberalisation and openness of goods and capital markets, the reduction of the role of the state in the economy (deregulation, privatisations and fiscal adjustments), the absence of protection for the national production facing foreign competition, a reduction in the real income of workers, and the deregulation of working conditions. In the Argentinian economy, these policies resulted in a strong deindustrialisation process, the disappearance of a large number of national enterprises (mainly small- and medium-sized businesses) that produced for the domestic market, an unprecedented increase in unemployment and, consequently, the impoverishment and social exclusion of large sectors of the Argentinian population.

The organisations of the social economy were greatly harmed by the neoliberal policies. Due to the fact that they are organisations promoting democratic and participative relations at the community level, the 1976 coup considered them a potential enemy and, for that reason, it left them unprotected and legislated against their interests. For example, an act forced more than 400 cooperative credit unions to turn into commercial banks in order to continue operating, and another act forbid cooperatives to be media licensees (Plotinsky 2017). With the policies of market openness and deregulation, the organisations of the social economy were forced to compete against big corporations in concentrated markets; as a consequence, many credit, farmers' and consumer cooperatives ceased to exist, lost their members or sacrificed a significant part of their cooperative identity in order to survive (Levin and Verbeke 1997). Only one type of organisation of the social and solidarity economy grew strongly in number: worker cooperatives and entrepreneurial initiatives self-managed by their workers, which became associative alternatives sheltering their members from unemployment and spaces of resistance. A good example hereof are the "recovered enterprises" (*empresas recuperadas*, i.e. enterprises taken over by their workers, usually after a capitalist company closure) that emerged in the 1990s.

The neoliberal policies plunged Argentina into a long and deep economic crisis, which reached its peak with the social and political outburst of December 2001, which expressed a popular rejection of the model of the time and a demand for a radical change in public policies. So, between 2003 and 2015, during the Peronist governments of Néstor and Cristina Kirchner, the liberal recipes were abandoned, and policies were implemented to reindustrialise the economy and to protect employment and domestic consumption, as well as to support state intervention of a redistributive character oriented towards the expansion of the public welfare system. This happened in the context of a regional trend towards popular and/or left-wing governments in almost all South America (Chávez in Venezuela, Lula in Brazil, Evo Morales in Bolivia, Correa in Ecuador, etc.), which brought about significant processes of expansion of rights and improvements in the majorities' well-being, after decades of degradation brought about by the neoliberal era.

In this context and during this period, the organisations of the social and solidarity economy were strongly fostered by the state. Policies to encourage associative initiatives through the massive granting of credits and subsidies were introduced as a strategy to reduce poverty. Furthermore, the creation of a great number of worker cooperatives was promoted in order to carry out public works (urban infrastructure, housing, sanitation networks, etc.) in low-income neighbourhoods, providing income and employment opportunities for a population excluded from the labour market. On the other hand, the redistributive policies, which increased the income of several sectors of the population, resulted in a considerable growth of consumption and favoured the national enterprises that produced for the domestic market, such as small- and medium-sized businesses, cooperatives and "recovered enterprises". There were also generally favourable legislation changes for the sector. For example, the bankruptcy law was modified, providing a legal framework that expedited the process of enterprise recovery by workers having lost their jobs, through the setting up of worker cooperatives.

Finally, at the end of 2015, a political alliance of a different ideological orientation came into power. This alliance clearly favours neoliberal policies and represents the interests of the most economically and financially powerful sectors. This takes place in the larger context of a change in the tendency at the South American level, with new right-wing governments (even established, in some cases—as in Brazil—through parliamentary coups), which encourage the re-emergence of the neoliberal programme, coming into power. This new political scenario presents huge challenges for the organisations of the social and solidarity economy, which will be discussed in the following pages.

2. Relevant Concepts in the Argentinian Context

As we have stated in the introduction, the concept of "social enterprise" is limited in Argentina to a particular type of initiatives, which aim at the integration of people with disabilities and mental health problems by means of their work. Towards the end of the 1990s and the beginning of the 2000s, under the impetus of international cooperation agencies and of some NGOs linked to these, the experience of "Italian social cooperatives" began to spread in Argentina.[3] The organisations promoting the concept suggested that it would be beneficial for Argentina to encourage the formation of organisations that would pursue the social integration of the "disadvantaged" by means of their own work. One idea of the local advocates of this notion was that the concept of "disadvantaged" should include not only people with mental health problems or disabilities, but also the homeless, long-term unemployed and other workers excluded from the formal labour market. This understanding of social enterprise is very close to the concept of work-integration social enterprise (WISE) (Defourny and Nyssens 2006). Since the country was undergoing a major employment and social crisis at the time, this proposal struck a chord and gave rise to several initiatives as well as to the Network of Argentinian Social Enterprises (*Red de Empresas Sociales Argentinas*, or REDESA), which gathered them.

There was also academic research at the time that adopted the concept of "social enterprise" in a more comprehensive way than the usual meaning of work-integration initiatives, with a view to identifying a group of organisations existing in the country and to analysing their characteristics and potentialities by framing this kind of experiences in a broader field, namely that of the "social economy".[4] It was precisely during those years that the concept of social economy began to gain strength within the national context, and it managed to bring together several experiences that had emerged as a response to the crisis. In this way, the use of the concept of social enterprise was rapidly reduced and, since then, it has only had a marginal use in the country, both in the academia and in the field of alternative economic practices.

By the turn of the 21st century, the use of the concept of social economy had grown significantly in Argentina, because of the popular responses that had been emerging in the face of the crisis.[5] At university level, 2003 saw the creation of the first Master's Degree in Social Economy. According to its proponents, "the Master's Degree received the name *social economy* to indicate that it would have an alternative focus, different from the neoliberal economic perspective, and that it would contribute to the development of a new, multidisciplinary, academic and professional field, able to account for the new forms of economic organisation and action in the process of building Another Economy".[6]

This re-emergence of the concept of social economy in Argentina did not occur without tensions: the cooperative and mutualist sectors had been using this denomination for a long time in the country, and it took them several years to accept the new emerging initiatives under the same conceptual and terminological framework they had traditionally been using (Plotinsky 2015).

Moreover, since 2001, the social, political and academic movement formed around the World Social Forum of Porto Alegre, where Argentinian participation proved to be very important, has been very influential. In this forum, there was a significant number of people and collective projects identifying with the idea that "another world is possible" and which, in particular, were part of the collective shaping of "another economy"—an alternative to the economy established by neoliberal capitalism. Through the exchange of experiences and literature with neighbouring countries and other places in Latin America, the notion of "solidarity economy", widely used in these close national contexts, and particularly in Brazil, made a strong entrance in the Argentinian landscape.[7]

Around the first decade of the 21st century, the overarching concept of "social and solidarity economy" emerged and spread rapidly in Argentina as a concept able to include a wide and diverse range of practical experiences and theoretical proposals. The term "social and solidarity economy" (SSE) has since gradually gained acceptance and it is now the most widely used denomination, both by academia[8] and by the members of the organisations that make up this field.

However, it must be underlined that, when the term SSE is used in Argentina, it does not always refer to the same idea. Nowadays, it is a polysemic concept (Pastore 2010), which is used in several ways:

- The concept is first used to denote a group of economic *experiences* (productive, financial, commercial, consumer initiatives) which have certain characteristics (they are associative, self-managed, democratic, inclusive, sustainable, etc.) and which aim at the satisfaction of needs, not at the accumulation of capital. It is this sense of the term that we adopt in this work, since it refers to the organisations that make up this "sector" of the economy and which can be empirically observed and comparatively analysed and studied.
- Secondly, "SSE policies" is a term used to designate a variety of *public policies* geared towards the promotion of productive activities that provide income to the poorest sectors of the population. These kinds of policies began to be implemented in 2003 and grew in number within the context of state strategies of social welfare and assistance, and they permeated into different levels of the state (local, provincial, national) and administrations of different political parties.
- Thirdly, the term SSE is also used to designate a *proposal for social transformation* that expresses radical criticism of the capitalist system and which suggests the need and the possibility to shape an alternative—"another economy" (Vázquez 2009). This utopian meaning of the term SSE—mainly used in activist spaces and political debate—puts a strain on the previous senses, which inevitably function within the frame of the capitalist system that they strive to overcome.
- Finally, within the context of a paradigmatic debate in the field of economic theory, the SSE is considered a critical *perspective*, opposed to the dominant neoclassical paradigm. The SSE theoretically challenges the definition of what the economy is and the way in which economic activities and institutions are organised. It points out the need to broaden the perspective and to adopt a more plural and substantive approach, able to include non-commercial or non-monetary practices, as well as practices guided by a reproductive economic rationality.

Social and solidarity-economy organisations (SSEOs), which constitute the main focus of this work, are a wide and diverse group of experiences that embody the first of the four meanings listed above. However, to a greater or lesser extent, the other meanings are also at stake, since most of these organisations are committed to a project of social transformation or have a connection with public policies to promote the SSE.

Before concluding this section, we want to indicate that the concept of "popular economy" is also widely used in Argentina. We can distinguish two different views about this concept in the country: one is a currently influential point of view—both at the academic and political levels—that characterises the popular economy as the group of activities carried out by workers excluded from the labour market, with a view to generating income, usually in an independent way (either individually or collectively), and often outside of legal frameworks (to this extent, it can be included in the informal sector), with survival as the main driver (Grabois and Pérsico 2014). The other perspective states that the popular economy is the collection of resources, activities, knowledge and networks that the workers' domestic units bring into play, so as to achieve an expanded and solidarity-based reproduction of the life of its members (Coraggio 1999). This approach does not refer only to the poorest and most excluded citizens, but also to everyone who makes a living out of their work (including wage-earners). Both perspectives criticise how the capitalist economy works, but only the second view highlights the potential of an actually existing popular economy, based on a reproductive and solidarity-based logic, in the domestic sphere, and explicitly conceives it as a platform for the creation of the SSE, understood as an alternative-economy project.

3. Five Different Models of SSEO in Argentina

In this third and central section of this chapter, we present a proposal for the classification of all SSEOs in Argentina in five models or "ideal types". This characterisation takes into account certain aspects of SSEOs which enable a comparative analysis within the framework of the ICSEM Project and which are related to the conceptual definitions presented in the introduction. Those aspects are: governing principles and lines of action; social mission and legal form adopted; resources and strategies for sustainability; forms of management and governance; institutionalisation processes and channels; and participation in public and political spaces.

We identify different characteristic features that make up five different models of SSEO in Argentina. It is worth clarifying that these features do not appear empirically to the same degree in each of the concrete organisations of each model; in this sense, these models are "ideal types" and not an exact reflection of empirical realities. This classification of SSEOs may be discussed and improved and, at the same time, it may be useful for comparisons with other national and regional realities.

The five models of SSEO that we propose are the following: (a) workers' self-managed organisations; (b) entities of the traditional social economy; (c) cooperatives for social inclusion related to state policies; (d) social businesses led by social entrepreneurs; and (e) associative and family popular initiatives. Below, we characterise each model, before presenting a table summarising this classification.

3.1. Workers' Self-Managed Organisations

The main feature of workers' self-managed organisations is that, in these SSEOs, all the members are at the same time workers, who own the means of production and voluntarily assume the self-management of the organisations under democratic and cooperative principles, which constitute their dominant logic. The main social mission of this type of SSEO is to generate self-employment and income for their members, who seek to live from this job, which is their main occupation. In many cases, the missions of these SSEOs are closely linked to the development of the local communities to which they belong.

Most of these organisations adopt the legal form of "worker cooperative", even though a significant number as well are registered as "associations". In both cases, they assume a similar statute, based on internal democracy. Each member has one vote in the general assembly, which is the sovereign governing body that elects the representatives for the board of directors. This model is present in almost every sector of the economic activity in Argentina: there are workers' self-managed SSEOs not only in the primary sector, but also in the industrial sector, as well as in the production of different types of services.

Most of these organisations' income comes from the sale of their products in the market, which obviously puts a strain on this type of SSEO because of the inescapable need to be competitive with capitalist enterprises operating in the same markets. A part of these organisations' struggle as a sector is to be recognised by the state as economic experiences that provide social benefits. This is why they demand laws and policies supporting their sustainability and growth, while contending for the allocation of public resources to the sector, as well as for their inclusion as suppliers in state purchases. Thus, their resource mix is mainly based on market income, with some state resources in the form of public subsidies or purchases. Their sustainability strategy also aims at a closer relationship with local communities, which is reflected both in solidarity consumption of SSEOs' products as well as in political support for their projects.

Most SSEOs of this type promote the active participation of all their members in strategic decisions by holding relatively frequent assemblies and providing information to every associate. Some of the workers themselves assume responsibilities in everyday management, a task that presents important challenges, such as the lack of specific training in management and the need to innovate in the adaptation or creation of new management tools that differ from conventional ones, as they should be more consistent with the principles of the SSE.

This model of SSEO has grown significantly in number and visibility since the mid-1990s in Argentina, first as a workers' grassroots response in the face of the employment crisis and, after the crisis of the neoliberal model, with some support from the state, which (partially) included them as subjects of progressive public policies.

Nowadays, workers' self-managed SSEOs are an emergent political player, with a certain capacity of organisation and mobilisation both to resist neoliberal policies and to foster the development of strategies towards an alternative economy. In the last few years, they have formed second- and third-degree organisations (federations and networks) as a way to express their interests publicly and to have an influence on public policies.

Several empirical groups of SSEO can be included in this first model: recovered enterprises, "from-the-outset" worker cooperatives (see next paragraph), associations of small producers and family farming, direct producers' fairs, fair trade and solidarity consumption organisations of SSEO products and small microfinance institutions (communal little banks). To conclude the characterisation of this first model, we briefly present some empirical cases that are very prominent in the Argentinian landscape.

In the field of the SSE, worker cooperatives constitute the most frequently encountered legal form in Argentina, with over 15,000 worker cooperatives currently grouping more than 500,000 workers (Acosta *et al.* 2013; Guarco 2013). That being said, among worker cooperatives, three groups can be distinguished: (1) the first group includes the thousands of worker cooperatives specifically created for the implementation of public policies; (2) the second group brings together worker cooperatives created by workers in the process of enterprise recovery; and (3) the third group is that of initiatives that were worker cooperatives from the outset, and were created by workers who voluntarily decided to organise themselves as a cooperative so as to produce and generate employment and income on a self-managed basis. In this case, cooperativism is a voluntary decision, not a need imposed by external circumstances. According to official information, nowadays in Argentina, there are more than 7,500 active cooperatives belonging to this third group, and they are present in almost all the production sectors. In the last few years, worker cooperatives have grown significantly in number (many were founded in periods of high unemployment, but more continued to be founded in contexts of increased employment). Their sectoral organisation has also improved over time; they are currently grouped in networks by sector of activity in more than 60 federations and in one big confederation at the national level, the National Confederation of Worker Cooperatives (*Confederación Nacional de Cooperativas de Trabajo*, or CNCT).

"Recovered enterprises" (*empresas recuperadas*, hereafter referred to as "RE") are experiences initiated by workers who, faced with the closure of a company of which they were wage-earning employees, decide to organise themselves as a self-managed group to produce and sell their products in the market again. These practices grew significantly in frequency and visibility during the end-of-the-century crisis, but they later became part of the workers' "struggle repertoire" and more REs continued to emerge even during moments of economic growth. Nowadays, there are 368 REs in Argentina, which gather together around 15,000 workers. Their level of social recognition in the country is relatively high and they are seen as exemplary at the international level. Half of the REs are industrial goods producers (among these, metallurgic, food and graphic initiatives stand out) and the other half are service providers (with gastronomic initiatives standing out) (Ruggeri 2014). Almost all of them managed to be sustainable over time, with a good level of production and commercial integration. They are grouped in several federations and have managed, as political players, to have an influence on some state interventions, such as a modification of the bankruptcy law that eases the processes of recovery and self-management by the workers who become unemployed. They usually carry out cultural and educational activities and are deeply rooted in their communities.

3.2. Entities of the Traditional Social Economy

In this second model of SSEO, we group the organisations identified in Argentina as "entities of the social economy". This group includes many organisations, legally registered as mutuals and cooperatives of different kinds (agricultural, public service, housing, credit, insurance, consumer cooperatives), whose working logic can be characterised as "mutualist", since they aim at mutual benefits for their members.

This type of SSEO emerged as a cooperative solution to satisfy the needs of groups of producers or local communities. The sectors where their presence is stronger are the provision of urban public services (electricity, phone, water, sanitation, etc.) and the agricultural sector (grain storage and commercialisation, production of agro-industrial goods, insurances for producers, etc.). These initiatives' relationship with their territorial communities is important, since these entities have had, and still have, a central role in their communities' historical development.

Generally, entities of the social economy aim to achieve self-sustainability; to that end, they rely almost completely on the market income obtained from the sale of their products or services to their own associates or other consumers, complementing these incomes with the periodical collection of members' fees. In these SSEOs, the associates are not the workers (who are usually wage-earners), but the consumers of the goods or services. This is why the relationship between these organisations and their members is often more distant than in the previous model. Their governance is formally democratic, since it relies on the annual General Assembly, which elects its representatives for the Board, but in general, most of the associates do not participate actively. The management of these SSEOs is generally in the hands of professional managers, who often come from within the organisation but have experience and training in conventional management.

These SSEOs emerged at the beginning of the 20th century, fostered by European immigrants, and they grew and developed in the heat of an industrialisation process, focused on the domestic market, that developed intensely from 1930 until the 1976 military coup, when the economic model took a turn towards neoliberalism. Since then, the sustainability of these SSEOs has become conditioned by the need for survival in open and deregulated markets and in a context that was very hostile for national and cooperative production. Many SSEOs of this type disappeared between 1976 and 2001, and those that managed to survive did so by ensuring their competitiveness, in some cases at the expense of certain solidarity-linked identity features.

Given their long history, these initiatives have a very solid structure of second- and third-degree entities (federations and confederations), as well as quite a high degree of financial autonomy and a certain capacity to have an influence at state level; in fact, it is this type of organisation that participates in the Board of Directors of the National Institute for Associationism and the Social Economy (*Instituto Nacional de Asociativismo y Economía Social*, or INAES), the public body that regulates and promotes the social and solidarity economy at the national level. In this institutional context, it is interesting to highlight these initiatives' approach to the other SSEO models in the last few years: they have opened up to the reality of a very diverse sector, with a large number of emerging initiatives, to face the crisis of the national economy.

Public service cooperatives constitute an empirically important type of initiatives in this category: there are indeed around 1,200 public services cooperatives in the country, including almost 600 electrical cooperatives, which serve more than 7 million people and distribute 50% of the electricity of the most populated province of the country (Buenos Aires) (Guarco 2013), and they also have a dense network of second- and third-degree organisations (federations and confederations), which makes them central players in the national SSE, with regional and international reach.[9]

Agricultural cooperativism also plays a major role in the Argentinian SSE. A big national confederation (Coninagro) groups together federations and cooperatives that produce milk products, *yerba mate*, wine, tobacco and many grains, as well as services for the rural sector. Some of these cooperatives are very large; the agricultural cooperative AFA, for example, has 36,000 associates and 1,600 employees, and it provides production and commercialisation support services to its members, such as the storage of 5 million tons of grains and the production of agricultural inputs for its associates. This sector grew considerably under the progressive governments; however, agricultural cooperatives usually share interests with the agricultural export sectors, which results in political tension with the rest of the SSE sector.

Finally, among the SSEOs belonging to this model, we can highlight the existence of the cooperative bank "Credicoop" and of the large consumer cooperative "Cooperativa Obrera de Consumo", two big organisations with thousands of associates and a rich history. They are also two of the few entities that have survived the 25 years of neoliberal policies which led to the disappearance of a huge majority of the several hundreds of financial and consumer cooperatives that existed until 1980.

We consider these first two models—workers' self-managed organisations and entities of the traditional social economy—to be the most significant ones in Argentina, given their number and the quality of their experiences as SSEOs, as well as their capacity for political action and the resources they mobilise. The following three models of SSEO are less important in the country's landscape, but they are part of a comprehensive overview of the SSE.

3.3. Cooperatives for Social Inclusion Related to State Policies

Organisations belonging to this third model are characterised by their strong connection with certain state policies, which explains, to a great extent, their emergence as well as their sustainability. These SSEOs are conceived to provide jobs and income to workers who are particularly underprivileged or excluded from the labour market (long-term unemployed people with a low education level, mothers who are heads of households, disabled people, etc.).

These organisations' dominant logic is redistributive. They are the tangible expression of certain state interventions that encourage the social inclusion of people and groups whose basic rights are critically affected. Their productive activities are financed by means of public subsidies sustained over time. In some cases, their logic can also be considered as an answer to social demands, when the marginal groups themselves organise to claim for and obtain the state resources that allow them to operate as a productive organisation.

These SSEOs' strong dependency on redistributive state funding is also explained by the fact that they produce goods and services devoted to the improvement of the popular habitat, be it housing for those who do not have access to housing in the market, collective equipment (health centres, schools, squares, etc.), or infrastructure (asphalt, sidewalks, drainages, etc.) in the suburbs inhabited by a poor population. As a consequence, the state is the main (and sometimes the only) contractor and buyer of their products, which is a great weakness in terms of sustainability, as these SSEOs and their members thus depend on third parties' political decisions and budget allocations.

Another sensitive aspect in SSEOs of this type is that their origins are to be found in "external" initiatives. Their members are invited to participate in the organisation—be it a worker cooperative or an association—as a requisite to benefit from a social policy and, consequently, they have little autonomy to make a voluntary decision as regards their incorporation in the organisation. Once they become members, they may go through a process of appropriation of the organisation's cooperative character, or gradually come to terms with their power to decide autonomously in assemblies or boards, but frequently, this process does not take place, due to a lack of knowledge or interest on the part of the members themselves (or of most of them) or of the public servants who are in charge of the implementation of these social policies.

The governance of these SSEOs is formally in the hands of their members, who elect their governing bodies in the assembly, but in practice these bodies' decisions often depend on state actions and decisions. As a result, this type of SSEO usually has a low level of autonomy, even though there are cases of groups of workers who develop and assume the cooperative identity and who struggle to gain more autonomy from the state. In other cases, the SSEOs are politically included in territorial social movements that assume the representation of the cooperative's members and, by means of direct actions (pickets and roadblocks, encampments in front of public buildings, etc.), they call for an increase in resources and decision-making autonomy in the definition and implementation of their action plans.

This model of SSEO grew significantly in Argentina during the governments of the Kirchners, between 2003 and 2015. These governments promoted the creation of more than 15,000 cooperatives (protected by specific norms) to build social-interest housing and carry out improvement work on popular habitat. These cooperatives thus constitute a phenomenon of great magnitude in terms of both the population involved (it is estimated that more than 200,000 people were involved in these cooperatives) and the public budget allocated to finance these organisations. In a political scenario that has changed dramatically since 2016, many of these SSEOs are becoming political players with a growing degree of organisation and integration in second-degree organisations, for example, through the Confederation of Popular Economy Workers (*Confederación de Trabajadores de la Economía Popular*, or CTEP), which aims to represent them. They occupy the public space to defend their interests, call for the recognition of their experiences and demand their continuity in the face of a government that reduces their budget.

Other empirical cases of SSEO that can be included in this model are protected workshops (*talleres protegidos*) for disabled workers and many communal organisations that provide childcare services (*guarderías*), food (*comedores*) and recreation (clubs and cultural centres) for free to families in popular neighbourhoods. These organisations depend on public finance provided through different social policies.

3.4. *Social Businesses Led by Social Entrepreneurs*

Nowadays in Argentina there is a group of organisations (not very large in number but increasingly influential) that are inspired by the perspectives of the "social innovation" school of thought and the "earned income" school (Defourny and Nyssens 2012). These experiences aim to develop enterprises (social businesses) capable of generating social benefits for poor or excluded sectors by means of market activities. These social benefits can be obtained, for example, by fostering businesses capable of generating employment or income for socially vulnerable people or by facilitating the poor's access to certain products or services, with a view to improving their living conditions (Ashoka undated). In other words, this type of SSEO aims at solving social problems by means of business initiatives that are, at the same time, profitable.

These experiences rely on the leadership capacities of certain individuals (usually called "social entrepreneurs") who also have access to financial and training support networks rooted in the business world. They are inspired by the idea that social problems can be solved through individual creative and innovative initiatives that emerge from within the capitalist business system but which prioritise social and environmental objectives and limit the distribution of profits.

The form of governance of these organisations, which adopt the legal form of foundations or commercial enterprises, is generally centred on the decisions of the founder, entrepreneur or leader. Consequently, their governance is usually not strictly democratic, although they usually consider it useful that the different stakeholders (consumers, employees and beneficiaries) participate in the decision-making spaces by contributing their opinions. For their administration, they rely on professional teams with training and experience in business management, which are essential to "guarantee" the quality of the work of these organisations.

The leaders of these social businesses believe that attaining their social aims should not restrain their initiatives from being profitable—or at least self-sustainable—enterprises, thanks to the sale of their products in the market. However, external resources from private donations, business foundations or even the state are usually an essential support in the initial stages of these initiatives. The "social business" perspective affirms that this sector of social enterprise—which is complementary to the for-profit sector—can be socially responsible and a generator of social change.

In Argentina, this social-business model was first promoted in the 1990s by the international networks Ashoka and Avina, which select social entrepreneurs and leaders and provide them with support through financing, training and contacts in the business world so that they face less obstacles in the development of their projects. The current Argentinian government has strongly adopted this entrepreneurial perspective, together with neoliberal policies of deregulation of the markets and state adjustments, and is financing projects and proposing new legal instruments favourable to this type of SSEO.

As a particularly relevant empirical case among the experiences that can be identified with this model of SSEO, we can mention "El Arca",[10] an association created by a social entrepreneur of the province of Mendoza who was supported by the Ashoka network. This organisation supports more than 100 productive initiatives of small producers by promoting them among consumers with high expectations in terms of product quality, who show their solidarity with the producers through their willingness to pay a price considered to be fair.

A more recent experience, which has grown exponentially in the last few years, is the so-called Sistema B, a network bringing together enterprises, consultants, accountants, lawyers and workers with the declared mission of "creating a favourable ecosystem for B Corps and other economic players that use the power of the market to solve social and environmental problems".[11] B Corps are for-profit companies that meet rigorous standards of social and environmental performance, accountability and transparency. Today, there is a growing community of more than 2,100 Certified B Corps from 50 countries and over 130 industries. In Argentina, the Sistema B network gathers more than 120 enterprises and various actors who encourage this model of SSEO in the country. They are currently working closely with the national government in the formulation of a new law that encourages the creation of this type of organisation.

3.5. *Associative and Family Popular Initiatives*

This last model of SSEO refers to a type of organisation that is very widespread in Argentina and Latin America: small associative initiatives launched by workers excluded from the formal labour market, people with a low educational level and in a situation of relative poverty. These SSEOs are usually composed of family members or neighbours from popular neighbourhoods on the outskirts of cities. We are including in this SSEO model the microenterprises made up of workers who have some associative practices, either in the production of goods or services (associative entrepreneurship), in commercialisation (for example, commercialisation through self-managed fairs) or in financing (for instance, micro-credit groups).

The dominant logic and purpose of these initiatives is to provide income to the participating families as part of a complex strategy of solidarity-based reproduction of the domestic unit which combines different activities, resources and income to guarantee their subsistence (simple reproduction) or, in the best of cases, their expanded reproduction.[12] According to Coraggio (1999), these initiatives can be understood as an "extension" of the members' domestic units, since their economic logic aims at satisfying family needs and not at generating profit (and, least of all, at accumulating capital).

This can be noticed in several aspects. An example is the fact that, in most cases, the workspace is the house of one of the members, and the organisation's tools and equipment become intermingled with those of the home. Many of these initiatives are carried out by women to complement the household income, and they combine their productive activity with caring for their children and fulfilling domestic and communal tasks. Resorting to the initiative's funds to cover family expenses in the face of emergency situations is also common.

These organisations usually operate without registration in the legal and tax systems. In other words, they are "informal", because they cannot bear the costs associated with the formalisation of the initiative and of the self-managed work within the conventional legal frameworks. But it can be observed that, when special normative frames are created to protect and extend the rights of vulnerable groups, as it was for example, the case with the implementation of the so-called single social tax (*monotributo social*),[13] many of these workers take advantage of the opportunity that is offered to them to formalise their activity to improve their living conditions and their possibilities of increasing their incomes by selling to clients who demand legally valid documents.

Generally, SSEOs of this type produce or commercialise low-complexity goods and services (food, clothes, building services, etc.), resorting to machinery, tools and facilities of simple or obsolete technology, as compared to more capital-intensive productive units. Their products are commercialised in local markets and in their neighbourhoods, where the level of competition is high, due to the large number of bidders trying to sell to clients who look for the lowest price. In fact, the most frequent problem of these SSEOs is their difficulty to sell their products, which forces them to reduce their production (their aim is not to sell what they can produce, but to produce what they can sell). As a result, the sales revenues of this type of popular initiatives are so close to the costs which they incur that it seriously limits their capacity to produce a surplus. Consequently, the income to be distributed among workers is low, to the point that many family workers do not even receive a monetary remuneration for their (usually part-time) dedication to the initiative.

In Argentina, a series of public policies have been implemented since 2003 to strengthen this model of SSEO. Basically, machinery and equipment are provided for free by means of subsidies of relatively small amounts to facilitate production in easily accessible sectors (shops, gastronomy, clothing, etc.). However, these measures do not solve the problem of the commercialisation of products or of the resulting low income. To sum up, these initiatives' resource mix consists mainly of market income, family resources and limited state contribution.

The governance of this model of SSEO is not very structured and it is strongly conditioned by (and embedded in) the pre-existing power structures underlying the members' families. The business management is, logically, highly informal and unprofessional.

As regards their institutionalisation process in Argentina, as we have said, these types of activities usually grow and develop during stages of employment crises. They become a refuge for workers excluded from the labour market or a solution for the popular sectors to generate complementary income to deal with worsening living conditions. Such development took place with great intensity during the turn-of-the-21st-century crisis of the neoliberal model, and it is happening again nowadays as a consequence of a new wave of neoliberal policies in Argentina.

During progressive governments (2003–2015), different policies were implemented to strengthen this type of SSEO financially (by means of micro-credits), commercially (through fairs, collective brands, state purchases) and in terms of social security (through the implementation of the single social tax), among other aspects. The inclusion of initiatives of this kind in public policies gave more visibility to their work and needs, but the sector remains "scattered", and it lacks the capacity of expressing its interests to the state and the rest of society in a unified manner. Today, these initiatives do not stand as an identifiable "political player", with explicit adherence to a socially transformative project. Up to now, their integration into second-degree organisations has remained scarce, although it has been increasing during the last few years, since the Confederation of Popular Economy Workers (*Confederación de Trabajadores de la Economía Popular*, or CTEP) has been publicly voicing their reality and needs (Grabois and Pérsico 2014), as well as assuming their representation to the governments, with a growing visibility and capacity for exerting political pressure.

Following the characterisation of the five models of SSEO that we have identified in the Argentinian context, we present a table (table 1.1) with a comparative summary of the different types of organisation, elaborated on the basis of the major elements of analysis considered in this section and with the goal of enabling the comparison with organisations from different countries within the framework of the ICSEM Project.

Table 1.1 Five different models of social and solidarity-economy organisations (SSEOs) in Argentina

Characteristic features \ Model	1. Workers' self-managed organisations	2. Entities of the traditional social economy	3. Cooperatives for social inclusion related to state policies	4. Social businesses led by social entrepreneurs	5. Associative and family popular initiatives
Dominant logic	Self-managed cooperative logic	Mutualism	Redistributive logic	Entrepreneurship and market logic	Internal reciprocity in the domestic unit
Main social mission	Work and income generation for the members	Local and community development	Social integration of excluded populations	Addressing social problems through profitable enterprises	Income generation for reproduction
Legal form(s) adopted	Worker cooperatives and associations	Different types of cooperatives and mutuals	Cooperatives promoted by the state	Commercial enterprises and foundations	Informal organisation or single-social-tax payers
Activity sectors	All sectors of the economic activity	Urban services and agricultural production	Housing construction and improvement of popular habitat	Sectors that allow to conduct business with a social impact	Low-complexity goods and services
Resource mix and sustainability strategies	Mainly market income, although they demand state resources	Self-sustainability on the basis of market sales and associates' contributions	Mainly state subsidies and contracts	Self-sustainability or commercial profitability + initial donations	Neighbourhood market + family resources + state support

Predominant forms of governance and management	Democratic and participative self-management; challenges and innovations as regards management	Formal democracy but with limited actual participation, active councils and professional management	Scarce member participation and autonomy; dependence on public servants	Governance based on the founder's leadership, with the support of professional teams in management	Governance embedded in cultural and family power structures; informal management
Processes and pathways of institutionalisation	Emergence in crises; expansion and consolidation with progressive policies	Dynamic cooperative movement since 1920; in decline since 1976	Social policies that promote the social economy for poor populations	Individual initiatives and support from business networks and neoliberal governments	Emergence and role of refuge in times of crisis; supported by progressive policies
Participation in public and political spaces	Recent integration in federations and networks aiming to influence public policies	Highly consolidated federations and confederations with great power in the sector	Pickets and encampments to demand state resources; growing inclusion in worker unions and federations	Promotion of social entrepreneurship and corporate social responsibility	Scarce, but incipient, integration in second-degree organisations
Empirical cases of SSEO that are representative of the model	Recovered enterprises, worker cooperatives, direct producers' fairs, family farming associations	Public services cooperatives, agricultural cooperatives, Cooperativa Obrera de Consumo, Credicoop Bank	Cooperatives arising from social and infrastructure policies; cooperatives within social movements	Enterprises led by social entrepreneurs, Ashoka and Avina networks; B Corps	Small productive and commercial initiatives of workers in popular neighbourhoods

4. The Argentinian SSEOs From a Global Perspective

On the basis of the different models that have just been identified, we present, in this section, some considerations and conclusions about SSEOs. This helps to outline some global features of the Argentinian SSEO landscape within the frame of the international comparison proposed by this book and the ICSEM Project.

According to the National Institute for Associationism and the Social Economy (*Instituto Nacional de Asociativismo y Economía Social*, or INAES),[14] the first three models presented above—namely workers' self-managed organisations, entities of the traditional social economy and cooperatives for social inclusion related to state policies—are the three most important groups in terms of number of organisations. The experiences that can be classified under the associative and family popular initiatives are also numerous; however, since they lack formal registration, it is not easy to assess how many there are in the country. The CTEP estimates that around 500,000 people are working in small initiatives of this type (Grabois and Pérsico 2014). The organisations that can be included in the fourth model (social businesses led by social entrepreneurs) are growing in number, but they are still few in comparison to the other SSEOs.

Taking these data into account and on the basis of what has been described, we can identify some predominant characteristic features of Argentinian SSEOs:

- In a very significant proportion, Argentinian SSEOs are *self-managed* experiences implemented by workers (first and fifth models). Self-management is a horizon to reach for in the case of cooperatives that have emerged from social programmes (third model), but not a factual current reality.
- In the same line, the predominant form of governance (first, second and third models) is that based on the *assembly of associates* where, with more or less active participation, the organisations' representatives for daily management, with varying degrees of professionalisation, are *democratically* elected.
- The *cooperative*, in all its variants, is the legal form most commonly adopted by SSEOs, and among cooperatives, the largest group is that of worker cooperatives, which account for almost two thirds of the currently existing cooperatives.
- The most frequent social objectives and missions are *income and employment generation* for different groups of workers (first, third, fourth and fifth models). In many cases, the intention is to include in the initiative workers who are excluded from formal employment (third and fifth models).
- For most of the SSEOs, the market is the main source of income. The exception is the third model, whose resources come almost entirely

from the state. However, in all OESS models, there are sustainability strategies that seek to hybridise resources, complementing the predominant source with the development of other sources (state subsidies in the first and fifth model, community's contribution in the first and second model, market sales in the third model and private donations in the fourth one).

- In a national context of relatively intense political mobilisation, SSEOs seek to become *social and political players* and to influence the public agenda so as to defend their rights and interests or to promote transformations. However, institutional fragmentation due to internal differences is also common.

In figure 1.1, we attempt to locate the five models of SSEO identified in Argentina within the so-called welfare triangle, which illustrates the complexity of principles, resources and logics of action with which these types of organisation operate (see Defourny and Nyssens 2012).

The analysis derived from the representation of the Argentinian models of SSEO in the welfare triangle indicates that most of these models include *formally registered organisations*, except for the fifth model, where informality predominates.

It also indicates that *not-for-profit* organisations (i.e. organisations not owned by shareholders) are predominant, with the partial exception of the SSEOs inspired by the social-business perspective.

Thirdly, these organisations belong to the private sector (even though their objectives are of public interest), although in the case of SSEOs

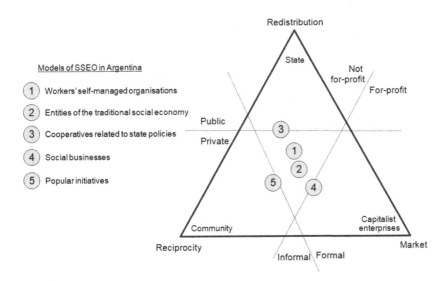

Figure 1.1 Models of Argentinian SSEOs in the "welfare triangle"

belonging to the third model, their strong connection with and dependence on state policies should be noted, both during their establishment stage and subsequently.

On another level, the figure shows that SSEOs differ from capitalist enterprises (although, in the case of the fourth model, they are strongly connected), from state institutions (with a strong connection in the case of the third model) and from community institutions, such as families or domestic units (although in the case of the fifth model, they can be considered as extensions of the domestic unit). That being said, all SSEOs work on the basis of principles and logics of action that are characteristic of such organisations, and the resources that make them viable result from the combination of practices of redistribution (they nearly all request and receive state support), practices of reciprocity (they develop a permanent exchange with the communities to which they belong) and market practices (their main source of income). For all these reasons, we can consider that SSEOs are experiences of *plural sustainability* (Vázquez 2010, 2016).

In figure 1.2, we have located the five models of SSEO in another triangle, which represents the diversity of principles of interest and resources at stake in this type of organisation (see Defourny and Nyssens 2016 and in this book).

This figure helps us to further examine the fact that, even though all SSEOs have strategies for resource hybridisation, market income is generally the dominant resource (the third model is again an exception), in

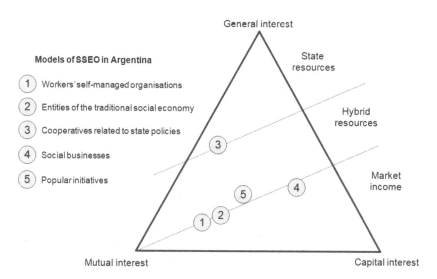

Figure 1.2 Models of Argentinian SSEOs according to their principles of interest and resource mixes

particular in the fourth model. This model also has stronger ties than the others to capitalistic logics, which may explain why organisations in this group tend to become stronger when these interests are predominant in government policies, as it is currently the case in Argentina. By contrast, the other models have a stronger link to the general and/or mutual interests. This also coincides with the fact that these types of SSEO (and in particular the first, second and third models) have undergone processes of growth and consolidation during the periods of history with predominantly progressive and redistributive policies aiming at protecting domestic production and consumption, as was the case during the Perón and Kirchners administrations, as has been explained in section 2 of this chapter.

Conclusion: Prospects and Challenges

Finally, to conclude this chapter, we want to share some thoughts and intuitions about the prospects and challenges that the different models of SSEO will face in the new national and regional political scenario.

This scenario is currently characterised by the rise of a group of neoliberal governments (Macri in Argentina, Temer in Brazil, Cartes in Paraguay, Piñera in Chile, etc.), all of which are introducing a series of "reforms" in laws, institutions and policies at different levels (labour, pensions, taxes, market, finance, etc.). They aim at deregulating markets and reducing state intervention in order to make room for financial capital and transnational companies and to enable them to deploy their accumulation strategies more freely than it was the case under progressive governments with popular roots. We consider that this new national and regional context will have a significant impact on the SSE sector, although this impact will vary depending on the model of SSEO considered.

In Argentina, businessman Mauricio Macri's administration is interested in promoting entrepreneurship of the "social business" type (fourth model), and some public resources that the previous government used to strengthen associative experiences (workers' self-managed organisations and cooperatives for social inclusion linked to state policies) are now being allocated to support for individual entrepreneurial initiatives.

As regards policies of social integration by means of cooperatives financed by the state (third model), the current government is pushing for a "de-cooperativisation" of beneficiaries by maintaining the subsidies, but only for the integration of individual and precarious workers through local state activities. The only cooperatives that are still being supported are those with ties to social movements that claim state resources by "direct-action" strategies (demonstrations, encampments, roadblocks, pickets, etc.).

Nowadays workers' self-managed SSEOs (first model) are facing enormous difficulties to obtain sufficient market income to secure their sustainability, and many are going through a serious crisis or simply closing. This is due to a combination of several factors: the falling demand for their products as a result of the decline in domestic consumption; the lack of state protection in the face of a massive and deregulated entry of cheap imported products; and the enormous increase in energy and public services costs (fuel, electricity, gas and water) due to the elimination of public subsidies and the deregulation of those markets. As a case in point, it is worth mentioning the critical situation towards which this government is driving workers' "recovered enterprises" by vetoing expropriation laws that favoured them.[15]

As regards entities of the traditional social economy (second model), there are cases of organisations that are benefiting from current policies, such as the agricultural cooperatives favoured by reductions in grain export taxes, while other SSEOs are being strongly affected by the decline in domestic demand and by rising costs. Medium and big cooperatives are also suffering under a new fiscal reform that levies on them taxes from which they were previously exempted.

Finally, family and associative popular initiatives (fifth model) are growing in number, since they represent today a refuge against growing unemployment and an answer to the need for income generation in the poorest sectors. This worsens the levels of saturation in neighbourhood markets and hinders the generation of sufficient income in a context of increasingly unsatisfied family needs.

In short, the majority of SSEOs in Argentina are going through difficult times that will test their capacity to defend their interests in the public sphere. The outcome will depend largely on their capacity to become strong political players by overcoming their fragmentations and articulating with other sectors of the population that are being negatively affected by this neoliberal offensive, as well as on their capacity to bring to light the practices and proposals that show that another economy is possible and necessary, by sharing them with the community as a whole and making them socially visible.

Acknowledgements

The author wishes to thank Luiz Inácio Gaiger, Marthe Nyssens and Sophie Adam for their useful corrections and suggestions.

Notes

1 This chapter was originally written in Spanish, and it was translated into English by the cooperative "Abrapalabra" (http://abrapalabra-sl.com/).
2 The capitalist world system can be characterised by the "centre-periphery" duality, where the central countries (industrialised and with a diversified production) establish relations of unequal exchange with the peripheral countries (specialised in primary production), configuring a dynamic that reproduces

peripheral countries' situation of dependence and underdevelopment. These explanations were developed by the Latin American structuralist economic school (by authors such as Raúl Prebisch and Celso Furtado) and then taken up by the world system theory (by authors such as Immanuel Wallerstein and Giovanni Arrighi).

3 The publication in Argentina of the book *La Empresa Social* ("The Social Enterprise"; de Leonardis *et al.* 1995) contributed to the local circulation of this perspective.

4 See the book *Empresas Sociales y Economía Social: aproximación a sus rasgos fundamentales* ("Social Enterprises and Social Economy: Apprehending their Fundamental Features"; Abramovich *et al.* 2003).

5 See the short text *La Economía Social como vía para otro desarrollo social* ("Social economy as a way to another social development"), written in 2002 as a document to start a debate about the different perspectives about the social economy (*Distintas propuestas de Economía Social*) at URBARED, available on www.coraggioeconomia.org/jlc_publicaciones_ep.htm.

6 See www.ungs.edu.ar/ms_ico/?page_id=5079. This Master's degree is directed by José Luis Coraggio, one of the most respected thinkers in this field in Latin America.

7 See for example Paul Singer's text *Economía Solidaria. Un modo de producción y distribución* ("Solidarity economy. A model of production and distribution"), published in the book *A economía solidária no Brasil: a autogestão como resposta ao desemprego* ("The solidarity economy in Brazil: Self-management as an answer to unemployment"; Singer and de Souza 2000).

8 This might have been influenced by the emergence, in 2005, of the Network of Latin American Researchers of the Social and Solidarity Economy (*Red de Investigadores Latinoamericanos de Economía Social y Solidaria*, or RILESS), which encouraged the organisation of different meetings and the creation of spaces for exchange, such as the journal *Otra Economía* (Another Economy), which was born in 2007. Later on, the University Network of the Social and Solidarity Economy (*Red Universitaria de Economía Social y Solidaria*, or RUESS; www.ruess.com.ar) was created in Argentina; it aimed to support the articulation, visibility, convergence and characterisation of the university practices (of intervention, research, teaching, community actions and territorial connection) related to the SSE.

9 The fact that Ariel Guarco, head of an electrical cooperative of Buenos Aires province, was elected president of the International Cooperative Alliance in 2017 offers a good example of such international influence (https://ica.coop/en/media/news/press-release-ariel-guarco-from-argentina-elected-president-of-the-international-co).

10 See www.elarcamendoza.com.ar.

11 See www.sistemab.org/argentina.

12 "At the level of a domestic unit, an expanded reproduction situation implies a process in which, above the simple reproduction level, a sustained development in the quality of life of the members takes place during a prolonged period (for example, one generation). The notion of 'simple reproduction' does not refer to mere subsistence, or reproduction of biological life, but denotes a quality of biological and social life considered as a socially accepted minimum below which no domestic unit belonging to the society under analysis should encounter itself". (Coraggio 1999: 1–2; author's own translation)

13 This special regime, subsidised by the state, enables workers to gain access to certain social security benefits (health and pension contribution) and to a legal status in terms of taxation by paying a low monthly contribution. In 2016, around 360,000 people were registered under this regime, including

workers in cooperatives (third model of SSEO, see section 3.3) and in popular initiatives (fifth model, see this section).

14 See the register of organisations on www.inaes.gob.ar
15 See www.lavaca.org/notas/las-empresas-recuperadas-en-la-era-macri/

References

Abramovich, A., Cassano, D., Federico Sabaté, A., Hintze, S., Kohan, G., Montequín, A. & Vázquez, G. (2003) *Empresas Sociales y Economía Social: aproximación a sus rasgos fundamentales*, Los Polvorines: UNGS.

Acosta, M. C., Levin, A. & Verbeke, G. (2013) "El sector cooperativo en Argentina en la última década", *Revista Cooperativismo y Desarrollo*, No. 21, Universidad Cooperativa de Colombia.

Ashoka. (undated) "Empresas Sociales. Aprendizajes sobre la Práctica de Emprendedores Sociales". Available HTTP: www.ashoka.org/es.

Coraggio, J. L. (1999) *Política social y economía del trabajo: alternativas a la política neoliberal para la ciudad*, Buenos Aires: UNGS, Miño y Dávila Editores.

Defourny, J. & Nyssens, M. (2006) "Defining social enterprise", in Nyssens, M. (ed.) *Social Enterprise: At the Crossroads of Market, Public Policies and Civil Society*, London and New York: Routledge, pp. 3–26.

Defourny, J. & Nyssens, M. (2012) "El enfoque EMES de empresa social desde una perspectiva comparada", *Revista de Economía Pública, Social y Cooperativa*, CIRIEC-Spain. Available HTTP: www.emes.net, EMES Working Papers Series, WP no. 13/01.

Defourny, J. & Nyssens, M. (2016) "Fundamentals for an international typology of social enterprise models", ICSEM Working Papers, No. 33, Liege: The International Comparative Social Enterprise Models (ICSEM) Project.

De Leonardis, O., Mauri, D. & Rotelli, F. (1995) *La Empresa Social*, Buenos Aires: Nueva Visión.

Gardin, L. (2006) "A variety of resource mixes inside social enterprises", in Nyssens, M. (ed.) *Social Enterprise: At the Crossroads of Market, Public Policies and Civil Society*, London and New York: Routledge, pp. 111–136.

Grabois, J. & Pérsico, E. (2014) "Organización y economía popular: nuestra realidad", CTEP—Asociación Civil de los Trabajadores de la Economía Popular, Buenos Aires.

Guarco, A. (2013) *El cooperativismo argentino: una esperanzadora mirada hacia el futuro*, Buenos Aires: Intercoop.

Laville, J-L., Lemaître, A. & Nyssens, M. (2006) "Public policies and social enterprises in Europe: The challenge of institutionalization", in Nyssens, M. (ed.) *Social Enterprise: At the Crossroads of Market, Public Policies and Civil Society*, London and New York: Routledge, pp. 272–295.

Levin, A. & Verbeke, G. (1997) "El cooperativismo argentino en cifras. Tendencias en su evolución: 1927–1997", Documents of CESOT, No. 6, Buenos Aires.

Pastore, R. (2010) "Un panorama del resurgimiento de la economía social y solidaria en la Argentina", *Revista de Ciencias Sociales*, Year 2, No. 18, Spring, Bernal: Universidad Nacional de Quilmes.

Plotinsky, D. (2015) "Orígenes y consolidación del cooperativismo en la Argentina", *Idelcoop magazine*, No. 215, Buenos Aires.

Plotinsky, D. (2017) "Argentina: políticas públicas y cooperativismo", paper presented at the VII Jornadas de la División de Historia de la Universidad Nacional de Luján, Mimeo.

Ruggeri, A. (2014) *¿Qué son las empresas recuperadas? Autogestión de la clase trabajadora*, Buenos Aires: Peña Lillo y Ediciones Continente.

Singer, P. & De Souza, R. A. (eds) (2000) *A economia solidária no Brasil: a autogestão como resposta ao desemprego*, São Paulo: Editora Contexto.

Vázquez, G. (2009) "La Economía Social y Solidaria en América Latina: Propuesta de Economía Alternativa y su aplicación al análisis de experiencias en Argentina", EMES Conferences Selected Papers Series, ECSP-B08-07. Available HTTP: www.emes.net.

Vázquez, G. (2010) "La sostenibilidad de los emprendimientos asociativos de trabajadores autogestionados. Perspectivas y aportes conceptuales desde América Latina", Master thesis, Los Polvorines: Universidad Nacional de General Sarmiento. Available HTTP: www.ungs.edu.ar/.

Vázquez, G. (2016) "La viabilidad y sostenibilidad de las experiencias de trabajo asociativo y autogestionado desde una perspectiva plural", *Revista de la Academia*, Vol. 21, pp. 31–55, Autumn, Santiago de Chile: Universidad Academia del Humanismo Cristiano.

2 Bolivian Cooperative and Community Enterprises

Economic and Political Dimensions

Fernanda Wanderley

Introduction

The Bolivian economy's plurality has long been the subject of analysis and debate in the country, due to the persistence and coexistence of economic units whose forms of ownership, governance structure, labour relations and objectives differ from those of capitalist enterprises and from the public sector. Agrarian communities based on family farming, producer associations and cooperatives have linked up with and existed alongside capitalist enterprises, forging a process of modernisation in which self-generated work still predominates today.

The victory of the "Movement for Socialism" (*Movimiento al Socialismo*) in the 2005 election marked the beginning of a new cycle in Bolivia's recent history—a period characterised by discursive, political and economic changes that were expressed in the Constituent Assembly with widespread popular participation. Great expectations were raised by the government's promise to implement a new model of development that would strengthen the economic diversity already present in the country. The new Constitution, approved in 2009, proposed to recognise, promote and protect what it named the "plural economy model", which comprised four major forms of economy: the state economy (state-owned enterprises and companies); the private economy (privately owned businesses and companies); the cooperative economy; and the community economy (social production and reproduction systems based on the particular principles and worldview of indigenous peoples, first nations and peasant communities).

Various collectives, with a long history of mobilisation, have worked to promote the new economic model by having new legislation drawn and approved. Through their political representation structures, each of these collectives demanded and/or participated in the drafting of specific laws recognising their economic organisations in the new legal typology. The new government promoted state-owned enterprises and the business sector supported privately owned enterprises through

DOI: 10.4324/9780429055164-4

various laws. The cooperative sector fostered cooperatives through the General Law on Cooperatives, approved in 2013. Three other collectives played a leading role to advance their economic organisations under the overarching legal concept of community economy: peasants and indigenous actors promoted their economic organisations (*organizaciones económicas campesinas*, or OECAs) through the Law on Sustainable Family Farming and Food Sovereignty, approved in 2013; farmers' unions promoted community economic organisations (*organizaciones económicas comunitarias*, or OECOMs) through the Law on the Productive Community Farming Revolution, approved in 2011; and artisans pushed for the Law on Artisans' Promotion and Development, approved in 2012.

This chapter has two objectives. The first is to analyse the four types of economic organisation whose forms differ from state-owned companies and privately owned businesses: peasant economic organisations (OECAs), community economic organisations (OECOMs), artisans' associations and cooperatives. We will characterise these economic organisations and illustrate their historical development as political subjects. Even though these forms can be considered as social enterprises, this concept is not used in the public and academic debates in Bolivia. Instead of this term, four concepts have been applied to identify this set of enterprises: the community economy, the social economy, the solidarity economy and the cooperative economy. Lack of clarity about how these concepts relate to each other in the plural economy framework has not been solved yet by collectives, policymakers and academics.

The second objective is to analyse the difficulties that prevent these collectives from linking up with each other to build a coherent, integrated, common public-policy agenda that would lead to the institutionalisation of these alternative forms of economy. The explanation focuses on the specific paths of collective action taken in the public sphere and in the overall economy by these four types of actors, established over the last ten years against the backdrop of an exceptional economic bonanza. This context fostered the drive to defend group interests in an unconnected manner, thus reducing the possibilities for building alliances between the different economic actors and for harmonising their interests with the aim of consolidating a broader collective project.

The chapter is structured in three sections. The first one summarises the main characteristics of the four types of economic organisation analysed here and listed above. The second section analyses the difficulties that prevent the collectives from forging links with each other. The third section focuses, through the lens of the political economy, on factors that intensify these actors' inability to connect and take forward a common agenda for a legal and public-policy framework to promote the plural economy. The chapter concludes with some final remarks.

1. Four Types of Economic Organisation

The process of demanding new laws and having them approved with a view to fostering different economic organisations within the plural economy model illustrates the lengthy political track record of the main economic actors. Not only do the different laws attest to the economic and political importance of these actors in Bolivian society; they also reveal the economic organisational types that these actors represent. To characterise the four types of organisation analysed here, the study followed the indicators put forward by the EMES network and used by the International Comparative Social Enterprise Models (ICSEM) Project, analysing three main dimensions: the social dimension, the economic one and the governance structure. A fourth dimension was included in the analysis, namely political action in the public sphere.

The sources for the study were secondary literature, statistical data and qualitative research. Bolivia does not have a census or survey aimed at mapping the plural economy and, therefore, the statistic sources are not only varied but also uneven.[1]

Table 2.1 summarises the characteristics of the four main types of economic organisation that differ from private for-profit and public enterprises in Bolivia.

1.1. Peasant Economic Organisations (OECAs)

Political Dimension

Peasant economic organisations (OECAs) date back to the 1930s and 1940s. Starting in the 1980s, however, the number of OECAs increased significantly, due mainly to the support they were receiving from non-governmental organisations (NGOs) at a time when international cooperation funding was plentiful. NGOs took on the role of providing support and services, in coordination with the public sector, for communities affected by structural adjustment policies (Muñoz Elsner 2004). Following a lengthy campaign for official recognition, Law 338 on Peasant and Indigenous Economic Organisations (OECAs) and Community Economic Organisations (OECOMs) for the Integration of Sustainable Family Farming and Food Sovereignty was approved in 2013.

OECAs are organised politically on three levels. The first level comprises small-scale farmers from one or more communities organised as a group of producers to address their production and/or marketing problems collectively. Their work mainly concentrates on technical issues. At the second level are the federations and confederations of farmers' organisations. Their main role is to provide technical support to producers in different economic categories and to represent them politically. The third level is that of national-level representative organisations.[2]

Social Dimension

OECAs are a form of association of farming families. OECAs are set up in three main ways: at the initiative of a local group, as a result of a government policy or as part of an international cooperation project. Since the 1980s, however, this last way has been prevailing: NGO projects financed by international donors account for a significant proportion of the OECAs established.

OECAs' main objective is to increase their members' income. Their activities may include marketing, the purchase of inputs, technical assistance, processing, storage and representation of their members in dealings with the state, NGOs and international donors. Their representative organisations offer regular courses for members on social and political issues such as leadership and gender equity, health insurance and other benefits for members.

Economic Dimension

OECAs operate in agriculture (61.2%), livestock farming (23.8%), handicrafts (12.2%), community tourism sectors in rural areas (1.5%) and forest harvest (1.3%) (CIOEC 2009). It is estimated that there are approximately 800 OECAs in the country as a whole, with 102,000 members, 59% of whom are women and 41% are men.

The members are these organisations' main workers, but OECAs also contract non-members for administrative and specialised technical tasks. In smaller OECAs, production is organised by each farming family and the OECA's main role is to collect and sell the produce. There is a preference for employing family members in OECA jobs, in keeping with the objective of bringing in new generations of members, but this often gives rise to tensions regarding the workers' capability and objectivity in dealings with partners.

The main activities of the majority of OECAs are joint marketing and political representation, with only a limited degree of cooperation in the stages of production (Flores and Ton 2015). The largest and most well-established OECAs tend to aim for vertical integration and seek to control the entire production chain, from inputs to marketing. One of the advantages many associations offer is the sale of pest-control products to their members at prices below the market price, as well as the provision of credit. Training services are also mentioned, although they are not provided regularly in most cases.

As just said, the sale of produce in the market is OECAs' main activity, although some of the food produced is for the families' own consumption. OECAs are highly diverse in terms of their size and market participation. A sample of OECAs studied by Flores and Ton (2015) included organisations ranging from 20 to 300 members, with annual sales (for the year 2012) worth between US$2,200 and US$1,700,000.

Table 2.1 Summary of the characteristics of community and cooperative enterprises

Dimensions	Types of economic organisation	Peasant economic organisation (OECA)	Community economic organisation (OECOM)	Artisans' organisation	Cooperative
Political dimension	Self-definition as regards the "plural economy model"	Community economy	Community economy	Community economy	Cooperative economy
	Political representatives	Peasant economic associations	Community autonomous governments	Artisans' associations	Cooperatives
	Public history	Lengthy organisational history dating back to the 1930s; weak institutional and public-policy support in the long run	Lengthy organisational history dating back to the 1980s; strong institutionalisation; and strong public-policy support since 2006	Lengthy organisational history dating back to the 1930s; weak institutionalisation and public-policy support in the long run	Lengthy organisational history dating back to the 1930s; strong institutionalisation; and public-policy support since 2006
	Post-2006 laws approved	Law 338, on Sustainable Family Farming and Food Sovereignty	Law 144, on Productive Community Farming Revolution	Law 306, on Artisans' Promotion and Development	Law 356—General Law on Cooperatives
Social dimension	Objectives	To increase the members' income by cooperating on marketing, purchase of inputs, technical assistance, processing, storage and political representation; and to obtain benefits for mefmbers	To increase the members' income and benefits by setting up community enterprises	To increase the members' income and benefits by cooperating on marketing, purchase of inputs, technical assistance, processing, storage and political representation	To generate income and to obtain benefits for members

		Associations of farming families	Community enterprises run by indigenous and rural communities whose territorial rights are recognised	Associations of family-run workshops	Wide range of cooperatives; low level of compliance with international cooperative principles and national laws
	Type of organisation	Associations of farming families	Community enterprises run by indigenous and rural communities whose territorial rights are recognised	Associations of family-run workshops	Wide range of cooperatives; low level of compliance with international cooperative principles and national laws
	Initiative	Members, government policy, international cooperation	Community government, government policy, international cooperation	Members, government policy, international cooperation	Members, government policy
Economic dimension	**Sector of activity**	Agriculture, livestock farming, forestry, handicrafts, community tourism	Management of common resources (land, water), agriculture, livestock farming, hunting and gathering, fishing, forestry, handicrafts, community tourism, production	Textiles, wood, pewter, jewellery, leatherwork, ceramics, silver- and goldsmithing, plasterwork, metalwork, food, weavings, paintings, hides, precious stones, musical instruments	Production sector, service sector, public services sector. Most important sectors: mining, savings and credit
	Resources	Mainly sales in the domestic and international markets Production for families' own consumption Resources from international cooperation Public funds	Mainly sales in the domestic and international markets Production for families' own consumption Resources from international cooperation Public funds	Mainly sales in the domestic and international markets International cooperation Public funds	Mainly sales in the market Public funds

(Continued)

Table 2.1 (Continued)

Dimensions	Types of economic organisation	Peasant economic organisation (OECA)	Community economic organisation (OECOM)	Artisans' organisation	Cooperative
Governance structure	Work relation	Family labour Member-workers Limited salaried work	Family labour Community workers	Member-workers Limited salaried work	Member-workers Limited salaried work
	Membership	Membership is voluntary and based on similar interests	Membership is compulsory due to membership of a territorial community	Membership is voluntary and based on similar interests	Membership is voluntary and based on similar interests
	Decision-making	Members' assembly Organisational structure similar to a trade union, with a president and secretaries Autonomous organisation	Community governments Organisational structure similar to a trade union, with a president and secretaries Autonomous organisation	Members' assembly Organisational structure similar to a trade union, with a president and secretaries Autonomous organisation	Management in most cooperatives does not abide by current laws. Insufficient respect for the principle of democratic control
	Leadership	Self-management Rotating leadership	Self-management Rotating leadership	Self-management Rotating leadership	Self-management Rotating leadership
	Legal arrangements	65% are civil associations 9% are cooperatives 26% are informal groups	Legal personality of the indigenous, first-nation, rural, intercultural or Afro-Bolivian communities	Civil associations Cooperatives	Limited-liability system as defined by the Code of Commerce

Source: Compiled by the author.

The market may be domestic or international, depending on the product category. In the domestic market, sales to the public sector have been gaining in importance, mainly thanks to the school breakfasts scheme run by municipal governments. OECAs have also been developing economic relationships with supermarket chains, which distribute the community organisations or associations' products in two ways: under the organisation's own brand or under the supermarket's brand. Other important sales outlets are street markets and the organisations' own shops (Borth and Elías Argandoña 2014). In the export market, the best-established OECAs are able to access the fair-trade market, mainly through certification by Fair Trade International (FLO) and World Fair Trade Organisation (WFTO) (Bishelly and Salazar 2006).

According to the members, prices are set based on consultation with all the members and tend to favour the producer. Members consider the prices set by the OECAs to be fair and stable, in contrast to those practiced by intermediaries or companies, which set prices without consulting producers and prioritise their own interests. Producers are paid according to the quantity of produce they deliver.

Part of the profit is reinvested in the association and the rest is redistributed in cash or under the form of services such as health insurance, training courses or scholarships for the members' children (Muñoz Elsner 2004; Pari 2017; Flores and Ton 2015).

Governance Structure

Membership is voluntary and based on the similarity of members' interests. OECAs are managed according to the principle of self-management, and they usually operate on the basis of the principle of rotating leadership among the members. This reflects the strong influence of the farmers' union, whose structure is similar—a structure that is also used by the next type of organisation analysed here. Most OECAs have similar leadership posts: a president, a vice-president, a records secretary, a finance secretary, a secretary dealing with the productive activity and ordinary committee members. It is also common for them to have a gender agenda. The most important decisions are taken in the general assembly, in which all the members participate. The management posts are not usually paid and the principle of rotating leadership creates management efficiency problems. In well-established OECAs, the rotation of the management committee is the subject of a debate and many organisations are choosing to hire an executive manager who is not a member.

According to the CIOEC census (2009), 65% of OECAs are legally registered as civil associations and 9% as cooperatives, while 26% are informal groups without any legal recognition. In legal terms, the organisations have two alternatives: to register as non-profit organisations, which means that they are not allowed to make a profit from their activities, or to register as cooperatives. This poses a problem for the organisations. The majority choose to register as non-profit organisations because the requirements to register as cooperatives are very onerous. This legal situation means that, legally speaking, they do not differ fundamentally from NGOs, even though their aim is to generate surplus income and to distribute it, in a controlled way, to their members (Wanderley *et al.* 2015).

1.2. Community Economic Organisations (OECOMs)

Political Dimension

OECOMs are part of the community autonomous governments, which have been a very important political actor in Bolivian history and remain so today. Community governments play two main roles: regulation of the social, economic and political relations of the group of people who live in a given territory, and political representation of these people in dealings with the state. These roles have been recognised by the Bolivian state throughout the country's history (Albó 1999, 2000). At the local level, community governments are known by different names, depending on the social and cultural characteristics of the communities concerned: farmers' unions, *ayllus*, *capitanías*, peasant communities, indigenous communities and other terms. At the second level of the representation structure are the local-level union organisations, referred to as *ayllus*[3] or cantons. At the third level are the regional farmers' unions—*marka* or *ayllu mayor*. Provincial federations or regional organisations constitute the fourth level; departmental federations, the fifth level; and confederations or umbrella organisations, the sixth—national—level (Gros and Foyer 2010).

The legal form of community economic organisation (OECOM), created by Law 144 in 2011, has its origins in the 1980s, under the leadership of the Single Trade Union Confederation of the Peasant Workers of Bolivia (*Confederación Sindical Única de Trabajadores Campesinos de Bolivia*, or CSUTCB). During the National Congress on Agrarian Reform, in 1984, the Small-Scale Farming Corporation (*Corporación Agropecuaria Campesina*, or CORACA) was established with the aim of acting as the economic arm of the farmers' unions (community governments), thus expanding their social and political roles to include economic roles as community enterprises. In the years following the 1984 Congress, the state recognised the CORACAs by awarding them legal personality, and many were set up by the farmers' unions in several regions of the country (Devisscher Leroux 1996).

Law 144 takes up the idea of the CORACA as an economic organisation run by community governments. The CORACA can thus be considered as the "predecessor" of the OECOM. There were many and varied experiences with CORACAs, and many of these turned into voluntary associations with members from one or more communities or cooperatives, thus becoming increasingly similar to OECAs. New OECOMs are few, and they tend to take the form of local projects in the process of being developed. The most important OECOM initiatives form part of the establishment of autonomous community territories by indigenous peoples.

An important characteristic of the community autonomous government is the management of common resources, such as land and water. Community cohesion is based mainly on the regulation of land ownership rights, both in the case of land owned by families and individuals (the majority) and in the case of community-owned land (Colque 2007). The management of water includes building infrastructure such as irrigation ditches and tanks, washing facilities and crop collection centres, as well as buying tools that are owned by the community. There is less collective experience of managing or regulating productive activities; this is a complex, long-term learning process.

There is no available statistical data about OECOMs.

Social Dimension

The overall mission of OECOMs is to create community enterprises in indigenous or peasant areas, backed by these communities' right to territory such as it is recognised in a series of laws passed in the 1990s.[4] The objective is to build economic organisations involving everyone in each community territory. As a political project, it is left to each community or autonomous territory to define the specific nature of the community economic organisation (OECOM) they want to create. One of the few new experiences so far is located in the autonomous territory of Raquaypampa. According to its statutes, this OECOM is defined as follows:

> It is a not-for-profit organisation set up by the community for its own benefit, under the principles of democratic participation, solidarity, reciprocity and equity. It was created following a decision by the majority of the organisations in Raqaypampa and is established as the organisation that guarantees their recognition as productive economic actors capable of generating self-employment, direct and indirect employment and earnings, as a solidarity-based response to other models of productive development.
>
> Calvo (2017: 26), quoting from the OECOM Statutes

The main objectives of the Raqaypampa OECOM are to increase the family income, improve agroecological farming production, strengthen food security, boost the recovery of biodiversity, promote women's participation in economic activities, process and add value to agricultural produce, diversify food production through processing, look for and consolidate markets at the local, regional, departmental and national level, promote organic farming that respects and looks after Mother Earth, ensure that the OECOM is participatory, fair and democratic in its structures and management, and help to reduce malnutrition and improve people's overall state of health by promoting healthy eating habits, based mainly on local agro-biodiversity resources (Calvo 2017).

Economic Dimension

Because an OECOM is a local economic enterprise, its work depends on the ecosystems in its particular territory and the activities practised there. These may be agriculture, livestock farming, hunting and gathering, fishing, forestry (logging or non-timber forest products), handicrafts, community tourism or other occupations. Likewise, the organisations may be involved in cultivation, collection, processing, industrialisation, distribution, exchange and/or marketing.

Decisions on price setting, sales and earnings distribution are taken collectively at the meetings of the community government or in the relevant structures set up specifically to manage the OECOM, as is the case in Raqaypampa (Calvo 2017).

The older experiences, which started as CORACAs, such as Productos Totolima-Altamachi (PROTAL), changed gradually over time from a community government principle of obligatory membership (OECOM) to a principle of voluntary membership (OECA). In PROTAL, which mainly aims to guarantee market access for its members' produce, prices are set by the producers in an assembly meeting, based on production costs: the price is judged "fair" by the members when it includes some profit for the producer, as well as an additional percentage for the CORACA (Devisscher Leroux 2017). This approach to setting prices allows the organisation to support the development of the enterprise in a systematic way (working capital, technological innovations, etc.) and provide additional services to members (a limited number of production support and social services) (Calvo 2017).

Governance Structure

OECOMs are economic organisations set up by all the members of one or more communities for economic purposes. According to the law, membership of the OECOM is compulsory for everyone who belongs to a territorial community. This is the main difference between these organisations and the OECAs, where membership is voluntary and depends on the shared interests and objectives agreed upon by a group of people who belong to a territorial community or several communities.

The community governments (farmers' unions or *ayllus*) are responsible for the management of the OECOM. OECOM management is a process that is still under development and depends on the specific characteristics of the territorial communities involved. In the indigenous and peasant community territories (*territorios indígena originario campesinos*, or TIOCs), the constitution of a new OECOM is closely linked to the process of developing the autonomous indigenous territory and designing the mechanisms for self-government, which in turn are closely related to the territorial plan. This process is gradually becoming formalised as the procedures for legally registering autonomous territories are carried out.

The process of setting up and launching the OECOM in Raqaypampa was taken forward collectively through the existing community governments, with the whole community participating. It was a lengthy and difficult process, which required more than 50 meetings:

> *Another issue that needed a lot of discussion in the local unions was how to define the organisational structure, because everyone in the communities wanted to be represented in the decision-making structure. Thus, they ended up with an organisational arrangement linked to the union's organisation at the territorial level, where the leadership committee includes representatives (men and women) from each of the lower-level unions. This committee—whose president acts as the legal representative—directs and supervises the work at the operational level, and has its own operations manager and staff team.*
>
> Calvo (2017: 29)

The regional organisational structure of CORACA-PROTAL includes the posts of president and vice-president, production officer, industrialisation and marketing officer, and infrastructure and services officer. The leadership committee was sworn in by the Single Trade Union Federation of Peasant Workers of Cochabamba. The organisation has about 150 member families and holds a General Assembly of Delegates, whose participants are leaders and authorities from the community CORACAs in four communities (Qhory Mayu, Carmen Pampa, Maiqa Monte and San Julián) and two working groups (Porvenir and Jaythasiri). The assembly has decision-making power and designs the association's overall policies. There is also a management committee, which is the organisation's executive arm and is made up of seven members: four with management responsibilities and three who play the role of a quality-control committee (Devisscher 2017).

Supreme Decree No. 2849, enacted in 2016, establishes the regulations for the process of legally registering an OECOM. For indigenous, first-nation, peasant, intercultural or Afro-Bolivian communities to be accredited to exercise the rights and duties corresponding to an OECOM, they must present the legal document recognising the legal existence of the relevant community (*personería jurídica*), a document awarding broad power of attorney conferred by the community government and a certificate of membership awarded by their umbrella organisations (federations and confederations) in keeping with their own norms and procedures.

1.3. Artisans' Associations

Political Dimension

The first collectives politically representing artisans date back to the second half of the 19th century, when they obtained the official approval as grassroots organisations and thus became established as a valid interlocutor in dealings with the state (Van Der Veen 1993). The artisans then began to organise around the objectives of cooperation and mutual assistance. As well as promoting informal rules governing sectorial activities, they formulated the first demands towards the state to defend their market and ban imports. Artisans have become established as a collective able to express their group interests and demands and pursue common objectives. In the process, they have developed their own institutions, structured in accordance with current laws and, at the same time, influenced the design of such laws. As a social group, they have evolved over time and adapted their ideological leanings and aspirations in accordance with changing political, social and economic circumstances (Wanderley 2005).

After a 25-year campaign, the artisans achieved approval of the Law on Artisan Promotion and Development (Law N° 306) in 2012. This law covers:

> *all natural or legal persons, individuals and collectives engaged in artisanal trades* [and its purpose is to] *recognise, protect, foster, promote and encourage the sustainable development of the artisan sector's activities, in all their locally-specific forms,* [by] *facilitating access to finance, technical assistance, training and markets for the artisan sector, promoting the recovery and dissemination of artisans' knowledge, skills, aptitudes and abilities as part of the integrated development of the Plurinational State, and raising public awareness of their economic, social and cultural importance.*

The location of artisans' associations within the plural economy model is not mentioned in the 27 articles that constitute this law. However, these organisations' participation in the plural economy is assumed in principle as the law stipulates that among the roles of autonomous territorial governments is the duty to promote and foster *the principles of solidarity, complementarity and cooperation, membership of associations and the development of synergies between the different actors involved in artisanal trades.*

The artisan sector is organised on three levels of representation: the first level is that of grassroots organisations, including associations, unions, cooperatives, centres, mutual societies and trade guilds. In the production sector, the association is the most important form of organisation, while in the services sector, the trade guild is the most common. At the second level are the federations, which bring together the grassroots organisations connected with a specific activity or set of activities. This means that there is a wide variety of federations in each department or region of the country. At the third level are the umbrella organisations, which may be sectoral or multisectoral in nature.[5]

There is no statistical data about artisans' associations.

Social Dimension

There is a great diversity of organisational forms in the artisan sector, from family-run workshops to small-scale businesses and associations. Their mainly peasant and indigenous origins place most artisans in the low-income sectors with ancestral ties to rural communities, although there are important differences depending on their geographical location.

The main objective of artisans' associations is income generation, but these associations tend to be set up with three secondary objectives. The first one is the joint marketing of the products in domestic or international markets. The second goal is to liaise with public authorities, private institutions, non-governmental organisations and international cooperation agencies. The third objective is to achieve joint production among the members by coordinating purchases of raw materials, processing and placement of the products in the market.

However, choosing to form an association is not motivated solely by expectations of higher monetary returns. Associations are non-hierarchical, transparent and participatory, and they offer very important social and personal benefits, such as a space for sharing and mutual support, especially in the case of the associations whose members are women (Wanderley 2014).

Artisans' associations are set up in three main ways: at the initiative of a local group, as a result of a government policy or as part of an NGO project with international cooperation funding. Like OECAs, from the 1980s onward, many associations have been set up at the initiative of NGOs financed by international cooperation.

Economic Dimension

The artisan sector produces food, clothes, wooden objects, jewellery, metalwork and popular art. Associations are very diverse in terms of their production and sales patterns. While some manage to keep production and sales going throughout the year, for others, production is seasonal and concentrated in certain months. Some associations are involved in both local and international markets, while others aim solely at the domestic or the export market. The stability of exports throughout the year also varies: while some organisations export all year round, others do so only sporadically or in very small quantities. Only a few have managed to enter the fair-trade market, mainly through FLO and WFTO certification (Bishelly and Salazar 2006).

There are two main production arrangements: members working individually in their homes, and members working together in a shared workplace. Those who work individually do so whenever they have time in between household chores, as one artisan explains: "At home, we have to do the cooking and the cleaning, and we fit in the knitting around that. The times when we do the most knitting are early in the morning and at night" (quoted by Wanderley 2014). Artisans often diversify their work by, for example, selling their products in street markets and engaging in other occasional income-generating activities.

Those who work together organise their work in different ways: some meet every day and spend eight hours in a workshop, while others meet a few times a week and work for three or four hours. Full-time collective work takes place in those associations that have a workshop of their own and regular, continuous orders throughout the year. Associations with seasonal markets engage in part-time collective work, a few times a week, when they have orders for their products. Working together is valued by the members because it enables them to correct mistakes in time, share technical knowledge and skills, make their products more quickly and improve these products' quality (Wanderley 2014).

Governance Structure

Membership of artisans' associations is voluntary, and these organisations bring together people engaged in the same area of work. Two main types of associations can be identified. The first type comprises associations that actually operate like a micro or small enterprise, where the president acts as the owner and deals with the management and administration, maintaining a top-down relationship with the workers. In these "associations", the accounts are not shared with the "members", who are therefore unaware of the administration costs, the profits or the percentage accounted for by labour costs.

In the second type of association, the members have a non-hierarchical relationship with each other and are owners, managers and producers at the same time. These associations tend to be characterised by rotating leadership, openness with regard to the accounts and a more participatory style of management, which is shared by all the members. These are the associations that belong to the universe of the community, social, solidarity and cooperative economy. Many of them were set up following experiences with the first type of associations—i.e. those operating like micro or small enterprises. Because these did not meet the producers' expectations of transparency and fairness, these producers decided to form their own associations (Wanderley 2014).

The organisational structure of this second type of artisans' associations, just like that of OECAs, is strongly influenced by trade unions' organisational model: they usually have a president, a vice-president, a records secretary and a finance secretary. Most associations are heavily dependent on the leader in charge, who usually holds the post of president or head of the group. These leaders take most of the responsibility for managing the association, although they do not always have the necessary level of education and training.

Artisans' associations are registered as legal persons under different arrangements regulated by the Civil Code, the Code of Commerce and the General Law on Cooperative Societies. They face a dilemma similar to that faced by OECAs when it comes to their legal registration: indeed, they have to choose between registering as a non-profit organisation, which means that they are not allowed to make a profit from their activities, and registering as a cooperative, which entails high setting-up costs.

Many first-level artisans' associations make use of the legal personality of the second-level organisation until they obtain their own. To obtain legal personality, the organisations need to have statutes and internal regulations. These are defined (and can be subsequently modified) by the general assembly, as also happens in OECAs. Compliance with legal regulations is patchy: artisans' associations tend to abide by some and not others. Few meet all the requirements or go through all the procedures defined by the legal framework (legal personality, tax registration, registration with the Ministry of Labour, health certification, business card); one of the strategies used by associations to avoid problems with the state is to comply with at least one of the legal requirements. A direct relationship can be noted between how well-established the associations are and the degree to which they comply with legal requirements. The reasons for the low level of formal registration of economic units belonging to the community, social and solidarity economy must be sought in the state institutions, which are characterised by inefficiencies and inconsistencies, as we will analyse later.

With regard to internal formalities, not all associations have basic documentation such as a founding charter, statutes, minutes books, accounts books, balances, attendance records, sales records, production records and asset inventories, even though they may be aware of the usefulness of all these documents and plan to introduce them at some point. Many of these records are kept by hand, as most associations do not have access to computer systems (which would make it easier to update, monitor and consult this information).

1.4. Cooperatives

Political Dimension

The first cooperatives to be established in Bolivia were the farming cooperatives set up in the 1930s (Moller 1986). The Decree-Law on the Creation of Cooperatives and Health Assistance was enacted in 1939 and the cooperative model then expanded rapidly to different sectors, such as factories, mining, public services and telecommunications. New decrees were enacted in subsequent years, including the Supreme Decree on Consumer Cooperative Societies in 1941 and the Supreme Decree on the Organisation and Use of Technical Services for Trams and Telephones in 1944. In 1944 as well, the legal status of the Bolivian Cooperatives Institute was officially recognised. Following the National Revolution of 1952, the General Directorate of Farming Communities and Cooperatives and the first Federation of Farming Cooperatives were set up. The Cooperative Societies Law was enacted in 1958 and the National Cooperatives Directorate (*Dirección Nacional de Cooperativas*, or DNC) was created as its executive arm. The following year saw the establishment of the National Cooperatives Institute (*Instituto Nacional de Cooperativas*, or INALCO), linked to the public universities, and in 1960, the National Cooperatives Council, reporting to the President of the Republic, was created (Moller 1986). Several reforms followed over the next two decades. In the 1980s, new sectoral federations were created. The General Law on Cooperatives was approved in 2013, following a process of consensus-building aimed at adapting the law to the plural economy model introduced by the 2009 Constitution.[6]

The cooperative system comprises first-tier (grassroots) cooperatives, second-tier cooperatives (grouping cooperatives in a local area), third-tier cooperatives (regional and departmental federations) and fourth-tier cooperatives (made up of national federations in each economic sector); the National Confederation of Bolivian Cooperatives (CONCOBOL) constitutes the fifth tier. Finally, there are recognised auxiliary institutions providing support to the whole system through education, development centres, technical training and assistance, support to cooperative administration and environmental management, as well as financial institutions promoting cooperative development, etc. (Wanderley *et al.* 2015).

Social Dimension

The General Law on Cooperatives and its specific regulations establish the principles of organisation and management more clearly than the various laws regulating the other types of organisation. According to the law, the cooperative is a not-for-profit association of natural and/or legal persons who join voluntarily. It is based on solidarity and cooperative work to meet the members' needs in terms of production and services, and its structure and operations are autonomous and democratic.

However, many studies, such as the one by Guzmán (2005), point to insufficient compliance with the principles of cooperativism in Bolivia, including the principle of open and voluntary membership. The delivery of social benefits to the members and contracted workers is very uneven among cooperatives: large cooperatives have social-protection mechanisms that work better than those in small cooperatives. The latter do not usually comply with the regulatory framework, such as covering workers against risk, for example. Working conditions are even often unsuitable and safety measures are deficient, as is well known in the mining sector (Mongrevo and Vanhuynegem 2012).

As far as the principle of members' participation in the economic benefits is concerned, practices vary a great deal among cooperatives and according to the sector under consideration. Although oversight and control mechanisms are very deficient in some cooperatives, especially the smaller ones, they work better in larger ones. For example, larger cooperatives are more likely to comply with the requirement to invest 5% of their profits in social spending, in education or in services for the community, such as building day-care centres for children, parks and other works of infrastructure (Mongrevo and Vanhuynegem 2012).

Economic Dimension

On the basis of the 2007 Census of Cooperatives, which covered 70% of active cooperatives, it was estimated that a total of 2,280,015 people were members of cooperatives in Bolivia, which represents 22% of the country's population; 80% of cooperative members are men, and 20% are women. In 2010, 1,444 cooperatives were registered in the National Register of Cooperatives, and in 2008, their assets amounted to US$2.037 billion. As far as their distribution by sector is concerned, 49% are mining cooperatives, 18% are farming cooperatives, 10% are transport and services cooperatives and 7.5% are savings and credit cooperatives (Mongrevo and Vanhuynegem 2012). According to the same source, 94% of members belong to cooperatives in the tertiary sector: 40% are members of services cooperatives (electricity, telephone and water services), 32% belong to savings and credit cooperatives and 22% are members of telecommunications cooperatives. The remaining 6% are members of mining and farming cooperatives.

According to the current law, the cooperative members' working tools may be individually or collectively owned. The law emphasises the fact that producer cooperatives may only hire administrative, advisory and technical services staff, while services and public services cooperatives can contract staff under the terms and conditions of the General Labour

Law; the law also recalls that cooperatives are obliged to comply with the social laws currently in force.

However, overall, compliance with the principles that govern labour relations in cooperatives is very deficient in Bolivia. In the case of mining cooperatives, workers are often hired by the cooperative's members under highly insecure and precarious conditions, and a high percentage die inside the mines. The work of mining cooperatives is not overseen, controlled or regulated by the state, and failure to comply with labour and environmental laws is therefore common (Porrez Padilla 2014).

Governance Structure

According to the law, all cooperative societies—local cooperative associations, federations and the National Confederation—must carry out their activities in keeping with an economic plan approved in their general assemblies. The law also established a social fund, which is fed by all cooperatives' compulsory and voluntary contributions and donations.

Although the law sets out the principles of cooperative governance in detail, cooperative leaders stated in an interview that cooperatives have lost sight of their identity and of the principles of cooperativism, as far as management and the organisation of production are concerned; according to a study by Guzmán (2005), the principle of democratic control by the members is not sufficiently respected by the cooperatives. The Regulations attached to the General Law on Cooperatives, approved in 2014, provide that cooperatives fall under the limited-liability system and this must be expressed in their statutes and regulations by placing the initials "R.L." (*responsabilidad limitada*) after their name. According to the Code of Commerce, they can have between 2 and 25 founding members, and the society's capital, divided into shares of equal value, worth BOB100 or multiples of BOB100, must be paid in full when the cooperative is founded.

2. Difficulties Preventing Collectives From Forging Links With Each Other

The analysis in the previous section demonstrates the importance and persistence of a diversity of economic organisations whose forms differ from state-owned companies and traditional privately owned businesses. Each of these various types of economic organisation has its own representation structures and a lengthy track record of campaigning for state recognition and support. The continual disputes or connections between these collectives' political representatives and successive governments led to processes of distancing or coming together and a constant redefinition of collective identities and alliances among them, throughout the 20th and 21st centuries.

After 2006, these political actors built platforms to promote the new model of the plural economy. One of the most outstanding of these platforms was the Unity Pact (*Pacto de Unidad*), which brought together the most important peasant and indigenous organisations in the country[7] and became the main interlocutor with the MAS government in its early years. Another was the Bolivian Multi-Sector Platform for the Promotion and Development of the Solidarity Economy and Fair Trade, later renamed the Bolivian Solidarity Economy and Fair-Trade Movement (*Movimiento de Economía Solidaria y Comercio Justo de Bolivia*, or MESyCJB), whose main members were the OECAs and the artisans' associations. Both platforms sought to position themselves as the main representative of the plural economy model.

In parallel with this, the cooperative movement conducted its relationship with the government independently, seeking to officially secure its place in the legal framework of the plural economy. Likewise, entrepreneurs achieved a space for the private economy in the new legal framework, while the government created state-run enterprises.

It is interesting to note the distance between the cooperative movement and the social and solidarity-economy movement in Bolivia, despite the affinities between the principles that underpin both types of organisation. This distance has not been explicitly analysed by social actors, academics or decision makers, but an initial assessment of the reasons that could account for it points to the fact that, in the collective Bolivian mind, cooperativism is associated with the mining, savings and credit sectors, because of their significant leadership, and these sectors have lost legitimacy in Bolivian society due to practices that distort the cooperative principles. A consequence of this is that producer cooperatives, mainly in the agricultural and livestock sectors, prefer to identify themselves as peasant economic organisations (OECAs), belonging to the social and solidarity economy, and they are also covered by the specific law that OECAs campaigned for.

In fact, cooperatives differ from the other types of organisation analysed here by the significant capacity to lobby and negotiate with governments which they have demonstrated since the mid-1950s and, more recently, with the MAS government in particular. Since 2006, the cooperative sector, led by mining cooperatives, has become a firm ally of the government, receiving economic and political benefits in return. Such benefits include funding for the sector in the form of equipment, tools and ambulances, as well as a commitment, on the part of the government, not to interfere in or regulate the mines, the working conditions there or their environmental impact, such as the pollution of water sources and alluvial soils in the area surrounding the mines (Porrez Padilla 2014). Equally significant is the participation of miners' representatives in government's decision-making on mining policies: many hold office as senators, deputies or in the executive branch of the government (Mongrevo and Vanhuynegem 2012).

In this political context of "parallel" representation structures, a collective effort was made to bring together all actors to approve a common legislation. This resulted in the adoption, in 2010, of a Ministerial Resolution on the Plurinational Strategy for the Solidarity Economy and Fair Trade. This strategy was promoted by the solidarity-economy and fair-trade platforms and drawn up by the Vice-Ministry of Domestic Trade and Exports, which is part of the Ministry of Economic Development and the Plural Economy, where a well-known leader of the solidarity-economy and fair-trade movement held the post of minister at the time. The coming together of OECAs and artisans' associations in the solidarity-economy and fair-trade movement did not last long, however, and although a strategy was designed and approved by means of a Supreme Decree, it gathered dust on the shelf and was never implemented (Wanderley *et al.* 2015).

At this time, the way in which the plural economy—and specifically the community, social and solidarity economy—should be interpreted was the subject of dispute, not just among and within the different collectives, but also within the government. The social and solidarity economy continued to be seen as marginal, while the concepts of community, cooperative, public and private economy were considered to be the dominant elements of the plural economy legal framework, despite the lack of consensus about what they meant and about the relationship between them. These semantic disputes reflected conflicts related to dialogue with the state and access to public resources. These disputes cut short any coordination effort between the collectives to campaign for a common objective: a different economic model, based on the plurality of organisations that were neither traditional private companies nor public enterprises (Wanderley *et al.* 2015).

With the exception of the cooperative movement, the various platforms started to fragment. The Unity Pact broke up when two of the most important indigenous organisations withdrew their support for the MAS government,[8] and the political map of the social movements was redefined with the formation of two blocs: the first comprised the organisations that supported the MAS government unconditionally, while the second included the organisations that had withdrawn their support for the government. The solidarity-economy and fair-trade movement split into two groups in 2012. The largest and most well-established organisations broke away from the Bolivian Solidarity-Economy and Fair-Trade Movement platform (MESyCJB) to form the Bolivian National Coordinating Committee for Fair Trade (*Coordinadora Nacional de Comercio Justo de Bolivia*, or CNCJ). The smaller organisations and initiatives continued in the MESyCJB, but they are also having serious problems coordinating with each other (Wanderley *et al.* 2015).

Thus, the efforts to bring together all the organisations in the MESyCJB platform and give it an institutional shape were frustrated in recent years by splits in the range of organisations that form part of the solidarity-economy and fair-trade movement, leading to the creation or strengthening of other platforms. Several platforms exist today: the Bolivian Solidarity-Economy and Fair-Trade Movement (MESyCJB), the Bolivian National Coordinating Committee for Fair Trade (CNCJ), the Fair-Trade Platform (*Plataforma de Comercio Justo*) and the Coordinating Committee for the Integration of Peasant and Indigenous Economic Organisations (*Coordinadora de Integración de Organizaciones Económicas Campesinas, Indígenas y Originarias*, or CIOEC).

The difficulty of linking up the different economic actors in the ambiguous universe of the community, social, solidarity and cooperative economy in Bolivia is acknowledged by the actors themselves. A Peasant Economic Organisations Coordinating Committee executive says that

> *bringing the movement together around a common agenda, as a political as well as an economic alternative, is a difficult task.* [It means uniting the different experiences, histories, ideologies and objectives] *that ought not to divide those of us who are committed to the struggle for an alternative economy in this country. That should not be a reason for the networks and organisations to remain separate. We ought to be speaking the same language, in order to build a high-profile movement able to exert an influence.*
>
> Quoted by Wanderley *et al.* (2015: 109)

The clearest and most visible expression of the difficulties preventing these actors from linking up with each other is the fact that specific laws were developed and approved for each of the collectives, as described above. Although this process required a huge effort by the different actors, these laws did not represent progress towards integrated public policies. Not only do these laws contradict each other; most of them have never been translated into public policies (Wanderley 2013). Furthermore, the laws have had a negative impact on the identities, interactions and collective actions of the actors involved in the community and solidarity economy. One of these effects was the worsening of conflicts and splits within the social movements, which made it difficult for them to set aside circumstantial political disputes and reach consensus on their shared interests. One of the most significant of these conflicts is the dispute between the OECAs and OECOMs over which of them is to be considered the legitimate actor in the community economy.[9] These political struggles between representatives of the umbrella organisations of the farmers' union movement, representing OECOMs, on the one side, and the producers' associations, representing OECAs and identified with the solidarity economy and fair trade, on the other, do not necessarily correlate with the experiences and views of the organisations at the grassroots level.

From an international comparative perspective, it is clear that Bolivia has not yet made significant progress in developing a suitable legal framework and policy strategy to strengthen the plural economy legal framework. No progress has been made, for example, towards a form of legal recognition that would take into account the specificities of the organisations in the community, social and solidarity economy. In other words, the legal recognition of these actors is not consistent with the stated intention—itself not devoid of contradictions—expressed by the state of recognising them as a substantial part of the plural economy. This legal vacuum has meant that these actors have had—and still have—to decide whether to register as not-for-profit organisations (NGOs), as civil associations, or as cooperatives, even though the requirements and obligations linked to each of these legal forms are not suited to their structures. Nevertheless, the key problem is not just the absence of regulations suited to these organisations' way of working, economic arrangements and economic and social purposes, but rather the divorce between their identity as an organisation and the characteristics imposed on them by their legal recognition (Wanderley *et al.* 2015).

3. The Political Dynamic of the Community, Social, Solidarity and Cooperative Economy

The question that arises from the analysis in the previous sections is the following: which factors do explain the difficulties that are preventing actors in the community, social, solidarity and cooperative economy from coming together around a common agenda to demand the fulfilment of the political commitments made by the MAS government and the effective implementation of a coherent policy strategy that would benefit them all? The difficulty of linking up the different actors is rooted in the Bolivian political governance, which has reinforced the diversity of interests and demands among the actors that make up this universe, as well as their parallel structures of collective identity and action.

The first factor is the significant diversity of economic units in terms of ownership, governance structure, labour relations, forms of production and criteria for earnings' distribution. This diversity is compounded by the organisations' disparate levels of involvement in local, national and international markets and the degree to which their economic units are consolidated, as reflected in their trade volumes and income flows. This in turn is reflected in differences in earnings and their ability to meet the needs of individual members and their families. Likewise, their geographical location (urban or rural), the area of the country in which they work and the type of activity in which they engage (e.g. handicrafts, agriculture and livestock farming, services and commerce) mean that they have specific needs, interests and priorities, which are expressed in their membership of a range of representative organisations and in the construction of different platforms representing them.

The second factor that can account for the difficulty of linking up the different actors and the fragmentation of collective actions to build an alternative economy concerns the different structures of political representation analysed in this chapter, which in turn are the result of these various organisations' relations with the state over the course of Bolivia's history. Nevertheless, these factors are not sufficient to explain the inability of the different collectives to come together in a more unified movement, considering the experiences of other countries that have made progress with collective action in a more unified way.

The reproduction of these conditions is rooted in the relationship between the state and society in managing power that has persisted throughout Bolivian history, and which is characterised by relations that have veered from confrontation with the government in office to close contact between social and political leaders and those in public office, based on clientelism and patrimonialism. Equally important and closely related to this is the absence of intermediate spaces for institutional coordination between the different actors and the state. Although the Bolivian Trade Union Confederation (*Central Obrera Boliviana*, or COB), under the leadership of the miners, used to channel the demands of many economic and social organisations and was the principal mediator between society and the state from the 1950s until the 1980s, at a time when it played a very important role in the struggle against the dictatorships and for the return of democracy, it has later become weaker, and no other umbrella organisation or platform has taken up its mediation role yet. Since the 1990s, the public space comprises a diversity of actors, whose relationships with the government are characterised by bilateral relations, in the absence of intermediate spaces for formal coordination between the different political subjects.

After 2006, the Movement-for-Socialism government maintained bilateral relations with social and political collectives. Indeed, it intensified its relations with each actor or sector. This model of public management favoured the pursuit of corporate interest rather than a general one. It also perpetuated rent-seeking behaviours and the discretional distribution of benefits or special privileges in return for corporate political support. This model of governance has entrenched the "capture" of policies, programmes and projects by collectives with more political weight, through top-down, non-democratic procedures.

The backdrop of the economic bonanza favoured these practices. Between 2006 and 2014, the financial resources available in the Bolivian economy increased exponentially in comparison to the previous period (1996–2005): on average, public spending and investment in one year of the Evo Morales government was equivalent to four years in the previous period. The injection of public funds into the economy occurred mainly through spending on infrastructure, buying capital inputs for state-owned enterprises, expanding public-sector employment, boosting redistribution policies (especially cash transfers in the form of benefits), subsidising petrol, natural gas for domestic use and electricity, and creating funds to provide direct transfers to territorial communities, such as the Development Fund for Indigenous Peoples and Peasant Communities (better known as the Indigenous Peoples' Fund).

In this context, relations between the government and the collectives tended to undermine the latter's independence as organisations through co-optation mechanisms, such as sharing out "quotas" of power through jobs in ministries and other state institutions, the offer of jobs in the public sector, and the distribution of funds and business opportunities in shady deals that bypassed official procedures and accountability mechanisms. This model of public management encouraged bilateral relations in defence of group interests and worked against the idea of coming together to promote the public good. Most importantly, no intermediate spaces for collective linkages and deliberation were developed during this time, at either the national or the subnational level. In other words, the model of governance over the last twelve years has revived the dynamic of bilateral relations between social collectives and decision makers, with the result that it has become even more difficult for the actors in the community, social, solidarity and cooperative economy to come together and act collectively in an integrated way.

Conclusion

As this analysis has shown, a plurality of economic organisations whose forms differ from state-owned companies and traditional privately owned businesses have long been present in Bolivian society. The new context ushered in 2006 raised great expectations that these other types of economic organisation would be strengthened as part of the model of a plural economy, even though many conceptual doubts remained about economic pluralism, the solidarity economy, the community economy, the cooperative economy and the role of the state. But there was a lack of clarity about how these various types of organisation related to each other in the plural economy framework. Moreover, the new laws created the potential for conflict by not awarding equal status to all economic actors, thus triggering disputes between the territorial organisations (OECOMs) and the peasant economic organisations (OECAs). This process has had a negative impact on the identities of the various types of organisation, their interactions and their willingness to set aside circumstantial political disputes to reach consensus on shared interests.

Due to a type of governance in which the government engages in bilateral relations with the different actors, leading to disputes among them to be seen as the legitimate interlocutor with the state, no institutionalised spaces have been set up for discussion and consensus-building on the various actors' demands or the development of integrated legal and public-policy frameworks. This has had perverse effects by weakening incentives for dialogue and encouraging disputes among the actors. It has also aggravated a culture of distrust by reinforcing long-standing practices of engagement through patronage and clientelism, which operate through short-term demands and immediate benefits in the form of protection and rents in return for votes and political support.

This political dynamic has favoured defensive social capital and hindered the different representative structures from linking up to push for public policies and institutional changes that would lead to an enabling environment for promoting the plural economy and especially the community, social, solidarity and cooperative economy. By limiting their actions to short-termist, defensive demands, producers and their organisations are failing to take advantage of opportunities to coordinate with public and private sector institutions to promote integrated, effective policies for building another economy sustainably.

In such a political field, the movements working for another economy in Bolivia are facing challenges. As the analysis shows, these challenges are both bottom-up, as they are linked to the relations between alternative economic organisations and their representatives, and top-down, as they are also related to government projects and initiatives and their impact on socio-economic and political processes.

A series of questions arise from Bolivia's recent experience, whose particularity lies in the tensions and contradictions between far-reaching discursive changes, on the one hand, and continuities in the orientation of economic policies and political practices, on the other—in other words, the experience of a government that raised great expectations of a different economic model and promoted very progressive changes in legislation, but which, in practice, increasingly departed from the principles set out in these laws. We need to redefine our questions and analytical frameworks to explain what happened in this process and gain a deeper insight into the relations between the established power and diverse economic organisations, between political discourse and practice, and thus improve our understanding of the complex challenges posed by the aims of ethical and political transformation towards another economy.

Acknowledgements

This chapter is based on research carried out by the author with Ivonne Farah and Fernanda Sostres as part of the CIDES-UMSA and HEGOA Project, 2014–2016.

Notes

1 A new economic census will be implemented in Bolivia in 2018 with the aim of mapping the plural economy in rural and urban areas.
2 The most important of these are the Bolivian Peasant Economic Organisations' Coordinating Committee (*Comité Integrador de Organizaciones Económicas Campesinas de Bolivia*, or CIOEC), the Bolivian Association of Organic Farmers' Organisations (*Organizaciones de Productores Agroecológicos de Bolivia*,

or AOPEB), the Small Producers' Liaison Committee (*Comité Enlace de Peque-ños Productores*), the National Association of Camelid Farmers (*Asociación Nacional de Productores de Camélidos*, or ANAPCA) and the National Association of Quinoa Producers (*Asociación Nacional de Productores de Quinua*, or ANAPQUI) (Muñoz Elsner 2004).

3 "*Ayllus*" can thus refer both to first-level and second-level organisations.

4 The main legal landmarks include: the March for Territory and Dignity in 1990; the ratification of ILO Convention 169 through Law 1257; the Constitution approved in 1994, which recognises indigenous peoples' right to territory and their right to apply their own norms; Law 1700, which recognises exclusive forestry rights on indigenous territories; Law 1715 of 1996, which recognises indigenous peoples' right to own their territories and the system of indigenous and peasant community territories (*territorios indígena originario campesinos*, or TIOCs) as collectively owned territories that are indivisible, immune from seizure and governed by their own norms; and the 2009 Constitution, which enshrines all the rights recognised previously and establishes the right to indigenous autonomy. Specifically, Article 289 of the new Constitution defines autonomy as consisting of self-government and the exercise of free determination by indigenous peoples, first nations and peasant communities, while Article 190 states that self-government by the autonomous indigenous and rural territories shall be exercised according to their own norms, institutions, authorities and procedures, in keeping with their powers and competencies, in harmony with the Constitution and the law.

5 An example is the Single Trade Union Confederation of Artisan Workers of Bolivia (*Confederación Sindical Única de Trabajadores Artesanales de Bolivia*, or CSUTAB), founded in 1989, which includes several sectoral umbrella organisations.

6 The main organisations pushing for the new law were the National Confederation of Bolivian Cooperatives (*Confederación Nacional de Cooperativas de Bolivia*, or CONCOBOL) and the National Federation of Mining Cooperatives (*Federación Nacional de Cooperativas Mineras*, or FENCOMIN).

7 The Unity Pact was forged in 2004 with the challenging goal of bringing together the country's peasant and indigenous movements and campaigning to hold a Constituent Assembly that would be "foundational, sovereign and participatory" and approve a constitution based on the recognition of the prior existence of the indigenous peoples and first nations.

8 The organisations that left the Unity Pact were CONAMAQ and CIDOB. They withdrew as a result of the conflict between the MAS government and indigenous peoples in 2011 regarding the proposal to build a road through the Isiboro Sécure National Park (TIPNIS, located in the departments of Beni and Cochabamba), which is an indigenous territory belonging to the Mojeño, Yuracaré and Chimán peoples. The indigenous peoples denounced the violation of the constitutional principles of prior consultation, free consent and autonomy on indigenous territory, as well as the negative social and environmental impacts of this mega-project.

9 The main problem with the law promoted by the farmers' unions was that it considered OECOMs as the only legal type of organisation in the community economy and excluded OECAs, which had a more solid track record as economic organisations, though much less political weight than the farmers' unions. OECAs had to fight for the approval of Law 338, two years later (in 2013). These laws are similar, but the new development in Law 338 was that it also took into consideration OECAs, which were not included in the earlier law—though they were still left in a secondary position by Law 338. In the process, the dispute between the two groups for the right to legitimately represent the community economy in dealings with the state became more pronounced (Wanderley *et al.* 2015).

References

Albó, X. (ed.) (1999) *Raíces de América El mundo aymara*, Madrid: Alianza América Unesco.

Albó, X. (2000) "El sector campesino-indígena, actor social clave", in *El sindicalismo en Bolivia: presente y futuro. Serie Opiniones y Análisis N° 52*, La Paz: Fundación Hans Seidel & Fundemos.

Bishelly, E. & Salazar, C. (2006) *Datos y experiencias sobre Comercio Justo Bolivia*, Documento de Trabajo, La Paz: CIPCA.

Borth, P. J. & Elías Argandoña, B. (eds) (2014) *Las compras públicas ¿Alternativas de mercado para la agricultura familiar campesina?* La Paz: Agrónomos y Veterinarios Sin F ronteras AVSF.

Calvo, L. M. (2017) "La Organización Económica Comunitaria de Raqaypampa. Un nuevo paso en la larga marcha", in Farah, I. (ed.) *Economía solidaria y compromisos con la equidad de género: experiencias y debates desde países andinos y País Vasco*, La Paz: CIDES-UMSA, HEGOA & AVCD.

CIOEC (2009) *Primer Censo Nacional de Organizaciones Económicas Campesinas, Indígenas y Originarias*, La Paz: Coordinadora de Integración de Organizaciones Económicas Campesinas de Bolivia.

Colque, G. (2007) "La Cohesión Comunal", in Urioste, M., Barragán, R. & Colque, G. (eds) *Los Nietos de la Reforma Agraria. Tierra y comunidad en el altiplano de Bolivia*, La Paz: CIPCA & Fundación Tierra.

Devisscher Leroux, M. (1996) *La Problemática de la gestión en las organizaciones económicas campesinas. Un análisis comparado en Bolivia*, Cusco: Centro de Estudios Regionales Andinos Bartolomé de las Casas.

Devisscher Leroux, M. (2017) "La experiencia de Coraca-Protal", in Farah, I. (ed.) *Economía solidaria y compromisos con la equidad de género: experiencias y debates desde países andinos y País Vasco*, La Paz: CIDES-UMSA, HEGOA & AVCD.

Flores, L. & Ton, G. (2015) *Inteligencia Organizativa y Desempeño Económico de Organizaciones Económicas Campesinas*, La Paz: CIOEC.

Gros, C. & Foyer, J. (eds) (2010) *¿Desarrollo con identidad? Gobernanza económica indígena. Siete estudios de caso*, Lima: IFEA.

Guzmán, W. (2005) *Principios y doctrina del cooperativismo y de la economía social*, La Paz: Editorial Universitaria.

Moller, E. (1986) *El cooperativismo como proceso de cambio: de la comunidad tradicional a la cooperativa moderna*, La Paz: Editorial Los Amigos del Libro.

Mongrevo, R. & Vanhuynegem, P. (2012) *Visión panorámica del sector cooperativo en Bolivia: Un modelo singular de desarrollo cooperativo*, La Paz: OIT, Oficina de la OIT para los Países Andinos, Alianza Cooperativa Internacional—ACI.

Muñoz Elsner, D. (2004) *Organizaciones económicas campesinas y políticas públicas. Un estudio comparativo*, La Paz: Plural Editores.

Pari, N. (2017) "La Central de Cooperativas El Ceibo Ltda. Recorrido con el sello del comercio justo: de los granos a un fino chocolate", in Farah, I. (ed.) *Economía solidaria y compromisos con la equidad de género: experiencias y debates en países andinos y país vasco*, La Paz: CIDES-UMSA.

Porrez Padilla, F. (2014) "Precariedad e informalidad en el mercado laboral: la sustentabilidad de las cooperativas mineras en Bolivia", in Barragán, R. & Mendieta, P. (eds) *Mundos del trabajo en transformación entre lo local y lo global*, La Paz: CIDES-UMSA 30 años.

Van Der Veen, H. (1993) "¿La Fuerza de Bolivia está en nuestras manos? El rol de las organizaciones artesanales", graduation thesis, Amsterdam: University of Amsterdam.

Wanderley, F. (2005) "Solidarity without cooperation—small producer networks and political identity in Bolivia", doctoral thesis, New York: Columbia University.

Wanderley, F. (2013) *¿Qué pasó con el proceso de cambio en Bolivia?— Ideales acertados, medios equivocados y resultados trastocados*, La Paz: CIDES-UMSA, Colección 30 años. Available HTTP: https://ucbcba.academia.edu/FernandaWanderley.

Wanderley, F. (2014) "El autoempleo y la asociatividad en Bolivia. Vías asociativas para la inserción laboral de mujeres en el área urbana", *Revue d'Economie Solidaire*, No. 7.

Wanderley, F., Sostres, F. & Farah, I. (coord) (2015) *La economía solidaria en la economía plural: discursos, prácticas y resultados en Bolivia*, La Paz: CIDES-UMSA, HEGOA & Plural Editores. Available HTTP: https://ucbcba.academia.edu/FernandaWanderley.

3 Brazilian Social Enterprises

Historical Roots and Converging Trends

*Adriane Ferrarini, Luiz Inácio Gaiger,
Marília Veríssimo Veronese and
Paulo Cruz Filho*

Introduction

This chapter presents the main models of social enterprise in Brazil; the analysis is based on previous empirical research and conceptual studies carried out by the authors over the last years. Its main empirical support is the database of the second National Mapping of the Solidarity Economy (Gaiger *et al.* 2014; Gaiger 2015), whose analysis will make it possible to establish a retrospective view of experiences in the solidarity economy in the country and identify its main current expressions. The analysis will also focus on other organisational forms that make up the social-enterprise field in Brazil, namely those related to the third sector and "social-impact enterprises". The latter include non-profit organisations creating, managing and expanding mission-based and market-related economic activities to ensure their financial sustainability, as well as a new generation of for-profit enterprises created to fulfil a social mission. In order to contextualise the typology, we will first examine some Brazilian historical aspects, such as the predominance of cooperativism since the early 20th century, the recent development of the popular and solidarity economy, and some new trends that have been emerging in the last years, like social-impact enterprises. This will explain why the term "social enterprise" is unusual in Brazil, both as a concept and as a legal form. It will be used in the next pages as a comprehensive ideal-typical concept, through adjustments to the EMES approach, with a view to using it for typological purposes.

Throughout the chapter and in the closing comments, some topics will be highlighted and discussed in more detail, as they are particularly relevant in the Brazilian case and typical of a Southern context: the entrepreneurship of excluded people, who are often both members and beneficiaries of the initiatives (a fact that redefines the meaning of profit distribution as a way to accomplish the very social mission); the meaning and the role of the informal economy, in which quite a few experiences take place that are driven by the solidarity inherent in the family and community, giving room to a singular integration between the economic

DOI: 10.4324/9780429055164-5

principles of domesticity and reciprocity such as they were put forward by Karl Polanyi; and the strong political dimension of the initiatives, both at the internal level (through self-management) and at the external one (through active participation in community and society). Pointing out these aspects will help us understand that the economy is plural and larger than the market, and that it is not ineluctably "antisocial". The primacy of social aims must be pursued as a matter of building an *embedded* economy.[1]

1. Historical Roots of Brazilian Social Enterprises

In Brazil, social-mission-driven economic practices have existed for a long time. Although the current initiatives might be perceived as a recent phenomenon, due to their expansion in the last decades, such perception would be misleading. Indeed, we might consider that they have a long-running history, beginning with pre-Columbian indigenous forms of production and collective systems adopted by freed slaves. Since the late 19th century, in parallel to the increasing expansion of capitalism, associative and cooperative strategies have sought to ensure decent living conditions for large population groups and to prevent the principles of goods production, labour organisation and circulation of wealth from being governed only by the strict rationality of capital. It must be recognised, however, that this historical resistance, guided by bitterly defended values, has sometimes been unable to prevent deviations from its initial route and important concessions regarding its original principles.

Having in mind the historical "tripod" of the social economy in Europe (*associations, cooperatives* and *mutual-aid* organisations), we should state from the outset that mutuals are rather unusual in the Brazilian context.[2] A few mutual-aid initiatives—such as collective funds pooled by workers—have been developed primarily by family farmers and urban labourers, but they are considered as part of the associative and cooperative sectors and do not constitute a specific mutual sector *per se*. In certain cases, these initiatives have persisted as indigenous forms of organising and enhancing communities. However, the services provided, particularly in health and education, have generally been incorporated into new institutional dynamics, primarily linked to private (mainly religious) and public philanthropy. Moreover, they have eroded into paternalistic patterns and have contributed, through clientelism, to preserving the hegemony of the social and political elites.

Associativism, in turn, has played a vital role in the country, especially for small family farmers, from the moment they started occupying agricultural areas, in the course of the 19th century. However, legally speaking, associations correspond to an extremely broad legal framework, which encompasses all the bodies bringing people together to carry out ordinary activities, provided they differ from more specific organisations (churches, foundations and political parties) and they have non-lucrative purposes. Analogously to the third sector as a whole, associations are often defined in Brazil by what they are *not* (or cannot be) rather than by what would characterise and unify them (Fernandes 1994; Gaiger 2015).

As such, associations have remained, throughout Brazilian history, devoid of individual personality and overall representation mechanisms, and have often been encouraged to function as a cog in the wheel for oligarchic domination. It is a sector with no encompassing social identity and no oversight bodies keeping statistical records (Gaiger 2015: 217). However, as shown by some studies (Pinto 2006), the associative act goes beyond the fight against the hegemonic strategies of the elites or a purely pragmatic spirit among the associated members. It shows a collective path in which identities and reciprocity practices are forged and may be revalued. In rural areas, for instance, associations in general fit into broader collective structures, which allows them to overcome the condition of abandonment and isolation that is typical of micro and small popular organisations. In urban areas, especially in the last decades, associative organisations have been created to solve collective problems such as homelessness, abuse of women and children, the low level of employability of low-income youth, etc. Several associations are part of the new types of social enterprises, as we will see in sections 3 and 4.

There are many stories behind associations; one of them is popular associativism. Since the 1970s, in the context of the demographic flows that resulted in the current urban landscape, associations have been a popular instrument of organisation and struggle for the right to housing and for decent living conditions. Similarly, in rural areas, associations of small farmers have long supported collective enterprises in production, trading or service activities. As a rule, these initiatives have been restricted to their original purposes and areas of operation, preserving the associative culture. The role played by community organisations is a visible "pillar" of wider social mobilisations, such as the democratic struggles and electoral clashes that led to the renewal of political parties and a shift of governments along the right-left spectrum. Simultaneously, associations functioned as the driver of local initiatives, giving them impulse and institutional backing. Community projects for generating income and enhancing economic development, when benefiting from the support of associations, are often intertwined with the latter. The result is a hybrid form of organisation: social community activities that essentially pursue economic enterprise aims and which, as such, operate in a legal grey zone, insofar as they effectively distribute surpluses to their members. The most common compromise is to use the legal form of association, to avoid full informality and to postpone the formalisation of the enterprise, thereby foregoing the privileges and benefits conferred upon the lawful exercise of economic activities (Gaiger 2015).

Cooperativism was originally introduced in Brazil by European immigrants, in the late 19th century, as a way to overcome situations of poverty and destitution. In these early days, consumer cooperatives emerged—and so did credit and farming cooperatives—especially in the south of the country. Consumer cooperatives expanded in the 1950s and 1960s. Subsequently, urban cooperativism showed signs of stagnation, due to a lack of public support that resulted in a number of barriers to its economic viability and survival, such as insufficiency of financial and technical assistance. In addition, as economic development has since favoured the expansion of capitalist corporations, it boosted the latter to offer services previously provided by cooperatives, such as credit and marketing support (Schneider and Lauschner 1979).

In contrast, farming cooperatives were gradually encouraged, primarily by military governments, which sought to boost exports by means of improved agricultural yields. Since 1970, farming cooperativism has been prevailing in Brazil and it has strengthened the dominance of the conservative elite, traditionally focused on the agribusiness export economy, and has served as a corporate alliance extremely sensitive to economic power. This explains the strong dependence of farming cooperativism on government policies and on the skills of its leaders to negotiate and deal with the state.

This framework was supported by a policy of social control and state intervention that brought no significant change to cooperative workers in rural areas. On the contrary, the model spread distrust about cooperativism amidst small farmers, who had in the prior decades valued this instrument of economic development and community strengthening. Meanwhile, the urban movement was given a new impetus, with the creation of many worker cooperatives in the 1980s. At the height of the proliferation of these cooperatives, several studies indicated that they were utilised mainly to make working relations more flexible, to outsource services and to cut labour costs (Lima 2007). Nevertheless, new genuine cooperatives were also identified, such as *recovered factories*,[3] which appeared as one of the first strands of the solidarity economy in Brazil.

Today large cooperatives function similarly to private companies; they aim at profitability in the market and are engaged in professional and efficient management. At the other extreme, small cooperatives in urban peripheries, focused on the socio-economic inclusion and basic needs of poor populations, have an egalitarian nature, appreciate the fact of governing themselves collectively and identify themselves with the solidarity economy (Nunes 2001; Anjos 2012). Alongside these, there are also "false" cooperatives, which use the legal framework to exploit manpower at low cost and preserve the hierarchy as well as the social division between capital and labour in the enterprise (Leite and Georges 2012; Gaiger and Anjos 2012). The Brazilian cooperative sector is thus heterogeneous with regard to the nature and scale of the organisations' activities, complexity and, more fundamentally, ideological principles (Gaiger 2015: 220).

When cooperatives carry considerable weight, they face significant obstacles to maintain their own structure and role as an alternative to the prevailing forms of economic enterprise. Their predominant function over time has been that of strengthening the market economy, or they have served as an instrument to compensate for the social ills caused by economic development. In this contradictory context, a new generation of cooperatives appeared in the 1990s, constituted by labour cooperatives, agricultural production cooperatives of the Landless Rural Workers' Movement and recycling cooperatives. Most of the members of these cooperatives were motivated by the belief that, though imperfect, this format was the most comprehensive self-management model for worker-owned enterprises and constituted the basis of a system capable of catering to their needs. The viability of these solidarity and self-managed cooperatives in the future will depend on their ability to create favourable socio-economic environments.

Before addressing more recent trends in Brazil that contribute to the present social-enterprise landscape, let us say a few words about the third-sector concept, which has been in the limelight since the 1990s (Fernandes 1994), to the extent that many civil organisations with different origins and models of management came to be framed into it. According to the canonical definition adopted in Brazil, such third-sector organisations act on public interest topics and issues; are autonomous from the standpoint of their constitution, management and dissolution; and are non-profit-oriented. Combining morphological and institutional criteria with an interpretive approach of the fundamental principles incorporated in this definition, it is possible to distinguish four historical subsectors in the Brazilian third sector: (1) a broad range of charitable or associative entities, such as traditional philanthropic organisations, without direct connection with the recent phenomenon of the third sector; (2) a great number of non-governmental organisations, or NGOs, whose action is strongly guided by social transformation goals; (3) particularly since the end of the 1990s, a growing number of entrepreneurial associations developing non-profit business models that ensure their economic sustainability while fostering their social and/or environmental impact; and (4) business foundations and institutes guided by a social-responsibility focus. Their actions normally complement social policies, addressing issues included in what such organisations define as the "social awareness agenda".

The concepts of "social enterprise" and "third sector" correspond to non-identical sets of organisations, even though they overlap in some cases and present important similarities, especially as regards entrepreneurial civil-society organisations (CSOs)[4]—the new legal denomination for entities that develop social projects with a public purpose. Most CSOs are legally registered as associations or foundations, and include also many NGOs (the Portuguese acronym, ONG, is still very usual in Brazil). Moreover, there are pathways between the two sets of organisations: third-sector organisations are private-law entities that do not seek to generate pecuniary benefits for their members but aim to respond to collective demands. They choose a particular social mission and fulfil it, based on values of gratuity, respect of human rights, equity, etc. They usually create representative bodies through decentralised horizontal connections respecting the plurality and the singular vocations of each organisation. They thus share many characteristics with social enterprise. However, third-sector entities generally fail to comply with some defining features of social enterprise, not only because these entities usually do not belong to the associated members who work in the organisation (unlike what is the case in most solidarity enterprises), but also because they often do not develop an explicit economic activity. Besides, the democratic character of their management is variable; it is often mitigated or relegated to formal procedures. In certain cases, their institutional and economic dependency on for-profit companies responsible for their creation is obvious.

2. The Popular and Solidarity Economy

The solidarity economy, a concept born during the 1990s, gave new impetus and continuity to an extensive history featuring countless experiences of popular solidarity. The changing social landscape of Brazil in the last decades has amplified the factors favouring the development of solidarity-based economic initiatives, from those determined by the precarious conditions suffered by salaried workers to those born under circumstances in which communities predominate and seek to protect their lifestyle and to shy away from the anti-social and deleterious logic of the prevailing economy. In addition to the more distant "predecessors" examined in the previous section, new social mobilisations made the solidarity economy a public fact, which was actually preceded, at the height of the 1980s, by similar initiatives, generally linked to social programmes of civil entities—primarily NGOs or religious institutions such as Christian churches. At the beginning, these initiatives were scattered and run in parallel, without connections among them. They spread across impoverished rural areas and urban peripheries and foreshadowed the significant emergence of solidarity-economy organisations recorded from the 1990s onwards. Although less well known than today's solidarity enterprises, they have been the seminal sources of these initiatives and, one can say, of a specific, relevant field of Brazilian social enterprise. Therefore, a retrospective of the solidarity economy should account, at least briefly, for the social processes of recent decades that gradually culminated in a new field of social practices, social innovation and new expectations.

As mentioned, the solidarity economy emerged in Brazil gradually, with a deep-rooted—even though not always continuous—history of solidarity-oriented values. The most prominent factors that influenced the solidarity economy within the macroeconomic scenario of the last quarter of the 20th century are the changes in the pattern of capitalist accumulation and their effects on work relationships, production chains and global reconfiguration of markets and geopolitics. Another factor that can account for the increasing number of initiatives observed over the last years (Gaiger *et al.* 2014) is the structural crisis that hit the Brazilian labour market and whose impacts were reinforced by the withdrawal of the state. Another important reason lies in the mobilisation of social movements, labour unions and citizen entities, unwavering in their commitment to establish and foster mutual-help and economic-cooperation practices (Gaiger 2015: 206). The solidarity economy essentially aspires to such ways of living and engages to either salvage them or work towards their creation.

On an ideological level, the failure of socialist experiments challenged the intervention strategies of many left-wing activists, opening possibilities towards innovative social experiences and new patterns of analysis and of strategic formulation. The evolution of pioneering grassroots experiences of solidarity economy, confirming their viability and ability to benefit their members and social surroundings, awakened the sensitivity of social actors and intellectuals and created a stimulating environment in which entities and networks promoting the solidarity economy have grown and multiplied.

Nowadays, the concept of solidarity economy evokes a wide range of economic organisations, representative bodies, and civil-society and state organisations. Since its inception, the social movement of solidarity economy has questioned official cooperativism. The legal frame of the cooperatives fails to provide adequate solutions for solidarity-economy enterprises (Gaiger 2015: 218–219). That is why, since the 1990s, solidarity-economy enterprises have been searching for their institutional identity and a legal framework compatible with their specific characteristics. Gaiger sums up this point as follows:

> [Solidarity-economy] enterprises usually adopt one of the available institutional formats—basically an association or cooperative—precisely because they lack alternatives more suited to their goals and their sui generis dynamics. This is an uncomfortable stopgap solution they find to avoid informality.
>
> Gaiger (2015: 207)

In its expansion, the solidarity economy has come to include different social categories and organisational arrangements, such as informal income-generation group units, farmer and consumer associations, local exchange systems, and cooperative indigenous farming communities, dedicated to producing goods or providing services such as commercialisation and credit. The solidarity economy currently comprises a multitude of social segments, agents and institutions. Solidarity enterprises are generally referred to as "solidarity economic enterprises"—hence the acronym SEE, which we will use hereafter.

SEEs include cooperative banks, service and goods exchange initiatives based on reciprocity, commercial networks and, above all, countless informal or formal associations of people who freely come together with the goal of developing economic activities, creating jobs and experimenting solidarity-based relations. The concept of solidarity economy usually refers to economic organisations aiming not only at financial gain for their members but also at benefits in terms of quality of life and citizen participation. They integrate economic and social dimensions, due to their sociocultural foundations and to their specific rationality, in which efficiency and welfare, productivity and participation are linked. They achieve their goals mainly through significant efforts that include the permanent engagement of the associated workers, users or consumers. Moreover, thanks to their social embeddedness, these initiatives also fulfil functions in the fields of health, education and environmental protection, among other areas (Gaiger 2016: 1–2).

According to reference studies (Singer and Souza 2000; Gaiger 2004; Veronese 2008), the priority of solidarity in these ventures is evident in the members' involvement in day-to-day management, the socialisation of productive resources and the adoption of principles of equity. When extended to the initiative's surroundings, solidarity encourages broader reciprocity practices, where practical experience in managing common goods lends new value to the notions of justice and public interest. The collective action involved in solidarity-economy initiatives mobilises individuals in the workplace, in class strategies and citizenship struggles, and in response to concerns over welfare, recognition and a meaningful life (Gaiger 2015).

Like in other countries, several types of organisation in Brazil could theoretically be classified as social enterprises. In the particular context of the solidarity economy, most initiatives are created and maintained through the voluntary association of workers, consumers and users to meet their needs and pursue shared economic, social and cultural aspirations. In those organisations, it is often those belonging to the target populations (such as the unemployed, small-scale family farmers, waste pickers or artisans) who, of their own accord, decide to act collectively. Therefore, the presence of non-member participants tends to be minor, and the majority of members are usually workers, consumers or users, who are themselves responsible for overall and capital management, and their activity enables them to obtain earnings or save on household expenses (Gaiger 2016: 7).

The specific features of SEEs are: the emphasis these organisations put on their economic functions and activities; their goal of achieving economic results and the legitimacy of profit redistribution amongst members, primarily in exchange for the work provided by these members; the need to distinguish the surplus produced and distributed collectively from the private generation and appropriation of profit; the fact that solidarity enterprises are managed by the workers (or consumers, or users) themselves, who participate in their activities and are both members and holders of capital, thus implementing a model of self-management that goes beyond democratic governance.

An important point to be mentioned is the importance of the informal economy within the popular and solidarity economy. In 2013, informal groups accounted for 30% of all enterprises surveyed by the second Brazilian National Mapping of the Solidarity Economy. Informality characterises the popular economy, which is a major "source" of the solidarity economy in Brazil, as well as more generally in Latin America and in Africa. The history of informality in Latin America is usually considered to span over the last five decades, during which populations migrated from rural areas to urban spaces at a rapidly growing rate. More often than not, the formal labour market in the cities proved incapable of absorbing the majority of people seeking work. Many people were thus left to their own devices and forced to subsist on temporary labour. This process has modified the urban landscape, giving rise to peripheral neighbourhoods and expanding the informal economy into a phenomenon of great magnitude (Véras de Oliveira *et al.* 2011).

Over the years, however, the spread and persistence of informality led to the belief that it was also, in some way, a choice intentionally inserted into popular strategies of life, economic resistance and social mobilisation. Informality was then reinterpreted as being part of the so-called popular economy, which had its own social logic of promoting community ties and reinforcing social cooperation.

Coraggio (1999), for example, considers the popular economy to have a rationality of its own that is guided towards the formation of a collective labour fund, namely through individual and collective strategies that are inseparable from the mesh of social relations in which small-scale economic agents act. The effectiveness of such strategies, then, is seen to depend on the relative freedom prompted by informality.

Gaiger (2015: 213)

The material and social assets that are typical of the informal economy should not be underestimated, but rather valued as means or tools of local effective social transformation. In other words, despite poverty, informal entrepreneurs may recognise themselves as being able to create new situations and to contribute to local changes. Doing so, they lead SEEs to overcoming the instability and uncertainty affecting the informal economy, to the extent that the entrepreneurs attenuate their subordination to the dictates of the prevailing economy and redistribute a portion of the surplus value to the workers. From the viewpoint of economic culture, we might state that such informal enterprises support the rationalisation of solidarity since they stimulate intentional and everyday practices of solidarity (Gaiger 2006, 2015).

According to Defourny and Nyssens (2013: 12), the concept of social enterprise can encompass informal organisations: "When examining areas connecting formal and informal organisations, it is possible to observe trajectories of pioneering social enterprises that informally invent new responses to social demands". Their evolution may involve some types of tension, such as those resulting "from difficulties in combining early informal involvement of various stakeholders and subsequent strictly defined decision-making processes". This leads these authors to the conclusion that the

> *area between informal and formal organisations could also be of interest with a view to analysing the heuristic power of the concept of social enterprises to grasp socio-economic logics of collective initiatives embedded in the informal sector, in developing countries. In the latter, indeed, large sections of the population, living on the margin of the formal economy, are involved in various types of economic practices based on self-help principles and aiming to generate income or to improve their living conditions.*
>
> Defourny and Nyssens (2013: 12)

3. Social-Impact Enterprises

During the first decade of this century, a new complementary chapter began to take shape in Brazil's social field. Organisations of different types but with a converging *modus operandi* became more organised, evolving into a subsector that would become known as the "social-impact-enterprise" field. These organisations are mainly characterised by the fact that they establish "impact models", inspired by market-based strategies and activities, to further their social and/or environmental impact. Three main developments explain the emergence of this field.

First, many of the Brazilian third-sector organisations started adopting market strategies and adapting them to their activities, especially in the early 2000s (Naigeborin 2013), in some cases even creating new "impact models", focusing on fostering their social impact while improving their economic sustainability. Many of these "impact models" are based on revenue generated by the provision of market-based products and services not only to individuals, but also to public institutions and especially for-profit companies.

Secondly, the traditional for-profit sector has gradually increased its investments in socially oriented projects, focusing in particular on improving the quality of social-responsibility actions, and in some cases exploring more recent trends such as the "base-of-the-pyramid" approach (Prahalad and Hart 2002; Cañeque and Hart 2015), shared-value strategies (Porter and Kramer 2011) and collective-impact initiatives (Kania and Kramer 2011). This tendency became stronger during the 1990s, when for-profit companies, corporate foundations and corporate institutes started to come together to explore, understand, orientate and improve their social impact and investments (Naigeborin 2013). Consequently, some socially orientated joint projects and programmes started being developed and co-created by entrepreneurial associations and for-profit companies; commercial transactions between them also increased.

Thirdly, new organisations, using the legal framework of for-profit companies but entirely oriented towards creating social and/or environmental impact, started emerging during the first half of the 2000s. This movement was strongly influenced by new young social entrepreneurs willing to solve societal problems and challenges using new business models, technologies and concepts, such as the collaborative, creative and shared economy. Interestingly, the for-profit legal framework in Brazil offers several advantages when compared to that of associations, such as easiness of incorporation, fewer formal obligations and lower taxation regimes over some economic activities, tax-free dividends, open access to all the traditional start-up ecosystem and eligibility to apply for social-impact investments.

These three main trends, influencing each other, shaped the emergence of the social-impact-enterprise field in Brazil. Since the mid-2000s, this terminology has been gradually adopted by several stakeholders from and linked to the social sector and the academic sphere, favouring the strengthening of the field in itself. Nowadays, the social-impact-enterprise field in Brazil can be described by the combination of two main elements:

- On the one hand, the field is made up of organisations whose purpose is to generate a social and/or environmental impact and which explore an economic activity generating financial resources to guarantee their sustainability and the expansion of their impact. These initiatives develop specific "impact models" that allow them to create a social impact in their particular and unique way.
- On the other hand, social-impact enterprises are a set of organisations that are conceptually located between CSOs and for-profit companies. At the CSO end of the continuum, there are entrepreneurial

associations developing innovative market-based activities, products, services and projects aimed at funding and improving their social impact. They are normally recognised in Brazil as third-sector organisations but they are also gradually being classified as social-impact enterprises. At the other end of the continuum, where we find the typical capitalist for-profit enterprises, there are for-profit companies that aim to run a business capable of sharing value to multiple stakeholders, and have a social impact attached to their main activity, like certified B Corps.

Being located between the two poles of this continuum, social-impact enterprises can be legally constituted as for-profit companies, but entirely focused on solving a social problem directly through their main economic activities; they can also be legally constituted as associations, and some cooperatives and even some foundations are increasingly being considered as being part of this field. As there is no legal definition of social-impact enterprises in the country, there are still important variations, depending on the actor defining the concept. As a result, with the exception of the consensus about the social purpose and the economic activity, other defining characteristics, such as those about governance, the nature of founding members and the scope/kind of impact are still borderline criteria and generate many "grey" areas in terms of definition. The "core" of the field of social-impact enterprise is, however, becoming gradually stronger. To illustrate this tendency, the case of the social-investment field is very enlightening. Since the early 2010s, the social sector in Brazil has witnessed the creation of many social-investment funds (such as Vox Capital, Sitawi, Bemtevi, MOV, Yunus) targeting social-impact enterprises legally constituted as for-profits, and owning part of the organisations' shares during the investment period. Recently, however, some of these funds have been considering—and even creating—new investment strategies (e.g. loan-based strategies) so that they can invest in some entrepreneurial associations that are considered as "social-impact enterprises".

In Brazil, as in many other parts of the world, there are different concepts and definitions used to explain the social-enterprise phenomenon. In particular, despite the apparent current tendency towards a consensus about the "social-impact enterprise" definition, other concepts, such as "inclusive business" and "social business", are also being promoted by specific actors in the social field.

In order to better understand the relationship between those concepts, it is paramount to explore the framework presented by Comini *et al.* (2012). Based on the works of Defourny and Nyssens (2010), these authors affirm that "[unlike what is the case in] Europe, where the term social enterprise prevails, and [in] the USA, where the term social business is normally applied to BoP-connected strategies, in emerging countries, the term inclusive business appears more strongly" (Comini *et al*. 2012: 390).

First, as explained earlier, the term "social enterprise" is unusual in Brazil. Secondly, the term "social business" has been adopted, used and promoted in the country by the Yunus initiative to refer to a specific subset of social-impact enterprises that fulfil the seven principles of social business such as they are defined by Yunus (Yunus Centre 2017). Thirdly, the term "inclusive business", adopted by the United Nations Development Program (UNDP), refers to organisations that are legally structured as for-profit companies with "a strong concern for poverty reduction initiatives, which must have a positive, effective and especially long-term social impact" (Comini *et al*. 2012: 390). A UNDP report also considers as inclusive business some "activities of inclusive business" that are projects including the base of the pyramid into the core business of for-profit companies (PNUD 2015). This subset would however be excluded from the "social-impact enterprise" field as social impact is not the main purpose of their business.

Another important clarification regarding the social-impact enterprise definition concerns the relation of this concept with the solidarity-enterprise field. In some cases, small social enterprises are created and owned by the beneficiaries; this is for example the case of cooperatives or associations with strong elements of self-management, whose success is expected to transform the standards of living of the population they serve and to insure their economic sustainability. Their purpose is then primarily mutual, because they aim to improve the quality of life of the members, who are usually from low-income social categories. There is then a clear intersection between the field of solidarity enterprises and that of social-impact enterprises, the former bringing to the latter the participatory governance principle, besides the social purpose and the explicit economic activity. Those two concepts thus share similarities and are complementary to understand the social-enterprise field in Brazil.

It is clear that many different concepts and definitions are being explored and used in Brazil to refer to the recent developments linked to the social-enterprise field. Each actor of the social-enterprise ecosystem establishes and promotes the definition that better suits its objectives and activities. Such behaviour is understandable, considering the relative conceptual ambiguity and newness of the social-enterprise phenomenon. There are, however, convergences between those various approaches, and the "social-impact enterprise" definition emerged as a collective construction able to encompass this diversity. Similarly, the "social enterprise" notion may conceptually work as an encompassing concept, allowing to bring together the different Brazilian "social-enterprise-related" traditions, as will be discussed further in the next section.

4. The Main Models of Social Enterprise

Each organisation in Brazil that is considered as a social enterprise, independently of its historical roots, aims to deliver social benefits or to generate a positive environmental impact for a specific target public or for society as a whole. And all of them develop and function according to specific patterns that allow them to produce the intended effects. The analysis of these different patterns reveals that there is one unequivocal particularity that defines two major fields of social enterprise in the Brazilian context: the relation between the promoters and the beneficiaries of the organisation.

In some cases, the organisation is owned and controlled by its associated members, be they workers, consumers or users, who manage the organisation so as to generate benefits for themselves and sometimes for a broader public. Most of the employees are members and consequently have both a share in the profits generated and a voice in the governance of the enterprise. The democratisation of ownership and the cooperation among worker-owners, sustaining models in which the worker-owned or self-managed enterprise becomes the dominant economic unit, materialise an ideological and strategic element. The protagonists are at the same time promoters and beneficiaries. Considering that the protagonists in general are poor or excluded people, the social mission and the economic mission merge. This pattern is typical of solidarity-economy enterprises, but it is also a common trait amongst associations and cooperatives. It can be considered as a *cooperative and self-managed pattern*.

In other cases, beneficiaries are mainly a "target public", while the providers are professionals or volunteers working in the organisation in order to supply products and services. This pattern is typically found in third-sector organisations driven by altruistic purposes and addressing social missions related to social services, environmental protection and other causes. The same basic pattern can also be found amongst social-impact enterprises, albeit with some innovations in the overall approach and in the role assigned to beneficiaries. Sometimes, the beneficiary becomes a sort of client, normally paying a subsidised fee for a service s/he would not be able to obtain otherwise. Sometimes, there is a triangulation between at least one category of beneficiaries and other stakeholders who receive some recompense and are in charge of covering, totally or partially, the costs of the benefits offered to the original target public. As mentioned above, in some cases, small enterprises are created and owned by the beneficiaries; they are thus self-managed organisations that aim to improve their owner-beneficiaries' standards of living through market strategies. Both third-sector organisations and social-impact enterprises develop a *social-oriented and market-based pattern*.

Each pattern encompasses a few models of Brazilian social enterprise. The first pattern mainly includes the solidarity-economy organisations, but also the cooperative sector as a whole and countless associations spread throughout the country; it is impelled by very active social movements, such as the Landless Rural Workers' Movement. The second pattern refers to third-sector entities and to social-impact enterprises. Models corresponding to this pattern combine different sources of resources (high level of economic "plurality") and often have a high level of explicit social commitment, including the traditional non-distribution constraint. Some organisations belonging to the second pattern, such as charities and foundations (to which we referred in a previous section), are more likely to include "defective" initiatives that would not fit completely into the concept of social enterprise. Regarding NGOs (or CSOs, under the current nomenclature), although they are not, properly speaking, economic organisations, they can manage economic activities involving their beneficiaries and distribute profits to the latter and to the organisation, under different modalities.

4.1. Models Under the Cooperative and Self-Managed Pattern

*SEEs Providing Services and Enhancing
Community Development*

SEEs providing services and enhancing community development are basically rural associations, and the most important groups among their members are family farmers and social policies beneficiaries, followed by traditional peoples and communities. These initiatives' collective activities aim to provide goods, services and benefits (such as domestic consumption items or sociocultural and educational services) contributing towards the well-being of their members, or to foster local associative and community development.

This model corresponds to historical forms of local solidarity, which witnessed significant waves of cooperation previous to the dramatic expansion of the solidarity economy in the 1990s. These initiatives seem to be less frequent nowadays, but research findings (Gaiger 1996) indicate that they generate other experiences, including new types of SEEs. As they are mostly located away from urban centres and are somehow "distant" from organised civil society, they take relatively little part in social mobilisations directly connected to the solidarity economy and, for this reason, they are not very present in debates and in intervention structures in the public setting. At the same time, the cooperative sector, led by the Brazilian Cooperative Organization (OCB), has promoted many similar initiatives since the 1950s in the consumption, educational, housing, infrastructure and health services fields. Another important source of initiatives over the past three decades has been the Landless Rural Workers' Movement.

SEEs Supporting Their Members' Productive Activities

The main collective purpose of SEEs supporting the productive activities of their members is to provide services, resources or benefits for the individual or family economic activities of their members, in areas such as product exchange, trade and collective use of equipment or productive infrastructure. With the exception of initiatives dedicated to trade and products exchange, which are mostly urban, this model presents a predominance of SEEs located in rural areas, and it is characterised by a relatively high concentration of old initiatives, which have been in operation for ten to twenty years and are mostly registered under the legal form of association. In addition to the predominance of family farmers in rural SEEs belonging to this model, a proportionally high presence of recyclable waste collectors and of craftsmen is noticed in urban initiatives of this type.

This model illustrates the fact that the solidarity economy works as a means to leverage and strengthen the productive activities of different categories of low-income workers through their free association and collective participation in self-managed enterprises. In addition to the Landless Rural Workers' Movement and the National Union of Cooperatives of Family Agriculture and Solidarity Economy, which bring together thousands of cooperatives and associations of family farmers, agricultural cooperatives belonging to this model are numerous to the point of being the main branch of the aforementioned OCB system.[5]

SEEs Providing Work and Generating Income for Their Members

The main collective activity of SEEs providing work and generating income for their members is the production of goods, trade or service provision; depending on the SEE, such activity can represent the most important source of income for the members, or only a secondary source of income. The activities are developed, at least partially, based on the socialisation of the means of production and the collectivisation of work, be it in execution or in management tasks. The main motivation for the setting up of these initiatives, mostly located in urban areas, is the search for alternative solutions to fight unemployment, but also the will to create economic organisations in which the workers are the business' owners, without depending on bosses or third parties.

Globally speaking, this is the model in which cooperatives stand out, as a legal form of reference as well as in terms of numbers. This model is frequently considered as an ideal example in the solidarity economy, since it meets, in theory, all the requirements of an alternative production conducted by the workers through self-management and partial or full socialisation of the means of production. However, many of these enterprises are small, informal, low-yielding and do not represent a decisive economic activity for their members, even if they may play an important role as experiences of social participation that foster the formation of new actors (Ferrarini and Veronese 2010).

SEEs Providing Social Integration Based on Work and Sociocultural Activities

The main purpose of SEEs providing social integration based on work and sociocultural activities is to promote the social integration of individuals in particular situations of risk or vulnerability through psychosocial and professional rehabilitation measures, based on human development processes, resocialisation dynamics, and occupational and training activities. In addition to social cooperatives, whose formalisation in Brazil was inspired by the Italian model, there are many associations providing social assistance, community philanthropic institutions, various organisations in traditional communities, and entities linked to the third sector. The motivations behind these initiatives can be social, philanthropic and/ or religious.

Initiatives close to the solidarity economy put an emphasis on the right to health and work as a way to achieve social justice and to strengthen citizenship. The economic activity carried out by the beneficiaries is basically a methodological resource to achieve their resocialisation and social integration, although it may also be a complementary source of income and, potentially, of future financial autonomy. In this model, there is a greater presence of specialised professionals, volunteers and other partners, which entails a social and functional distinction between managers and beneficiaries, with different forms and levels of participation. Links with government policies, public agencies and private entities are also typical in this model. However, there is also an active involvement of the beneficiaries in participatory bodies, such as networks and councils, as well as in specific social struggles related to mental health, ethnic or gender issues, children and elderly people. Social cooperatives—the flagship of this model—are legally obliged to implement democratic management through collective decision-making, and to insure equal distribution of benefits to all members.

SEEs Providing Financial Services

The main activity of SEEs providing financial services is to provide financial goods and services (such as credit, savings and transfers of benefits from government programmes) to their associated members, other participants and citizens. They have been created over the last two decades and work mostly in rural areas, serving mainly family farmers. Although, in this model, cooperatives prevail, within the solidarity economy, these coexist with other forms of organisation, such as community banks and solidarity funds. The originality of the solidarity economy is to promote financial organisations of various types, stimulating popular initiatives and keeping the SEEs close to current dynamics and local needs. In addition, such organisations function as interaction devices that agglutinate interests, which positively affects other initiatives based on community ties or class solidarities.

In the solidarity economy, there is a predominance of credit cooperatives, such as those belonging to the National Association of Credit Cooperatives for the Family and Solidarity Economy (*Associação Nacional do Cooperativismo de Crédito da Economia Familiar e Solidária*, or ANCOSOL) and to the System of Rural Credit Cooperatives with Solidarity Interaction (*Sistema de Cooperativa de Crédito Rural com Interação Solidária*, or Cresol Central), which gather hundreds of cooperatives, in addition to the credit branch of the OCB system. Due to the legislation and control mechanisms regulating financial companies in Brazil, credit cooperatives have considerable institutional and functional homogeneity. This situation produces an effect of isonomy in relation to private-market institutions, stimulating competitive strategies and leaving sometimes in a secondary plane the democratic and participative spirit of cooperatives.

4.2 Models Under the Social-Oriented and Market-Based Pattern

Third-Sector Organisations Providing Social Services

The model of third-sector organisations providing social services refers to the provision of care and promotion of social integration for people with disabilities, children, elderly people, etc. Such services are targeted mainly—but not exclusively—at populations in situation of poverty or social vulnerability. Most of the services offered are related to health and social assistance; education and training are also important areas. Services in the cultural area are expanding because of the growing importance of this field in society (especially among young people—a significant share of the public of these TSOs) and due to the emergence of the concept of "creative economy" in Brazil, which has generated public and private financing lines for these activities. Many organisations have also focused on advocacy lately: facing high social inequality and many kinds of discrimination, they incorporate in particular the defence and protection of the rights of minorities among the services they offer, in order to be more effective in their social mission.

Heterogeneity is very high among organisations belonging to this model, which includes both initiatives corresponding to traditional conceptions, inherited from the church, and other, more professionalised approaches. Especially since the Constitution of 1988 was adopted and new conceptions of social assistance as a right were introduced in the 1990s, these organisations have had to meet technical criteria in order to receive state funding. Finally, we should mention the recent emergence of new organisations, more business- and management-oriented, but totally focused on their social purposes.

Third-Sector Organisations Protecting the Environment

This model is focused on environmental protection, which often stimulates social mobilisations. In general, these organisations understand sustainability in a multidimensional way. Therefore, in some cases, the protection of the traditional communities and the preservation of their knowledge and values are parts of the organisation's mission. In others cases, processes aiming to help or empower people, mainly through educational actions, are regarded as a means to achieve the organisation's main purpose. Considering that environmental protection is a relatively new subject in the social agenda, these organisations usually incorporate new management forms and demonstrate a high willingness to connect with other public, private and multilateral organisations. There is a strong tendency, among organisations in this group, to becoming involved in international networks and events, which can be explained by the understanding that "the environment knows no borders".

Financial and Advisory Third-Sector Organisations

The main activity of financial and advisory third-sector organisations is to provide financial goods and services but, unlike organisations belonging to the SSE that provide financial services, these organisations are not specifically geared towards rural areas. They also offer technical or material support to social projects and programmes. They can be considered as making up a new kind of organisation, since they usually hire private organisations when they need advisory services in different areas, such as legal issues, management, financial questions, marketing and technology.

Social-Impact Enterprises Providing Access to Goods and Services

Among social-impact enterprises, the ones that provide access to goods and services represent the most common type. They enable people to get access to a good or a service, such as education, language courses, accessibility tools (e.g. accessible software for blind people) and health care. This model is closely related to that of "third-sector organisations providing social services"; their main difference concerns the legal form in which the organisations are respectively constituted: in the case of the latter, as non-profit associations; in the case of the "social-impact enterprises providing access to goods and services", as for-profit companies entirely focused on solving a social or environmental problem.

Social-Impact Enterprises Providing Support and Empowerment

Social-impact enterprises in this group provide support and empowerment, usually to a specific group of beneficiaries, such as immigrants and refugees, low-income people or patients suffering from a specific disease. The delivery of services occurs in two ways. The first one corresponds to the situation in which the beneficiaries become a special kind of client, normally paying a subsidised fee for a service they would not be able to obtain otherwise. The second way in which the services are delivered is based on a triangulation between the provider, at least one category of beneficiary, and another stakeholder who covers, totally or partially, the costs of the service provided to the beneficiary. This second way of service delivery is also used by entrepreneurial associations providing social services and constitutes a bridge between these evolving models.

Social-Impact Enterprises Providing Mediation for Conflict Resolution

Social-impact enterprises belonging to this model focus on the delivery of mediation services for conflict resolution, based on a particular model that has proven its usefulness in solving complex and hitherto unresolved situations. One example is "Terranova", an enterprise that has created an innovative mediation process to peaceably resolve land conflicts between landowners and squatters: the landowners are compensated for their property losses, while the squatters acquire formal property titles for the land they live on. Another case is "Renascer", which deals with the relationship between companies managing new infrastructure projects passing through pre-existing communities, advocating and negotiating interests from both sides.

Conclusion

Brazil is one of the most unequal countries on the planet; it is also a huge country, characterised by an immense diversity, originated from the miscegenation of indigenous, African and European ethnicities, among others. The diversity of social, economic and political conditions explains the multiplicity of conceptions and organisational formats encountered among civil-society initiatives. In the construction of a worldwide typology of social enterprise, Brazil may contribute both knowledge on initiatives that correspond to "mainstream" models identified in the North and analysis of innovative elements.

To better understand the complexity of this social landscape, we should remember from the outset that, in 1940, only about one third of Brazilians lived in urban locations. Around 2003, that number had nearly tripled: over 80% of Brazilians were urban dwellers. Among other factors, such a rapid growth of urbanisation has undoubtedly contributed to the poor quality of life in modern urban Brazil, and to the weaknesses of the public sphere in the country (Nettuno 2011). But this trend towards urbanisation has also had more positive effects: it has been strongly linked to the emergence and development of social movements and solidarity enterprises, both in rural and urban contexts. It is important to reflect on the plural configuration of these grassroots initiatives, considering the different social actors in focus, trying to take into account their cultural diversity as well as their multiple origins and the challenges they are currently facing. For this purpose, in this final section, we will focus on solidarity-economy organisations, having in mind some of their specificities in the country.

As a first point, according to the second Brazilian Mapping of the Solidarity Economy, completed in 2013, about 30% of solidarity enterprises are informal groups. They are not regulated by any legal provisions, but by their own internal norms. In such circumstances, there are no established or widely accepted criteria for the purpose of distinguishing and classifying the initiatives. Broadly speaking, there is a wide range of initiatives still in search of institutional identity and a consistent legal framework, and which do not fit in the traditional cooperative or third-sector fields. The creation of an adequate legal framework for the solidarity economy has been at the centre of the agenda of the solidarity-economy social movement for at least a decade. Despite controversies on this subject, such legal evolution would undoubtedly remove obstacles to institutional innovation in Brazil, particularly with a view to designing and implementing a more inclusive public agenda, open to the diversity of solidarity enterprises.

Some progress has been made in some sectors, such as that of labour cooperatives, but obstacles and difficulties persist, and the adoption of a specific national law has been postponed several times. In addition to disputes among social actors involved in the solidarity economy, there is a strong opposition from the traditional cooperative sector, whose institutionalisation occurred during the military dictatorship (1964–1985), and which benefits from unique representation and economic advantages. As far as the rural sector is concerned, the development of conventional Brazilian agribusiness, led by large producers and landowners, promoted a potentially predatory economic model. Its rise is achieved through the destruction of traditional communities and the appropriation of work and nature by capital (Christoffoli *et al.* 2013).

Regarding small farmer collective enterprises, a more adequate legislation, providing for different production and marketing models and legitimating and facilitating the diversity of formats would be desirable. The current legal model dates back to 1971; it is enshrined in the national law on cooperatives, enacted during the military dictatorship. This model aimed at benefiting the project of "conservative modernisation" of Brazilian agriculture. The cooperativism that emerged from there has not incorporated popular or solidarity experiences, leaving aside small family farmers (peasants), forest extractives communities, river dwellers and other social groups, without any possibility of creating cooperatives to solve their problems. Popular sectors then created the National Union of Cooperatives for Family Agriculture and Solidarity Economy (*União Nacional das Cooperativas da Agricultura Familiar e Economia Solidária*, or UNICAFES), that aims to bring together new associative experiences of popular economy and family farmers that have been created without support from traditional cooperativism (Alves 2014).

A second point concerns the Brazilian civil society in which, referring in particular to social entrepreneurship, we have to take into consideration the weight of grassroots organisations and of popular protagonists.[6] As Santos highlights, for the last 30 years, the most progressive struggles have featured subaltern social groups: indigenous people, peasants, women, Afro-descendants, miners and unemployed people. These groups often organised themselves in ways differing from those of political parties and unions (Santos 2012: 46). In these civil-society experiences, solidarity economy entrepreneurs move into a deeper level of participatory citizenship, becoming actors of social changes. In terms of political rights, the solidarity ties that emerge from participation in solidarity enterprises support collective action and the strengthening of citizenship. Some initiatives are provisional and precarious, whereas other experiences achieve consolidation, successes and possibilities for expansion. It should be pointed out that the experiences and networks grow within a field of social regulation and are carried out by the actors in the space located between the unregulated, free market, on the one hand, and state planning, on the other hand (Vinha 2003).

That being said, this chapter leads to the general—and crucial—conclusion that, although the concept of social enterprise is not usual in Brazil, it is possible to consider Brazilian organisations through the lens of the social-enterprise concept and to employ the EMES ideal type of social enterprise as a methodological tool.

On the one hand, some social enterprises in Brazil are similar to those typical of the North, with a high degree of institutionalisation and formalisation. They can be analysed and understood using the theoretical approaches—mainly North American and European—that have traditionally been called upon in this scientific field. Some of the Brazilian "new social-mission-based enterprises" fit well into the American mainstream approach according to which a social objective can be achieved by non-profit companies through market strategies and resources (Austin *et al.* 2006), or even by for-profit enterprises (Dees 1998; Salamon and Young 2002). For the latter, profit-making is desirable for the fulfilment of the mission, without necessary links with the type of economic activity or with the governance structure. Other Brazilian initiatives developing entrepreneurial activities while pursuing social missions (associations, mutual and cooperatives) are more in line with the European mainstream approach embedded in the tradition of the social and solidarity economy, which places limits on the distribution of economic benefits to the partners and emphasises democratic governance, as well as the relevance of partnership with public policies, with some degree of interaction with the institutional environment.

On the other hand, there is a heterogeneous set of initiatives with characteristics that are typical of Brazil in particular and of Latin American countries in general, and which tend to remain invisible or undervalued in light of canonical conceptions of Schumpeterian entrepreneurship and of the market economy. Such initiatives have acquired legitimacy under the theoretical and conceptual umbrella of the solidarity economy and they brought novelty into the "mainstream" field of social enterprise. Solidarity enterprises can present and articulate rationalities from indigenous and African worldviews (such as those of *quilombolas* and traditional communities of fishermen) to cultural and economic patterns assimilated by peripheral capitalist societies. These initiatives are taken by excluded people through associative entrepreneurship, with scarce material and immaterial resources (Gaiger and Corrêa 2010; Ferrarini and Veronese 2010). Their gains are not restricted to the economic dimension (or cannot be grasped in the light of formalist economic references), since the provision of subsistence is inseparable from the virtuous, extra-economic and systemic effects of cooperation. As a rule, the initiatives are self-managed and the ownership of capital is collective. There is a clear predominance of the economic principle of *domesticity* (Polanyi 1977), reinforced by a great presence of women. In addition, for the reasons already explained above, there is a high degree of informality among solidarity enterprises, and supporting public policies are clearly insufficient. As a consequence, solidarity enterprises should be understood as potentially innovative instituting practices, aiming at building emancipatory alternatives.

As regards empirical analysis, preliminary data and previous theoretical reflections (Gaiger 2015; Laville *et al.* 2016) allow us to state that solidarity enterprises could be conceptualised as social enterprises through an adaptation of some indicators of the EMES definition.

With respect to the economic dimension, the valuation of work is the common element that most strongly stands out in solidarity enterprises.

However, other key elements should be added to better characterise solidarity enterprises under the EMES model, such as: the emphasis on the plurality of economic principles, with renewed attention to the domesticity principle and the simultaneously conservative and emancipatory sense that this principle acquires, particularly in patriarchal societies (Hillenkamp 2013); the consistency of economic, social and environmental commitment; and finally, the recognition of the members' need for remuneration, as part of the social mission.

In light of this last argument, it seems obvious that simply limiting the distribution of profits among members would not make sense: explicit goals of benefiting the community are not contradictory with the aim of providing work and income for the members of the solidarity enterprise. Moreover, the search for means of subsistence in solidarity enterprises is carried out in a perspective of social transformation, of promoting a counter-hegemonic movement based on solidarity alternatives in terms of life and production. In a context in which formal equality is not materialised in the daily life of these groups, it should be emphasised that self-management and cooperation provide an experience of substantive equality, an exercise of rights and of access to basic services.

As for the political dimension, the participatory nature of the solidarity economy is promoted mainly by self-management in the enterprises. A key element that solidarity enterprise can add to the social-enterprise approach concerns the fact that the economic and social activities are driven by a political project of society, under principles of solidarity and sustainability. This is expressed: (1) within the enterprise, by the prevailing collective spirit and by the reluctance to consider the enterprise as a private organisation in the strict sense; (2) in society, as the solidarity economy is a social movement that works through democratic deliberation instances; and (3) in the workers' permanent pursuit of co-constructed democratic public policies. Addressing social problems leads to projective views of a more inclusive and fair society and to a commitment to social transformations.[7]

Last but not least, a particularity of the Brazilian case lies in the fact that the epistemological dimension—understood as the diversity of modes of knowledge, human life and social relations generated by and embedded in different cultural traditions (Santos 2012; Solomon 1994)—may contribute to a broad and multicultural theoretical analysis of social enterprises through the challenging North-South dialogue carried out within the frame of the ICSEM Project.

Notes

1 See also Gaiger *et al.* (2015).
2 And unlike what is the case in Europe, the term *social economy* is alien to Brazilian institutions, social actors and academic environments, with a few exceptions (Dowbor and Kilsztajn 2001). Even one of the rare conceptual elaborations in this regard (Serva and Andion 2004, 2006) acknowledges that

the term is unusual in the country, despite the fact that organisations operating on the border between the economic and social spheres constitute a vivid phenomenon, increasingly noticeable both from the theoretical and practical standpoints.

3 See chapter 1, on Argentina, for information on the same type of experience in this country.

4 The name CSO was originally adopted by the Inter-American Development Bank, in the early 1990s (Naigeborin 2013).

5 Many cooperatives are run by agricultural companies linked to agribusiness, with salaried labour. In this case, they function as a lucrative instrument of accumulation of capital by private companies and can only be identified to some limited extent—or even not at all—as social enterprises.

6 Emblematic examples include the Landless Rural Workers' Movement, family farmers' new associative organisations, recycling initiatives and urban social movements fighting for rights like affordable housing or quality public transportation.

7 When the organisation focuses on "social-repair processes", the main objective is to provide palliative assistance to poor or vulnerable people. In this case, notwithstanding the benefits provided to the target public, the way in which the activities are managed will hardly lead to significant levels of emancipation and autonomy.

References

Alves, A. F. (2014) "Sustentabilidade das cooperativas da agricultura familiar e economia solidária no Brasil: o caso da União Nacional de Cooperativas da Agricultura Familiar e Economia Solidária (UNICAFES)", *Anais do IX Congreso Sociedades Rurales Latinoamericanas*, pp. 6–11.

Anjos, E. (2012) "Práticas e sentidos da economia solidária. Um estudo a partir das cooperativas de trabalho", Tese de Doutorado em Ciências Sociais, São Leopoldo: Unisinos.

Austin, J. E., Leonard, B., Reficco, E. & Wei-Skillern, J. (2006) "Social entrepreneurship: It's for corporations too", in Nicholls, A. (ed.) *Social Entrepreneurship, New Models of Sustainable Social Change*, Oxford: Oxford University Press, pp. 169–180.

Cañeque, F. C. & Hart, S. L. (2015) *Base of the Pyramid 3.0: Sustainable Development Through Innovation and Entrepreneurship*, London: Greenleaf Publishing.

Christoffoli, P., Nines, P., Rambo, A. & Costa, T. (2013) "Family farm's associative experiences in Southern Brazil as strategies for sustainable rural development", *Revista da ABET*, Vol. 12, No. 2, pp. 96–114.

Comini, G., Barki, E. & Aguiar, L. (2012) "A three-pronged approach on social business: A Brazilian multi-case analysis", *Revista de Administração*, Vol. 47, No. 3, pp. 385–397.

Coraggio, J. (1999) *Política social y economia Del trabajo*, Madrid: Miño y Dávila Editores.

Dees, J-G. (1998) "Enterprising nonprofits", *Harvard Business Review*, January–February, pp. 55–67.

Defourny, J. & Nyssens, M. (2010) "Conceptions of social enterprise and social entrepreneurship in Europe and the United States: Convergences and divergences", *Journal of Social Entrepreneurship*, Vol. 1, No. 1, pp. 32–53.

Defourny, J. & Nyssens, M. (2013) *The International Comparative Social Enterprise Models (ICSEM) Project–Invitation to Join the "ICSEM" Project*, Liege: The International Comparative Social Enterprise Models (ICSEM) Project.

Dowbor, L. & Kilsztajn, S. (eds) (2001) *Economia Social No Brasil*, São Paulo: Editora SENAC.

Fernandes, R. (1994) *Privado, porém público: o Terceiro Setor na América Latina*, Rio de Janeiro: Relume-Dumará.

Ferrarini, A. & Veronese, M. (2010) "Piracema: uma metáfora para o microempreendedorismo associativo no Brasil", *Outra Economía*, Vol. IV, No. 7, pp. 131–152.

Gaiger, L. (ed.) (1996) *Formas de combate e resistência à pobreza*, São Leopoldo: Unisinos.

Gaiger, L. (ed.) (2004) *Sentidos e experiências da economia solidária no Brasil*, Porto Alegre: UFRGS.

Gaiger, L. (2006) "A racionalidade dos formatos produtivos autogestionários", *Sociedade& Estado*, Vol. 21, No. 2, pp. 513–544.

Gaiger, L. (2015) "Collaborative research between civil society, state and the academia: Lesson from the Brazilian mapping of the solidarity economy", in Bouchard, M. & Rousselière, D. (eds) *The Weight of the Social Economy: An International Perspective*, Brussels: Peter Lang, pp. 205–230.

Gaiger, L. (2016) "Global and Brazilian approaches of the social and solidarity economy enterprises", *Iberoamericana*, Vol. XXXVIII, No. 1, pp. 1–14.

Gaiger, L. & Anjos, E. (2012) "Solidarity economy in Brazil: The relevance of cooperatives for the historic emancipation of workers", in Piñero, C. (ed.) *Cooperatives and Socialism: A View from Cuba*, Hampshire: Palgrave Macmillan, pp. 212–234.

Gaiger, L. & Corrêa, A. (2010) "A História e os sentidos do empreendedorismo associativo", *Otra Economía*, Vol. IV, No. 7, pp. 153–176.

Gaiger, L., Ferrarini, A. & Veronese, M. (2015) "Social enterprise in Brazil: An overview of solidarity economy enterprises", *ICSEM Working Papers*, No. 10, Liège: The International Comparative Social Enterprise Models (ICSEM) Project.

Gaiger, L., Kuyven, P., Ogando, C., Kappes, S. & Silva, J. (2014) *A economia solidária no Brasil. Uma análise de dados nacionais*, São Leopoldo: Oikos.

Hillenkamp, I. (2013) "Le principe de *householding* aujourd'hui. Discussion théorique et approche empirique par l'économie populaire", in Hillenkamp, I. & Laville, J-L. (eds) *Socioéconomie et démocratie. L'actualité de Karl Polanyi*, Toulouse: Erès, pp. 215–239.

Kania, J. & Kramer, M. R. (2011) "Collective impact", *Stanford Social Innovation Review*, Winter, pp. 26–41.

Laville, J-L., Hillenkamp, I., Eynaud, P., Coraggio, J. L., Ferrarini, A., França Filho, G., Gaiger, L., Kitajima, K., Lemaître, A., Sadik, Y., Veronese, M. & Wanderley, F. (2016) "Théorie de l'entreprise sociale et pluralisme: L'entreprise6sociale de type solidaire", *Revue Interventions économiques*, Vol. 54.

Leite, M. & Georges, I. (eds) (2012) *Les nouvelles configurations du travail et l'économie sociale et solidaire au Brésil*, Paris: L'Harmattan.

Lima, J. (2007) "Workers' cooperatives in Brazil: Autonomy vs precariousness", *Economic and Industrial Democracy*, Vol. 28, No. 4, pp. 589–621.

Naigeborin, V. (2013) "O papel das organizações da sociedade civil na criação e no desenvolvimento de negócios com impacto social", in Barki, E., Izzo, D.,

Torres, H. G. & Aguiar, L. (eds) *Negócios com impacto social no Brasil*, São Paulo: Peirópolis, pp. 100–118.

Nettuno, D. (2011) "The threat to democracy in Brazil's public sphere", graduate thesis, Tampa: University of South Florida.

Nunes, C. (2001) "Cooperativas, uma possível transformação identitária para os trabalhadores do setor informal", *Sociedade & Estado*, Vol. 16, No. 1/2, pp. 134–158.

Pinto, J. (2006) *Economia solidária: de volta à arte da associação*, Porto Alegre: UFRGS.

PNUD (2015) *Mercados inclusivos no Brasil. Desafios e oportunidades do ecossistema de negócios*, Brazil: PNUD.

Polanyi, K. (1977) *The Livelihood of Man*, New York: Academic Press.

Porter, M. E. & Kramer, M. R. (2011) "Creating shared value: How to reinvent capitalism and unleash a wave of innovation and growth", *Harvard Business Review*, Vol. 89, No. 1/2, pp. 62–77.

Prahalad, C. K. & Hart, S. L. (2002) "The fortune at the bottom of the pyramid", *Strategic + Business*, Vol. 26, No. 1, pp. 1–14.

Salamon, M. D. & Young, D. (2002) *The State of Nonprofit America*, Washington, DC: Brookings Institution.

Santos, B. de S. (2012) "Public sphere and epistemologies of the South", *Africa Development*, Vol. 37, No. 1, pp. 43–67.

Schneider, J. & Lauschner, R. (1979) "Evolução e situação atual do cooperativismo brasileiro", in *O cooperativismo no Brasil: enfoques, análises e contribuição*, Rio Grande do Sul: Friedrich Neumann, Associação de Orientação às Cooperativas, pp. 1–58.

Serva, M. & Andion, C. (2004) "Por uma visão positiva da sociedade civil: uma análise histórica da sociedade civil organizada no Brasil", *CAYAPA—Revista Venezolana de Economía Social*, Vol. 4, No. 7, pp. 7–24.

Serva, M. & Andion, C. (2006) "Uma delimitação do campo da economia social no Brasil: história, correntes e atores", Anais do 30° Encontro da ANPAD, Salvador.

Singer, P. & Souza, A. (eds) (2000) *A economia solidária no Brasil: a autogestão como resposta ao desemprego*, São Paulo: Contexto.

Solomon, M. (1994) "A more social epistemology", in Schmitt, F. (ed.) *Socializing Epistemology: The Social Dimensions of Knowledge*, Lanham: Rowman and Littlefield Publishers, pp. 217–233.

Véras de Oliveira, R., Gomes, D. & Targino, I. (eds) (2011) *Marchas e contramarchas da informalidade do trabalho: das origens às novas abordagens*, João Pessoa: Editora da UFPB.

Veronese, M. (2008) *Psicologia social e economia solidária*, São Paulo: Ideias e Letras.

Vinha, V. (2003) "Polanyi e a nova sociologia econômica", *Econômica*, Vol. 3, No. 2, pp. 207–230.

Yunus Centre (2017) "Seven principles of social business". Available HTTP: www.muhammadyunus.org/index.php/social-business/seven-principles.

4 Social- and Solidarity-Economy Organisations in Chile

Concepts, Historical Trajectories, Trends and Characteristics

Michela Giovannini and
Pablo Nachar-Calderón
with the contribution of Sebastián Gatica

Introduction

Historically, in Chile, there has been a great wave of organisations that can be considered as social enterprises (SEs), even though this term has not been frequently employed in the country. The institutionalisation of this type of organisation has faced several hurdles, since legal forms provided for by the Chilean legislation are not always appropriate in order to define and identify SEs. Furthermore, the level of visibility and legitimacy of SEs is low, and national studies on this sector remain very scarce.

The aim of this chapter is to present the historical and legal background against which the organisations that can be considered as SEs have developed in Chile, to analyse the main related concepts employed in the country, and to identify and characterise SEs in such a context, highlighting new emerging trends, namely the (re)emergence of community enterprises and the emergence of B Corps.

Against this background, it is relevant to analyse the existence of these types of entities as solutions to community problems from different perspectives, and to study the reasons for their existence, their mode of operation, and the beneficial impact they have on the communities within which they operate.

The chapter is structured as follows: First, we present a conceptual approach to the phenomenon in Chile, as influenced mainly by the European concept of social economy, the Anglo-Saxon approach to the third sector, the social- and solidarity-economy (hereinafter SSE) approach, derived *inter alia* from the Latin American conceptual tradition, and the concept of popular economy, which has been frequently employed in Chile. We then focus, in the second section, on the historical context for the emergence of civil-society organisations in Chile. The third section is dedicated to the analysis of the legal approach, with the specific objective of evaluating which of the different legal forms provided for by Chilean law comply with the EMES approach to social enterprise. We then try, in

DOI: 10.4324/9780429055164-6

the fifth section, to synthesise these different approaches, and we propose a framework of analysis of the different models of SSE organisations specific to the Chilean context. The sixth section presents and analyses two very different emerging trends in the SSE scenario in Chile: new cooperatives and B Corps. Finally, some concluding remarks close the chapter.

1. Conceptual Approach: Popular Economy, Social Economy, Third Sector or Social and Solidarity Economy?

All enterprises are generally seen as problem-solving devices that address unsatisfied needs through the production of various types of services and goods. In the last decades, due to the fact that for-profit and public enterprises were either unwilling or unable to address a number of specific societal needs, new, non-conventional forms of enterprises with specific social aims have started to emerge in different settings and in different countries; the characteristics of these enterprises are shaped by the specific context in which they emerge.

In Chile, similarly to what happens in other countries, several terms are employed to identify civil-society initiatives that operate under the form of organisations aiming to address unsatisfied societal needs, emerge from civil society and are independent from the government and from the for-profit sector.

From the conceptual point of view, four main trends have influenced the denomination of these civil-society initiatives: (1) the "popular economy" concept, used to define the informal sector; (2) the "social economy" concept, which mainly derives from the European, and especially French, school of thought; (3) the "third sector" or "non-profit sector" concept, which is influenced mainly by the US stream of thought; and (4) the "social and solidarity economy", a concept originally coined in parallel in Latin America and Europe in the 1990s.

As the different denominations confirm, conceptualisation is rather problematic, and a shared definition, able to draw a delimitation among the different concepts, is still a matter of discussion.

The concept of *popular economy* is employed to refer to those informal experiences that arise from civil society in order to meet needs of income generation, generally without any margin of accumulation. These autonomous, community-based initiatives address their members' needs of subsistence, and social relations appear crucial in this context, because they are conducive to appropriate solutions to problems linked to actual living conditions. The concept of popular economy has been widely employed in Chile to refer to a phenomenon that emerged—as it did in other contexts of the global South—at the end of the 19th century, but it started to gain more importance from the 1970s onward. This is particularly true if we look at those experiences of popular economy that emerged at the initiative of *pobladores* (inhabitants of popular urban neighbourhoods) and which survived, and even increased in number, in the years of the dictatorship (Nyssens 1997).

Even though, in the past, the *social economy* concept was not frequently employed in Chile (Radrigán *et al.* 2010), the Chilean government has recently started to use this term by establishing the Associativity and Social-Economy Division (*División de Asociatividad y Economía Social*, or DAES), which is part of the Ministry of Economy, Development and Tourism. This implies a certain institutional recognition and representation of the organisations belonging to this sector. This Division considers that the following organisations are part of the social economy: cooperatives, consumer associations, professional associations (*asociaciones gremiales*),[1] fair-trade organisations, B Corps and other social enterprises (with no further specifications so far).

In the last 25 years, terms that have been largely employed in Chile are those of *third sector* and *non-profit sector*; their use was spread by a study carried out by the Johns Hopkins University on the third sector in about 40 countries, including Chile. The Johns Hopkins University developed a structural operational definition according to which non-profit organisations share five main features: they are organised, private, non-profit-distributing, self-governing and voluntary (Salamon and Anheier 1997). The part of the Johns Hopkins study carried out in Chile highlighted the importance of the Chilean non-profit sector, which has a considerable number of employees and volunteers. The services delivered by non-profit organisations concentrated in four main sectors of activity— health care, education, community development and social services—and the main source of revenues for these organisations was the government, through subsidies and reimbursements to the organisations for the services delivered (Irarrázaval *et al.* 2006).

At the Latin American level, the term *social and solidarity economy* (hereinafter referred to as SSE) was coined with the aim—among other reasons—of differentiating the sector from traditional cooperatives, which were becoming more and more similar to traditional for-profit enterprises, especially in the case of large agricultural cooperatives. The SSE concept benefited *inter alia* (Coraggio 1999, 2011; Gaiger 1999; Singer 2000; Guerra 2003; Arruda 2003) from theoretical and conceptual contributions by Chilean scholar Luis Razeto, who started to employ the term "solidarity-based popular economy" (*economía popular de solidaridad*) in the 1980s (see Razeto 1986). The material and relational assets on which popular-economy initiatives are based can constitute a fertile ground, on which more developed organisations of the SSE can build (Razeto 1993; Coraggio 1998). The social and solidarity economy (a concept that appeared in the 1990s) departs from the mere adaptation to circumstances that was characteristic of the popular economy in that it focuses on the economic activity as a vehicle capable of bringing about change. The entrepreneurial economic logic that emerges is based on cooperation and exploits the potential of social relations, based also on traditions and personal ties.

The SSE sphere includes cooperatives, cooperative banks, mutual organisations and, in general, associations of people who freely join to develop economic activities and create jobs on the basis of solidarity and cooperative relations, among themselves and in society at large. The main drive is to ensure the material conditions for the survival of people, fighting against poverty in order to create short- and medium-term socio-economic alternatives.

The analysis proposed in this chapter relies mainly on the term SSE, since this concept was born *inter alia* in the Latin American context and it thus seems to be the best adapted to grasp the specific characteristics of this sector and its transformative logic in the Chilean context. Up to now, the term SSE has been employed in Chile mainly in activist circles, but it is now starting to be employed, with increasing frequency, in institutional contexts as well, such as the government and universities.

2. Historical Approach

After having analysed this conceptual variety, it is interesting to understand the reasons for the emergence of SSE organisations as well as the reasons why they have increasingly become an important part of the Chilean society and economy. The origins of SSE organisations in Chile in a modern perspective are to be found in the colonial period (1598–1810), when charity organisations based on solidarity principles started to develop, mainly with the support of the Catholic Church (Irarrázaval *et al.* 2006). During the process of economic and political consolidation that the country underwent at the beginning of the independency period, in the early 19th century, all charitable, assistance and solidarity activities were carried out by these organisations. From around 1850 onward, SSE organisations started to gain greater attention, and non-profits were legally recognised for the first time (Irarrázaval *et al.* 2006).

This period also witnessed the emergence of the cooperative movement, under the influence of the European experience: the first Chilean cooperative, a consumer cooperative called La Esmeralda, was founded in 1887. The cooperative movement was also influenced by the trade union movement, which emerged in this period mainly due to the spontaneous effort of miners in the northern part of the country (Del Campo and Radrigán 1998), and by mutual societies, whose first expression was linked to typography workers, who supported the replication of the mutual model until the beginning of the 20th century (Martini *et al.* 2003).

During the 20th century, a phenomenon of greater diversification of civil-society organisations started, with the development of voluntary organisations, mutual societies, workers' organisations, unions and political parties.

A wider legal framework for SSE organisations was developed, in particular for cooperatives: the first cooperative law was enacted in 1924. A slow but steady development of this sector then began in Chile.

Inspired by Radrigán *et al.* (2010), who followed the approach proposed by the abovementioned "Comparative Non-Profit Sector Project", we analyse here the historical background of the SSE in Chile. However, while Radrigán and his colleagues focused only on non-profits, we aim to include in our analysis, as table 4.1 shows, all SSE organisations. The table describes six main periods or historical phases of SSE development, together with salient political, economic and sociocultural events that marked each phase.

The first phase was marked by the incidence of pre-Columbian economic practices, which were characterised by reciprocity, non-monetary and solidarity-based exchanges, and were often based on free collective work to the advantage of the whole community. These principles and practices survived through centuries, and they adapted to the new political, military and commercial relations imposed by the conquerors. They were incorporated into the indigenous conception of *buen vivir*, which describes a collective approach to well-being based on respectful exchanges between humans and the natural environment, on the promotion of collective rights, and on a community-based model of production (Gudynas 2011; Acosta 2013).

The second phase was characterised by a process of economic, political and social emancipation that followed independence from the Spanish crown. From the economic point of view, in this period, the beginning of the industrialisation process was marked mainly by the mining boom. From the political point of view, power was concentrated in the hands of the conservative sector. As far as civil society is concerned, several processes of civic organisation started in this phase; the most notable experience for the SSE was the emergence of the first mutual-aid societies, which appeared in Chile around 1840. They were closely linked to the nascent industrial working class and aimed to guarantee protection to the workers and their families in case of accident, invalidity, disease or death.

The third period was characterised by a strengthened role of civil-society organisations in the struggle for fundamental rights, as has occurred in other countries since the beginning and during the consolidation of the industrial revolution. This period saw the emergence of charities and advocacy organisations for basic social rights, especially concerning labour issues. The state began to implement a social-action strategy, which resulted in a series of social laws. Regarding more specifically the SSE, this period can be considered as the "golden age" of the mutual sector. In 1924, there were over 500 mutual societies in Chile, with more than 100,000 members. The mutualist movement was responsible for several innovative social measures, such as equality of treatment for women (mutual societies were the first Chilean organisations to recognise

Table 4.1 Historical phases of SSE development in Chile

Phase	Social, economic and political context	SSE
1. Origins: from pre-Columbian period to the War of Independence (1810)	Indigenous communities based on reciprocity, non-monetary exchanges and collective work	Embryonic forms of SSE: indigenous peoples have organisational structures similar to the SSE logic
2. Pre-industrial period and beginning of the Republic (1811–1850)	External economy, mainly focused on the export of saltpetre Societal, political and economic change after the process of independence and against the previous colonial model	The first mutual societies, closely linked to the labour sector, started to emerge; existence of several charity organisations linked to the Catholic Church and of informal productive organisations (popular economy)
3. Industrialisation and beginning of the welfare state (1851–1945)	Promotion of the national industry to replace the imports Emergence of a renewed vision of the government's role: need to generate social participation through societal channels of organisation Strong role of Catholicism	"Golden age" of mutualism, in parallel to the rise of the labour movement Emergence of the first cooperatives Adoption of the first law on cooperatives
4. From the welfare state to the democratic breakdown (1946–1972)	Consolidation of the state, which played a crucial role in the final process of industrialisation of the country	Progressive growth and differentiation of SSE organisational types Growth and differentiation of the cooperative sector
5. Dictatorship (1973–1990)	Military coup, rupture of the democratic tradition Neoliberal economy Two main transformations: (1) switch from a national, closed economy to an open, liberal economy and (2) end of the welfare state and privatisation of social services	Worst period for the SSE: most SSE organisations went bankrupt or were destroyed; however, many popular-economy organisations survived, and they even increased in number
6. Return to democracy (1990-present)	Recovery of democracy Switch from an authoritarian exclusionary neoliberal economic model to an inclusive democratic neoliberal economy	Restoration of the SSE, although in a neoliberal context that is not highly favourable to associative arrangements New wave of SSE organisations in the last decade, also revived by social movements

Source: Adapted from Radrigán *et al.* (2010) and Pizarro (2004).

the equality of rights between men and women) and the first experiences in the field of adult education, cultural activities and prevention of harmful behaviours (e.g. alcohol abuse and problem gambling). In the same period (more exactly in 1887), the first Chilean cooperative was founded, in Valparaíso; as explained above, it was a consumer cooperative called La Esmeralda (Del Campo and Radrigán 1998). The emergence of cooperativism was, like in other Latin American countries, linked to the social and labour movements that developed in reaction to the consequences of industrialisation, and it was influenced by the European experience brought by migrants. In 1925, the first law on cooperatives was approved, thus supporting a subsequent slow but constant development of the cooperative sector. The law provided for the creation of the Department of Mutual Societies and Cooperatives within the Ministry of Work and Social Security; this Department was formally constituted in 1927. The Department supported the creation of cooperatives in several sectors: agriculture, provision of drinking water, housing, electricity. However, a structured support to the cooperative sector was still lacking, and the state mainly sustained single and isolated initiatives.

The fourth phase saw the consolidation of the state as a resource provider, using SSE organisations as a way to provide social services or meet social needs. The 20th century witnessed a progressive growth and differentiation of organisational types in the SSE sector. The general Law on Cooperatives was elaborated in the 1950s, during Jorge Alessandri's government. This law was then modified in 1963 by the Agrarian Reform. President Eduardo Frei Montalva (1964–1970) made an important contribution in terms of support to the cooperative sector: during his term, although no coherent and comprehensive cooperative programme was implemented, cooperatives became an instrument supporting the reformist policies of the government. In this phase, the number of cooperatives grew constantly, and their action expanded into new and differentiated sectors of activity, with the creation, for example, of worker, housing and user cooperatives.

The fifth phase, which corresponds to the period of the dictatorship, was marked by the breakdown of civil-society movements and organisations, as well as by the repression of individual freedoms. The military coup marked a rupture in the process of organisation of civil society— a process which had already been threatened by the democratic breakdowns of 1891 and 1924–1925, which had limited the expansion and autonomy of civil-society organisations. During the dictatorship that followed the military coup of 1973, SSE and all civil-society organisations suffered their worst period; they were affected by the dictatorship's economic system, which also impacted their internal structure. Many of the existing organisations were forced to cease their activities and many cooperatives went bankrupt, also due to the economic crisis at the beginning of the 1980s. However, it is worth noting that several popular-economy organisations survived through the dictatorship, and even registered an increase in their workforce (in Santiago, the share of popular-economy organisations' workforce in the city's total workforce increased from approximately 15% in 1970 to 20% in 1982). Moreover, popular-economy strategies multiplied and qualitatively changed, with organisations engaging in new activities to address needs that were left unsatisfied in the new regime (Nyssens 1997).

Finally, with the return to democracy, in 1990, civil society and SSE organisations were also restored, with the aim of addressing new and differentiated societal needs. Since the beginning of the 1990s, the country has been experiencing a process of cultural transformation, whereby ordinary people have begun to assume the charge of solving the problems affecting the community, instead of presenting their claims to the state (Rodriguez and Quezada 2007). This process has resulted in the emergence of several initiatives by civil society, some of them belonging to the SSE.

However, the national constitution is still the one that had been inherited from the military regime, and it has a strongly neoliberal character. The restoration of democracy brought about a resurgence of civil-society initiatives and a review of the legal framework for SSE organisations, but there is no clear-cut breakaway from the period of the military regime. In 2015, the former Department of Cooperatives (founded in 1927) was incorporated into the newly created Associativity and Social-Economy Division (*División de Asociatividad y Economía Social*, or DAES). Until this date, no real effort had been made at the institutional level to recognise the importance of and support the sector. It is still too early to judge if this Division will have an impact on the SSE in terms of promoting public policies and specific legislative measures, but at least its setting up is a first step in the direction of giving more visibility to the sector.

According to Rodriguez and Quezada (2007), Chile has traditionally left the solution to community issues in the hands of the government. According to these authors, this situation is reflected, for example, in the fact that the industrialisation process was promoted at the governmental level, with the objective of modernising the country. However, in the late 20th century, the government abandoned its protective function (Rodriguez and Quezada 2007; Radrigán *et al.* 2010). According to this interpretation, the SSE sector in the Chilean context has developed within a framework of political and economic transformation, where the government has changed its role from a welfare model (*"modelo asistencialista"*) to a neoliberal model, where the satisfaction of societal needs is left to the private sector (*"modelo subsidiario"*) (Hernandez *et al.* 2003).

3. Legal Approach

In Chile, as in many other contexts, a plurality of economic and social organisations coexist. SSE organisations, which differ from traditional capitalist firms and from government institutions, include various types of activities and structures. For the purpose of this chapter, the main types of SSE such as they are provided for by the Chilean law will be identified and briefly defined, following the approach proposed by Radrigán and Barría (2005). These organisations will then be analysed by applying to them the EMES approach to social enterprise, with the aim of identifying types of SSE organisations that can be considered as social enterprises.

We hereby analyse the legal provisions that can refer to SSE organisations in Chile, identifying the following types: (1) neighbourhood associations and other community organisations; (2) cooperatives; (3) trade associations; (4) indigenous organisations; (5) mutual societies; (6) non-profit enterprises; and (7) non-profit foundations. Table 4.2 provides a brief definition of each of these types of organisation.

Not all the organisations reviewed can necessarily be considered as social enterprises, because each of them may show different logics of action. Employing the welfare triangle as a tool (and thus following

Table 4.2 Legal definition of the main SSE organisations in Chile

Type of organisation	Definition
Neighbourhood associations and other community organisations (*juntas de vecinos* and other *organizaciones comunitarias*)	Non-profit organisations with a legal personality, which aim to represent and promote the values and interests of the community. They have to respect the religious and political freedom of their members. There are two types of community organisations: 1) Territorial organisations: organisations that are representative of people in a neighbourhood, and whose goal is to promote community development, safeguard the interests and ensure the rights of neighbours. 2) Functional organisations: non-profit entities with legal personality that aim to represent and promote the values and interests of the community within the territory of the municipality or group of municipalities.
Cooperatives	Associations based on the principle of mutual aid that aim to improve the lives of their members. Cooperatives have the following key features: 1) Members have equal rights and obligations; cooperatives operate according to the "one person, one vote" principle; membership and retirement are voluntary. 2) The surplus generated by operations with members should be distributed to members in proportion to their transactions with the cooperative. 3) Cooperatives should observe political and religious neutrality, and they should seek to establish and develop cooperative education activities, including federal and inter-cooperative relations.

Type of organisation	Definition
Professional associations (*asociaciones gremiales*)	Organisations established by law, whose members are either natural and/or legal persons who aim to promote the rationalisation, development and protection of the activities they have in common, because of their profession, trade or industry production or services. These associations cannot engage in political or religious activities.
Indigenous organisations	Groups of people belonging to the same indigenous group and who satisfy one or more of the following conditions: 1) They come from the same family tree. 2) They recognise traditional leadership. 3) They own or have owned indigenous lands in common. 4) They come from a single ancestral settlement.
Mutual societies	The purpose of a mutual-benefit society is to achieve public interest benefits on a reciprocal basis between its members. There are three types of mutual societies: 1) Mutual-aid societies. 2) Mutual-protection societies. 3) Mutual-insurance companies.
Non-profit corporations	A non-profit corporation is made up of a number of associated individuals who pursue a common objective and determine the foundation and the mission of the organisation. Corporations have an ideal object—development or social progress, welfare, culture and education—but they cannot pursue trade union or for-profit objectives, or objectives that are defined by law as corresponding to other types of entities.
Non-profit foundations	A foundation is a patrimony administered by agents according to the will of the founder; such will also determines the organisation's goals, which must be directed to general-interest objectives. Foundations are not comparable to a corporate legal person. Most relevant in the figure of the foundation is the endowment of assets for the pursuit of a given objective set by the founder(s). People involved in the foundation are not owners of the organisation and must follow the objective determined by the founder(s), which has to be a general-interest, permanent and non-profit objective.

Source: Prepared by the authors on the basis of Radrigan and Barría (2005), DECOOP (2007), Ley 19.253 sobre protección, fomento y desarrollo indígena; Ley 19.832 sobre cooperativas; Ley 19.418 sobre juntas de vecinos y demás organizaciones comunitarias; Ley 2.757 sobre asociaciones gremiales.

Pestoff 1998, 2005) enables us to recognise the combination of actors (the state, private for-profit companies and communities), logics of action (market, redistribution and reciprocity)[2] and resources, and to understand that the set of organisations considered as social enterprises may be understood from different points of view. Figure 4.1 shows this combination and graphically represents the situation. Following this graphic representation, it is possible to position each of the organisations described in table 4.2 in the triangle.

However, in order to identify the set of organisations that can be considered as social enterprises following the EMES approach, it is necessary to evaluate whether these organisations display the three main characteristics put forward by the EMES Network, i.e. whether they have (1) an economic project, (2) a social mission and (3) a participatory governance. Table 4.3 analyses the organisations presented in table 4.2 according to these characteristics.

Following the legal approach (i.e. taking into account the legal forms traditionally considered as belonging to the SSE), it appears that only some types of cooperative, some indigenous organisations, some non-profit corporations and some non-profit foundations comply with the indicators of the EMES definition to such an extent that they can be considered as social enterprises. However, the legal approach is not sufficient to grasp the full array of organisational forms that belong to the SSE sector and that can be considered as social enterprises—whether they are regulated as such by Chilean law or not.

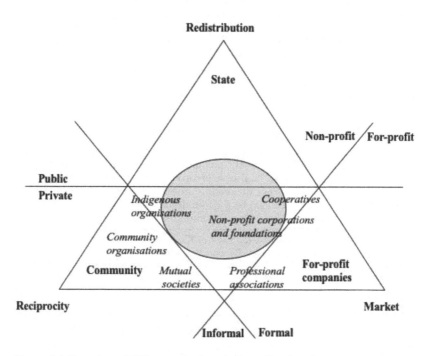

Figure 4.1 Location of SSE organisations in Pestoff's triangle

Table 4.3 Chilean SSE organisations (legal definition) and the EMES indicators of social enterprise

	Neighbourhood associations and other community organisations	Cooperatives	Professional associations	Indigenous organisations	Mutual societies	Non-profit corporations	Non-profit foundations
An economic project	**No**	**Yes**	**No**	**Some of them**	**No**	**Yes**	**Yes**
A continuous production	No	Yes	No	Some of them	No	Some of them	Some of them
Some paid work	No	Yes	No	Some of them	Yes	Yes	Yes
An economic risk	No	Yes	No	Some of them	No	Some of them	Some of them
A social mission	**Yes**	**Yes**	**Yes**	**Yes**	**Yes**	**Yes**	**Yes**
An explicit social aim	Yes	Some of them	Yes	Yes	Yes	Yes	Yes
Limited profit distribution, reflecting the primacy of social aim	No	Yes	Yes	Some of them	No	No	No
An initiative launched by a group of citizens or a third-sector organisation	Yes	Some of them	Yes	Yes	Yes	Yes	Some of them
A participatory governance	**Yes**	**Yes**	**No**	**Yes**	**Yes**	**Some of them**	**Some of them**
A high degree of autonomy	Yes	Yes	No	Yes	No	Yes	Yes
A participatory nature, which involves various parties affected by the activity	Yes	Some of them	No	Yes	Yes	Some of them	Some of them
A decision-making power not based on capital ownership	Yes	Yes	Yes	Yes	Yes	Yes	Yes
Can they be considered as social enterprises?	***No***	***Some of them***	***No***	***Some of them***	***No***	***Some of them***	***Some of them***

Source: Prepared by the authors.

4. Mixed—Empirical, Legal and Conceptual—Approach

Having said that, it seems more useful, with a view to identifying SSE models in Chile, to adopt a mixed approach, taking into account legal but also empirical and conceptual elements. Such a mixed approach allows us to identify four main types of social enterprise, by reference to the EMES ideal type:

- Traditional cooperatives—at least those that have an explicit social aim and/or are directed towards the welfare of the community in which they are embedded and do not only serve the interests of their members. The majority of agricultural and fishery cooperatives, worker cooperatives and credit cooperatives are thus excluded from this category, which comprises water and energy cooperatives, school cooperatives and open housing cooperatives. An interesting experience included in this category is that of rural water cooperatives. This case is particularly interesting as, in Chile, water provision was privatised during the military dictatorship (1981, *Codigo de Aguas*) and, to date, remains private. Nowadays, several water cooperatives—some of them active since the 1960s, when they were founded thanks to the direct intervention of the state—represent an actual alternative to the private model of water provision. Moreover, they are also providing a plurality of complementary services to the communities (such as public libraries, spaces that the community members can use for various activities and spaces for community celebrations).
- Non-profits (corporations, foundations, some NGOs). This category includes those organisations that operate under the legal form of foundation, non-profit corporation or NGO and aim to develop a common-interest activity. According to the EMES approach, this category includes at least those organisations that explicitly state a social goal beyond a mutual objective of satisfying the needs of their members. In this group, different "subtypes" of organisations, working as NGOs but operating under various legal forms (foundations, corporations, NGOs), can be distinguished, for example: non-profit foundations (Fundación Las Rosas, Fundación un Techo para Chile, Fundación de Ayuda al Niño Limitado . . .); non-profit associations (Corporación Nuestra Casa, Corporación Red de Alimentos . . .); and NGOs working on development issues (ONG de Desarrollo al Menor en Riesgo Social un Rincón de Alegría, ONG de Desarrollo Corporación de Beneficencia Jesús Niño . . .).
- B Corps or "Empresas B". B Corps are private for-profit organisations that, in general terms, seek to address socio-environmental issues of public interest. Four main characteristics of these organisations are highlighted by B Lab, the United-States-based non-profit organisation that created this certification and promotes it all over the world:

(1) they are committed to creating a positive impact on society and the environment; (2) they redefine this socio-environmental purpose in a binding way; (3) they have high standards of management; (4) they are oriented towards all stakeholders and long-term goals.[3] B Corps are thus defined as double-mission organisations, to the extent that they have an economic responsibility towards their shareholders and they must simultaneously create public value for other stakeholders (López Mayher 2013). Sistema B was created in 2012 with the vision of building a new economy where success is measured in terms of well-being of both the people and the planet. With the support of B Lab, Sistema B has made rapid progress in Latin America; it is now present in ten Latin American countries, supporting a community of B Corps' impact investors, academia, media, policymakers and traditional companies. In November 2018, there were 140 for-profit companies certified as B Corps in Chile.[4]

- Community enterprises. While the Chilean law identifies as community enterprises entities with the legal forms of neighbourhood associations (*juntas de vecinos*) or other community organisations, which cannot perform a stable economic activity (see table 4.2), this category also appears appropriate to include other types of organisation that can be considered as social enterprises but that operate under different legal forms. This category could indeed include the "new cooperatives" (Vieta 2010), based on self-management (*autogestión*) and on "horizontalised" labour processes and decision-making structures, that have started to emerge in the last decade in Chile.

5. Towards a Synthesis of the Different Types of SSE Organisations

The various approaches analysed so far all shed light, in a complementary way, on several aspects of SSE organisations. As explained in the previous section, we have chosen to integrate the conceptual and the legal approaches, without forgetting the historical trajectory of SSE organisations, in order to better understand the complexity of the SE phenomenon and to include in our analysis all the forms that appear compatible with the EMES definition of social enterprise.

As anticipated, from the conceptual point of view, the term SSE has to be preferred over other concepts, as this term is an original Latin American contribution, able to highlight the specificities of the phenomenon in this area. Moreover, this concept can also include those informal experiences that have not been officially recognised as social enterprises by Chilean legislation, like collective organisations belonging to the popular economy (Nyssens 1997; Razeto 1990). Even though the number of these grassroots organisations has been decreasing over the years (Bauwens and Lemaître 2014), they remain a phenomenon worthy of attention. By contrast, the legal approach has highlighted the lack of specific recognition and support for SSE organisations.

An analysis of existing literature and the observation of new phenomena emerging in the area make it possible to grasp the specificities of SSE organisations in Chile, some of which have also been observed in other Latin American countries. These can be summarised as follows:

- SSE organisations are influenced by the indigenous culture that derives from pre-Columbian economic non-monetary practices (for instance the *minga*, i.e. collective free work in favour of the community, which is still present in some communities in Chile) and the indigenous attachment to land and natural resources.
- SSE initiatives are characterised by a precise political connotation, which derives from their connection with social movements. The primary aim of SSE is to build new social and labour relations that do not reproduce inequalities and constitute an actual alternative to the capitalist economic system, questioning the existing socio-economic structures (Guerra 2003; Coraggio 2005).
- SSE initiatives are characterised by the presence of the "C factor" (Razeto 1998), understood as a factor of production as such, that is to say a factor that should be integrated in the economic models and analyses, together with work, capital and technology. The "C factor" (where C stands for community, cooperation, collaboration) involves several aspects, like cooperation in the labour environment, knowledge sharing, collective decision-making and additional non-monetary benefits for workers. A crucial aspect in this sense is self-management, intended as a revolutionary practice that questions the neoliberal system, to the extent that SSE initiatives are not based on the exploitation but on the free association of workers (Singer and Souza 2000; Vieta 2014).

As a consequence, SSE organisations are characterised by the pursuit of a plurality of goals, including environmental, political and community objectives, which are sometimes underestimated by some Anglo-Saxon schools of thought. Therefore, we propose to take into account, in our analysis, five major dimensions of these organisations, namely the social, economic, community, political and environmental aspects. Each dimension can be evaluated qualitatively on a scale ranging from low to high. It is worth specifying that we consider social enterprises as specific organisational types within the broader SSE sector.

In table 4.4, the five dimensions mentioned above are analysed; for each of them, the table highlights the beneficial impacts generated by SSE organisations, the risk that the organisations would face, should the related dimension prevail, and the protection mechanisms that help to maintain a balance among all the dimensions. We consider that, if one

Table 4.4 Dimensions of SSE organisations

Dimension	Beneficial impacts	Risks	Protection mechanisms
Social	Provision of goods and services to address unsatisfied needs	Inefficiency	Managerial tools consistent with the social goal pursued
Economic	Production of goods and services according to efficiency criteria	Predominance of profit-seeking behaviours	Participatory governance model
Community ("C factor": collectivity, cooperation, collaboration . . .)	Reinforcement of social cohesion and economic democratisation	Creation of closed or "exclusive" organisations	Exchange with external stakeholders
Political	Creation of alternative modes of production	Predominance of advocacy action	Stable and continuous production of goods and services
Environmental	Provision of environmentally sustainable goods and services	Predominance of advocacy action	Stable and continuous production of goods and services

Source: Adapted from Giovannini (2014).

of the five dimension prevails, the organisation can still be considered as belonging to the SSE sector, but it is not a social enterprise. For instance, if the environmental dimension is too strong, while the economic one is very weak or downright absent, we can talk about an advocacy environmental organisation (like an environmental NGO or a similar type of entity) that belongs to the SSE, but not about a social enterprise.

Traditional cooperatives score low on the political dimension and high on the economic dimension; some of them—depending on the specific cooperative considered—also score high on several other dimensions.

Non-profits score high on the social and community dimensions, while their scores regarding the other dimensions vary according to the organisation considered.

B Corps score very high on the economic dimension; the social and environmental dimensions are of an average level and vary according to the corporation considered, and the political and community dimensions are very weak.

Community enterprises score very high on the political, social and community dimensions, while the importance of the environmental and economic dimensions vary according to the type of good or service provided. In any case, the accent in these enterprises is on collective governance, consensus decision-making, creation of alternatives to the capitalist system thanks to the relation with social movements, and impact on the community.

6. Emerging Trends in Chile

6.1 Community Enterprises: The Case of New Cooperatives

In the last years, a new phenomenon has started to emerge in Chile: new organisations arising from the civil society that take the cooperative form with the objective of re-signifying and politicising this organisational arrangement. Although, from the legal point of view, not all of these organisations are cooperatives, all of them share the main characteristics of this organisational form, as further detailed below. New cooperatives are emerging from some sectors of the civil society, for instance those connected to the student movement of 2011. These sectors are trying to self-organise in order to address various needs such as job creation, accessible health and education, and food sovereignty. New cooperatives can be considered as experiments that seek to challenge the *status quo* of the neoliberal system through the construction of actual economic, political and social alternatives. The main characteristics of these organisations have to be found in the way in which they are managed, based on horizontal and democratic practices; in their ethical and political values, which stand in opposition to the neoliberal system; and in the strong connections they have with the local communities in which they operate and with which they exchange knowledge, products and experience (Vieta 2010). New cooperatives' aim is to generate political and social change through economic activity.

At the end of 2015, ten organisations that can be considered as new cooperatives were investigated in Santiago, adopting the ICSEM questionnaire as a tool to guide semi-structured interviews that were tape-recorded and transcribed. Since most of these organisations are recent and some of them have a light structure, we decided to employ semi-structured interviews, as this method allowed us to grasp more insights from the interviewees and give more space to the emergence of their point of view. The organisations investigated were grouped in three main categories, according to their sector of activity: work, food and consumption, and education. These sectors of activity are crucial in the neoliberal context of the Chilean state, since they are—together with the health sector—sectors in which, due to the incapacity and/or unwillingness of both the state and the market to provide credible responses, many citizens' needs remain unmet.

In the category of organisations active in the field of *work*, we investigated six organisations belonging to a federation of worker cooperatives called Federación Trasol (Trabajo Solidario). The federation was founded in 2015 and gathers fourteen cooperatives, which share the common goal of re-signifying the cooperative form in order to create fairer working conditions, based on self-management (*autogestión*), democracy and solidarity. They perform different activities, such as the provision of gas, electric and photovoltaic services, cleaning services, research and consulting. Most of these organisations are small and have between three and ten members. An interesting aspect is that some of these cooperatives were founded by former students who had participated in the student movement of 2011: the participation in this social movement appears to have played a crucial role in their becoming aware of the need for socio-political commitment—a need that was later canalised into the creation of cooperatives.

These organisations are devoted to creating dignified working conditions, antithetic with respect to the neoliberal model. They do not only have economic objectives of income generation, but also social, political and educational aims, which they pursue through the creation of fair and equal work and social relations, with an evident social and political stance. Decisions are often achieved by consensus instead of being based on the majority rule; salaries are equal; and the property of the means of production is collective. Members have different experiences and do not belong to the traditional cooperative movement (Vieta 2010), towards which they have a critical approach.

In the *food and consumption* category, we had interviews with two organisations: Cooperativa Semilla Austral and Juntos Compremos. The first one was constituted as a consumer cooperative in 2015, originating from the "Free Seeds Network" (*Red de Semillas Libres*), whose main aim is to protect biodiversity through the defence, reproduction and exchange of native seeds, and to revitalise ancestral Mapuche practices and ceremonies. The aim of the cooperative is to generate income in order to support the network through the sale of seeds, plants and books and the organisation of workshops and educational events. As for Juntos Compremos, it was a virtual community of consumers at the time of the interview, and it was later transformed into a consumer cooperative. The objective is to create awareness about responsible consumption, understood in the economic, social and environmental sense, and to provide members with consumption goods at lower prices.

As in the case of Federación Trasol, both experiences have been created by groups of people with a critical attitude towards the neoliberal model and who do not have any relations with the traditional cooperative movement. In these two cases, the economic dimension is weaker than in the worker cooperatives analysed, and the ethical and political dimensions prevail. Both organisations are well integrated into their local communities, and both create opportunities for exchange with the communities within which they operate, both in their daily activities and through special events. Horizontal practices are implemented in the governance of the organisations, which also resort to non-monetary exchanges (voluntary work and barter of seeds). Both organisations aim to diffuse a critical view of the neoliberal model in the food production and consumption sphere through the creation of different relations between consumers, producers and the communities in which they live.

The case selected in the field of *education* is an organisation called Preuniversitario Popular Víctor Jara (PPVJ). PPVJ is a non-profit foundation (*fundación sin fines de lucro*); it is not, legally speaking, a cooperative, but the logic behind its functioning is similar to that of cooperatives, and given its characteristics, it can be considered as a new cooperative. Its aim is to offer pre-university education to students who do not have sufficient economic resources to be able to afford training in a "commercial" school. The organisation was founded in 2001 by a group of university students who wanted to support potential peers who did not have sufficient resources to access the university, thus breaking the gap between families with higher and those with lower economic resources. In this case as in the others, founders and members do not have connections with the traditional cooperative movement, and they self-organised with a view to fighting the exclusion of large social groups from the educational model imposed by the neoliberal system. Relations between teachers and students in PPVJ are horizontal, not hierarchical, and they are not conditioned by the capacity to pay fees to access educational services. Decision-making is made by assemblies of teachers, where most decisions are achieved through consensus. PPVJ operates in seven locations in Santiago; it has strong relationships with the local communities and is pointing to social and political objectives such as social inclusion, inequalities reduction and free education.

Table 4.5 summarises the main characteristics of the organisations investigated. The six organisations interviewed belonging to Federación Trasol have been grouped in the table since they share, with only few differences, the same main features.

6.2. B Corps

When analysing the ESS trends in Chile today, a point that particularly draws the attention and interest of many actors has to do with new dynamics of entrepreneurship characterised by a strong search for new approaches to socio-environmental challenges. These dynamics, as put forward by Gatica (2015), can be identified, on the one hand, in new organisations that are being created today and that, from their inception, are conceptualised under hybrid logics. On the other hand, these dynamics also emerge within existing private companies, which seek to incorporate them or, in many cases, reaffirm a strong socio-environmental commitment by incorporating them in a central way in their business activity.

Table 4.5 Characteristics of the new cooperatives investigated

	Economic project: resources	*Governance*	*Social mission*
Federación Trasol *(6 organisations)*	Mixed: market resources and start-up funds from governmental calls for proposals	- Self-management - Consensus rule - Commissions	Cooperatives' "re-signification" through self-management and "work without a boss"
Semilla Austral	Mixed: market resources, voluntary work, barter	- Based on the Free Seeds Network - Still to be defined in the cooperative itself	- Protection of biodiversity - Increased awareness of ethical consumption
Juntos Compremos	Mixed: market resources, voluntary work	- Virtual community (light structure) - Commissions	Increased awareness of ethical consumption
PPVJ	Mixed: voluntary work, donations from some local institutions	- Assembly - Consensus rule	Reduction of inequalities through access to free education

Although such companies, which seek to renew capitalism, are still very few in numbers in Chile, there is little doubt that they are already provoking reactions in the ecosystem: universities, media, entrepreneurs' networks and even public institutions all begin to react to their existence. Beyond the difficulties encountered by the different bills discussed in the Chilean parliament about the creation of a new legal form for these organisations, various government agencies have been responsible for promoting this type of social venture. Several initiatives contributed to the rapid development of these organisations in Chile, enabling them to reach a position of leadership on these matters in Latin America; today, nearly one third of all B Corps in Latin America are located in Chile.

In order to gain better knowledge of this new phenomenon, its characteristics and different trends, some B Corps were contacted, and two cases—Triciclos and Pegas con Sentido—were studied using the ICSEM questionnaire. Semi-structured interviews in each of the companies were also conducted; these interviews were recorded and then transcribed.

Triciclos is a private for-profit organisation that defends the adoption of market principles to solve public problems—an approach that is coherent with this organisation's origins in the private sector. Triciclos regularly provides services of public interest related to its mission, which is to achieve a "zero-waste" goal in the geographical zones where it operates. The services provided by the organisation can be considered to be of public interest as they solve complex public problems encountered by Chile, such as the issue of pollution produced by economic development, which has become a particularly serious concern in the last 40 years—a period over which Chilean GDP per capita has explosively accelerated its growth.

The organisation recycles "valuable" and "non-valuable" materials. The collection of valuable materials subsidises both the development of technology and the organisation's operative capacity, which will ultimately allow recycling around 90% of all solid waste produced in the Santiago Metropolitan Region—a goal which benefits all citizens in the Region.

This profitable market activity allows Triciclos to have autonomy in its management. This management is closely linked to a decision-making structure based on the company's ownership. Nevertheless, different elements within its operation over time reveal a certain path towards a more participative nature. This is the case of its approach towards involving relevant stakeholders, such as recyclable material collectors, territorial organisations or the company's own employees.

Pegas con Sentido is a public limited company that seeks to respond to a particular social problem. Since its inception, the organisation has supported societal change through promoting a new path for purpose-driven young people entering the professional world. Pegas con Sentido's team has been working to help these people find job opportunities within organisations whose main goal is not only to maximise financial returns, but also to contribute to solving socio-environmental challenges through the implementation of a sustainable business model.

Pegas con Sentido also wants to be a place where people not only find a job, but also receive information, advice and referrals. The organisation's

Table 4.6 Characteristics of the B Corps investigated

	Economic project: resources	Governance	Social mission
Triciclos	Market resources	- Decision-making power based on capital ownership - Participative approach to their stakeholders	Zero-waste goal
Pegas con sentido	Mixed: market resources and start-up funds from governmental calls for proposals	- Decisions are made by shareholders - "One member, one vote" rule	Connecting purpose-driven professionals to companies committed to a better society

mission is to articulate the link between professionals and institutions that seek to be pioneers of a new culture of sustainability, thus managing talents for a new economy.

In 2016, after five years of operation, Pegas con Sentido already had more than twenty employees and had engaged in an expansion process in Latin America. Important decisions are made by the members; they take part in the decision-making process because they hold shares in the corporation, but the number of votes is not linked to the number of shares held, and the "one member, one vote" rule applies.

Conclusion

This chapter has followed a mixed approach, combining legal, historical and conceptual perspectives, as we considered that each of these perspectives, taken alone, would not allow us to grasp the full richness of the SSE in Chile. On this basis, we have identified four main types of social enterprise in the Chilean context: traditional cooperatives, non-profit organisations (corporations and foundations), B Corps and community enterprises.

Despite this apparent organisational variety, complexity and relative importance of the SSE in Chile, it is worth mentioning that the level of visibility and recognition of this sector remains low, and national studies on the sector are still very few in number (Gatica 2011). So far, academic and governmental institutions have not been able to really go beyond declarations and to promote and implement effective public policies. Though it is true that the governmental Associativity and Social-Economy Division (DAES) has been trying to promote the concept of social economy, effective economic measures to support it remain limited. Some studies have been carried out and published (see for example DAES 2014a, 2014b, 2015a, 2015b) with the main aim of describing the characteristics of cooperatives and other social-economy organisations, and this entails a certain improvement towards a greater visibility of the sector, but the methodologies employed have been only partially adapted to the actual processes that are happening on the field. Moreover, the concepts employed by the DAES are still not sufficiently clear nor explained, and this is reflected by the scarce impact that these concepts have on the public opinion.

Another limit of the Chilean SSE sector is that it is characterised by a scarce presence of networks and integration structures (such as second-level organisations), especially at the regional and local levels.

SSE experiences, as we have tried to illustrate, are taking different shapes depending on their promoters and main aims. We believe that these experiences, which are being promoted at different levels, deserve greater attention, promotion and further in-depth investigation.

Acknowledgements

The authors would like to thank Nicolás Gómez (Universidad Central de Chile) for his more than precious support and commitment in the empirical work.

Notes

1 In Chile, the term *gremial* has a specific meaning, which differs from its meaning in other Spanish-speaking countries, where *asociaciónes gremiales* usually refers to trade unions.
2 A fourth logic, namely "householding", can also be mentioned; it refers to economies where production is centred on individual households—a kind of domestic economy. In Polanyi's work, this logic sometimes appears as a separate logic, and is sometimes included in reciprocity.
3 See https://bcorporation.net/about-b-lab (2016).
4 Source: Juan Pablo Larenas, executive director of Sistema B.

References

Acosta, A. (2013) *El Buen Vivir: Sumak Kawsay, una Oportunidad para Imaginar Otros Mundos*, Barcelona: Icaria Editorial.
Arruda, M. (2003) "What is a solidarity economy?" *Fórum Social Mundial*, January 23–28, Porto Alegre. Available HTTP: www.tni.org/es/archives/act/511 (accessed on November 16, 2012).
Bauwens, T. & Lemaître, A. (2014) "Popular economy in Santiago de Chile: State of affairs and challenges", *World Development*, Vol. 64, pp. 65–78.
Coraggio, J. L. (1998) *Economia urbana: la perspectiva popular*, Quito: Editorial Abya Yala.
Coraggio, J. L. (1999) *Política social y economía del trabajo. Alternativas a la política neoliberal para la ciudad*, Madrid: Miño y Dávila Editores.
Coraggio, J. L. (2005) *Es posible otra economía sin (otra) política?, El Pequeño Libro Socialista*, Buenos Aires: Editora La Vanguardia.
Coraggio, J. L. (2011) *Economía social y solidaria: El trabajo antes que el capital*, Quito: Ediciones Abya-Yala.
DAES (2014a) *Estudio de caracterización del sector agroalimentario de la Economía Social y Cooperativa*, Santiago: Subsecretaria de Economía y Empresas de Menor Tamaño, Ministerio de Economía, Fomento y Turismo de Chile.
DAES (2014b) *Estudio caracterización del Sector de la Pesca en la Economía Social y Cooperativa*, Santiago: Ministerio de Economía, Fomento y Turismo de Chile.
DAES (2015a) *Caracterización de la Asociatividad y la Economía Social de los Pueblos Indígenas*, Santiago: División de Asociatividad y Economía Social del Ministerio de Economía, Fomento y Turismo de Chile.
DAES (2015b) *Participación de las muejres en cooperativas y empresas de la economía social*, Santiago: División de Asociatividad y Economía Social del Ministerio de Economía, Fomento y Turismo de Chile.
DECOOP (2007) "Paralelo entre cooperativas y otras formas asociativas", Departamento de Cooperativas, Ministerio de Economía, Fomento y Turismo,

Gobierno de Chile. Available HTTP: www.decoop.cl/Portals/0/pdf/20070 924ParaleloEntreCooperativasYOtrasFormas Asociativas.pdf (accessed on April 16, 2014).

Del Campo, P. & Radrigán, M. (1998) *El Sector Cooperativo Chileno: Tradición, Experiencias y Proyecciones*, Santiago de Chile: CONFECOOP-CCA.

Gaiger, L. I. (1999) "La solidaridad como una alternativa económica para los pobres", *CIRIEC España, Revista de Economía Pública, Social y Cooperativa*, Vol. 31, pp. 187–205.

Gatica, S. (2011) "Emprendimiento e Innovación Social: construyendo una agenda pública para Chile", *Pontificia Universidad Católica de Chile*, Año 6, No. 48, Centro de políticas Públicas UC.

Gatica, S. (2015) "Understanding the phenomenon of Chilean social enterprises under the lens of Kerlin's approach: Contributions and limitations", *Social Enterprise Journal*, Vol. 11, No. 2, pp. 202–226. Available HPPT: https://doi. org/10.1108/SEJ-02-2014-0013.

Giovannini, M. (2014) "De la Economía Popular a la Economía Social y Solidaria: el Caso de los Recicladores de Base en Santiago de Chile", *Euricse WP*, No. 73|14.

Gudynas, E. (2011) "Buen Vivir: Today's tomorrow", *Development*, Vol. 54, No. 4, pp. 441–447.

Guerra, P. (2003) "Economía de la Solidaridad: Construcción de un camino a veinte años de las primeras elaboraciones", paper presented at the III Jornadas en Historia Económica, July 9–11, Montevideo. Available HTTP: https://emes. net/content/uploads/publications/Guerra_Historia_E_S_031.pdf.

Hernandez, L., Oyanedel, J. C. & Perez, E. (2003) "Asociatividad y desarrollo. Para una caracterización del sector asociativo en Chile", presentation at the XXIV Congreso de la asociación Latinoamericana de Sociología, Limarp.

ICSEM (2013) "The international comparative social enterprise models, (ICSEM) project: A broad research project funded by the Belgian science policy office to be extended to a large international research community in partnership with the EMES European research network", Interuniversity Attraction Pole (IAP) on Social Enterprise (SOCENT) 2012–2017.

Irarrázaval, I., Hairel, E., Wojciech Sokolowski, S. & Salamon, L. (2006) *Estudio comparativo del sector sin fines de lucro—Chile*, Santiago de Chile: Johns Hopkins University, PNUD, Focus Estudios y Consultorias.

Ley 19.253 de 05/10/1993, *Ley Indígena*, Ministerio de Planificación y Cooperación, Gobierno de Chile.

Ley 2.757 de 04/07/1979, *Normas sobre asociaciones gremiales*, Ministerio del Trabajo Previsión Social, Gobierno de Chile.

Ley No. 19.418 de 09/01/1997, *Ley sobre juntas de vecinos y demás organizaciones comunitarias*, Ministerio del Interior, Subsecretaría de Desarrollo Regional y Administrativo, Gobierno de Chile.

Ley No. 19.832 de 17/02/2004, *Ley general de cooperativas*, Ministerio de Economía, Fomento y Reconstrucción, Gobierno de Chile.

López Mayher, C. (2013) "¿Qué aportan las empresas B al desarrollo social y/o medioambiental? Análisis de tres casos de estudio", Master thesis in development management, Washington: American University. Available HTTP: https://www.sistemab.org/wp-content/uploads/2013/07/Articulo-Empresas-B. Cristina-Lopez-Mayher.30-Julio-2013.pdf.

Martini, G., Pérez, E. & Radrigán, M. (2003) "Situación Actual del Cooperativismo en Chile", Programa Interdisciplinario de Estudios Asociativos Pro—Asocia, Santiago de Chile: Universidad de Chile.

Nyssens, M. (1997) "Popular economy in the South, third sector in the North: Are they signs of a germinating economy of solidarity?" *Annals of Public and Cooperative Economics*, Vol. 68, No. 2, pp. 171–200.

Pestoff, V. (1998, 2005) *Beyond the Market and State: Civil Democracy and Social Enterprises in a Welfare Society*, Aldershot, UK and Brookfield, NJ: Ashgate.

Pizarro, R. (2004) "El Tercer Sector en Chile. Las organizaciones de acción social en el ámbito comunal", PhD thesis in sociology, Granada: Departamento de Sociología, Universidad de Granada.

Radrigán, M. & Barría, C. (2005) "Situación y proyecciones de la economía social en Chile", Programa Interdisciplinario de Estudios Asociativos—PRO-ASOCIA, Santiago de Chile: Universidad de Chile.

Radrigán, M., Barría, C., Hernández, L. & Lagarrigue, A. (2010) "Informe diagnóstico nacional de Chile. Claves para un desarrollo con equidad en América Latina—El caso de Chile", in Monzón, J. L. (ed.) *Economía social y su impacto en la generación de empleo: claves para un desarrollo con equidad en América Latina*, Madrid: FUNBIDES.

Razeto, M. L. (1986) *Economía Popular de Solidaridad*, Santiago de Chile: Edición Conferencia Episcopal de Chile.

Razeto, M. L. (1990) *Las Organizaciones Económicas Populares 1973–1990*, Santiago de Chile: Ediciones PET.

Razeto, M. L. (1993) *De la Economía Popular a la Economía de Solidaridad en un Proyecto de Desarrollo Alternativo*, Mexico: Instituto Mexicano de Doctrina Social Cristianao.

Razeto, M. L. (1998) *De la Economía Popular a la Economía de Solidaridad en un Proyecto de Desarrollo Alternativo*, Santiago de Chile: Ediciones PET.

Rodriguez, D. & Quezada, S. (2007) "Cultura en las organizaciones del tercer sector chileno", *Revista Española del Tercer Sector*, Vol. 6, pp. 121–151.

Salamon, L. M. & Anheier, H. K. (1997) "In search of the nonprofit sector: The question of definition", in Salamon, L. M. & Anheier, H. K. (eds) *Defining the Nonprofit Sector: A Cross-National Analysis*, Manchester: Manchester University Press.

Singer, P. (2000) "Economia solidária: um modo de produção e distribuição", in Singer, P. & Souza, A. (eds) *A Economia solidária no Brasil; a autogestão como resposta ao desemprego*, São Paulo: Contexto.

Singer, P. & Souza, A. (2000) *A Economia solidária no Brasil; a autogestão como resposta ao desemprego*, São Paulo: Contexto.

Vieta, M. (2010) "The new cooperativism", Editorial, *Affinities: A Journal of Radical Theory, Culture, and Action*, Vol. 4, No. 1, pp. 1–11.

Vieta, M. (2014) "The stream of self-determination and autogestión: Prefiguring alternative economic realities", *Ephemera: Theory & Politics in Organisation*, Vol. 14, No. 4, pp. 781–809.

5 Popular and Solidarity Economy in Ecuador

Historical Overview, Institutional Trajectories and Types of Organisation

María-José Ruiz-Rivera and
Andreia Lemaître

Introduction

The notion of "social enterprise" is unusual in Ecuador.[1] So far, social actors and practitioners engaged in promoting alternative economic models (not assimilated to the private for-profit model nor to the public-statist model) have recognised themselves through historically established concepts (e.g. cooperativism and associations) or more recent expressions such as the "popular and solidarity economy". The latter emerged from seminal theoretical contributions by Latin American scholars (e.g. Coraggio 1999; Razeto 1984; Singer 2000) who analysed economic practices developed by popular groups not driven by the sole purpose of profit maximisation, but by a plurality of goals reconciling economic, social, political and environmental objectives. In South America, the concept of "solidarity economy" spread during the 1990s, through the creation of international academic networks. It also gained relevance within the public debate through the rise of anti-neoliberalism activism by civil-society organisations in the last three decades, and more particularly in the wake of the first World Social Forum, organised in 2001.

Moreover, since the second half of the 2000s, the rise of the so-called new left governments in Latin America (Ellner 2012; Coraggio and Laville 2014; Stoessel 2014) has encouraged some particular trajectories of institutionalisation of the solidarity economy[2] (for examples in the region, see Coraggio 2015; Lemaître *et al.* 2011; Wanderley *et al.* 2015). As regards the Ecuadorian case, since the adoption of a new Constitution in 2008, as a part of a project of state transformation driven by an apparent post-neoliberal turn (Ettlinger and Hartmann 2015; Molyneux 2008), the term of "popular and solidarity economy" (*economía popular y solidaria*—for simplification, hereafter referred to by its Spanish acronym, EPS) has been explicitly used by Ecuadorian state officials for public-policy design as well as bureaucratic intervention (Nelms 2015). In this context, the EPS legally encompasses collective forms of

DOI: 10.4324/9780429055164-7

organisations operating in the fields of production, exchange, consumption of goods and services, and finance, and which are registered as cooperatives, associations and community organisations.[3]

The question of institutionalisation has often been related to the evolution of public policies, through approaches in which the state is at the centre of the analysis as a one-sided source of political recognition of the target organisations. However, in previous work (Ruiz-Rivera and Lemaître 2017), we have argued that the institutionalisation of EPS in Ecuador has not been merely the result of a proactive strategy driven by the state. This process has rather been the outcome of a mutual relation—in tension—between state intervention and organisations aiming to achieve their own recognition in the public sphere and through public policies. At a given stage, this process shaped the conditions in which EPS organisations scaled up without endangering their values; at another stage, it affected the nature of these initiatives. Therefore, adopting a historical approach appears necessary to understand the construction of what is nowadays acknowledged as the EPS in the Ecuadorian landscape.

In this chapter, we focus on identifying the types of organisation that claim to be part of the EPS and on analysing the functioning logics that characterise them. In order to do so, we answer some preliminary questions: Where do these organisations come from? In particular, are they rooted in any specific institutional trajectory that would explain their emergence, and which may have shaped different profiles of organisations?

Our study consisted of a review of the existing literature on the popular and solidarity economy in Ecuador as well as documentary and data analysis. Indeed, primary data was collected through 64 semi-structured interviews carried out in three waves of fieldwork (between 2015 and 2017), with leaders and members of EPS initiatives, government officials and representatives of networks and NGOs advocating EPS interests in the public sphere. Afterwards, we carried out an in-depth analysis among a sample of sixteen organisations (four emblematic cases stemming from each institutional trajectory), in which, among other techniques such as direct observation, we conducted the ICSEM survey with founder members, managers or other decision makers.

The aim of this chapter is twofold. First, we identify the main trajectories followed by different groups of economic initiatives that led to their institutionalisation. Secondly, in the light of the ideal type proposed by EMES (Defourny and Nyssens 2012, 2017) and of the work of authors debating on a solidarity-type social enterprise (Coraggio *et al.* 2015), we present the analytical framework—regarding the economic, social and political dimensions—underpinning our subsequent EPS typology. We then propose four major models of EPS organisations in Ecuador, each one linked to one of the institutional trajectories previously presented. We place a particular emphasis on the public dimension of each model, as this aspect allows to grasp the specific interplay between organisations and their institutional environment; i.e. their potential in terms of political embeddedness. Those types of interaction may prove themselves one of the most defining features that distinguish one type of EPS organisation from another. The four models are then briefly illustrated in different fields of activity, both established and emerging in the Ecuadorian context. We conclude by some remarks regarding the question of institutionalisation and the popular and solidarity-economy research agenda.

1. EPS Institutionalisation: A Historical Overview

Following a diachronic perspective, we argue that organisations that currently recognise themselves as being part of the EPS in Ecuador have been inspired by four particular institutional trajectories:

- the cooperative tradition, which has mostly been institutionalised via the state since the first half of the 20th century;
- a trajectory that has been rooted in the popular economy since 1970 and supported by grassroots NGOs, international cooperation and the Catholic Church;
- the social movements tradition, which, in the late 1980s and in the 1990s, led to the networking of a variety of actors bearing a political project of transformation;
- the emergence and multiplication of new forms of entrepreneurial ventures in the wake of the adoption of the new Constitution in 2008 and of the Law on the Popular and Solidarity Economy (*Ley Orgánica de Economía Popular y Solidaria*, or LOEPS) in 2011.

1.1. The Cooperative Tradition

The work of Da Ros (2007) and Miño (2013) retraces the trajectory of cooperativism in Ecuador since its origins, in the first half of the 20th century. In urban areas, cooperatives emerged as small-scale groups, composed of wage-earning workers and merchants. The aim of these organisations, which were founded by liberal, socialist and anarchist activists, was to grant mutual aid and professional defence to their members, in a context characterised by the lack of public social programmes. In rural areas, during the 1930s, peasant groups gradually organised themselves into agrarian unions in order to pursue their claims to land ownership and political representation (Miño 2013). Their mobilisation eventually resulted in the adoption of legal frameworks legitimising their demands (e.g. the first National Cooperatives Act and the Labour Code were both announced in 1937) (Clark and Becker 2007).

From the 1960s onward, the state and international aid agencies (e.g. the United States Agency for International Development, or USAID) played a key role in the institutionalisation of the cooperative model in the fields of production and finance. Following the two agrarian reforms of 1964 and 1973, the state financially supported producer cooperatives with the aim of transforming precarious forms of production into modern collective organisations, so as to increase productivity and contribute to the expansion of cocoa and banana in a primary-export-led growth model (Da Ros 2007). The existing peasant unions thus regrouped under the legal form of producer cooperatives to access land redistribution. However, as soon as the land property rights were assigned, cooperatives tended to divide themselves, not legally but *de facto*, into a series of individual farms—though these maintained areas of communal use (Oleas 2016). As regards international aid agencies, they acted as intermediate structures that financially supported the creation of federations, which regrouped cooperatives by different fields of activity,[4] particularly during the 1970s (Mills 1989).

Despite the expansion of the cooperative model, it was a project of material accumulation that prevailed in the practices of organisations, resulting in clientelistic relations with the state (Miño 2013), and in 1973, when US funding and government support were interrupted, only a quarter of registered cooperatives survived (Oleas 2016). We relate this phenomenon to a hypothesis of political opportunism, as Coque-Martínez (2001) suggests in his work on cooperativism in Africa and Asia: cooperatives were historically instrumentalised as implementers of governmental programmes serving the interests of socio-economic elites.

Concerning savings and credit cooperatives, most of them arose during the agricultural sector's modernisation of the 1960s, but it was during the oil boom of the 1970s that these organisations experienced their most dynamic growth in terms of increase in membership[5] (Da Ros 2007). During this period, the members' profile also underwent a transformation, from a predominantly rural population to an urban one (Miño 2013). Moreover, in the aftermath of the most significant Ecuadorian financial crisis, in 1999, which strongly affected the banking system,[6] cooperatives became an institutional alternative for depositors who had lost confidence in traditional financial institutions (Jácome *et al.* 2004).

Case studies carried out in emblematic cooperatives created in the 1960s and 1970s in the fields of production and finance and still operating today suggest that, since public policies aiming at modernisation demanded consistent levels of growth, cooperatives adopted practices of market isomorphism, i.e. they started "imitating" an accumulation model specific to market-driven capitalistic enterprises (Bidet 2003). In addition, cooperatives did not manage to secure mechanisms of democratic control by their members, which led them to compromise their autonomy from external actors while scaling up.

1.2. Popular Organisations and the Role of Intermediate Structures

The trajectory of popular organisations is rooted in the popular economy and refers to forms of self-generated work reflecting a specific rationality, not only based upon growth-oriented aims. As pointed out by Coraggio (1999), popular actors are domestic units developing socio-economic strategies with the aim of securing the "reproduction of life", by meeting their own material and immaterial needs. The inclusion of these initiatives in the public debate was mostly supported by civil society, such as the progressive Catholic Church and development-oriented NGOs.

As far as the role of the Catholic Church is concerned, after the Second Vatican Council, in the 1960s, advocated the relation between evangelisation and social commitment, priests professing the theology of liberation helped people in precarious situations to organise collectively with the aim of gaining access to raw materials, training and equipment as necessary conditions to generate income (Calvo and Morales 2013). "Gruppo Salinas" could be considered as a representative example of ecclesiastical initiatives which worked directly with rural populations: it is a cluster of community-based agro-industries located in the Ecuadorian highlands that emerged in 1970, with the support of the Salesian mission. The production of raw material is developed at the family level and all the transformation process happens at a collective, organised level.

As regards NGOs, some of them were religiously affiliated organisations, and they were often financed by development cooperation programmes. They promoted community production and trading practices in urban and rural areas (these activities were subsequently—during the 1990s—articulated into fair-trade networks). The "Tiendas Camari Solidarias"—i.e. shops that are part of the "Fondo Ecuatoriano Populorum Progressio" (FEPP)—and the "Maquita Cushunchic" Foundation (MCCH) emerged respectively in 1981 and 1985 and provide a good illustration hereof. "Tiendas Camari Solidarias" is an initiative focused on the development of trading circuits, led by suburban groups of Quito and the progressive Catholic Church. As for MCCH, this organisation aims to provide organisational support and technical assistance to producers with similar or complementary productive activities. Both structures organise and bring together producers and consumers to create spaces in which direct commercialisation can happen, such as neighbourhood and community stores, consumer cooperatives, local fairs and fair-trade networks (Espinosa 2010).

Moreover, intermediate structures have been decisive for the empowerment of producers. They have contributed to the collective action of popular organisations and to their gradual inclusion in the public sphere, by promoting the adoption of internal democratic structures (which often took the form of general assemblies) and through the creation of public micro-spaces based on proximity (e.g. neighbourhood fairs *qua* meeting places for generating income but also for debating issues of mutual concern), prompting these initiatives to evolve from mere survival tactics to more political strategies.

During the 1990s, popular organisations undertook a phase of networking, encouraged by intermediate structures to challenge exclusion in the context of structural adjustment programmes following the Washington Consensus. According to Andino (2017), those structures acted as interlocutors between popular organisations claiming redistributive policies (such as the implementation of a social-protection system) and policymakers. We put forward the hypothesis that, despite this recognition of popular organisations in the public debate, the pursuit of a political objective, including the participation of these initiatives in the building of public policies, might remain, for initiatives, secondary in relation to the achievement of their economic and social objectives. The economic fragility of these initiatives raises the question of the extent to which an objective of economic reinforcement has remained predominant to ensure their sustainability, at the expense of any political objective.

1.3. EPS' Embeddedness in Social Movements

During the 1980s and the 1990s, social movements in Ecuador often had to deal with state repression or co-optation mechanisms by the political parties in power (De la Torre and Ortiz Lemos 2015). Despite that, some political platforms (e.g. the Confederation of Indigenous Nationalities of Ecuador—*Confederación de Nacionalidades Indígenas del Ecuador*, or CONAIE) supported popular resistance processes against the neoliberal agenda, thus stimulating the articulation of economic organisations to social movements, which in turn gave rise to intense collective mobilisation. While the goal of popular organisations is job creation and income generation in a context of vulnerability, social movements explicitly pursue social change. However, these two types of actors agree on a radical critique of neoliberalism as a model of development and on the importance of the quest for alternatives. Popular organisations as well as cooperatives eventually became linked to social movements as a way of expanding new forms of collective action and of developing a more normative vision of EPS, relating to another way of producing, trading and consuming, based, beyond non-utilitarian practices, on an explicit political project: a shift of the development paradigm (Disney and Williams 2014).

Several networks (whose demands include the implementation of gender equity, the development of fair trade and ethnic claims, among others) have arisen with a conception of the solidarity economy as fulfilling a role as a political actor (Scarlato 2013). Their shared political discourse explicitly addresses social transformation, which according to Andino (2017: 114–118) is possible only if economic practices founded on reciprocity, solidarity, complementarity and cooperation are implemented. For example, in 1991, under the impulse of MCCH (see previous section), the Latin American Network of Community Trading (*Red Latinoamericana de Comercialización Comunitaria*, or RELACC) was founded with the aim of articulating community production forms through a structure for commercialisation, as an alternative to the inequality of exchanges in the international trade (Espinosa 2010).

Scarlato (2013) points out three issues that have been internalised by social movements in Ecuador, especially since the first decade of the new century: environment, ethnicity and migrants' rights. The Ecuadorian Movement of the Social and Solidarity Economy (*Movimiento de Economía Social y Solidaria del Ecuador*, or MESSE) provides a good illustration of such evolution. The MESSE is a social platform that appeared in 2006. Its creation was financially and technically supported by NGOs (namely VECO, AVINA and the International Federation for Alternative Trade, or IFAT), upon the initiative of two Ecuadorian fairtrade actors (MCCH and RELACC), and umbrella organisations related to agroecology. The MESSE gathers individual and collective economic initiatives and supports organisations involved, in most cases, in fair trade, agroecology and ethnic and gender actions. Beyond the formulation and management of community projects (for example, the creation of economic circuits), political action is one of MESSE's main lines of action.

The embeddedness in social movements represents for the EPS the concretisation of collective action, allowing socio-economic initiatives to achieve greater political participation. We argue that, as they became increasingly interconnected within networks at different levels, organisations have begun to convey a common discourse, based on solidarity. Beyond its normative value, solidarity is considered here as an operating principle within organisations, in which the main mode of economic integration is horizontal reciprocity among members.

1.4. New Wave of Organisations Following EPS Promotion Policies

During the 1990s and the first half of the 2000s, the Ecuadorian public debate was focused on tensions concerning the failure of neoliberal policies.[7] After recurrent periods of political instability[8] and dynamic social mobilisation (led principally by the indigenous movement, in opposition to the free-trade agreement that was then to be imminently concluded with the US), President Rafael Correa was elected in 2006. He presented himself as a detractor of neoliberal approaches and advocated the important role of the EPS in the national economic system (Becker 2011).

One of the most relevant actions undertaken by the government as a starting point for state transformation was the establishment of a

Constituent Assembly in 2008. This Assembly's primary goal was to rewrite the national Constitution; in the new version, *Buen vivir*[9] is pointed out as the macro social horizon in a post-neoliberal perspective (Acosta 2010; Gudynas 2011). Through iterative working sessions, practitioners (mainly community leaders, cooperatives managers, and social movements and networks' representatives) were consulted about issues of general interest—among which, for example, their comprehension of the EPS itself (Andino 2017). As a result of this process, the 2008 Ecuadorian Constitution asserted significant claims. For example, it was the first Constitution worldwide to underline the rights of nature and its—no longer functionalist—role in human well-being (Becker 2011). From this point onward, solidarity was assumed to be part of the logics guiding public action, opposed to a neoliberal rationale (Oleas 2016).

To operationalise a part of this project, which scholars (Escobar 2010; Yates and Bakker 2014) have called a "shift to the left" in state politics, the Law of Popular and Solidarity Economy (LOEPS) was passed in 2011. This Law is considered to result from a process of legislative co-construction: seventeen nationwide workshops were conducted, with the participation of around 1,800 representatives of the government, social movements and EPS networks (Muriel 2012). The latter managed to relay grassroots initiatives' demands within those deliberative public spaces. Indeed, the process of the LOEPS' redaction presented itself as a historical moment of participation, which was intended to embody the reflection of practitioners about their own initiatives as well as the position of state officials about a socially embedded economy (Nelms 2015: 107–113).

The LOEPS initiated a process of institution-building, which involved an explicit inclusion of EPS in regulatory frameworks and development agendas. In this regard, specific state bodies were entrusted with the coordination, promotion, control and financing of EPS initiatives. Through the creation of the National Institute of Popular and Solidarity Economy (*Instituto Nacional de Economía Popular y Solidaria*, or IEPS), a series of policies for the promotion of the sector were defined. Overall, we argue that the current national programmes aim at alleviating poverty by strengthening the economic dimension of EPS, hence fostering entrepreneurship. More precisely, programmes carried out by IEPS focus on enabling organisations to access markets and production means (e.g. assets and working capital).

In addition, the Super-administration of the Popular and Solidarity Economy (*Superintendencia de Economía Popular y Solidaria*, or SEPS) has undertaken in 2012 a process of setting up a national register whose initial target was cooperatives and associations. The process was based on the updating of administrative information about organisations (e.g. registration of members and board of directors) in a first phase, and the updating of financial information in a second phase. The objective of this registration process was twofold: (1) to quantify and map EPS organisations in Ecuador, and (2) to enable them to operate legally, so that they would qualify for participation in public programmes (Jácome and Ruiz-Rivera 2013).

This process was the starting point for a rise and proliferation of what we can refer to as a new wave of popular-economy ventures. Indeed, IEPS officials have been focused on linking socio-economic initiatives with potential markets, such as the public one, through what is called "inclusive markets" (*ferias inclusivas*) and, since 2014, through the adoption of the "inclusive purchase catalogue" (*catálogo dinámico inclusivo*). Both tools constitute ways of implementing the public purchasing programme, which provides that any state institution can place an order for a particular good or service (e.g. uniforms or cleaning services), previously entrusted to private capitalist subcontractors, directly with potential EPS providers, without them being put in competition with other providers such as medium and large companies. The IEPS serves as a mediator for and provider of technical assistance to EPS initiatives, so that they can deliver that order. When local manufacturers are informed about a public call, they are invited to register in the "inclusive purchase catalogue".[10]

Since formalisation is a condition for EPS initiatives to be included in these programmes, individual or family undertakings tend to reorganise and register as associations.[11] According to IEPS officials, one of the main reasons for choosing this legal form rather than the cooperative one lies in the fact that the legal form of association involves lower transaction costs (e.g. costs of the procedures required to create the organisation) than other legal forms. In this context, the number of producer associations rose from 2,839 in 2012 to 6,369 in 2017 (SEPS 2018). We argue that this new wave of associations reflects a pragmatic logic, stimulated by the current public policies, since the institutional framework represents a new path of public recognition for these popular ventures.

2. EPS Organisations: Four Models

2.1. Analytical Framework

After presenting the contextual background related to the historical construction of EPS in Ecuador, we argue that the trajectories reviewed in section 1 might have led to the emergence of four models of EPS in Ecuador. To support this hypothesis, drawing on some of the indicators of the ideal type proposed by EMES (Defourny and Nyssens 2012, 2017), we describe the operating logics that characterise and distinguish each of the types of EPS organisation coexisting in Ecuador. We outline three key dimensions: the economic project, the social aim and the political dimension (table 5.1). In addition, we call on the work carried out by Coraggio *et al.* (2015) on the solidarity-type social enterprise. These

Table 5.1 EPS analytical framework

Dimension	Variable	Description	
Economic	Activity and coherence with the mission	The initiative is directly involved in the production of goods or the provision of services on a continuous basis. The activity thus represents the reason for the existence of the organisation, and it must be coherent with the social mission and with any other kind of goal (environmental and/or political) pursued by the organisation.	
	Economic risk	A balance must be achieved between fulfilling the initiative's mission and achieving financial sustainability. This aspect can be observed by investigating whether a certain type of resources—and which one—dominates in the operation of the initiative, analysing the proportion of income coming from sales (market logic), from public grants (redistribution logic), from philanthropic sources (reciprocity logic) and from domestic-type units (householding logic).	
	Valorisation of work	Members are both associates and workers of the organisation; and the majority of workers are members as well (the use of hired labour force is limited).	
Social	Mission and principles of interest	The aim of the initiative is to explicitly serve a particular group of people: it is responding to a mutual interest among its members or, beyond members' interests, to the interest of the community in which it operates (or even the general interest). This variable opens a discussion about the way in which and the level at which the organisation balances those different drivers of its productive activities.	
	Profit distribution	There is a constraint on the distribution of the revenue surplus among members to avoid practices of profit maximisation. This constraint can refer to a total non-distribution constraint or to a distribution to a limited extent only (surpluses might be allocated to funding collective activities favourable to the mission).	
Political	Participation and governance	Decision-making	The decision-making power is not based on capital ownership. Members actively participate in the definition of matters of common interest. Beyond its members, the initiative might operate on the basis of a participatory logic, which involves various parties affected by the activity.

Dimension	Variable	Description	
Public dimension	Explicit political goal	Beyond work and income generation, the initiative explicitly tackles, through its mission, a transformation of the political, economic or social order.	
	Creation of public spaces	The initiative seeks to achieve political impact, beyond the interests of the organisation, through participation in deliberation processes in the public sphere. Members take part in autonomous micro public spaces (e.g. based on proximity) and intermediate public spaces (wider arenas, e.g. structures of mediation with other actors).	
	Articulations with other actors and autonomy	Relationships with other actors (to get access to resources, to markets, to financing or to technical or managerial knowledge) should not compromise the control of the organisation by its members.	

Source: The authors, based on Defourny and Nyssens (2012, 2017) and Coraggio *et al.* (2015).

authors' approach is similar to the EMES perspective in that it is based on the identification of indicators in the social and economic fields, but its additional contribution concerns the analysis of the political dimension, beyond the field of governance (which is related mostly to internal choices). These authors discuss the public dimension of EPS organisations, which includes the latter's ability to enrol in the public debate, to act as a political actor and to participate in the development of public policies—in other words, their political embeddedness (Lemaître 2009).

On such basis, we propose a classification that distinguishes four EPS ideal types in Ecuador. Each model follows a particular path of institutionalisation; the four models should be considered as operating alongside one another, in a non-hierarchical order.

Before presenting each model and its distinctive features, we first underline some points of convergence among all the categories.

Production Activity

In all four EPS ideal types, there is a continuous activity of production of goods and/or services. This feature is in fact a *sine qua non* condition, since it makes it possible to distinguish EPS initiatives from other types of organisations—such as support organisations (e.g. foundations or NGOs)—pursuing a social (or political) mission but not carrying out any economic activity.

Main Mission and Subsidiary Goals

Regardless of the model to which they belong, the studied initiatives explicitly claim to pursue a mission of job creation and income generation, which they all consider as the main goal of their economic activities. This mission corresponds to the finality of improving the quality of life of the organisation's members and of their households by meeting their material needs, such as the needs for food and housing, among others. It is also the reason why EPS organisations are currently the target of public policies that aim to promote social inclusion and poverty alleviation. The social dimension could also be connected to other objectives for meeting immaterial or subjective needs, which, according to Bauwens and Lemaître (2014), entail a symbolic value, such as the creation of community bonds.

Mix of Economic Relations

We refer to what actors consider as the main source of revenue (including both monetary and non-monetary resources) that allows the organisation to fulfil its mission and foster its sustainability. However, the analysis may not be limited to the stance of resources, but rather it is addressed, following Polanyi's (1944) substantive approach, in terms of interdependences among various economic logics: reciprocity, which refers to practices of complementarity voluntarily instituted (e.g. support between symmetrical groupings); redistribution, which indicates interactions within centralised systems, such as interactions with the state; the market, understood as the interactions between buyers and sellers through price fluctuations; and householding (Hillenkamp *et al.* 2013: 5–6), which corresponds to the interdependence within the domestic unit, based upon self-provisioning for and by the group members. We argue that this approach allows to recognise how the four models of EPS organisations are embedded in several economic logics, intertwine different resources and connect with diverse external actors.

Decision-Making

In all the EPS models presented below, decision-making is, by principle, not based on capital ownership; however, each type of organisation has some specificities, which may depend on the legal form (if the organisation is legally registered) adopted by the initiative. It should be emphasised that all types of organisations, except cooperatives, might navigate between self-management practices and indirect economic democracy. Self-management refers to the fact of being "totally managed, in equal parts, by the workers" (Lemaître and Helmsing 2012: 755), while indirect economic democracy entails the establishment of representation bodies.

2.2. Cooperatives

This model encompasses the organisations formally registered under the legal form of cooperatives. The production activity is the primary motive for their existence. Concerning the field of activity in which cooperatives operate, there are producer, service, housing and savings and credit cooperatives. Those organisations are composed of a group of persons, voluntarily united, and explicitly seeking to meet the members' common economic, social or cultural needs through practices of cooperation and mutuality. By December 2018, in Ecuador, there were 2,654 registered non-financial cooperatives and 641 savings and credit cooperatives (SEPS 2018).

Members are therefore the main beneficiaries of the economic activity. In fact, the specific feature of cooperatives is the double status of their members (Gui 1991), who act both as co-owners (or associates) and as users. For instance, in consumer cooperatives and housing cooperatives, members get direct access to the goods or services produced by and within the organisation. In producer cooperatives (e.g. coffee and cocoa cooperatives), associates make use of the organisation to gain access to raw material (e.g. seeds) and to transform and commercialise their production. In agricultural cooperatives, harvests are delivered to the cooperative by all members; the organisation provides in turn the infrastructure for the storage and transformation of their production. In saving and credit cooperatives, however, most users of the financial services provided by the organisation are clients-like (not associates), i.e. they do not take part in the decision-making processes. Moreover, in cooperatives, workers are *a priori* members. This can however vary from one field of activity to the other. For example, paid work is significant in transport cooperatives, in which bus drivers operate as employees and do not (or barely) take part in the management of the organisation (Ruiz-Rivera 2014). Concerning the membership composition, most interviewed associates consider themselves as belonging to the middle-class segments of the population.

Concerning the social mission, it explicitly responds to a mutual interest among members, since it refers to job creation and income generation as a means of securing members' livelihoods as well as those of their families. Consequently, the social mission hardly meets the interests of groups beyond the organisation's members. Market resources from sales are the main economic source sustaining cooperatives' activities. Those organisations attempt to obtain the highest margin from their economic transactions. A minor proportion of reciprocity resources (e.g. local voluntary work or donations from actors such as foundations) could be identified. By contrast, the presence of resources from redistribution, mostly under non-monetary forms (such as training services provided in the framework of public programmes), is rather significant.

As regards the distribution of the revenue and surplus, the instituted norms among members respond to legal requirements as provided for in the LOEPS. In cooperatives, specific rules regulate the distribution of net income and surpluses. Those organisations must contribute to a so-called indivisible legal reserve fund, which serves to face economic contingencies. Contributions to this fund correspond to at least 50% of the annual surplus. Cooperatives are also constrained to contribute up to 5% of their annual surplus to the Super-administration (SEPS). Besides those legal requirements, the most common practice regarding surplus distribution is to reinvest revenue in the organisation. Yet, net income is equally shared among cooperatives' members in some specific cases (e.g. to increase motivation or to face crisis).

Cooperatives appear to operate as jointly owned organisations, but within an indirect economic democracy framework, that is to say through setting up representative bodies. Indeed, the LOEPS requires that cooperatives set up representation bodies for the decision-making process: a general assembly, a board of management and a supervisory board. During assemblies, members elect—following the "one member, one vote" rule—the representatives to whom they delegate the decision-making power for the day-to-day management of the organisation. By doing so, members follow not only the national regulations regarding EPS, but also the principles defined by the International Cooperative Alliance (ACI).[12]

2.3. Community-Based Organisations

Community-based organisations are cooperative-like organisations rooted in the popular economy. Under the current legal framework, some of these initiatives are being registered as cooperatives, some as associations;[13] yet, most of them remain informal. Linked by a plurality of bonds based on family, ethnicity, culture or gender, members are workers, and the majority of workers are also members. The presence of paid work is negligible since those initiatives deliberately focus on limiting the use of hired labour force. Most members self-identify as being part of the lower middle class of the population, though amongst them, there are some who consider themselves as poor.

Like cooperatives, community-based organisations seek to ensure the improvement of their members' livelihoods through, in the terms of Sarria Icaza and Tiriba (2006), the use of the members' workforce and of available resources. One distinctive feature of this model, compared with the cooperative one, is that, beyond a common interest for income generation among members, the mission here also targets other actors at the local level and occasionally tackles larger societal challenges. For example, some agricultural organisations relate their economic goal to the provision of collective services for improving not only the livelihood of their members, but also that of their community. They provide irrigation channels in rural areas for use by people in the community, regardless of their relation to the organisation (whether or not they are members). Initiatives in the area of community-based tourism provide another example of organisations balancing more than one driver of economic activities: they deliberately combine the goal of improving their members' income (local tourist guides and family hosts) with the purpose of promoting the consumption, by the tourists, during their stay, of organic products from local farmers and shops—a goal which is also related to an environmental challenge. In this regard, beyond market-driven aims, the purpose of these organisations embraces what Hillenkamp *et al.* (2013) describe as "community embeddedness" (or "amplification of social capital", in Evans and Syrett's [2007] words) through durable relations with local actors.

In addition, community-based organisations pursue members' empowerment, and this is a vital part of their mission. As highlighted by Lemaître and Helmsing (2012: 754–755), "the economic activity in organisations [could appear] as a means to empower workers and for them to access citizenship [. . .] They gradually realise their capabilities by becoming aware of their reality of economic, social and political exclusion". In fact, the participation of these initiatives in training programmes focused on professionalisation and "awareness-raising",[14] mostly linked to umbrella organisations (e.g. regional federations of producers) and networks (e.g. the Ecuadorian Fair Trade Coordination, or *Coordinadora Ecuatoriana de Comercio Justo*), might allow them to progressively gain access to the public sphere.

As regards financial sustainability, members of community-based organisations identify the market as their main source of revenue. Initiatives of this type are more likely than others to be linked to fair-trade circuits. Resources coming from redistribution and reciprocity relations are also significant for the fulfilment of the mission. Redistribution-based resources are generally mobilised in the form of training activities led by state officials or local NGOs, while reciprocity-based resources take forms such as the free provision of premises or diverse donations by the community (e.g. by the village church or neighbourhood councils). Interviewees declared that it seemed unlikely that their organisations might be able to access public monetary resources (e.g. grants or funding) under the current stringent conditions regarding credit guarantees.

Concerning the allocation of revenue, it is distributed according to productivity, following criteria such as the number of hours worked or the number of units produced, or according to specific conditions enshrined in (formal or informal) contracts. The possibility that a portion of income remains in the organisation (as a sort of accumulation) is not common among these initiatives. If there are surpluses at the end of the year, those resources are allocated to collective events organised for members and their families, and involving as well other actors in the community.

As regards governance, and especially the decision-making power, community-based organisations appear to be willing to practice self-management. Cooperative principles are often put into practice by this type of initiatives, despite their not being formally registered as cooperatives. In this regard, members express their will to achieve an active participation in the definition of the organisation's mission and of the means to accomplish it. They also consider that participation should concern the sharing of knowledge (e.g. about customers, suppliers and support organisations, among other stakeholders).

2.4. Organisations Embedded in Social Movements

Organisations embedded in social movements—be they rooted in the popular economy or in the cooperative tradition—are engaged in the production and commercialisation of goods and/or services. The distinctive feature of this type of organisation, compared with community-based initiatives, is their deep-rooted relation with social movements, but also with platforms and networks of actors pursuing an explicit political goal. Therefore, amongst their members, there are usually some intellectual activists.

In this regard, as part of their social mission, organisations embedded in social movements target an ethical purpose. They tend to balance and integrate economic, social and political purposes and strategies. As Defourny and Nyssens (2017: 2483) state, "the general interest component may be considered to be embedded in the very nature of the production". In this regard, we argue that economic organisations linked to grassroots social movements are more concerned with awareness about collective rights and capabilities for the common good in the medium and long term than with immediate and pragmatic interests (prioritised by the aforementioned other EPS types). This appears to be the case for producer associations linked to the agroecological movement, in which membership does not only entail advocacy for organisational benefits, but also a space to question the vision of development (Intriago *et al.* 2017). Various organisations of this type are members of the Ecuadorian Committee for the Defense of Nature and the Environment (*Comité Ecuatoriano para la Defensa de la Naturaleza y el Medio Ambiente*, or CEDENMA).

Indeed, initiatives in this category are characterised by their political commitment; they might appear as new forms of collective action, pursuing an explicit project: the quest for social, economic and political change. We further discuss this matter in section 2.6, which addresses the political goals that EPS initiatives might pursue.

Compared with community-based organisations, initiatives embedded in social movements rely more on relations based on reciprocity (e.g. local donations) and (indirect) redistribution[15] (e.g. public funding coming from international development cooperation, provided mostly by local social platforms) as a significant source of revenue. However, those organisations' resource mix also includes an important proportion of market resources, arising from short circuits, and which play a significant role for their sustainability. In addition, like community-based organisations, initiatives embedded in social movements are not particularly dependent on national public grants. Their members consider that there are many obstacles, in terms of eligibility criteria, to accessing public monetary resources.

Concerning decision-making processes, these organisations generally aim to operate according to self-management principles. Likewise, revenue is distributed here according to productivity and following particular norms (formally or informally) instituted by the members. Potential surpluses (when existing) are allocated to funding activities supporting the organisation's members, such as training programmes and technical assistance.

Initiatives embedded in the Ecuadorian Movement of the Social and Solidarity Economy (MESSE) provide a good illustration of organisations linked to the "social movements" tradition. In 2014, this platform brought together 1,300 members (both individual and collective popular-economy initiatives and support organisations), located in 15 of the 24 Ecuadorian provinces. Members include organic producers (or producers engaged in the transition towards organic production techniques), artisans, promoters of popular education, fishermen, community tourism initiatives, a housing cooperative, consumers and several NGOs. Their shared political discourse explicitly addresses social transformation. According to MESSE's leaders, such transformation involves the formulation and dissemination of concrete proposals in participative forums at the local, national and regional levels (Andino 2017: 116).

2.5. New Popular-Economy Ventures

New popular-economy ventures mostly refer to urban undertakings and small family businesses, which are experiencing a formalisation process under the current institutional framework. As stated in a previous section (see section 1.4), these initiatives appear to pursue formalisation by adopting the legal form of associations in order to gain access to the benefits linked to public policies.

These initiatives serve individual or group needs. Workers are not systematically members and there is a significant presence of paid work. This is the case, for example, for textile manufacturing ventures, in which workers have the status of employees. Production activities during the periods of state purchasing programmes (e.g. uniform-making for public schools) require a significant recourse to subcontracted or outsourced work.

This model encompasses mostly market-driven initiatives. Members of newly formalised organisations tend to self-identify as incipient entrepreneurs willing to transit from subsistence conditions to a stage of economic growth. As regards their financial sustainability, members clearly identify resources originating in a redistributive relation (fees resulting from public purchasing programmes)[16] as essential for their operation. They do not mention the existence of reciprocity resources from the community but identify householding relations as an important strategy for their subsistence, especially during periods of vulnerability (e.g. during periods in which there are no contracts with the state).

Concerning governance, newly registered associations are legally obliged to set up democratic bodies (a board of management and a supervisory board elected by the general assembly). Yet, processes of decision-making usually do not involve all the members. Interviewees here describe a more pragmatic approach: members prefer to delegate power to a representative leader, who is tasked with assuming management responsibilities. In fact, as stated by Kervyn and Lemaître (2018), principles of association might be combined with a capitalistic entrepreneurial logic, with a constant superposition of values. Moreover, there are no systematic rules regulating the distribution of the net income. The actual practice is that revenue is distributed according to the work performed by members. These initiatives are characterised by organisational volatility and by fragility in terms of both creating stable jobs and generating stable income, and they do not (or barely) generate surpluses. However, it is important to highlight the fact that, in organisations having achieved sustained participation—at least nine months a year—in public purchase programmes, members often receive a monthly remuneration equivalent to the legal minimum wage (US$386/month for the year 2018).

New popular-economy ventures self-identify as part of the EPS, alongside traditional cooperatives and popular organisations (be they rooted or not in social movements). For this new wave of undertakings, the EPS means the formal overarching category created by the state and through which it implements its intervention. In this regard, the mission of generating jobs is considered by these organisations' members as the element that legitimates their being part of the EPS.

2.6. *Public Dimension*

Political-type criteria (see table 5.1) appear necessary to characterise the EPS in Ecuador. These criteria refer to these organisations' participation in the public sphere, which involves external actors to discuss and deliberate on common issues and to make decisions beyond the organisation itself (Laville 2005). The public dimension of the solidarity economy might help avoid the separation that Habermas (1986) operates between the political and the economic spheres, and it might offer a scenario of co-construction of public action, which would thus no longer be produced by the state alone but would also be driven by initiatives. This public dimension, as highlighted by Coraggio *et al.* (2015), concerns the pursuit of an explicit political goal, the creation of autonomous public spaces (based on proximity), and the participation of the organisations' members in intermediate public spaces, eventually with a view to achieving institutional change.

As regards cooperatives, they are usually officially members of sectorial federations (intermediate public spaces), which should make it possible for them to engage in collective action in the public sphere. However, any political project might be threatened by an actual risk of co-optation of organisations' leaders by governments or political parties. Those practices are likely to hinder the preservation of organisations' autonomy and democratic control by the members. Moreover, interviewees consider the pursuit of a political goal to be secondary to their economic and social objectives. Leaders from cooperatives who actively participated in the elaboration of the LOEPS consider this process as the historical concretisation of a political goal of institutional recognition. Nowadays, what remains of a political project might appear implicit, as it refers to facing challenges in members' attempts to build collective action, and it is not necessarily shared by all the members.

Members of community-based organisations and organisations embedded in social movements all declare to support the creation of autonomous public spaces (e.g. producers/farmers' markets) in which, besides carrying out trading activities, they discuss and deliberate on common concerns such as price policies, low levels of productivity, opportunities to engage in quality certification processes adapted to EPS, limited access to credit, limited administrative and accounting capabilities, among other issues. Such collective action might make it possible to continuously assess and redefine the organisational interests, and eventually to build a long-term political agenda.

Members of community-based organisations identify the pursuit of a political goal among their organisational purposes. Yet, they make the pursuit of such goal conditional on the existence of relations with umbrella organisations and networks. Indeed, it seems that what defines and circumscribes the extent of any political project in community-based organisations is their interaction with intermediate structures willing to foster dialogue spaces with a plurality of actors (including public authorities), in which they advocate the organisations' needs and aspirations. For example, popular banks (which collect members' savings and then use them to lend to members) systematically tend to adhere,

Table 5.2 Ideal-typical EPS models in Ecuador

Criteria	Models	Type 1 Cooperatives	Type 2 Community-based organisations	Type 3 Organisations embedded in social movements	Type 4 New popular-economy ventures
	Main legal form	Cooperatives	Mostly informal organisations	Mostly informal organisations	Family/small ventures, recently formalised as associations
Economic	Main resources sustaining the activity	(1) Market sales	(1) Market sales (2) Voluntary resources	(1) Voluntary resources (2) Market sales	(1) Public grants
	Type of dominant market	Classic capitalist market	Fair trade	Short circuits Fair trade	Public markets
	Valorisation of work: status and minimum number of members	Usually, members = workers, but it depends on the field of activity Minimum 20 members in production and services cooperatives, 50 in savings and credit cooperatives	Members =/≠ workers Minimum number of members not defined	Members =/≠ workers Minimum number of members not defined	Members ≠ workers Minimum 10 members when the legal form is that of association
Social	Social mission and principles of interest	Cooperation and mutuality (meeting members' needs)	Job creation and income generation serving members' and community needs	(More radical) societal change towards an inclusive/ecological . . . society (general interest)	Job creation and income generation serving individual/group needs

Governance	Surplus distribution	Limited surplus distribution	Revenue distributed according to productivity If there is a surplus, it is usually used for collective activities decided by the general assembly	Revenue distributed according to productivity It there is a surplus, it is usually used for collective purposes decided by the general assembly	Revenue distributed according to productivity Usually no surplus
	Decision-making	Democratic governance (general assembly)	Democratic participation in decision-making (general assembly) and in the management of the organisation	Democratic participation in decision-making (general assembly) and in the management of the organisation	Democratic bodies when the legal form is that of association
Political	Pursuit of a political goal	Not explicit	Implicit in terms of empowerment	Explicit: institutional change	None or not explicit
	Participation in public spaces	Intermediate public spaces	Autonomous micro public spaces	Autonomous micro public spaces and intermediate ones	(newly created) intermediate public spaces
	Articulation with external actors	Formal membership in umbrella organisations (e.g. federations)	Support structures, mostly NGOs, social platforms and networks	Formal adherence, through commitment to a Chart of principles, to social movements and networks	Federative dynamic resulting from relations with state officials while taking part in national programmes

Source: The authors.

in their discourse, to the critics made by social platforms regarding the exclusion of some people from the formal banking system. However, most intermediate structures might tend to defend the rights of a historically marginalised population, proposing short-term aid, rather than pursuing long-term aims for the common good. Concerning the relation with umbrella organisations such as sectorial unions or federations, community-based initiatives describe a possible membership as being driven by the opportunity to access markets and training, and not by any political motivation.

As concerns organisations embedded in social movements, their political goal is explicitly reflected in their ability to both create autonomous public spaces and participate in intermediate public spaces with policymakers. Interviewees consider it as an important role of the organisation to seek iterative contacts with multiple actors outside the organisation (e.g. local public authorities) to discuss public issues. For instance, some women associations of handicraft production are embedded in the Ecuadorian Popular Women Movement (*Asamblea de Mujeres Populares del Ecuador*), and organic-producer associations are embedded in the Ecuadorian Agroecological Movement (*Colectivo agroecológico del Ecuador*). By developing periodic encounters with social movements, these initiatives are able to translate their concerns for gender justice and agro-biodiversity (respectively) into practical local action. Those movements play a role of political lobbying for the initiatives, relaying actors' demands and proposals into the public sphere. Organisations of this type might also have a transnational dimension (Scarlato 2013), due to the contribution their members make to the regional debate on poverty and the Millennium Development Goals (MDGs) agenda.

It should be noted that nowadays there is a variety of networks and social platforms encompassing EPS initiatives; yet they have not so far constituted a unified political movement, nor have they achieved a collective identity. Their opening up to deliberative processes risks remaining limited to the level of their member organisations themselves, without a constant participation of policymakers in local, regional or national public spaces.

Most of the new popular-economy ventures are not likely to be linked to intermediate structures such as federations and social platforms. They do not have either any goal of political participation, since they are not rooted in their territory—according to Hess (2004), being rooted in a territory goes beyond the fact of sharing a common geographical location and involves community embeddedness. Interviewees here declare to sometimes engage in direct discussions with state officials regarding their participation in public programmes, particularly *ex-ante* and during the intervention. These articulations seem to follow a pragmatic logic and not to result from an explicit political motivation. Thus, faced with uncertainties regarding possible changes in public procurement policies,

Table 5.3 Examples of EPS initiatives in Ecuador by models and fields of activity

Models / Fields of activity	Type 1 Cooperatives	Type 2 Community-based organisations	Type 3 Organisations embedded in social movements	Type 4 New popular-economy ventures
Production	Agricultural production cooperative	Craft manufacturing association (usually operating in a fair-trade circuit)	Economic circuit based on agroecology	Family venture, textile manufacturing association
Services	Housing cooperative	Community tourism project	Association aimed at popular education	Family venture involved in catering or cleaning services
Finance	Savings and credit cooperative	Popular bank	Social currency exchange device	–

Source: The authors.

new popular-economy ventures have recently undertaken, under the tutelage of IEPS and the National Department for Public Procurement (*Servicio de Contratación Pública*, or SERCOP), the creation of so-called EPS networks and regional EPS chambers. The aim of these actions is to formally bring together registered associations; however, it remains to verify whether these networks and chambers respond to the organisations' motivation or to a proactive initiative on the part of current public authorities.

Table 5.2 sums up the characteristics of each type of EPS organisation according to the aforementioned criteria.

These models can be illustrated in different fields of economic activity. Table 5.3 presents examples of EPS initiatives in the Ecuadorian landscape.

Conclusion

Through this chapter, we highlighted the relevance of a historical approach to characterise the EPS in Ecuador. Indeed, this perspective led us to identify some significant trajectories followed by organisations in their attempts to achieve recognition and to find their place in the current field of public-policy design. The process of EPS institutionalisation appeared to be dynamic and to be a long-term one. It results from relations of mutual influence between different categories of actors: EPS organisations, intermediate structures (operating in the public sphere) and state authorities.

Our findings suggest that different types of organisation, having evolved along different institutional trajectories, all recognise themselves nowadays as part of the EPS. As regards the participation of these organisations in the field of public-policy design, although the LOEPS itself could be pointed out as the result of long-lasting bottom-up relations involving different categories of actors, the current policymaking derived from this law is underpinning a top-down intervention. Two major issues could be at stake in this regard.

First, particular public programmes (such as calls for tenders targeting EPS potential providers) are resulting in the creation of a new wave of organisations, less identified with a democratic project, and reshaping the existing ones. There appears to be a risk of institutional isomorphism as organisations tend to mimic the dominant institutional norms regarding operation, management and governance, because this could enable them to fulfil the expectations of their key stakeholders (Gordon 2015)—in the Ecuadorian case, governmental authorities that define the eligibility criteria to get access to resources. Secondly, these interventions might be over-stimulating the mobilisation of market and redistribution resources to the detriment of reciprocity and householding relations. This is contradictory to the official acknowledgement of economic pluralism (related to the notion of *Buen vivir*).

Through this chapter, we also aimed to provide a first contribution to a classification of EPS organisations that would go beyond the current legal classification established by the LOEPS since 2011. The origins of each of the categories are related to a specific institutional trajectory, which also shaped a particular profile. In order to further support our typology, we carried out—in addition to the historical overview—an examination of the organisations' practices at the micro level that completed what actors shared in their discourses. Adopting such perspective, we put forward a typology distinguishing four types of EPS initiatives in the Ecuadorian context. It should be noted that, rather than defining clear-cut frontiers between the different categories, this contribution aims to emphasise some particular traits about what practitioners portray as EPS. These features give insights into the economic, social and governance dimensions put forward by the EMES approach (Defourny and Nyssens 2012, 2017) and feed into the debate some criteria developed by Coraggio *et al.* (2015) regarding solidarity economy's political dimension, with a view to grasping how EPS organisations interact with their institutional environment.

We hope that our proposal of an EPS typology may contribute to a deeper understanding of the diversity of initiatives combining economic, social and political aims in Ecuador. The challenge remains to continue developing more exhaustive empirical research on both the evolving institutional contexts in which the EPS is being institutionalised and the logics, practices and strategies of these forms of organisations, including their ability to become embedded in public action.

Notes

1 However, there is a recent opening up to the term of "social entrepreneur" as a label promoted by business incubation programmes undertaken by private companies, which includes projects addressing both economic and social goals. These projects are mostly for-profit start-ups.

2 The question of institutionalisation refers to what brings about the stabilisation and recurrence of particular socio-economic practices (Salamon and Anheier 1998). Scholars (e.g. Castelao Caruana and Srnec 2012) point out that the phenomenon of institutionalisation includes, in particular, the building process of legislation and state apparatus as part of the environment in which organisations operate. Most of the actual research following the solidarity-economy approach focuses on the various ways in which organisations adopt legal frameworks and, to a lesser extent, on the ways in which those organisations modify their institutional environment (Ruiz-Rivera and Lemaître 2017).

3 The EPS also includes individual undertakings. However, this last subcategory remains unclear in terms of operationalisation within the current legal framework.

4 According to Hübenthal (1987), the number of cooperatives rose from 2,280 organisations operating in 1963 to 4,378 cooperatives in 1972.

5 Between 1973 and 1982, the number of members of credit unions increased from 87,000 to 445,000 (Miño 2013). However, it should be kept in mind that one person can be a member of several unions simultaneously.

6 Under the impulse of the Washington Consensus, deregulation reforms in the financial system led to the bankruptcy of 20 banks out of 27 (Jácome *et al.* 2004).

7 Poverty levels increased by 12.8% between 1995 and 1999; the share of poor in the population reached 52.2%. This increase could be correlated to factors such as the effects that "El Niño" had on Ecuador in 1998 and the 1999 banking crisis. Regarding incomes, between 1990 and 2006, the first eight deciles of the population experienced a reduction of their income level; households belonging to the ninth decile kept their share of income at 16.2%, while the richest decile saw their incomes increase, from 35.5% to 41.8% of the country's total income (Ramírez 2008).

8 The dismissal of President Abdala Bucaram by the Congress and the popular protests of 1997 led to a series of weak brief governments: in 2000, after one year and a half of term of office, President Jamil Mahuad was ousted by a civilian-military coup d'état. Then in 2005, popular protests overthrew President Lucio Gutiérrez after two years in office. Among the arguments explaining those episodes, Blake and Morris (2009) point out the exclusion, from public action, of important segments of the population, corruption and patronage.

9 *Buen vivir*, or *Sumak Kawsay*, is a polysemic concept, still contested and under construction in the scientific literature. It carries out alternative propositions to the dominant notion of development—based on material well-being

and anthropocentrism—integrating indigenous cosmovisions that understand well-being as the harmony between humans and the natural environment (Gudynas 2011).

10 In order to be registered as providers, EPS manufactures must prove that (1) their production takes place within the territory where the demand is expressed (i.e. at least 50% of raw material and inputs come from the province where the order is placed); (2) they have the equipment and workforce necessary to meet the demand; (3) they function legally. The total amount of goods demanded through the public call is distributed according to the production capacity of several available organisations. One single organisation is usually not able to fully meet the demand, so another organisation from the catalogue is randomly added. Such procedure is repeated until the demand is fully met; the allocation procedure is then automatically closed.

11 Between June 2015 and December 2016, 3,301 organisations were registered, 93% of which were associations that might potentially participate as providers in the inclusive purchase catalogue (SEPS 2018).

12 Those principles are: voluntary and open membership; democratic member control; member economic participation; autonomy and independence; education, training and information; cooperation among cooperatives; and concern for community.

13 By December 2017, there were 9,651 registered associations (66% operating in the field of production, 34% in the field of services) (SEPS 2018).

14 By "awareness-raising" (*sensibilización*), the actors refer to those training activities focusing on acquiring awareness of what makes participation possible.

15 Redistribution includes what Lemaître and Helmsing (2012: 750) call "delegated redistribution", that is, public funds coming from international cooperation and targeted at economic initiatives in the South through support to local organisations. Moreover, when support to those organisations is financed by the capital of the international civil society (e.g. NGOs in the North), the authors call it "voluntary redistribution". Indeed, although this support is not collected in a compulsory way, it is not reciprocity since those resources are not related to symmetric relations between those giving and those receiving. It rather has to do with the centrality that is characteristic of redistribution: the resources are collected by a central entity, which then allocates them according to some criteria.

16 Markets whose functioning is not based on the "supply-demand-price" mechanism but on patterns of reciprocity or redistribution can exist. In Polanyi's substantive theory, exchange and market are not coextensive; they have independent empirical characteristics, to be studied separately (Polanyi 1944, cited by Hillenkamp 2009: 36–38): a demand group, a supply group (both necessarily present in "price-creating markets", but not systematically in other configurations; e.g. an auction entails a group of bidders, but only one offeror); the exchange rate (a more general category for the price) that may be fixed or variable (the latter established by bargaining mechanisms); and the existence (or not) of competition. In the case of public procurement programmes, there is a supply group (EPS organisations), but only one petitioner (a central entity). Moreover, although organisations receive revenues in exchange for the provision of goods or services (market relation), prices are standardised and not the result of competition among providers. Actually, all registered organisations can potentially be assigned a contract. The relation here is what is called "decisional exchange" and is aimed at democratising public resources.

References

Acosta, A. (2010) "El Buen Vivir en el camino del post-desarrollo. Una lectura desde la Constitución de Montecristi", Policy Paper, No. 9, Quito: Fundación Friedrich Ebert. Available HTTP: http://library.fes.de/pdf-files/bueros/quito/07671.pdf.

Andino, V. (2017) "De palabras con poder y acciones con libertad. Análisis de los posibles efectos del marco legal en el sector de la economía popular y solidaria en el Ecuador y propuestas para seguir actuando en libertad", in Fernández Villa, M., Guridi Aldanondo, L. & Jubeto, Y. (eds) *Políticas públicas territoriales para la economía social y solidaria en Loja*, Bilbao: Hegoa, pp. 11–145.

Bauwens, T. & Lemaître, A. (2014) "Popular economy in Santiago de Chile: State of affairs and challenges", *World Development*, Vol. 64, pp. 65–78. Available HTTP: https://doi.org/10.1016/j.worlddev.2014.05.015.

Becker, M. (2011) "Correa, indigenous movements, and the writing of a new constitution in Ecuador", *Latin American Perspectives*, Vol. 38, No. 1, pp. 47–62. Available HTTP: https://doi.org/10.1177/0094582X10384209.

Bidet, É. (2003) "L'insoutenable grand écart de l'économie sociale. Isomorphisme institutionnel et économie solidaire", *Revue du MAUSS*, Vol. 21, No. 1, pp. 162–178. Available HTTP: https://doi.org/10.3917/rdm.021.0162.

Blake, C. H. & Morris, S. D. (2009) *Corruption and Democracy in Latin America*, Pittsburgh: University of Pittsburgh Press.

Calvo, S. & Morales, A. (2013) "The social and solidarity economy in Ecuador: Opportunities and challenges", Working Paper, Quito: Living in Minca. Available HTTP: http://base.socioeco.org/docs/minca_ecuador.pdf.

Castelao Caruana, M. E. & Srnec, C. C. (2012) "Public policies addressed to the social and solidarity economy in South America: Toward a new model?", *Voluntas: International Journal of Voluntary and Nonprofit Organizations*, Vol. 24, No. 3, pp. 713–732. Available HTTP: https://doi.org/10.1007/s11266-012-9276-y.

Clark, A. K. & Becker, M. (2007) "Indigenous peoples and state formation in modern Ecuador", in Clark, A. K. & Becker, M. (eds) *Highland Indians and the State in Modern Ecuador*, Pittsburgh, PA: University of Pittsburgh Press, pp. 1–21.

Coque Martínez, J. (2001) "El cooperativismo rural en zonas desfavorecidas: una panorámica de los orígenes y situación actual en África, Asia y los antiguos países socialistas del este de Europa", *Cuadernos de Desarrollo Rural*, No. 47, Pontificia Universidad Javeriana.

Coraggio, J. L. (1999) "La economía popular es más que la suma de microproyectos", *Política y Sociedad*, Vol. 31, pp. 133–141.

Coraggio, J.-L. (2015) "L'économie sociale et solidaire et son institutionnalisation en Amérique latine : cinq pays, cinq processus", *Revue Française de Socio-Économie*, Vol. 15, No. 1, pp. 233–252. Available HTTP: https://doi.org/10.3917/rfse.015.0233

Coraggio, J. L., Eynaud, P., Ferrarini, A., de França Filho, G. C., Gaiger, L. I., Hillenkamp, I. & Wanderley, F. (2015) "The theory of social enterprise and pluralism: Solidarity-type social enterprise", in Laville, J-L., Young, D. R. & Eynaud, P. (eds) *Civil Society, the Third Sector and Social Enterprise: Governance and Democracy*, London and New York: Routledge, pp. 234–249.

Coraggio, J. L. & Laville, J-L. (eds) (2014) *Reinventar la izquierda en el siglo XXI: hacia un diálogo Norte-Sur*, Los Polvorines: Universidad Nacional de General Sarmiento.

Da Ros, G. (2007) "El movimiento cooperativo en el Ecuador. Visión histórica, situación actual y perspectivas", *CIRIEC-España, Revista de Economía Pública, Social y Cooperativa*, No. 50, pp. 249–284.

De la Torre, C. & Ortiz Lemos, A. (2015) "Populist polarization and the slow death of democracy in Ecuador", *Democratization*, Vol. 23, No. 2, pp. 221–241. Available HTTP: https://doi.org/10.1080/13510347.2015.1058784.

Defourny, J. & Nyssens, M. (2012) "The EMES approach of social enterprise in a comparative perspective", *EMES Working Papers*, No. 12/03, EMES Network.

Defourny, J. & Nyssens, M. (2017) "Fundamentals for an international typology of social enterprise models", *Voluntas: International Journal of Voluntary and Nonprofit Organizations*, Vol. 28, No. 6, pp. 2469–2497.

Disney, J. L. & Williams, V. S. (2014) "Latin American social movements and a new left consensus: State and civil society challenges to neoliberal globalization", *New Political Science*, Vol. 36, No. 1, pp. 1–31. Available HTTP: https://doi.org/10.1080/07393148.2013.864897.

Ellner, S. (2012) "The distinguishing features of Latin America's new left in power: The Chavez, Morales, and Correa governments", *Latin American Perspectives*, Vol. 39, No. 1, pp. 96–114. Available HTTP: https://doi.org/10.1177/0094582X11425333.

Escobar, A. (2010) "Latin America at a crossroads: Alternative modernizations, post-liberalism, or post-development?" *Cultural Studies*, Vol. 24, No. 1, pp. 1–65. Available HTTP: https://doi.org/10.1080/09502380903424208.

Espinosa, B. (2010) *Agir dans une pluralité de mondes: le cas du commerce équitable en Équateur*, Louvain-la-Neuve: Presses universitaires de Louvain.

Ettlinger, N. & Hartmann, C. D. (2015) "Post/neo/liberalism in relational perspective", *Political Geography*, Vol. 48, pp. 37–48. Available HTTP: https://doi.org/10.1016/j.polgeo.2015.05.009.

Evans, M. & Syrett, S. (2007) "Generating social capital? The social economy and local economic development", *European Urban and Regional Studies*, Vol. 14, No. 1, pp. 55–74. Available HTTP: https://doi.org/10.1177/0969776407072664.

Gordon, M. (2015) "A typology of social enterprise 'Traditions'", *Working Paper*, No. 18, p. 36. Available HTTP: http://iap-socent.be/sites/default/files/Theory%20-%20Gordon.pdf.

Gudynas, E. (2011) "Buen Vivir: Today's tomorrow", *Development*, Vol. 54, No. 4, pp. 441–447. Available HTTP: https://doi.org/10.1057/dev.2011.86.

Gui, B. (1991) "The economic rationale for the 'third sector'", *Annals of Public and Cooperative Economics*, Vol. 62, No. 4, pp. 551–572. Available HTTP: https://doi.org/10.1111/j.1467-8292.1991.tb01367.x.

Habermas, J. (1986) *L'espace public: Archéologie de la publicité comme dimension constitutive de la société bourgeoise* (M. de Launay, Trans.), Paris: Payot.

Hess, M. (2004) "'Spatial' relationships? Towards a reconceptualization of embeddedness", *Progress in Human Geography*, Vol. 28, No. 2, pp. 165–186. Available HTTP: https://doi.org/10.1191/0309132504ph479oa.

Hillenkamp, I. (2009) "Formes d'intégration de l'économie dans les démocraties de marché: une théorie substantive à partir de l'étude du mouvement d'économie solidaire dans la ville d'El Alto (Bolivie)", doctoral dissertation, Geneva: Université de Genève.

Hillenkamp, I., Lapeyre, F. & Lemaître, A. (2013) *Securing Livelihoods: Informal Economy Practices and Institutions*, Oxford: Oxford University Press.

Hübenthal, D. (1987) "Ecuador", *Perspectiva Económica*, Vol. 22, No. 57, pp. 311–360.

Intriago, R., Gortaire, R., Bravo, E. & O'Connell, C. (2017) "Agroecology in Ecuador: historical processes, achievements, and challenges", *Agroecology and Sustainable Food Systems*, Vol. 41, No. 3–4, pp. 311–328. Available HTTP: https://doi.org/10.1080/21683565.2017.1284174

Jácome, H., Ferraro, E. & Sánchez, J. (2004) *Microfinanzas en la economía ecuatoriana: una alternativa para el desarrollo*, Quito: FLACSO.

Jácome, H. & Ruiz-Rivera, M. J. (2013) "El sector económico popular y solidario en Ecuador: Diagnóstico y modelo de supervisión", in Intendencia de Estadísticas y Estudios (ed.) *Estudios sobre Economía Popular y Solidaria*, Quito: SEPS, pp. 101–144.

Kervyn de Lettenhove, M. & Lemaître, A. (2018) "Micro-entreprises du secteur informel dans le Mono (Bénin): vers un approfondissement à travers une approche d'économie populaire", *Mondes en développement*, Vol. 181, No. 1, pp. 11-25. Available HTTP: https://doi.org/10.3917/med.181.0011

Laville, J-L. (2005) "Action publique et économie : un cadre d'analyse", in Laville, J-L., Magnen, J-P., De França Filho, G. C. & Medeiros, A. (eds) *Action publique et économie solidaire*, Ramonville Saint-Agne: Érès, pp. 17–46.

Lemaître, A. (2009) *Organisations d'économie sociale et solidaire. Lecture de réalités Nord et Sud à travers l'encastrement politique et une approche plurielle de l'économie*, Louvain-la-Neuve: Presses universitaires de Louvain.

Lemaître, A. & Helmsing, A. H. J. (2012) "Solidarity economy in Brazil: Movement, discourse and practice analysis through a Polanyian understanding of the economy", *Journal of International Development*, Vol. 24, No. 6, pp. 745–762. Available HTTP: https://doi.org/10.1002/jid.2865.

Lemaître, A., Richer, M. & França Filho, G. (2011) "L'économie solidaire face à l'État en Amérique latine: Les dynamiques contrastées du Brésil et du Venezuela", *Tiers-Monde*, Vol. 208, No. 4, pp. 159–175. Available HTTP: https://doi.org/10.3917/rtm.208.0159.

Mills, N. (1989) "El cooperativismo en el Ecuador", in *Cooperativismo Latinoamericano: antecedentes y perspectivas*, Santiago de Chile: CEPAL, Comisión económica para América latina y el Caribe (CEPAL), p. 371.

Miño, W. (2013) *Historia del cooperativismo en el Ecuador*, Quito: Ministerio de coordinación de la Política Económica.

Molyneux, M. (2008) "The 'Neoliberal Turn' and the new social policy in Latin America: How neoliberal, How new? The neoliberal turn and the new social policy in Latin America", *Development and Change*, Vol. 39, No. 5, pp. 775–797. Available HTTP: https://doi.org/10.1111/j.1467-7660.2008.00505.x.

Muriel, P. (2012) "Cambio de época, la Economía Popular y Solidaria y el Sector Financiero Popular y Solidario tienen su propia ley", *Actuar En Mundos Plurales*, Vol. 8, pp. 27–28.

Nelms, T. C. (2015) "The problem of delimitation: Parataxis, bureaucracy, and Ecuador's popular and solidarity economy", *Journal of the Royal Anthropological Institute*, Vol. 21, No. 1, pp. 106–126. Available HTTP: https://doi.org/10.1111/1467-9655.12149.

Oleas, J. (2016) "La economía social y solidaria en el Ecuador: una mirada institucional", in Rhon, F. (ed.) *Economía solidaria. Historias y prácticas de su fortalecimiento*, Quito: SEPS, Vol. 4, pp. 51–81.

Polanyi, K. (1944) *The Great Transformation*, New York: Farrar & Rinehart.

Ramírez, R. (2008) *Igualmente pobres, desigualmente ricos*, Quito: Programa de las Naciones Unidas para el Desarrollo.

Razeto, L. (1984) *Economía de solidaridad y mercado democrático*, Santiago de Chile: PET.

Ruiz-Rivera, M. J. (2014) "El sistema de Caja Común y el cooperativismo", *Apunte*, No. 1, Quito: Superintendencia de Economía Popular y Solidaria, p. 14. Available HTTP: www.seps.gob.ec/c/document_library/get_file?uuid=94b227c9-8a8f-447f-8895-c503b3337b06&groupId=613016.

Ruiz-Rivera, M. J. & Lemaître, A. (2017) "Institutionnalisation de l'économie populaire et solidaire en Équateur: une lecture historique de l'encastrement politique des organisations", *Mondes en développement*, Vol. 179, No. 3, pp. 137–152. Available HTTP: https://doi.org/10.3917/med.179.0137.

Salamon, L. M. & Anheier, H. K. (1998) "Social origins of civil society: Explaining the nonprofit sector cross-nationally", *Voluntas: International Journal of Voluntary and Nonprofit Organizations*, Vol. 9, No. 3, pp. 213–248. Available HTTP: https://doi.org/10.1023/A:1022058200985.

Sarria Icaza, A. M. & Tiriba, L. (2006) "Économie populaire", in Laville, J-L. & Cattani, A. D. (eds) *Dictionnaire de l'autre économie*, Paris: Gallimard, pp. 258–268.

Scarlato, M. (2013) "Social enterprise, capabilities and development paradigms: Lessons from Ecuador", *Journal of Development Studies*, Vol. 49, No. 9, pp. 1270–1283. Available HTTP: https://doi.org/10.1080/00220388.2013.790962.

SEPS (2018) "Una mirada al desarrollo de la economía popular y solidaria", *Boletín*, No. 12, Quito: Superintendencia de Economía Popular y Solidaria, p. 10. Available HTTP: www.seps.gob.ec/documents/20181/455927/Boletín+SEPS+12.pdf/b552608c-d049-442e-a4d3-f14131223cde?version=1.0.

Singer, P. (2000) "Economía dos setores populares: proposta e desafio", in Kraychete, G. & Costa Lara, B. (eds) *Economia dos setores populares: entre a realidade e a utopia*, Petrópolis: Vozes.

Stoessel, S. (2014) "Giro a la izquierda en la América Latina del siglo XXI: Revisitando los debates académicos", *Polis* (Santiago), Vol. 13, No. 39, pp. 123–149. Available HTTP: https://doi.org/10.4067/S0718-65682014000300007.

Wanderley, F., Sostres, F. & Farah, I. (2015) *La economía solidaria en la economía plural. Discursos, prácticas y resultados en Bolivia*, La Paz: Plural Editores.

Yates, J. S. & Bakker, K. (2014) "Debating the 'post-neoliberal turn' in Latin America", *Progress in Human Geography*, Vol. 38, No. 1, pp. 62–90. Available HTTP: https://doi.org/10.1177/0309132513500372.

6 Social Enterprise in Mexico
Origins, Models and Perspectives

Sergio Páramo-Ortiz

Introduction

Although the term "social enterprise" (*empresa social*) is not commonly used by the general public in Mexico, in the last decade, some actors from different sectors of society—including a few government entities, a growing number of universities, researchers and organisations from the private and third sectors—have increasingly incorporated it into their agendas and in their official communication, publications, reports and calls.

Fieldwork shows that, although no consensus exists about the meaning of the term, these actors largely coincide on two common attributes of the entities embodying it. First, in one way or another, all social enterprises aim to contribute to solving social and/or environmental problems. Secondly, they also aim to generate the majority of their income through an economic activity. However, when asked about the types of organisation that embody these two attributes, actors refer to different kinds of initiatives; these differences are mainly rooted in the different schools of thought—or, in other words, to the different stances from which the various types of entities operationalise their solutions to social/environmental issues.

Other concepts sharing certain attributes with that of social enterprise (SE) are also present in the country, such as the concepts of impact business (*negocio de alto impacto*) (INADEM 2013), social business (*negocio social*) (Yunus Centre 2014), social entrepreneurship (*emprendimiento social*) (Conway and Dávila 2018; Portales 2018), community enterprise (*empresa comunitaria*) (Orozco-Quintero and Davidson-Hunt 2010), social economy (*economía social*) (Conde Bonfil 2016) and solidarity economy (*economía solidaria*) (Oulhaj 2015).

This diversity in terms of nomenclature and understandings around the social-enterprise concept is also tangible in academic research produced on this topic. Conde Bonfil (2013, 2016), in a pioneering research, approached the analysis of social enterprise from a social-economy perspective, more specifically analysing the relevance of the legal framework for the social economy in Mexico. Vázquez-Maguirre and Portales (2014) addressed the topic from an indigenous perspective, analysing the

DOI: 10.4324/9780429055164-8

mechanisms implemented by indigenous social enterprises to support the sustainable development of their communities. Orozco-Quintero and Davidson-Hunt (2010) analysed social enterprise from the perspective of the commons and their relation to indigenous enterprises. Wulleman and Hudon (2016) used the typology put forward by Zahra *et al.* (2009) to classify social entrepreneurships in Mexico. More recently, seventeen authors, coordinated by Conway and Dávila (2018), addressed the topic from the perspective of social entrepreneurship, developing a compendium of the multifaceted expressions of the phenomenon in Mexico.

The diversity of understandings is also visible in non-academic research and public communication from government entities. With a view to disclosing the causes that lead Mexican social enterprises to fail, the Failure Institute (2017) analysed social enterprises using the conceptual framework put forward by the Schwab Foundation for Social Entrepreneurship (2016). This approach, which is built around individuals combining traditional business practices with innovation and accountability practices to address other people's social problems, is contrasting with the official communication of the National Institute of the Social Economy (*Instituto Nacional de la Economía Social*, or INAES), which also uses the term "social enterprise" but to refer to those enterprises rooted in the social economy (see chapter 7 in the present volume).

As a consequence of the above, a heterogeneous understanding of the social-enterprise term and of those related prevails in Mexico, and studies, reports, books and peer-reviewed publications on this organisational phenomenon uphold a collection of diverse—and, in some cases, contrasting—visions of what social enterprises represent, and of the types of economic and social activities they are meant to perform.

The general social and economic background in Mexico is that of an increasingly adverse national context. Among the many problems, the most pressing ones are the immovable high rates of multidimensional poverty, with 53.4 out of 122.5 million people living under the poverty line (CONEVAL 2016); the high rates of income inequality and other types of inequalities, which place Mexico in the first quartile at global level in terms of income inequality (Esquivel 2015); the stagnating and precarious salaries, with more than half of the wage-earning population living under the monetary poverty line; and the loss of purchasing power of the salaries (between 2012 and 2017, the purchasing power of workers with a university degree decreased by 14.4%; see Teruel *et al.* 2018). On top of that, the violence associated to drug cartels—and which some observers link to the government's controversial anti-drug strategy—skyrocketed; it reached a peak in 2017, with 70 murders a day on average; in total, between 2007 and 2018, the death of almost 250,000 people could be linked to confrontations among drug cartels and between these and the army (Tierrablanca and Lara 2018). Finally, the high rates of corruption in the government, at all levels, place Mexico among the 20 countries with the most corrupt public officers, out of 102 countries analysed in a large study on this topic (World Justice Project's Research Team 2015). Paradoxically, Mexico is today the fifteenth largest economy in the world in terms of GDP, with an average annual growth rate of 2.37% in the last two decades (World Bank 2018).

The objective of this chapter is to go beyond the observed diversity of terminology and understandings to present some major SE models which coexist in Mexico. Using an empirical approach, the chapter attempts to better understand these models from the point of view of both their organisational dimension and their institutional context. The analysis builds on primary data from 45 semi-structured interviews conducted with stakeholders of the SE sector; it also relies on secondary data, composed by publicly available grey and peer-reviewed literature, and material handed over by the interviewees. Based on the analysis of these data, four SE types appear to emerge prominently in Mexico:

- private enterprises owned and controlled by social entrepreneurs who rely on innovation to create a product or a service with the objective of addressing a social issue through a market-based business model;
- collective organisations with a land-based identity, which originate from and are embedded in the social structure of indigenous communities;
- non-profit organisations that develop economic activities to complement their sources of income;
- collective organisations that operate under the principles and values of the social economy, and which emerge from a collective effort of a group of members with the primary purpose of creating social benefits for themselves.

The organisational attributes of the first three models are drawn using the three dimensions of the EMES "ideal type" of SE (Defourny and Nyssens 2012); in other words, each model is characterised from the point of view of its social, economic/entrepreneurial and governance dimensions. Each model's institutional context is also depicted, tracing back the institutional forces behind its emergence in Mexico and around its current state of existence. Finally, the challenges, limitations and threats that each model faces are exposed. The fourth model, i.e. the one linked to the social economy, is analysed in the next chapter, by Conde Bonfil and Oulhaj.[1]

1. Market-Oriented Social Businesses

In Mexico, three understandings of the "market-oriented social business" approach can be identified: the "Yunus-inspired social business" understanding, the "impact business/social start-up" understanding and the "B Corp" understanding. The different meanings are compared in table 6.1.

Table 6.1 Market-oriented social businesses' understandings in Mexico

	Impact business/social start-up	Yunus-inspired social business	B Corp
Year of emergence in Mexico	2012	2014/2018	2016
Main promoters in Mexico	INADEM, Socialab Mexico, New Ventures and Intituto Irrazonable, among others.	Social Business Summit (2014), UABC-YUNUS Centre (2018) and Yunus Innovation Pathway Centre of the University of Monterrey (2018)	Sistema B
Business model	Private enterprises owned and controlled by social entrepreneurs who rely on innovation to create a product, service or business model that both: • aims to address an environmental issue or the social need of a vulnerable group of society; and • aims to be commercially viable in the marketplace. The maximisation of profits is not restricted (but not necessarily desired) as long as the maximisation of social impact is also pursued.	In Mexico, Yunus centres support two types of models. • Type 1: micro-businesses owned and operated by disadvantaged/poor families. The support provided aims to help them to maximise their business profitability as a strategy to improve the household's economic situation, and potentially lift the family out of poverty. Therefore, profit maximisation is desired. • Type 2: private companies that provide a social benefit to a disadvantaged group through the provision of products or services in the market. These companies follow the principle of "no loss, no dividend", and therefore profit distribution to owners is restricted.	There is no specific business model promoted by the Sistema B network. Its approach rather focuses on encouraging (social or traditional) enterprises to create positive impacts in the community and the environment and on the employees through the enterprise's day-to-day operations. Through an impact measurement system, enterprises can obtain the "B Corp" certification, which differentiates them from traditional enterprises in the marketplace. This certification also links them together into the Sistema B network. Profit distribution to owners is not restricted.

Source: Compiled by the author.

Such social enterprises are private businesses created by a (group of) social entrepreneur(s) operating under the market conventions and who aim primarily to contribute to solving a social or environmental issue through the commercialisation of a product or a service. In such perspective, the terms "social enterprise" and "social entrepreneur" are closely linked. The process of designing, prototyping and then validating in the field the effectiveness of the product or service proposed by the social entrepreneur is known as social entrepreneurship. This last term is sometimes used as a synonym of that of social enterprise. Yet, for others, "social entrepreneurship" does not necessarily incorporate a commercial dimension.

1.1. Context and Origin

In the last decade, a booming network of organisations supporting this type of social enterprise has emerged in Mexico. The pioneer in this regard was Ashoka, which started operating in the country in 1987, introducing the "social entrepreneurship" concept such as it is understood by Bill Drayton. In 2004, New Ventures (NV), originally from the USA, established itself in Mexico with the aim to provide support to environmentally driven businesses. In 2006, inspired by Prahalad's book (Prahalad 2006), NV broadened its scope to support socially oriented businesses. In the following years, an array of other national and foreign actors (mostly from the US) emerged or started operating in Mexico. Between 1987 and 2018, some 30 organisations—umbrella organisations, networks, platforms, impact-investment funds, incubators, consultancy firms, knowledge networks and specialised media—appeared in the country. Organically, they configured themselves as a support network for social entrepreneurs. Today, they fulfil the functions of an SE ecosystem.

Academia has also played an important role in the shaping of the field. In the last decade, top universities have actively joined the ecosystem, creating social-business labs, academic programmes, research centres and even whole new teaching divisions, such as the School of Social Entrepreneurs of the National Autonomous University of Mexico, set up in 2012. In 2001, the Monterrey Institute of Technology and Higher Education (ITESM) joined, as a founding member, the Social Enterprise Knowledge Network (SEKN)—a research network initiated by Prof. James E. Austin from the Harvard Business School that brings together business schools from leading universities of Ibero-America. In 2018, two Yunus centres opened in the north of Mexico (University of Monterrey and University of Baja California).

As far as governmental institutions are concerned, in 2012, the federal government created, through the Ministry of Economy, the National Institute of the Entrepreneur (*Instituto Nacional del Emprendedor*, or INADEM). Bringing in a different vision of support to micro and small enterprises, the government's new approach shifted from support to entrepreneurship by sector to support by type of enterprise. Following this line, the INADEM issued the first call for high-impact entrepreneurship (*emprendimiento de alto impacto*), defined as:

> [a] company that has a double-nature scalable business model, which means that, on the one hand, it pursues an economic goal (generation of wealth and employment) and, on the other hand, it seeks a social, environmental or cultural benefit (generation of values, meaning and identities). [High-impact entrepreneurship initiatives] are globally replicable business models based on innovation (being this component a distinctive trait of their sector). [High-impact entrepreneurship] generates 360-degree value for its partners, workers, customers and the community.
>
> INADEM (2013)

This active involvement of the government through INADEM legitimised, for the first time, the nascent sector into the public agenda through three different events: first, the conclusion of an agreement with Ashoka to create the first national-range government call specifically directed to social entrepreneurs; secondly, the commissioning of a study on social entrepreneurship to EY Mexico; and thirdly, the participation of INADEM—as host and partner—in the organisation of the Social Business Summit in 2014. In the following years, the INADEM supported annually an average of 150 organisations, reaching 172 in 2017 (INADEM 2017). When the new government took office, in December 2018, the new Minister for Economic Affairs announced that the INADEM would disappear but that support to entrepreneurs would be maintained; however, specific programmes for impact entrepreneurship have not been announced yet.

In 2015, Mexico joined the Global Steering Group for Impact Investment, and the Alliance for Impact Investment was created. Today, providers of a variety of equity instruments designed to support social enterprises keep emerging. In 2016, the Latin American counterpart of B Corps, Sistema B, opened a branch in Mexico, bringing a slightly different approach to social enterprise. Through an annual evaluation that can lead to a certification, the B Corps network encourages both traditional for-profit enterprises and social-purpose-driven businesses to pursue efforts to reduce their negative externalities in their day-to-day operations, while simultaneously encouraging positive impacts on key stakeholders. At the end of 2018, 31 certified B Corps operated in Mexico.

1.2. Social Mission and Economic Activities

Precise data about the number of market-oriented social businesses operating in Mexico are not available. However, a survey carried out by the

Aspen Network for Development Entrepreneurs (ANDE 2018) found 867 social ventures. Regarding economic activities, the main sectors in which social ventures were operating were: financial services (18% of enterprises), health (17%), agriculture (9%), education (8%), environment (7%) and information and communications technology (6%) (ANDE 2018). As for these enterprises' social mission, the following ones were observed: to generate employment (32% of enterprises), to increase productivity and income (29%), to foster community development (21%), to improve health (21%), to increase equality and empowerment (20%) and to improve access to financial services (19%) (*ibid.*).

1.3. Ownership and Governance

The governance structure of this type of SE is shaped by the interplay of different elements.

The first and most important one is the commitment of the owner(s) towards fulfilling the social mission. In this regard, and although final decisions are usually made by the owners or the board of directors, incorporating stakeholder participation mechanisms into the decision-making processes is considered as highly desirable—and even seen as good practice—among social entrepreneurs.

Secondly, the legal conditions and obligations dictated by the legal form chosen by the initiative are also key elements. So far, no legal form specifically designed for social businesses has been created in Mexico. In the majority of cases, social businesses operate under a commercial legal form; some are registered under a non-profit legal form;[2] and a few others operate under a combination of a commercial and a non-profit legal forms (ANDE 2018).

Thirdly, any mission-protection mechanism can be voluntarily included in the organisation's articles of incorporation. Such governance mechanisms are being pioneered in Mexico by the B Corps system. The network indeed encourages their members to include two specific clauses into their legal statutes: the first clause secures the statement of either a social mission or a business mission that incorporates efforts aimed at impacting positively and tangibly the environment or society; the second clause requests that the board of directors consider the potential negative externalities of the enterprise's operations over an array of stakeholders, including employees, the environment and clients (Sistema B 2018). Social enterprises may also implement specific guidelines to obtain and maintain other types of certification and/or support from external organisations/networks.

The last elements that might influence the governance structure are the terms, conditions and participation mechanisms of external capital investors, which vary depending on the financial instrument in place.

1.4. Challenges, Threats and Weaknesses

From the point of view of the availability of financial resources, some players in the ecosystem argue that, although financial mechanisms and portfolios for social enterprises are emerging today, there is still a long way to go as, on the one hand, traditional investors, who could potentially fund this type of venture, are still not aware of the possibility of or interested in investing in social enterprises and, on the other hand, most of the social ventures in Mexico are in a very early stage of development and are not yet ready to receive funding through financial instruments.

From an organisational perspective, the business and financial skills of those launching social ventures seem to be weak. Some accelerators and incubators report that they quite commonly receive applications submitted by social entrepreneurs with an "aversion to fly on their own" and that they have noticed that, for some social entrepreneurs, it seems to be easier to jump from incubator to incubator than to venture into the real market and reach financial sustainability.

From a governmental perspective, apart from INADEM (whose closure had been announced by the time this chapter was being written) and some regional agencies such as the Ministry of Innovation of Jalisco, the majority of (federal and regional) governmental agencies are unaware of the existence of this type of enterprise and therefore do not encourage the creation of favourable conditions for their growth.

From a legal perspective, most of the players agree that a specific legal form, tailored to the needs of social enterprises, is needed. Some advocate for the creation of a completely new legal form, while others believe that it would be easier to add some extra features to existing commercial forms in order to enable social enterprises to differentiate themselves on the market and to operate under a more favourable taxation scheme.

2. Indigenous Social Enterprises

Indigenous social enterprises, which are also known as indigenous communitarian enterprises, community-based enterprises or commons enterprises, are the result of a process through which an indigenous community creates and operates an enterprise embedded in its existing social structure (Orozco-Quintero and Davidson-Hunt 2010; Peredo and Chrisman 2006). The enterprise's management and governance support are aligned with the economic, social and political goals of the community (*ibid.*).

2.1. Context and Origin

Mexican indigenous social enterprises have long been extensively documented by academics. Special focus has been placed on indigenous coffee growers and forest management indigenous enterprises. Indigenous forestry enterprises emerged around the late 1970s, when indigenous communities, refusing the logging practices of the state and private companies, fiercely opposed the renovation of the private logging concessions and claimed their land rights (Antinori and Rausser 2010; Chapela 2012; PNUD 2012). This claim was made possible by the agrarian reform, a state-directed large transfer of forests rights to communities over the 20th century (Antinori and Bray 2005). In order to restore their land rights to the communities, the state created the "social property" regime, a special land tenure regime that differs from both private and public property (Reyes *et al.* 2012): whereas private property refers to land granted by the nation to individuals and public property refers to land owned by the state, social property refers to land that belongs to and is managed by communities (*ibid.*). Communities are of two types: *ejidos* (literally, "common land"), composed by peasant groups, and *comunidades* (literally, "communities"), composed by indigenous communities (Antinori and Rausser 2010). *Comunidades* cannot sell nor lease their land since it belongs to the community and it can only be farmed by the *comuneros*, i.e. the members of the community (Morett-Sánchez and Cosío-Ruiz 2017). It is estimated that there are 2,344 *comunidades* in Mexico (Reyes *et al.* 2012). Mexico is considered to be a virtually unique case in this regard, as this social property regime, which includes forests, jungles and shrubland, encompasses 48% of the nation's territory and represents 80% of Mexico's forests (Bray *et al.* 2003).

As for those indigenous social enterprises that produce coffee, many emerged as a counteractive response from indigenous communities to the abolition of the Mexican Coffee Institute (*Instituto Mexicano del Café*, or Inmecafé) in 1989 (Jaffee 2014). Inmecafé was a public agency that had been created in 1952 to provide support and protection from market forces to small coffee growers (*ibid.*). Although it brought about a rapid increase in the number of coffee producers, its paternalistic approach, together with corrupt practices, resulted in a high dependence and vulnerability of coffee growers (Alvarado 2009; Jaffee 2014). The dissolution of Inmecafé was triggered by the collapse of the International Coffee Agreement and by the adoption of neoliberal economic policies aiming to reduce the regulatory power of the state (Jaffee 2014; Vázquez-Maguirre 2012).

2.2. Social Mission and Economic Activities

The economic activities of indigenous forest enterprises primarily derive from community logging. A few very competitive enterprises have been able to vertically integrate sawmills and furniture and moulding workshops while operating under the Forest Stewardship Council certification (Bray *et al.* 2003). Some enterprises in the Oaxaca region, using profits from the logging activity, have diversified their economic activities, creating water bottling, ecotourism and resin-tapping companies (*ibid.*). Successful indigenous coffee producers, popular in the southern states of Mexico (Jaffee 2014), have set up over time processing, transportation and technical services, financial and commercialisation companies and, in some cases, coffee shops and eco-touristic centres (Vázquez-Maguirre *et al.* 2018). There are success stories among coffee producers, such as the Union of Indigenous Communities of the Isthmus Region (*Unión de Comunidades Indígenas de la Región del Istmo*, or UCIRI); this cooperative, working along with Frans Vanderhoff, participated in the creation of the Max Havelaar label, and thus became a precursor of the fair-trade movement worldwide (Alvarado 2009). UCIRI was created in 1983 with the participation of 17 villages; by 2009, there were more than 3,000 coffee growers affiliated, from 52 communities (*ibid.*).

Indigenous social enterprises have demonstrated that they are able to generate social, political, cultural and environmental benefits (PNUD 2012).

The social objective of these enterprises is to improve the living conditions in their communities (Berkes and Davidson-Hunt 2010). Such improvement mostly derives from the generation of employment (with better wages, access to benefits and permanent positions) and from investment made by the enterprise in public goods and infrastructure and in social welfare programmes (*ibid.*). At the regional level, strengthening and improving indigenous communitarian enterprises could help to bring down the migration rates of indigenous populations to the United States and the northern regions of Mexico (Vázquez-Maguirre *et al.* 2018).

Political benefits derive from the enterprise's capacity to secure, restore and preserve the indigenous community's commons, i.e. their land, their natural resources and their customary social relations—institutions, values and norms rooted in their territories (Berkes and Davidson-Hunt 2010; Orozco-Quintero and Davidson-Hunt 2010). There is evidence that the financial and social capital generated by some enterprises has helped to restore a relative social peace in the territories where these enterprises operate, which were previously exposed to violence linked to drugs and/or illegal logging (Bray *et al.* 2003).

Cultural benefits are associated to the preservation of the indigenous peoples' identity. This is fostered through the provision of training and education in the peoples' native languages. It can be also strengthened by counteracting external pressures that prompt the community to adopt utilitarian market values, such as giving higher value to individual production than to collective production or voting in favour of the privatisation of communal land instead of maintaining collectively the community's territory (Orozco-Quintero and Davidson-Hunt 2010).

Regarding environmental benefits, there is evidence that well-managed community forests, in which the logging activity is carried out by indigenous social enterprises in a sustainable way, can help to stabilise the forest cover in the community's territory, stop land-use change and contribute to broader biodiversity protection in the concerned territories (Bray *et al.* 2003).

2.3. Ownership and Governance

Indigenous enterprises' ownership is restricted to those who are officially considered as community members, normally by birth, and who also own the commonly held land and its resources. Such ownership thus differs from what can be observed in cooperatives, where membership is not tied to land tenure (Antinori and Bray 2005).

The governance of indigenous enterprises varies in structure and it is usually complex (Jaffee 2014). Due to the collective nature of these entities, which is coupled with their inherent function of managing a communal pool of resources, their governance configuration demands high levels of coordination and cooperation, frequently accompanied by high costs (Chapela 2012). Each particular governance arrangement reflects the community's quest to set up a local socio-economic optimum that goes far beyond achieving profitability or competitiveness in the marketplace and aims primarily to respond to the community's needs (Antinori and Bray 2005).

Indigenous enterprises' governance can either be "grafted" onto the community's governance framework or be independent from it (Bray *et al.* 2006). In the first case, all or an important part of the enterprise's decision and control processes occur inside the community's governance bodies, which are appointed by the Mexican Constitution: (1) the general assembly (*asamblea general*), where each registered community member has one vote, and decisions regarding general matters of community interest are taken; (2) the commission of common goods (*comisariado de bienes comunales*), which is in charge of executing the assembly's resolutions and of managing the community's territory and common goods; and (3) the surveillance council (*consejo de vigilancia*), which is in charge of auditing and monitoring the legality of the operations executed. In this type of governance, the community's governance and the enterprise's governance blend together, i.e. decisions regarding forestry activities, distribution of benefits, workloads, wage levels, sales, extraction, processing, etc. are taken at the community level (Antinori and Rausser 2010). In some cases, in parallel to the traditional governance structure, the community develops specialised bodies (such as a forestry council) to manage the productive activities more efficiently (Antinori and Rausser 2010). In the second type of governance, i.e. when the enterprise's governance is independent from the community's governance, working groups (*grupos de trabajo*) and individuals (*modo individual*) (Antinori and Rausser 2010) obtain specific rights to extract and manage limited parts of the community's logging forest. In this type of governance, the general assembly proportionally divides the community's annual authorised logging volume among the working groups and/or individual parcel holders (Antinori and Bray 2005). Then, each parcel holder (be it an individual or a group) contacts outside buyers and competes to get the best price (Antinori and Rausser 2010). These mechanisms tend to emerge as an alternative management plan to deal with the dissatisfaction with management of certain groups within the community (*ibid.*).

2.4. Challenges, Threats and Weaknesses

Most logging indigenous enterprises experience, to some degree, problems of corruption, lack of accountability, mismanagement, clandestine forest use, uncontrolled agricultural clearing and inefficient logging methods (Merino 1996). Tensions between hierarchy and community governance, between accountability and opacity and corruption, and between efficiency and traditional practices are among the most common problems (Antinori and Bray 2005). Local elites can exert "covert privatisation" of lands. Domination of communal institutions by elites through (violent) intimidation, elections' manipulation and threats are frequent as well (Klooster 1999).

This adverse panorama can be better understood by contextualising the current situation of indigenous peoples. In 2015, more than 12 million people (10.1% of the country's population) considered themselves as indigenous (CDI 2015). The majority (over 70%) speak at least one of the 68 indigenous languages present in Mexico (*ibid.*). These populations have structurally been placed in conditions of social, economic and political exclusion since colonial times (CONEVAL 2018; Quijano 2000); as a result hereof, today, more than 70% of them live in poverty or even in extreme poverty (CONEVAL 2018). Geographically, the majority of these populations are scattered in small and remote towns with poor communication (CDI 2015).

Not only have indigenous populations to overcome these challenging conditions, their social enterprises moreover need to operate in harmony with the community's social structure while simultaneously being competitive in the market and implementing locally designed institutional arrangements regarding management and governance (Antinori and Bray 2005).

3. Non-Profit Organisations with Economic Activities

The socio-political trajectory of Mexico from the 1980s onward appears relevant to understand the context of emergence of the so-called third sector, which includes, as will be shown, various types of civil-society organisations; it is also important to grasp the causes that may be leading some of these organisations to venture into market mechanisms to support their operations.

3.1. Context and Origin

The 1980s represented a turning point for the civil society in Mexico. At the beginning of this decade (in 1982), a severe financial crisis led the country to declare itself in default. Mexico, on the advice of the International Monetary Fund and the US government, then started its transition from a state-centred model of development to one that encouraged the liberalisation of the economy (Alberro 2010). This transition, which forced the state to reduce its social spending, also fractured the government's strong corporatism[3] that had prevailed in Mexico since the 1930s; this evolution resulted in turn in the emergence and quick multiplication of independent associations launched by civil society and seeking to engage into solidarity-related activities (Verduzco 2001). From the mid-1980s onward, due to the government's failure to respond adequately to the 8.1-magnitude earthquake that hit the country in 1985, many citizens organised themselves to respond to the tragedy by forming associations; this phenomenon fostered a sense of empowerment in society (Layton and Mossel 2015). At the end of the decade, the government in power (PRI Party) orchestrated a fraud in the national elections to maintain itself in power, and this triggered the emergence of civil-society organisations in the fields of human rights and democracy (*ibid.*).

During the 1990s, the country started to experience a slow democratic transition which brought about an increase in overall government tolerance towards the organisation of civil society, and which was followed in turn by an increase in citizens' participation in public life (Verduzco 2001). This context favoured the institutionalisation of the third sector (*ibid.*). The sector was first referred to as "organisations of promotion, assistance and development"; then, in the following decade, the terms "philanthropy" and "third sector" emerged and gradually started prevailing, as they better embraced the diversity of organisations composing the sector (Girardo and Mochi 2012; Verduzco 2001).

In the 2000s, after 70 years of rule by a hegemonic state-party, Mexico experienced for the first time political alternation. The new government developed a new approach to the third sector, unlocking the dialogue with several groups of civil society organisations which had been pushing for a legal framework during the previous eleven years. As a result of this, in 2003, the Federal Law for the Promotion of Activities Carried Out by Civil-Society Organisations (*Ley Federal de Fomento a las Actividades Realizadas por Organizaciones de la Sociedad Civil*, or LFFAROSC) (Aguilar Valenzuela 2006) was finally approved.

Despite the positive expectations raised by these developments, the third sector continued suffering from the same ills as in the past decades: the scarcity of financial support from the state and insufficient public policies to strengthen it (Natal and Sanchez 2013).

3.2. Social Mission and Economic Activities

The activities carried out by civil society organisations (CSOs) are plenty and very diverse. For explanatory purposes, in this chapter, CSOs in Mexico will be classified into "non-assistance CSOs" and "assistance CSOs". The former carry out religious, labour-related, political activities and other types of activity that are predominantly for-profit in nature but do not pursue commercial speculation, and they will not be taken into account in the analysis. The latter, by contrast, do not have a predominantly economic nature but are CSOs purposely created to improve the living conditions of vulnerable or at-risk populations or to pursue environmental causes.[4] Only these CSOs (i.e. "assistance CSOs") will be included in the analysis—and hereafter referred to simply as "CSOs".

In Mexico, the Federal Registry of Civil-Society Organisations maintains an annual record of the CSOs analysed in this chapter. In 2018, it registered 39,672 CSOs. The main activities of these organisations were: community development (37% of CSOs); promotion of an inclusive society and social cohesion (17%); culture, science and sport (16%); social assistance (15%); promotion of social and citizenship participation (8%); promotion of gender equality (5%); and civil protection (2%) (SEDESOL 2016). In this regard, it is possible to assert that CSOs are totally aligned with the EMES indicator that states that social enterprises have "an explicit aim to benefit the community" (Defourny and Nyssens 2012). As shown in table 6.2, CSOs can be created by a group of citizens but also by one citizen; it can thus be considered that CSOs only partially comply with the EMES indicator that states that social enterprises are "initiatives launched by a group of citizens or civil society". With respect to the indicator that states that social enterprises are characterised by "a limited profit distribution", CSOs do meet this indicator: indeed, they do not distribute profits, as the law obligates them to reinvest them all into the organisation.

Regarding CSOs' resource mix, few studies have investigated in detail how Mexican CSOs obtain their income. The latest information available is from Natal and Sanchez (2013) who, using data from the Mexican Centre for Philanthropy (*Centro Mexicano para la Filantropía*, or CEMEFI), show that CSOs in Mexico rely predominantly on self-generated streams of income, which represent between 73% and 80% of their total income. The rest comes from three other sources: public funding, that represents between 15 and 20% of CSOs' resources; corporate funding, which represents between 10 and 12%; and societal funding, which accounts for less than 10% (Natal and Sanchez 2013). Self-generated streams of income are composed mostly by fees paid by members and/or affiliates as well as by revenue from the provision of services to the beneficiaries (*ibid.*). Although these activities are not market-based/oriented, they represent together the major monetary source of income for CSOs; consequently,

Table 6.2 Legal forms, purpose and governance of CSOs in Mexico

Legal form	Purpose	Governance
Civil association (*Asociación Civil*, or AC)	Organisation created by a (group of) citizen(s) with a common interest. This interest has a non-lucrative nature. The organisation can generate economic income, but such income must be totally reinvested in the organisation.	Individual or collective administrative board composed of a director or directors. Each board member has one vote; decisions are taken by a majority vote.
Private-assistance institution (*Institución de Asistencia Privada*, or IAP)	Organisations created by a (group of) citizen(s) with the purpose of providing social assistance to individuals, families or populations that are vulnerable or at risk. The organisation can generate economic income, but such income must be totally reinvested in the organisation.	The founder(s) has/have the right to determine the services and activities of the IAP. IAPs can be managed directly by the founder(s), or by a board of trustees (*Patronato*), composed of at least five persons and appointed by the founder(s). Each trustee has one vote, and decisions in the board of trustees are taken by a majority vote.

Source: Prepared by the author, based on DOF (2012) and GODF (2014).

in the long run, CSOs' financial viability is directly linked to their capacity to self-generate resources of this type. This dominant economic and entrepreneurial dimension of Mexican CSOs aligns closely with the first two EMES indicators about the economic dimension of social enterprise (Defourny and Nyssens 2012). Indeed, CSOs in Mexico rely mostly on income from their continuous activity of provision of services to people and not from donations or public funding, which is in line with the EMES indicator stating that social enterprises have "a continuous activity producing goods and/or selling services". And the financial viability of CSOs directly depends on their capacity to self-generate resources, which is in tune with the EMES indicator about social enterprises assuming "a significant level of economic risk" to achieve financial viability, which ultimately depends on the capacity of their staff (volunteers and paid workers) to secure adequate resources.

Regarding the third EMES indicator about the economic dimension of social enterprise (Defourny and Nyssens 2012), which states that social enterprises should have "a minimum amount of paid work", data from the Satellite Account of Non-profit Institutions of Mexico (*Cuenta*

Satélite de las Instituciones sin Fines de Lucro de México, or CSIFLM) show that, from the total staff (paid workers and volunteers) that worked in CSOs in 2016, 74.1% (1,979,000) were volunteers, hence 25.9% were paid. In this regard, it can thus also be said that CSOs meet this indicator, as they do have paid workers.

The fulfilment of the aforementioned EMES indicators (Defourny and Nyssens 2012) by Mexican CSOs shows that, from the point of view of the economic and social dimensions, CSOs behave in the field very similarly to social enterprises. In order to assert if CSOs fulfil the three dimensions of the EMES indicators (*ibid.*), the governance dimension will be explored in the following section (3.3).

Aside from CSOs that behave similarly to social enterprises, there are also other cases—though fewer in numbers—in which CSOs realise that their expertise in the provision of services to disadvantaged people has the potential to become a highly valued service in the market, and they decide to engage in market activities as a new way to generate more resources to increase their social impact. The pros and cons of this approach are exposed below, in section 3.4.

3.3. Ownership and Governance

As was explained in the previous section (3.2), "non-assistance CSOs" and "assistance CSOs" coexist in Mexico, but they serve different purposes in society. Within the first group, in addition to those that serve religious, labour-related and political purposes, there are others that serve economic-related not-speculative purposes; since they are for-profit organisations, these initiatives, which are operating under the legal form of general partnerships (*sociedad civil*, or SC), will not be reviewed in this chapter. As for assistance CSOs, as already underlined above, they serve predominantly social or environmental purposes, and therefore, the study of their legal forms and governance mechanisms are of interest for the present chapter. Assistance CSOs (i.e., as previously explained, the CSOs taken into account in our analysis) operate under the civil association (AC) or the private-assistance institution (IAP) legal forms, due to the non-predominantly economic nature of their *raison d'être* (see table 6.2).

The legal forms analysed in table 6.2 reveal that CSOs are aligned to a large extent with two of the EMES indicators about SE governance (Defourny and Nyssens 2012): First, CSOs enjoy a high degree of autonomy. They are created by a group of people on the basis of an autonomous project, and they are governed by these people. Secondly, CSOs' decision-making power is not based on capital ownership, but on the "one board member, one vote" principle. In this regard, the only exception would be those CSOs that are created by one person: indeed, IAPs that are created by one person can be governed by their founder.

It can thus be concluded that CSOs in Mexico behave in the field in a way that is very close to the EMES ideal type of social enterprise.

3.4. *Challenges, Threats and Weaknesses*

CSOs in Mexico face an environment that is not very favourable to their growth and development. The National Survey on Philanthropy and Civil Society (Layton and Moreno 2013) revealed that 43% of the participants[5] did not trust organisations that ask for donations. When asked how they preferred to help/donate to others, 82% of interviewees said that they preferred to donate directly to people in need, and only 10% stated that they preferred to donate through an organisation. These and other results of the survey reveal that the sector does not enjoy the confidence of Mexican society.

Regarding public support, using the metrics from the Johns Hopkins Comparative Non-Profit Sector Project (Salamon *et al.* 1999), Layton and Mossel (2015) point out that in Mexico, the share of public funding in CSOs' resources is only half of the average for Latin America, and about one fifth of the average at the global level. Moreover, Mexico's tax system is complex, which requires CSOs to invest a great amount of resources into fulfilling fiscal requirements. From a regulatory perspective, critics underline that much of the legislation dates back to the 19th century and is thus outdated, and that it is scattered among federal and state-level regulatory schemes (*ibid.*).

The CSOs that realise that their expertise could be a highly valued service in the market and could thus potentially generate a new stream of income, with an important leverage effect on their social impact, face a legal dilemma. Indeed, they can either abandon their non-profit legal form and start operating under a for-profit form in order to venture into the provision of services for non-vulnerable populations (clients) and use that new stream of income to increase their social impact, with the drawback of losing their legal right to obtain donations from third parties, financial and technical support from the government and tax deductions. Or they can create a "parallel" for-profit enterprise, which they will use to provide services in the market, while maintaining, through the NPO, their legal rights to receive donations from third parties and support from the government. In this situation, the drawback is linked to the necessity to manage two structures, i.e. to file a double tax return, to support double operating costs and to hire specialised staff to manage the commercial enterprise.

Conclusion

In this chapter, it is argued that, beyond the diversity of terminology and understandings around the social-enterprise term, four salient models of social enterprise coexist in Mexico today, namely: market-oriented social businesses, indigenous social enterprises, non-profit organisations with economic activities and social-economy enterprises. As this last model is developed in the following chapter, it is not addressed in the present conclusion.

Institutional backgrounds differ greatly from one model to the other. The communitarian origins of indigenous enterprises, which are rooted in rural and indigenous environments, highly contrast with the more individual origins of market-oriented social businesses, which predominantly emerge within urban environments. The different models also emerged at different times and in different regions of the country. The emergence of the network that supports the market-oriented social-business model is recent, and this model's boom has been observed predominantly in Mexico City and Guadalajara City; by contrast, the first indigenous social enterprises were formed more than 40 years ago, and they are scattered throughout the country in indigenous settlement with forest territories.

Contrasting differences can be also found among the different models in terms of types of governance and social objectives pursued. Indigenous enterprises are mutual-interest organisations, embedded in the communities where they operate and managed by their beneficiaries. They collectively pursue the improvement of the living conditions of their members through an approach that is respectful of their customary social norms. These organisations emerge as a collective response to structural constraints. Market-oriented social businesses and non-profit organisations with economic activities aim to improve the living conditions of disadvantaged people on very specific aspects, such as access to education, clean water, housing or health services. These organisations are not managed by their beneficiaries but by people with access to more resources and opportunities than the majority of the population and who are aware of the alarming level of socio-economic inequalities in Mexico.

The different models also differ in terms of the extent to which they are "in tune" with the economic order of the country. The nascent market-oriented social-business sector—whose organisations are controlled and owned by one person or by a board of directors—seems to fit more easily into the predominant neoliberal economic model of Mexico, which favours international trade openness and the liberalisation of key sectors of the economy. Market-oriented social businesses are increasingly looking for capital investment through financial mechanisms as a way to scale up and grow more rapidly, as traditional start-ups would do but, unlike their private counterparts, some social businesses are experimenting with "social-mission-lock" mechanisms to ensure the continued prevalence of their social mission in the future. The evolution of market-oriented social enterprises towards more start-up-like behaviours may be part of the reason why social enterprises of this type seem to be very appealing to the Mexican millennial generation. Indeed, this model seems legitimate enough to fit the economic order, but also disruptive enough to challenge the traditional forms of addressing social or environmental issues. In this perspective, the question of developing a legal form adapted to their hybrid nature appears as a major challenge.

Indigenous enterprises seem to be the most distant from the predominant economic order, as they actively counteract the external pressure towards adopting utilitarian market values, and they favour democratic decision-making processes within their governance mechanisms. The structural conditions of exclusion in which the indigenous peoples have lived since colonial times seem to be the greatest barrier for their enterprises to fully integrate into the predominant economic order in Mexico. Internal issues such as corruption, lack of accountability, mismanagement, clandestine forest uses, uncontrolled agricultural clearing and inefficient logging methods can also raise doubts about their legitimacy.

As for non-profit organisations with economic activities, the lack of trust on the part of society, the scarcity of financial support from the government, an outdated and scattered legislative framework and a complex tax system seem to keep these organisations trapped in an institutional limbo, preventing them from expanding their participation in addressing social issues.

By the time this chapter was being written, a new national government had just taken office. After more than 80 years of right-wing governments, Mexico is experiencing for the first time a left-wing government, with a progressive agenda at the national level. Radical changes, with potential impact on these three types of enterprise and their contexts, may be just around the corner.

Notes

1 It has to be noted that the boundaries between the various models are sometimes blurred. In particular, two of the subtypes of SE described by Conde Bonfil and Oulhaj in chapter 7, and which would thus be included in this fourth model, are *"ejidos"* and *"communities"*, which are both collective organisations with a land-based identity and are also described here, in section 2.

2 Commercial legal forms available to social businesses are those of limited company (*Sociedad Anónima*, or SA), joint-stock company (*Sociedad por Acciones Simplificada*, or SAS) and public limited investment company (*Sociedad Anónima Promotora de Inversión*, or SAPI). Non-profit legal forms are those of civil association (*Asociación Civil*, or AC) and private-assistance institutions (*Institución de Asistencia Privada*, or IAP).

3 Corporatism refers here to the co-option and control of the labour, peasant and popular sectors of civil society exercised by the hegemonic political party that governed the country for 70 consecutive years, with the purpose of maintaining political control of the nation and favouring itself in electoral results.

4 There are nineteen activities approved by the Federal Law for the Promotion of Activities Carried Out by Civil-Society Organisations (LFFAROSC).

5 Size of the sample: 1,200 effective interviews. Study population: adult Mexicans with residence in the Mexican territory.

References

Aguilar Valenzuela, R. (2006) "Las organizaciones de la sociedad civil en México: su evolución y principales retos", PhD dissertation, Universidad Iberoamericana México.

Alberro, I. (2010) "Impacto de la economía política en la administración pública: Liberalismo económico y democracia", in Méndez, J. L., Ordorica, M. & Prud'homme, J. F. (eds) *Volume XIII, Políticas públicas: Los grandes problemas de México*, Mexico: El Colegio de Mexico, pp. 85–104.

Alvarado, J. (2009) "Fair trade in Mexico and abroad: An alternative to the Walmartopia?" *Journal of Business Ethics*, Vol. 88, No. 2, pp. 301–317.

ANDE (2018) *Acceleration in Mexico: Early Impacts on Mexican Ventures*, Washington, DC: Aspen Network of Development Entrepreneurs.

Antinori, C. M. & Bray, D. B. (2005) "Community forest enterprises as entrepreneurial firms: Economic and institutional perspectives from Mexico", *World development*, Vol. 33, No. 9, pp. 1529–1543.

Antinori, C. M. & Rausser, G. C. (2010) "The Mexican common property forestry sector", *UC Berkeley CUADRE Working Papers*, paper 1105.

Berkes, F. & Davidson-Hunt, I. (2010) "Innovating through commons use: Community-based enterprises", *International Journal of the Commons*, Vol. 4, No. 1, pp. 1–7.

Bray, D. B., Antinori, C. & Torres-Rojo, J. M. (2006) "The Mexican model of community forest management: The role of agrarian policy, forest policy and entrepreneurial organization", *Forest Policy and Economics*, Vol. 8, No. 4, pp. 470–484.

Bray, D. B., Merino-Perez, L., Negreros-Castillo, P., Segura-Warnholtz, G., Torres-Rojo, J. M. & Vester, H. F. M. (2003) "Mexico's community-managed forests as a global model for sustainable landscapes", *Conservation Biology*, Vol. 17, No. 3, pp. 672–677.

CDI (2015) *Indicadores Socioeconómicos de los Pueblos Indígenas de México*, Mexico: Comisión Nacional para el Desarrollo de los Pueblos Indigenas.

Chapela, F. (2012) *Estado de los bosques de México*, México, DF: Consejo civil mexicano para la silvicultura sostenible AC.

Conde Bonfil, C. (2013) "Reform to the law of social and solidarity economy of Mexico", 4th EMES International Research Conference on Social Enterprise, Liege.

Conde Bonfil, C. (2016) "Entendiendo las diferentes perspectivas de las empresas sociales en México", *Ciências Sociais Unisinos*, Vol. 52, No. 3, pp. 321–342.

CONEVAL (2016) "Resultados de pobreza en México 2016 a nivel nacional y por entidades federativas, Consejo Nacional de Evaluación de la Política de Desarrollo Social". Available HTTP: www.coneval.org.mx/Medicion/MP/Paginas/Pobreza_2016.aspx (accessed on August 17, 2018).

CONEVAL (2018) *Informe de Evaluación de la Política de Desarrollo Social. Resumen Ejecutivo*, México: Consejo Nacional de Evaluación de la Política de Desarrollo Social.

Conway, M. D-O. & Dávila, J. A. C. (2018) *Modelando el emprendimiento social en México*, Mexico City: LID Editorial.

CSIFLM (2016) "Cuenta Satélite de las Instituciones sin Fines de Lucro de México", *Instituto Nacional de Estadística y Geografía, Comunicado de prensa*, No. 131/18, March 20, 2018.

Defourny, J. & Nyssens, M. (2012) "The EMES approach of social enterprises in a comparative perspective", *EMES Working Papers Series*, No. 12/03.

DOF (2012) *Código Civil Federal*, DOF, April 9.

Esquivel, G. (2015) "Desigualdad extrema en México: concentración del poder económico y político", *Reporte de Oxfam México*, No. 23.

Failure Institute (2017) *Causas del Fracaso en Empresas Sociales Mexicanas*, México: Failure Institute, Promotora Social Mexico.

Girardo, C. & Mochi, P. (2012) "Las organizaciones de la sociedad civil en México: modalidades del trabajo y el empleo en la prestación de servicios de proximidad y/o relacionales", *Economía, sociedad y territorio*, Vol. 12, pp. 333–357.

GODF (2014) "Ley de Instituciones de Asistencia Privada para el Distrito Federal", Gaceta Oficial del Distrito Federal, November 28.

INADEM (2013) "Convocatoria pública para acceder a los apoyos del Fondo Nacional Emprendedor 2014", in Instituto Nacional del Eemprendedor, Secretaría de Economia, *Diario Oficial de la Federación*, México: INADEM.

INADEM (2017) "Informe trimestral de programas de subsidios. Listado de beneficiarios. Fondo Nacional Emprendedor", Cuarto Informe Trimestral 2017.

Jaffee, D. (2014) "Eating and staying on the land: Food security and migration", in *Brewing Justice: Fair Trade Coffee, Sustainability, and Survival*, Berkeley: University of California Press.

Klooster, D. (1999) "Community-based forestry in Mexico: Can it reverse processes of degradation?" *Land Degradation & Development*, Vol. 10, No. 4, pp. 365–381.

Layton, M. D. & Moreno, A. (9–10 September 2013) "Factores clave en la filantropía individual mexicana: Encuesta Nacional sobre la Filantropía y la Sociedad Civil (ENAFI)", in ITAM (ed.) *XIII Congreso de Investigación sobre el Tercer Sector*, UVM Campus Querétaro

Layton, M. D. & Mossel, V. (2015) "Giving in Mexico: Generosity, distrust and informality", in Wiepking, P. & Handy, F. (eds) *The Palgrave Handbook of Global Philanthropy*, Basingstoke: Palgrave Macmillan, pp. 64–87.

Merino, L. (1996) "Los bosques de Mexico, una perspectiva general", *Cuadernos Agrarios*, Vol. 14, pp. 157–162.

Morett-Sánchez, J. C. & Cosío-Ruiz, C. (2017) "Panorama de los ejidos y comunidades agrarias en México", *Agricultura, sociedad y desarrollo*, Vol. 14, No. 1, pp. 125–152.

Natal, A. & Sanchez, H. (2013) Ch. 3 "El entorno económico de las OSC en México", in Natal, A. & Muñoz-Grandé, H. (eds) *El entorno económico de las organizaciones de la sociedad civil en México*, Mexico: Fundación para el desarrollo del tercer sector A.C.

Orozco-Quintero, A. & Davidson-Hunt, I. (2010) "Community-based enterprises and the commons: The case of San Juan Nuevo Parangaricutiro, Mexico", *International Journal of the Commons*, Vol. 4, No. 1, pp. 8–35.

Oulhaj, L. (2015) "Miradas sobre la Economía Social y Solidaria en México. Breve revisión conceptual del tercer sector", *Repositorio Institucional Universida Iberoamericana Puebla*, pp. 17–27.

Peredo, A. M. & Chrisman, J. J. (2006) "Toward a theory of community-based enterprise", *Academy of Management Review*, Vol. 31, No. 2, pp. 309–328.

PNUD (2012) "Comunidad Indígena de Nuevo San Juan Parangaricutiro, Mexico", Equator Initiative Case Study, New York: United Nations Development Programme.

Portales, L. (2018) "Emprendimiento social, ¿alternativa o continuidad a las consecuencias del sistema neoliberal al que busca responder?" *RECERCA Revista de Pensament I Anàlisi*, No. 23, pp. 1–24.

Prahalad, C. K. (2006) *The Fortune at the Bottom of the Pyramid*, Upper Saddle River: Pearson Education.

Quijano, A. (2000) "Coloniality of power and Eurocentrism in Latin America", *International Sociology*, Vol. 15, No. 2, pp. 215–232.

Reyes, J. A., Gómez, J. P., Muis, R. O., Zavala, R., Ríos, G. A. & Villalobos, O. (2012) *Atlas de Propiedad Social y Servicios Ambientales en México*, Mexico: Instituto Interamiericano de Cooperación para la Agricultura, Cooperación Técnica Registro Agrario Nacional-Instituto Interamiericano de Cooperación para la Agricultura.

Salamon, L. M., Anheier, H. K., List, R., Toepler, S. & Sokolowski, S. W. (1999) *Dimensions of the Non-Profit Sector in Global Civil Society*, Comparative Nonprofit Sector Project, Baltimore: The Johns Hopkins Center for Civil Society Studies.

Schwab Foundation for Social Entrepreneurship. (2016) "What is a social entrepreneur?" Available HTTP: www.schwabfound.org/content/what-social-entrepreneur.

SEDESOL (2016) "Informe de labores 2015", in Secretaria de Desarrollo Social (ed.). Available HTTP: www.gob.mx/cms/uploads/attachment/file/172028/24052016_Informe.pdf.

Sistema B (2018) "Requisitos para ser empresa B. Modificaciones legales México". Available HTTP: https://sistemab.org/requisitos-para-ser-empresa-b/modificaciones-legales-mexico/2018.

Teruel, G., Reyes, M. & Lopez, M. (2018) *Policy Brief—Análisis de Coyuntura no.1 "México, país de trabajadores pobres"*, Ciudad de Mexico and Puebla: Observatorio de salarios EQUIDE.

Tierrablanca, C. & Lara, A. (2018) "El saldo de dos sexenios de guerra", *Animal Político*, April 12. Mexico. Available HTTP: www.animalpolitico.com/blogueros-el-foco/2018/12/04/el-saldo-de-dos-sexenios-de-guerra/.

Vázquez-Maguirre, M. (2012) "Indigenous social enterprises in subsistence economies", in "Capítulo 6. Administración del Desarrollo Regional y Sustentabilidad", in Fonseca-Paredes, M. (ed.) *Retos de las Ciencias Administrativas desde las economías emergentes: evolución de sociedades*, Mexico: Tecnológico de Monterrey, pp. 1–18.

Vázquez-Maguirre, M. & Portales, L. (2014) "La empresa social como detonadora de calidad de vida y desarrollo sustentable en comunidades rurales", *Revista científica Pensamiento y Gestión*, No. 37.

Vázquez-Maguirre, M., Portales, L. & Velásquez Bellido, I. (2018) "Indigenous social enterprises as drivers of sustainable development: Insights from Mexico and Peru", *Critical Sociology*, Vol. 44, No. 2, pp. 323–340.

Verduzco, G. (2001) "La evolución del tercer sector en México y el problema de su significado en la relación entre lo público y lo privado", *Estudios sociológicos*, Vol. 19, No. 55, pp. 27–48.

World Bank (2018) "Annual growth of GDP Mexico". Available HTTP: https://datos.bancomundial.org/indicator/NY.GDP.MKTP.KD.ZG?end=2017&locations=MX&start=1998.

World Justice Project's Research Team (2015) "The world justice project rule of law index® 2015", Report from The World Justice Project, Washington, DC.

Wulleman, M. & Hudon, M. (2016) "Models of social entrepreneurship: Empirical evidence from Mexico", *Journal of Social Entrepreneurship*, Vol. 7, No. 2, pp. 162–188.

Yunus Centre (2014) "Yunus to inaugurate global social business summit 2014 in Mexico". Available HTTP: http://muhammadyunus.org/index.php/91-news/1412-yunus-to-inaugurate-global-social-business-summit-2014-in-mexico.

Zahra, S. A., Gedajlovic, E., Neubaum, D. O. & Shulman, J. M. A. (2009) "A typology of social entrepreneurs: Motives, search processes and ethical challenges", *Journal of Business Venturing*, Vol. 24, No. 5, pp. 519–532.

7   A Legal Approach to the Social and Solidarity Economy in Mexico

Carola Conde Bonfil and Leïla Oulhaj

Introduction

In Mexico, many types of organisations engaged in social entrepreneurship coexist; they operate under various legal forms, such as *ejidos*,[1] communities, cooperatives, workers' organisations, civil associations and societies, private welfare and charitable institutions and social groups (not constituted as legal entities). These types of organisation differ in many ways (in terms of objectives, characteristics, process of constitution, structure, requirements, legal records, etc.) and are regulated by different laws.

From a historical perspective, two key moments are important to understand the emergence of this type of entrepreneurship. The first one is the *post-revolutionary period* (1920s and 1930s), during which the agrarian distribution started, *ejidos* were created and land that had been stripped by the great landowners before the armed movement was returned to communities; the restitution of their land was indeed the main demand of the farmers who took part in the Mexican Revolution. It was also in those years that the first cooperatives emerged: the first General Law on Cooperative Societies was passed in 1927 and the First National Cooperative Congress was organised in 1929. The second turning point is the *profound crisis of the Mexican economy* that hit the country in the 1970s and 1980s. Industrial restructuring was focused on deregulation in every way with a view to reorienting the productive apparatus towards a new scheme of accumulation in order to overcome the crisis. The crisis had two significant impacts for the emergence of the social economy in Mexico. On the one hand, it caused an abrupt entry of popular groups into the new national economic dynamics, which resulted in better integration and living conditions for some happy few, while the others were confined to a passive role (consumption) (Barkin 1988: 99). On the other hand, it drastically limited the state's ability to channel resources at its discretion, provide special services or subsidise the activities of its "loyal groups" and fractured several of the corporatist structures. Both these economic and political aspects led to the creation of civil society organisations, especially after the 1985 earthquake.

DOI: 10.4324/9780429055164-9

The historical context in which social enterprises have emerged and developed in Mexico—in different phases and during turbulent times—has led to many different empirical concepts being used, confusions and overlapping between these concepts and non-consistency between formulation in various laws and concrete use by various Mexican agencies.

We focus on one key example of such inconsistency and lack of clarity in legal texts and concepts by analysing the "social and solidarity economy" and "social sector of the economy", more specifically such as they are defined:

- in the Mexican Law on the Social and Solidarity Economy (*Ley de la Economía Social y Solidaria*, or LESS), which has been the national legal framework regulating the social and solidarity economy since 2012, and lists the organisations that compose the social sector of economy (*sector social de la economía*, or SSE) and
- in the Catalogue of organisms of the social sector of the economy (*Catálogo de organismos del sector social de la economía*, or COSSE), which allows to consider other types of organisations, which are not included in the LESS, as organisations of the social sector of the economy (*organismos del sector social de la economía*, or SSEOs).

Can all types of organisation recognised by the LESS and in the COSSE be considered as social enterprises (SEs)? The problem we address here is the lack of clarity that prevails in the country regarding social enterprise—a concept does not exist in the LESS nor in the COSSE. The specific objective is to contribute elements that would allow for an improvement of public policies, so that they would better recognise and strengthen social enterprise in the country.

This chapter is organised as follows: First, we review the legal forms recognised in the LESS and in the COSSE. Second, these legal forms are confronted with the attributes of SE such as they are described by the EMES International Research Network—an analytical framework that is used by the ICSEM Project, of which this research is part. Finally, we conclude with some considerations regarding the role of public policies.

1. Legal Forms Recognised in the LESS and in the COSSE[2]

The LESS was passed in 2012. This new law ordered the transformation of the National Fund for Support to Businesses in Solidarity (*Fondo Nacional de Apoyo para las Empresas en Solidaridad*, or FONAES) into the National Institute for the Social Economy (*Instituto Nacional de Economía Social*, or INAES) and instructed the Secretary of Economy to create the Programme for the Promotion of the Social Economy

(*Programa de Fomento a la Economía Social*, or PFES). This programme defines the social economy as:

> [a] system that implies a type of collective initiatives which prioritise the generation of collective well-being through economic profitability. It is constituted by social organisms endowed with legal personality and internally organised in a way that allows them to be autonomous from other economic actors and to make decisions, through democratic organs of governance, to control and organise their own activities [. . .] The [social sector of economy] operates as a socio-economic system constituted by organisms of social ownership, based on a relationship of solidarity, cooperation and reciprocity, where work and the human being are privileged, and which are shaped as associations and administrated as such to satisfy the needs of their members and the communities. Generating a return on capital is valued, but only as a means to generate jobs and welfare for people.
>
> DOF (2015)

The LESS offers a good illustration of the conceptual confusion that exists in Mexico: while its title includes the terms "social and solidarity economy", and despite the fact that the programme whose creation it foresees addresses the social economy, the text of the law does not mention this concept, and focuses instead on the "social sector of the economy" (SSE). The SSE is a concept that has been formally used since 1983; it is cited in Article 25 of the country's Constitution. This article states that "the national public sector, the social sector and the private sector will [. . .] participate in national economic development" and that "under criteria of social equity and productivity, companies in the social sector will be supported and promoted. [. . .] The law will establish mechanisms that facilitate the organisation and expansion of economic activity in the social sector" (INAES 2014).

The LESS itself does not contain a definition of the social economy; it simply lists the types of organisation that make up the SSE:

- *ejidos*;
- communities;
- organisations of workers;
- cooperatives;
- companies belonging largely or solely to workers; and
- in general, all forms of social organisation for the production, distribution and consumption of socially necessary goods and services (DOF 2015).

Before reviewing the main features of each of these types of organisation, it is important to mention that the INAES considers that organisations that are not listed in the LESS can be registered in the COSSE and are potentially eligible to the support and incentives granted by the Programme for the Promotion of the Social Economy (PFES), provided that they accept and respect the goals, values, principles and practices enunciated in Articles 8–11 of the LESS (INAES 2016).

1.1. Ejidos

Ejidos are composed by peasants groups and have legal personality and assets. They own the land they have been given or which they have acquired by any other title. An *ejido*'s assembly can decide to collectively work the *ejido*'s land; in this case, provisions about the way in which the work will be organised, the exploitation of the *ejido*'s resources, the mechanisms for the equitable sharing of benefits, the constitution of capital reserves and of social security or services reserves and the reserves that will be affected to common funds have to be determined beforehand.

1.2. Communities

Communities are also legal persons created by the redistribution of land to indigenous people. The community status creates a special protection regime for agrarian nuclei since the land becomes inalienable, imprescriptible and indefeasible; internally, the community determines the use of its lands, its division in various parcels according to various aims and the organisation for the use of its property. The community implies the individual status of "commoners" (*comuneros*) for its members and allows them the use and enjoyment of their land and the possibility to transfer their rights in favour of family and neighbours, along with the right to the use and benefit of common goods.

Communities, together with the *ejidos*, were the most important associative forms in rural Mexico during the 20th century *qua* associative forms generators of foreign exchange and guarantors of national food security. Indeed, their products were so abundant that they did not only guarantee national food security; they also generated foreign currency through the exportation of a significant share of their production. The neoliberal public policy, however, prioritised supporting more profitable private economic units and allowed the dissolution and alienation of the *ejidos* so—although they are still numerous—today they are only a form of subsistence.

1.3. Organisations of Workers

The LESS does not specify what is meant by "organisation of workers" but, in common parlance, it is considered to refer to trade unions and their associations, federations and confederations, none of which can be considered as SEs. For greater clarity in the presentation, the types of organisations that could be included here are presented in section 1.6, because they are outlined in the COSSE (and not in the LESS).

1.4. Cooperatives

The cooperative society is a form of social organisation composed of individuals and based on common interests and on principles of solidarity, own efforts and mutual help; it aims to meet individual and collective needs through economic activities of production, distribution and consumption of goods and services. There are three types of cooperatives: (1) cooperatives of consumers of goods or services; (2) cooperatives of producers of goods or services; and (3) savings and loan cooperatives (*sociedades cooperativas de ahorro y préstamo*, or SCAPs). Unlike private companies, which consider profit as an end in itself, the cooperative aims to strengthen itself, meets the needs of its partners and provides social benefits that are distributed evenly. Although cooperatives appeared in Mexico at the end of the 19th century, cooperative legislation only emerged in the 1930s, and without a real effort, on the part of the legislator, to protect these organisations. At the end of that century, the different laws that had been passed sought to eliminate the organisations belonging to the social sector of the economy, so the LESS can be considered as a success for cooperatives in that it states that cooperatives "will not be regulated by commercial law nor by the civil code" (Rechy unpublished).

1.5. Companies Belonging Largely or Solely to Workers

The General Law of Mercantile Societies recognises different types of mercantile companies.[3] For a mercantile society to be considered by the INAES as eligible to receive funds from the PFES, at least 51% of its shared capital must be held by organisms of the SSE. The kinds of organisation concerned by the LESS are not clearly defined, and some of those organisations may have specific legal forms, not listed in the LESS nor in the COSSE; this is for example the case of exclusively worker-owned companies or, among some mercantile societies, of companies whose workers hold at least 51% of the company's shares. These worker-controlled small and medium enterprises are referred to, in table 7.2, as SMEs.

1.6. Other Forms of Social Organisation for the Production, Distribution and Consumption of Socially Necessary Goods and Services

Since there is no definition of this category nor any specific term to refer to it in the law, it may include some associative legal forms or even groups not possessing any legal form (such as community-based organisms or social groups that their members integrate only to receive government support). We suggest to include in this category the legal forms and groups that the COSSE incorporates but which are not listed in the LESS.

- *Rural associations of collective interest (asociaciones rurales de interés colectivo*, or ARICs) are constituted by two or more *ejidos*, communities, rural-production societies or unions of any of *these* forms. Their goal is to integrate human, natural, technical and financial resources for the establishment of industries, exploitation and commercialisation systems and any other economic activity.
- *Rural-production societies (sociedades de producción rural*, or SPRs) are integrated by two or more partners (farmers, *ejidatarios*, commoners, smallholders, settlers, third-party investors, or a combination of these). They can produce, transform and commercialise goods and provide services in an associated form. They may receive public or private support to undertake, develop and consolidate productive and social-investment projects. They can also manage, purchase and administer economic functions such as financing, insurance, supplies, machinery, equipment and facilities.
- **Social-solidarity societies** (*sociedades de solidaridad social*, or SSSs) aim, among other goals, to produce, process and commercialise goods and services. They are constituted with assets of collective character; partners must be *ejidatarios*, commoners, landless peasants, agricultural smallholders (*parvifundistas*) and persons entitled to work.
- **Credit unions** (*uniones de crédito*, or UCs) are the oldest institutions providing financial services and, for many years, they have been the only source of credit for low-income producers.
- **Mutual societies** (*sociedades mutualistas*, or SMUs) are formed by groups of people acting voluntarily to build a fund of financial assistance, through regular cash contributions, by way of spontaneous collaboration. The aim of the fund is to financially support the members in case of disease, accident and other natural hazards; this assistance can be extended to family members when these are not self-sufficient. In Mexico, mutual societies appeared in the 1950s (before cooperative societies) but failed to establish strong bases; their position remained rather marginal. An important legal limitation of mutualism has been the impossibility of engaging in economic activities (industry, agriculture, commerce, etc.) or financial activities, which is why they focused on insurance activities. The main differences between these organisations and traditional insurance companies are that mutual societies do not have a profit motive and do not choose their members based on their individual risks.
- **Agricultural and rural insurance funds** (*fondos de aseguramiento agropecuario y rural*, or FAARs) cover damages in the agricultural and animal-farming industry and in the related branches covered by an insurance company; debtor-balance schemes and life schemes

for rural families in the branch of life operations; and the branch of personal injury. Their purpose is to offer supportive mutual protection for their shareholders through active operations of insurance or co-insurance.

- **Community financial societies** (*sociedades financieras comunitarias,* or SOFINCOs) are financial institutions composed of individuals and legal entities that are established as public limited companies restricted by collective ownership and run on a democratic basis. They operate under the principles of territoriality, solidarity and mutual support and are organised on a sector-specific basis. Their institutional design makes it possible for the savings collected in a community to be reinvested in the same region by means of credit, promotion and investment for economic development of rural communities.

- **Workers' savings associations** (*cajas de ahorro de trabajadores*) are an institutional mechanism set up in some companies or organisations to promote savings by the employees. The employees hold a general assembly at the beginning of the fiscal year to make decisions about the operation of the "cash desk": types of loans, duration, amount, payment of interest, etc. The savings association performs the savings and payments via payroll and, at the end of the year, it reimburses each worker's contributions and, based on these, a proportional fair share of the interest earned.

- **Social groups** normally function as self-managed collectives that form solidarity-economy movements and networks and implement productive projects. Indeed, due to the complexity of the legislation and the costs linked to the process required to adopt a legal form and fulfil the fiscal obligations linked hereto, many successful productive projects are implemented by groups that function as unregistered self-managed collectives. However, since many government programmes condition the delivery of grants and subsidies to the existence of a group, groups are also sometimes created "on paper" only and are dissolved as soon as they obtain the sought-after resources. In accordance with the Rules of Operation of the PFES, the COSSE takes into consideration social groups not constituted as legal entities and composed of at least two or three members (depending on modality); these groups are required to register legally only if their application for support by the PFES is approved.

2. Are Social and Solidarity-Economy Organisations Social Enterprises?

Can the different types of organisations included in the LESS and in the COSSE be considered as social enterprises? In order to answer this question, given the variety of terms in use in the LESS (and knowing that this law never mentions the concept of social enterprise) and the lack of consensus on them, we consider most relevant to confront the purposes, principles, values and practices of organisations listed in the LESS with the SE indicators put forward by the EMES International Research Network.

The comparison carried out in table 7.1. between the EMES indicators and the LESS reveals that, although the LESS highlights some elements that are close to the EMES indicators, a major difference appears

Table 7.1 Comparison between the EMES indicators and the characteristics of organisations listed in the LESS

EMES indicators (ICSEM Project)	*Mexico: purposes, principles, values and practices of organisations listed in the LESS (2015)*
Economic project	
A continuous production	Production, distribution and consumption of goods and services that are socially necessary (purposes)
Some paid work	Generation of sources of work and better ways of life for all people (purposes)
An economic risk	
Social mission	
An explicit social aim	Design of plans, programmes and projects for economic and social development (purposes)
Limited profit distribution, reflecting the primacy of the social aim	
An initiative launched by a group of citizens or a third-sector organisation	
Participatory governance	
A high degree of autonomy	Autonomy and independence from the political and religious spheres (principles)
A participatory nature, which involves various parties affected by the activity	Democracy (values) Participatory democracy (purposes) Participatory democracy regime (principles)
A decision-making power not based on capital ownership	Equitable distribution of benefits without any discrimination (purposes)

Source: Prepared by the authors.

regarding the place of the social mission, which is a key indicator that may distinguish a social enterprise from a traditional, for-profit enterprise: the primacy of the social mission is indeed not mentioned in the LESS. However, as just said, some of these organisations also have some things in common with social enterprise such as it is envisaged in the EMES approach. They coincide on some central aspects, such as the participatory nature of the initiatives, the primacy of the individual over capital and the ongoing production of goods or provision of services.

We confronted the actual behaviour of organisations, regardless of their legal form, with EMES indicators. In such perspective, we assigned different values to each indicator according to the frequency with which we could find it in the type of organisation considered (see table 7.2):

0:   The indicator is not present in this type of organisation.
1:   Among organisations of this type, some have this feature.
2:   Among organisations of this type, many meet this criterion.
3:   This criterion is a distinctive feature of organisations of this type.

In order to avoid results reflecting an individual and subjective perspective, once the assessment had been completed based on personal knowledge, the table was sent for validation to several specialists in rural, agriculture and forestry development; in cooperatives; and in civil society organisations and social groups.[4]

As expected, the higher values were obtained by production cooperatives (24), social-solidarity societies (SSSs) (23) and consumer cooperatives (22), which means that the majority of the organisations of each of these types behave as (or that their behaviour is close to that of) social enterprises. The reason why savings and loan cooperative (SCAPs) do not score as high as these other types of organisations is that, because of the current prudential regulation and the pressure exerted by financial authorities, some—or even many—of them treat their members as customers and are more concerned with complying with financial-management indicators than with cooperative principles. As for the legal form of social-solidarity society, it has made it easier for some (mainly rural) workers and social groups to acquire legal personality and to become qualified for specific benefits (linked to this legal form).

On the opposite end of the spectrum, among the three types of organisation with the lowest scores, two—namely rural associations of collective interest (ARICs) and worker-controlled mercantile societies (SMEs)—are entities in which profit distribution or the creation of social funds are not restricted by law; consequently, many of them may have been constituted with a purely economic purpose and for the sole benefit of those who constitute them. As for community financial societies (SOFINCOs), at the time of writing this chapter, only one organisation had been authorised to operate under this legal form (created in 2009); this obviously makes any reliable assessment difficult, and the low score obtained by SOFINCOs in the table should thus not be taken at face value.

Table 7.2 Analysis of the various types of Mexican organisation based on the EMES indicators for social enterprise

EMES indicators	Catalogue of organisms of the social sector of the economy (COSSE)													
	Organisms of the social sector of the economy (OSSE)								Other legal forms					Social groups
	Ejidos	Communities	Cooperatives		SCAP	SSSs	SPRs	ARICs	SMEs	Financial institutions				
			Consumption	Production						UCs	SOFINCOs	SMUs	FAARs	
Total score	17	17	22	24	17	23	18	13	8	21	13	16	14	18
Economic project														
A continuous production[1]	2	2	2	3	3	3	3	2	3	3	3	3	3	1
An economic risk	2	2	2	2	3	2	2	2	1	2	2	2	3	3
Some paid work	1	1	2	3	3	3	2	3	3	3	3	3	3	1
Social mission														
An explicit social aim	2	2	3	3	2	3	2	1	1	3	2	2	1	2
An initiative launched by a group of citizens or third-sector organisation(s)	1	2	3	3	2	3	3	2	0	2	0	1	1	2
Limited profit distribution, reflecting the primacy of social aim	2	2	3	2	1	1	1	1	0	1	0	2	2	1
Participatory governance														
A high degree of autonomy	2	2	2	3	1	2	1	1	0	2	1	1	1	3
A participatory nature, which involves various parties affected by the activity	2	2	2	3	1	3	2	1	0	3	1	0	1	3
A decision-making power not based on capital ownership	3	2	3	2	2	3	1	0	0	2	1	2	0	2
Number of indicators for which the score of 3 is reached by type of organisation	1	0	4	6	2	6	3	1	2	4	2	2	2	3

1 For organisations that are located in the tertiary sector, we take into consideration the continuous provision of services.

Source: Prepared by the authors based on COSSE (2016), with the validation of experts in different types of organisations.

Table 7.3 Types of social and solidarity-economy organisation (SSEO) that can/
cannot be considered as social enterprise (according to the EMES
indicators)

SSEOs that can be considered as SEs	SSEOs that cannot be considered as SEs
Cooperatives of consumption	*Ejidos*
Cooperatives of production	Communities
Social-solidarity societies (SSSs)	Savings and loan cooperatives (SCAPs)
Credit unions (UCs)	Rural-production societies (SPRs)
	Rural associations of collective interest (ARICs)
	Mercantile societies (SMEs)
	Community financial societies (SOFINCOs)
	Mutual societies (SMUs)
	Agricultural and rural insurance funds (FAARs)
	Social groups

Source: Prepared by the authors.

We can close this section with a brief summary (see table 7.3) of the types of social and solidarity-economy organisations that can/cannot be considered as social enterprises; for each type of organisation, we looked at the number of indicators for which the score of 3 was reached (see last line of table 7.2), considering as social enterprises the types that reached this score for at least 4 indicators.

Conclusion: Some Final Considerations Regarding the Role of Public Policies in the SE Field

In conclusion, we could point out that the LESS and the COSSE include a list of organisations that are not really social enterprises (like corporations or mercantile societies, which, by definition, do not comply with the indicator that states that the decision-making power should not be based on capital ownership) and, conversely, do not accept other types of organisation that, in many countries, are considered as SE and are close to the characteristics of SE.

These observations allow us to draw a first conclusion: in Mexico, the legal and fiscal framework is inadequate and ill suited to the realities of the SE field, so many initiatives end up opting for the legal form that is easier for them to adopt but that does not necessarily correspond to their organisational characteristics. The absence of a clear conceptualisation ultimately leads authorities to support organisations that do not comply with the very principles and values defined in the LESS—those SSEOs which are not SEs—and, conversely, not to support organisations that comply with these principles and values but are not listed in the LESS nor in the COSSE. Furthermore, it should be noted that social enterprise, as part of the social and solidarity economy, has been mixed up in Mexico with the fight against poverty.

This leads us to the second conclusion: the Mexican government is not looking for a true solution to the situation of poverty or extreme poverty (suffered respectively by more than 55 million and 11 million Mexicans in 2014, according to the National Council for Evaluation of Social Development Policy figures), given the limited budget assigned to this issue in relation to the magnitude of the problem. Rather, the public agenda tends to convert the "poor" into consumers of the global market or to use them for clientelist (*clientelares*) purposes (as occurred for example in the elections that took place in 2017 in the State of Mexico, the main bastion of the party in power at the national level until 2018).

There should be a programme whose general objective would be to strengthen practices of organised popular actors based on values such as solidarity and cooperation. In particular, such programmes should recognise explicitly these practices—which take the forms of cooperatives and other types of organisation of the social and solidarity economy—as SEs and support them in the challenges they currently face, the increase in the number of their actors and their integration as a sector (Oulhaj 2016). The biggest challenge for these SEs is to be able to legitimise their mission, i.e. to preserve their essence *qua* ESS organisations and to consolidate their position without becoming private companies, controlled by the demands of the market. This implies support modalities that go far beyond subsidies or credits for some productive projects, since these types of SE are a means to reach social ends and not an end in themselves (Oulhaj 2016).

In terms of public policies, a true co-construction with the actors and an acknowledgement of SEs' realities and needs are required. Therefore, in the current context of crisis in Mexico, it is urgent that universities deepen the issue of social enterprise in the country (as it is a recent academic topic in this country), its historical contributions and current realities and the dissemination of this "other economy".

In short, the enactment of the LESS can represent a step forward to the extent that it makes the characteristics of SEs visible (indeed, even though it does not mention the term "social enterprise", it casts light on a type of entrepreneurship that differs from the private one), but it cannot be considered as a suitable legal framework for a public policy strengthening this kind of actors, in particular SEs.

Notes

1 An *ejido* is a farm communally owned and operated by the inhabitants of a village.
2 For more information about legal forms, see Conde (2015).

3 Society in collective name; limited partnership; limited-liability company; public limited-liability company; limited-stock partnership; cooperative; and simplified joint-stock company.
4 Diana Elisa Bustos Contreras and Alfredo Tapia Naranjo of the National Institute of Forestry, Agriculture and Livestock (*Instituto Nacional de Investigaciones Forestales, Agrícolas y Pecuarias*, or INIFAP) for agricultural organisations; José Antonio Espinosa García, INIFAP (livestock); Jesús Zárate Mancha, independent consultant (forestry); Mario Rechy Montiel, former Advisor to the Economic Development Committee in the Senate (cooperatives and workers' organisations) and Alejandro Natal Martínez of the Universidad Autónoma Metropolitana Lerma (civil society organisations and social groups). Even though they each have a specific field of expertise, several of them expressed theirs view on all the legal forms.

References

Barkin, D. (1988) "El sector social: ¿al rescate de México?" en Labra, A. (ed.) *El sector social de la economía. Una opción ante la crisis*, Mexico: Siglo XXI Editores, pp. 98–114.
Conde, C. (2015) "Social enterprise in Mexico: Concepts in use in the social economy", *ICSEM Working Papers*, No. 22, Liege: The International Comparative Social Enterprise Models (ICSEM) Project. Available HTTP: www.iap-socent.be/sites/default/files/Mexico%20-%20Conde_0.pdf.
DOF. (2015) "Ley de Economía Social y Solidaria". Available HTTP: www.diputados.gob.mx/LeyesBiblio/doc/LESS.doc.
INAES (2014) "ABC de la economía social e INAES". Available HTTP: www.gob.mx/cms/uploads/attachment/file/102028/ABC_de_la_Econom_a_Social_e_INAES.pdf.
INAES (2016) "Catálogo de organismos del sector social de la economía". Available HTTP: www.gob.mx/inaes/documentos/catalogos-inaes.
Oulhaj, L. (ed.) (2016) *Avanzar en la inclusión financiera*, Mexico: Universidad Iberoamericana.
Rechy, M. (unpublished) *El sector social de la economía en México. Una recopilación de documentos sobre el último periodo de su resistencia, con sus alcances y limitaciones, 1997–2012*, Mexico.

8 Definition and Models of Social Enterprise in Peru

María Angela Prialé and Susy Caballero

Introduction

Despite official intentions and robust economic growth in recent years, Peru has made only limited progress in terms of social development. The Peruvian state has not succeeded in reducing social divisions, and gaps still exist in terms of meeting basic needs (Instituto Nacional de Estadística e Informática—INEI 2013; Ghezzi and Gallardo 2013). Some opinion leaders believe that, to deal with such a complex issue, deeper involvement is required from both the state and other social agents, specifically private enterprises (market) and civil society (non-profit sector). This context gives the social enterprise (SE) phenomenon an opportunity to position itself as a potential vehicle for reducing economic and social disparities (Borgaza *et al.* 2008) in the Peruvian society.

In this context, some research has been done in order to contribute to the understanding of the way in which SE is conceived and operates and of the characteristics of the institutional and social framework in which Peruvian SEs function. The latest research on these subjects includes the work carried out by Caballero *et al.* (2013), who approached the topic by focusing on the understanding of the role of personality traits, known as the Big Five in the social entrepreneurship process; by Farber *et al.* (2015), who made a first contribution to establishing SE operating models that explain the relationship between SEs, the market and the intended beneficiaries for SEs active in Lima (Peru); and by Vera *et al.* (2016), who studied and contextualised the social and economic circumstances that enabled the gradual consolidation of a Peruvian social-enterprise ecosystem, analysing the mission, activities, human capital and operational models of 460 social entrepreneurs working in Lima. However, despite these academic efforts, this field of knowledge is far from being consolidated.

This study attempts to gain a deeper knowledge of the Peruvian SE landscape and to present an analytical approach to Peruvian SE. In order to achieve these goals, the chapter first puts forward a definition based on a historical review of the roots of Peruvian SEs. In the second section,

DOI: 10.4324/9780429055164-10

four SE models are presented; they capture the variety and complexity of the social-enterprise field in terms of activities and of legal forms (or organisational types)[1] adopted by social entrepreneurs in the absence of a specific legal framework. The modelling includes a characterisation of these SE models as regards three major dimensions—namely, the economic and entrepreneurial, the social and the participatory governance dimensions—of the "ideal type" of SE put forward by the EMES International Research Network (Defourny and Nyssens 2012). Lastly, the chapter offers some conclusions and reflections regarding the SE movement.

The methodology used was qualitative. Based on the information collected in 26 interviews with government officials, social entrepreneurs, academics and non-governmental or multilateral aid delegates, a SE definition commonly accepted and adapted to the Peruvian context was built. The models were created through a qualitative comparison of the answers given by 32 SEs to some selected questions in the ICSEM questionnaire, across five of the six variables proposed by Kerlin (2010)—outcome emphasis, programme area focus, common organisational type, societal sector and strategic development base—and across different SE types—mutual-purpose, community-purpose, altruistic-purpose, ethical-purpose, private-purpose and public-statist-purpose types—in Gordon's (2015) tradition-related typology.

1. Understanding the Definition of Social Enterprise in Peru

Social-enterprise characteristics—and, as a result, the concept's definition—are based on the context in which the phenomenon develops (Defourny and Nyssens 2012; Kerlin 2010). This section explains how social enterprise is understood in Peru, based on literature, the perspective of the different actors in the SE ecosystem and the institutional origins that gave birth to it.

1.1. Social-Enterprise Definition

The use of the term "social enterprise" is relatively new in Peru. Fieldwork shows that only academics, multilateral agencies, a few non-profits and some social entrepreneurs are familiar with this denomination.

Locally, in academia, the most cited definition of SE is the one developed by researchers from the Social Enterprise Knowledge Network (SEKN), who define SEs as "private (and formal) organisations that employ market strategies to obtain financial resources, in order to achieve social value for [their] members and/or for groups or communities and which are legally chartered as non-profit or cooperative organisations" (Márquez *et al.* 2010: 97). Among practitioners, the definition that prevails was developed by the international non-profit organisation NESST and Digital Divide Data (2014: 9), which define SE as "an innovative business that seeks to resolve a social problem in a sustainable and profitable manner".

The academic and applied approaches share, in their respective definition of SE, the following two characteristics: (1) the existence of a social purpose, and (2) the search for economic self-sustainability through market mechanisms. In practice, the requirement of self-sustainability through market does not formally limit the possibility to get "non-market funding" nor the profit distribution. Hence, the intensity of market dependence raises two controversial aspects when it comes to constructing a definition of SE in the Peruvian context.

The first aspect is linked to the specific legal form of social enterprises and to the related issue of their profit-distribution policies. Regarding the legal form, some experts believe that SEs should be registered as non-profit organisations, while others favour a for-profit status. With respect to profit distribution, some actors believe that, in order to be considered as a SE, an initiative's profits should be wholly reinvested; others consider that profits can be distributed among shareholders; and a third group of actors are simply unconcerned about the profit dimension, as long as the social purpose remains central. Such differences of opinion can probably be accounted for by the fact that Peru has not developed a legal framework for SE as a sector, which forces organisations to operate under a variety of legal forms. Some use the umbrella of the General Corporation Law (*Ley General de Sociedades*—Law No. 26887 1997) or the Individual Limited Liability Company Law (*Ley de Empresa Individual de Responsabilidad Limitada/E.I.R.L*—Law No. 21621 1976), which govern all for-profit organisations and give them freedom to decide what to do with their profits. Others use the Civil Code, which regulates non-profits and requires them to reinvest revenues in the organisation (Legislative Decree No. 295 1984). A third group uses the General Cooperative Law (Law No. 29683 2011), and some SEs even combine two legal forms: it is indeed possible for an organisation to operate as a non-profit and as a corporation in tandem (with two separate legal persons) to achieve a single purpose (Farber *et al.* 2015).

As far as the legal aspect is concerned, a recent development is worth underlining here: in March 2018, Congressman Alberto de Belaunde presented a bill on societies of benefit and collective interest (*sociedades de beneficio e interés colectivo*, or BIC), with the purpose of establishing a legal framework for for-profit organisations, constituted within the framework of the General Law of Societies, that integrate in their purpose the generation of social and/or environmental benefit or reduce any negative impact they might have on the community and the environment. Strictly speaking, the bill proposes an extension of the enterprise corporate purpose in which commitment to economic value creation for shareholders is integrated with the social and environmental development of the country, and both aspects are given the same weight. The bill does not seek to grant tax benefits to BIC companies; its main purpose is to give them a stable and clearly defined legal basis upon which to operate in front of society and investors, safeguarding their long-term purpose, and to recognise and promote this type of company. It is expected that the proposed law will be debated and refined in the second half of 2018 (De Belaunde 2017).

The second controversial aspect to consider is linked to SE's origins and to the related question of whether, in the Peruvian context, an influence of any of the schools of thought identified by Defourny and Nyssens (2012) can be identified. In this regard, the predominant vision is that the Peruvian definition of SE is aligned with the school of thought that Defourny and Nyssens (2012), based on Dees and Anderson (2006), named the "earned-income" school. This school, developed in the United Sates, includes two forms of social enterprise: a "commercial non-profit" approach, which refers to a quest, among on-profit organisations, for a diversification in terms of financial resources; and a "mission-driven business" approach, referring to commercial companies with social objectives. Nonetheless, deeper analysis shows that—similarly to what Defourny and Nyssens (2012) report for SEs in Europe—in Peru, some of these organisations are rooted in the third sector, or social economy, particularly when their foundational aspirations take into account the Andean tradition of reciprocity. Therefore, it is realistic to state that the "Peruvian school of thought" on SE shares common traits with both the US "earned-income" school of thought and the European approach, and that these organisations' origins reveal a hybridisation process of the market and reciprocity logics.

The concept of SE in Peru is framed in the development and consolidation of the formalised third sector and the evolution of the social approach to commercial enterprises. According to findings presented in Peru and refined in a proposal by Farber *et al.* (2015), a SE is defined as a private and formal organisation with an entrepreneurial dynamic and market strategies whose aim is to tackle a social or environmental problem and which is economically sustainable, mainly thanks to the sale of a product or service in the market and, to a lesser extent, through the use of other public or private funds. Moreover, SEs' profit-distribution policy denotes a profound commitment to social or environmental purposes.

Figure 8.1 summarises the position of SEs as hybrid organisations operating under the umbrellas of the third sector, or social economy, on the one hand, and of the market economy, on the other.

The left side shows the path followed by for-profit organisations to social business. Basically, it reflects the incorporation of social and environmental concerns into the core of these organisations. The right side corresponds to the evolution of formal non-profit third-sector organisations; it shows the way in which non-profits have gradually integrated the

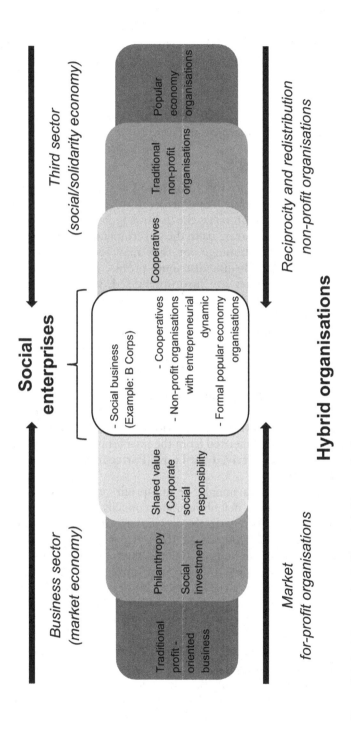

Figure 8.1 Social enterprise in Peru: hybrid organisations

Source: The authors, based on Alter (2003).

concern for self-economic sufficiency, which is now reflected in the sale of products and services in the market in combination with other public or private funds. SE is found at the meeting point of these converging trends; it is a hybrid organisational form that incorporates characteristics from both the social and market economies. The roots of that hybridisation will be explained in the next section.

1.2. The Roots of Social Enterprise in Peru

The Third Sector

One of the roots of Peruvian SE is to be found in the third sector. The Peruvian third sector is defined by Portocarrero *et al.* (2002) as the group of organisations that meet the following five characteristics: (1) they are private and separate from the government in their decision-making and internal functioning, but they may receive funds from the government; (2) they do not distribute profits, but reinvest them in the organisation; (3) they are institutionalised, with a stable and functional structure that can be legally formalised or not; (4) they are self-governed, i.e. they control their internal planning and execution; and (5) they have a voluntary constitution and promote voluntary jobs within the organisation. Similarly to what is the case in some European countries, as Defourny and Nyssens (2012) have highlighted, in Peru, the third sector is the same as the social economy (although the latter term is less frequently used in Peruvian literature) and its origins are grounded in the solidarity dynamics, reciprocity and redistribution principles of the ancient Peruvian civilisation. Peru indeed has a historical tradition of solidarity inherited from the Inca Empire—the "Andean reciprocity"—which has survived until now (Portocarrero and Sanborn 1998; Montoya 2017).

The third sector consists mainly of non-profit organisations, soup kitchens, mothers' groups, neighbourhood councils, foundations and charities, among others. As regards the specific case of cooperatives, Portocarrero and Sanborn (1998) consider them as part of the third sector because they are created and built on the tradition of solidarity and self-help among people with a view to overcoming government flaws. In the following paragraphs, we will develop the history and link to the SE phenomenon of three types of third-sector organisations—namely cooperatives, non-profit organisations and popular organisations.

Cooperatives   One of the most visible promoters of cooperatives was Victor Raul Haya de la Torre, leader of the political party *Alianza Popular Revolucionaria Americana* (APRA). Founded in 1919, APRA shared with José Carlos Mariátegui, one of the most renowned intellectuals of the history of Peru and founder of the Socialist Party, the dedication to look for socio-economic relations based on reciprocity, cooperation and solidarity instead of capital (Montoya 2017). According to Montoya (2017), Haya de la Torre proposed an anti-imperialist state based on the formation of a cooperative nationalised system. Later, in the 1940s and 1950s, several institutions—such as the Peruvian Cooperative Institute (*Instituto Cooperativo del Perú*), "Cooperar" Magazine, the Union of Cooperatives from Puno and the National Federation of Savings and Credit Cooperatives—were founded to promote the cooperative movement.

The theoretical promotion of cooperatives in the 1940s and 1950s was put into practice by General Juan Velasco Alvarado after he conducted a military coup and took control of the country in 1968. Velasco also led the Land Reform of the 1970s and, as stressed by Montoya (2017), one of his decisions was to develop cooperatives across the country, especially in the agricultural and industrial sectors. The organisational types that were promoted were mainly agricultural cooperatives of production, agricultural societies of social interest, industrial communities and socially owned enterprises. However, despite this initial impetus, over time, these organisations showed negative results in terms of productivity and as an employment generator (Montoya 2017; Schaller 2007). Furthermore, inequality persisted in Peruvian society and new forms of hierarchy emerged. This situation led these organisations to failure. By the 1980s, the cooperative movement, especially in the rural sector, was also being wrecked by two terrorist movements, Sendero Luminoso and Movimiento Revolucionario Tupac Amaru. During Fernando Belaúnde's presidency (1980–1985), terrorists started leading insurgency activities in rural areas and tried to appeal to and get the support of peasants (Conger *et al.* 2009; Instituto de Democracia y Derechos Humanos de la Pontificia Universidad Católica del Perú—IDEHPUCP 2009). Even though not all peasants were convinced and many sought to stay away from violence, terrorism generated a high economic and social cost to rural cooperatives: it destroyed their infrastructure and machinery and caused the loss of their link to the market, and their leaders and workers fled the violence (Mogrovejo *et al.* 2012). Later on, during Alan Garcia's presidency (1985–1990), which led the country to a terrible economic and political collapse (Cermeño and De la Cruz 1991; Crabtree 2005; Schydlowsky 1989), terrorists threatened, tortured and killed cooperatives' leaders and workers. This resulted in an exodus of cooperative workforce (Mogrovejo *et al.* 2012). During the 1990s, according to Mogrovejo *et al.* (2012), a new cooperative crisis emerged as a result of the neoliberal approach of Alberto Fujimori, who promulgated several laws that were unfavourable to cooperatives, and even omitted cooperatives from the constitution in 1993. This weakened cooperatives and led most of them to terminate their activities.

However, over the last two decades, after Fujimori left the government in 2001, cooperative institutions resurfaced, and in 2017, with the support of the Ministry of Production through the creation of the Cooperative Direction, cooperatives were redefined. Cooperatives are currently considered as autonomous non-profit associations, created voluntarily by individuals or legal persons (who must comply with some preconditions) to meet their own economic, social and cultural aspirations, through a jointly owned organisation that is democratically managed. The work of cooperatives is based on four main principles: the free and voluntary association of members; the economic self-sustainability of their operations; self-management (members must run their cooperative); and the absence of "for-profit" objectives, which means that, in Peru, all cooperatives exist only with the objective of being a source of work for their members (workers' cooperatives) or, alternatively, with the goal of delivering services to partners (users' cooperatives) (PRODUCE 2009). In the last years, the government has also come to understand cooperatives as an organisational model making it possible to develop and improve the competitiveness (especially in international markets) of small farmers in rural areas.

Nowadays, according to the 2017 national cooperative census, there are 1,245 cooperatives in Peru, and 90% of them are micro or small companies. Most of them are located in Lima and Callao (34.9%); the following towns by order of number of cooperatives are Junín (7.6%), Cusco (6.7%), Puno (6.7%), Cajamarca (6%) and Arequipa (5.1%). Concerning the sectors, agrarian cooperatives represent 29.7% of organisations; savings and credit cooperatives, 26.1%; multiple services cooperatives, 11%; and special services cooperatives, 9.9% (INEI and PRODUCE 2017). According to the Minister of Production in 2017, Pedro Olaechea, "the census confirms that cooperatives were born primarily in the agro-industrial sector to strengthen it by allowing easier access to credit, therefore opening the opportunity to access new markets, in a trend that has increased over the last 10 years with the support of the Ministry of Production". Cooperatives have more than 2.4 million members, 40% of which are women. They created 17,000 new formal job positions in 2016 (PRODUCE 2017). Olaechea also highlighted that "cooperatives [were] an important engine of growth and employment generator in Peru", and he mentioned that they were more concentrated in areas where traditional banks were not quite present (PRODUCE 2017). Savings and credit cooperatives are considered as microfinance institutions, along with other organisations such as non-profits, rural banks (*cajas rurales*) and municipal banks (*cajas municipales*). During the last years, savings and credit cooperatives have been highly questioned because there is no formal system to regulate them; indeed, there is no formal registration system for cooperatives, and of the 659 savings and credit cooperatives identified in the country, only 24% are voluntarily supervised by the Federation of Savings and Credit Cooperatives (*Federación de Cooperativas*

de Ahorro y Crédito, or FENACREP)—which is incidentally not authorised to sanction any misconduct (Gestión 2018). A bill has recently been
submitted that provides for the regulation of savings and credit cooperatives by the same authority that regulates banks. This is very important because it is suspected that some cooperatives launder money (La
República 2018).

Non-Profit Organisations   The second type of third-sector organisation,
namely the non-profit organisation or non-governmental organisation
(NGO),[2] has its origins in the influence of the renaissance of Peruvian
social sciences and the modernisation of the catholic principal of help-
ing others during the 1960s. First, non-profit organisations focused on
strengthening community-based organisations' (or popular organisations') capacities for popular education, social awareness and reporting
the political situation. These early organisations wanted to distinguish
themselves from the state, presenting an alternative development proposal (Portocarrero and Sanborn 1998; Sahley and Danziger 1999).

During the 1980s, non-profit projects motivated both by international
trends (donors' interest shifted from raising awareness to raising income)
and by the will to meet local needs (migrants looked for a means to survive in the city and became microentrepreneurs in the informal sector)
focused on production and technical assistance to help their beneficiaries
increase their income. In the late 1980s, terrorism generated a national
crisis, with various consequences for non-profit organisations. On the
one hand, community-based organisations' leaders were threatened and
often killed, so it was very difficult for non-profit organisations to work
with them. Non-profit organisations' workers were also threatened and
some of them were killed, which forced them to "scale down" their visibility and activities (Sahley and Danziger 1999). On the other hand,
the government suspected non-profit organisations of working with terrorists, because of these organisations' close links to community-based
organisations, some of which had been infiltrated by terrorists. In this
context, non-profit organisations focused on strengthening civil society
through the promotion of political citizenship, on supporting locally
based development projects and on defending human rights (Portocarrero *et al.* 2002).

In the early 1990s, non-profit organisations focused again on supporting the population's economic-survival strategies. They also supported
food kitchens and Glass-of-Milk[3] committees.

Under the government of President Alberto Fujimori, as Portocarrero
and his co-authors synthesise,

> the central government did not have a coherent conception of the
> existence and importance of a third sector as such, independent of the

state and the private for-profit sector. On the one hand, the climate of relative freedom of association that had predominated in Peru since the restoration of democracy in 1980 was maintained and there was no systematic interference of the state in private associative life. But on the other hand, there was no widespread recognition of this sector in the discourses of public authorities, and in practice, the concentration of power and resources in the central government reflected a widespread distrust toward autonomous and private initiatives. "Tolerance but distrust", then, could characterise the position of the Fujimori regime toward the majority of private non-profit organisations.

Portocarrero *et al.* (2002: 154)

In addition, Fujimori considered non-profit organisations "as [in] competition [with the state] for the minds and hearts of the poor" (Sahley and Danziger 1999: 18). Therefore, the government implemented many social programmes directly, although some were carried out by non-profit organisations that were subcontracted by the government, due to multilateral donors' requests (Sahley and Danziger 1999).

Later on, in 2008, as a result of an effective fifteen-year period of macroeconomic reforms, Peru was upgraded from "middle-income" to "upper-middle-income" country classification by the United Nations. According to COEECI (*Colectivo de ONG Belgas del Perú*—COEECI 2013), the new country classification led to a reduction and progressive withdrawal of international aid. As a result, traditional non-profit organisations, which were dependent on donors to survive, began to have trouble sustaining themselves economically: a lot of non-profit organisations had to face the challenges of economic survival by their own means. Because of that, and in order not to have to downscale their operations or even totally disappear, some of them chose to start selling products or services. Such evolution in the financing of their social activities makes these organisations one of the forerunners of social enterprise in Peru.

All non-profit organisations are regulated by the Civil Code (De Belaúnde and Parodi 1998). The Civil Code contemplates three legal forms under which any non-profit can register: The first one is the association, which is defined as a stable organisation of natural and/or legal persons, pursuing a non-lucrative purpose. The second form is the foundation, which is a non-profit organisation that seeks to meet religious, welfare, cultural or other social-interest objectives. The third form is that of committee, which is defined as an organisation of natural and/or legal persons, dedicated to the public collection of contributions for an altruistic purpose (Ministerio de Justicia y Derechos Humanos 2015). The most common legal form is that of association, because it is simple and flexible in terms of internal governance and regulation. Foundations have more restrictions in legal and administrative terms; they are regulated by the Council of Supervision of Foundations. Committees are less frequent, since they focus mainly on the public collection of contributions for a specific social aim, which in practice can be done under any of the two previous forms (Portocarrero and Sanborn 1998).

Popular Organisations The third type of third-sector organisations linked to SE is that of popular organisations or community-based organisations. According to Portocarrero and Sanborn (1998), the first popular organisations in the country—namely Glass-of-Milk committees and community kitchens (*comedores populares*)—emerged to respond to the social needs generated by the massive internal migration from rural to urban areas (especially Lima). In the 1972 population census, the internal mobility rate (i.e. the percentage of people who had moved from one area to another within the country) rose to 18% of the Peruvian population; this high figure can be accounted for by the land-reform crisis that manifested itself in the division of land, loss of productive capacities and even abandonment of thousands of hectares that had hitherto been productive. By the 1980s and 1990s, the internal mobility rate reached 20% of the country's population, as a result of migrants leaving the departments of Ayacucho, Huancavelica and Apurímac, which were the epicentre of the terrorist conflict (Sánchez 2015). Migrants, when moving to the cities, kept their tradition of cooperation, and they formed self-help groups to support the urban poor. Most of these groups were founded by underprivileged women as a means to survive and to request basic services from the state. The groups also assume the responsibility of guiding the new migrants, and they have built a considerable part of the urban infrastructure of the nascent slums that have begun to surround Lima (to the east to San Juan de Lurigancho district; to the south to San Juan de Miraflores, Villa María del Triunfo, Villa el Salvador, Pachacamac and Lurín districts; and to Ventanilla district on the seashore; see Sánchez 2015) and other cities in the provinces. Their activity, which has taken place in a grey area in terms of the legal formality required by public authorities, included the construction of houses, streets, schools, markets, public transport services, as well as the constitution of community-based patrols (*rondas urbanas*) to ensure the security of citizens and a certain level of administration of justice (Portocarrero and Sanborn 1998: 55).

Quijano (1998) also lists other types of popular organisation, such as associations of street vendors, micro productive workshops and associations of micro businessmen and small self-run businesses, also referred to as micro and small enterprises (MSEs). These organisations spread as a consequence of the employment crisis in the 1980s, and they were considered as a means of survival for the impoverished citizens excluded from the modern economic sector (Montoya 2017). Some of these organisations were informal and emerged as self-employment initiatives (Favreau *et al.* 2002).

The term "popular", used to refer to this type of organisation, represents social change and democracy, taking into account the needs and interests of the majority, a feeling of group identity, a community-based form to live together and make joint decisions (Ortiz 2002), and "the alternative" to an imposed system that only benefited a few rich people (Ayerbe and Dupas 2005). Nevertheless, the concept of "popular economy" was very diverse in itself because it brought together the majority of the population and the specific needs of many different groups (Guerra 2010). In 1991, Law No. 25307 provided a legal framework for popular organisations working in food-support services to formally register (De Belaúnde and Parodi 1998). Law No. 28015 was promulgated in 2003 in order to promote the action and formalisation of MSEs (Congreso 2003). In 2013, it was modified by Law No. 30056 (Congreso 2013), and in 2016, the government published Legislative Decree No. 1269, which creates the MSE Tax Regime (RPP 2016).

The Business Sector

Other roots of SE in Peru are anchored in the evolution of the business sector; enterprises in this sector have progressed in terms of their social orientation and of the way in which they see their role in the country's development. This social orientation reflects how Peruvian enterprises see corporate social responsibility (CSR). According to Portocarrero and Sanborn (1998), there is evidence that, after the agrarian reform and nationalisation of companies in the 1970s, the oligarchic Peruvian elites developed philanthropic initiatives based on the Christian mission of charity, on civic and moral concerns, as well as on a search for public recognition; this might have constituted the beginning of CSR in Peru. As mentioned by Portocarrero and Sanborn (1998), in the late 1980s, the social instability of the country was obvious; businessmen, realising that their prosperity was based on the political and social stability of the country, started focusing on implementing social-responsibility programmes in education, culture, environmental protection, community development and protection of children, as a renewed version of the philanthropic practices of landowners from the past.

Over the years, these philanthropic initiatives began to become institutionalised in different ways (Caravedo 2010). For example, the National Confederation of Private Business Institutions (*Confederación Nacional de Instituciones Empresariales Privadas*, or CONFIEP), was founded in 1984 to "promote and ensure the development of business activity aimed at the welfare of citizens"; it is "working for an ethical, competitive system and [is] committed to the development of the country" (Confiep 2017). The Peruvian Institute of Business Administration (*Instituto Peruano de Administración de Empresas*, or IPAE) promotes spaces to support the exchange of ideas between businessmen and university students, and with educational representatives (Sulmont 1999). In 1994, Peru 2021, a non-profit organisation, was founded by a group of young businessmen with the aim to contribute to the "national reconstruction" (Sanborn 2008), promote a long-term view of development and highlight the leadership role of the business sector in the transformation of the country (Sulmont 1999). Peru 2021 received the support of international cooperation agencies that saw in CSR an alternative to the traditional governmental social programmes (Sanborn 2008). In the following years, Peru 2021 signed alliances with IDB, USAID and AVINA, and it became the representative of the World Business Council for Sustainable Development (WBCSD) in Peru (Peru 2021 2017).

Corporate social responsibility (CSR) practices implemented by big enterprises operating in the country gained significant importance during the 1990s (Sulmont 1999). According to Sanborn (2008), there were several definitions of CSR at the time, but they all agreed on the fact that CSR is an applied management approach that integrates the concern for the enterprise's different stakeholders (such as workers, stockholders, suppliers, clients, communities and the environment, among others) and which surpasses their legal obligations. Sulmont (1999), quoting Baltazar Caravedo, refers to CSR as a way in which businesses relate to their context with the aim to promote win-win relationships in a long-term perspective. He also distinguishes CSR from philanthropy or humanitarian actions by the owners, and from social investment or responses to specific social or environmental requirements that have to be met in order for the enterprise to operate. Therefore, CSR has a greater scope than philanthropy and social investment.

Sanborn (2008) considered the 1990s as the first phase of CSR development in Peru, with the beginning of economic openness and the restoration of political order in an authoritarian way. The interest of companies to promote CSR responded to the country's general lack of sustainability, which was itself linked to the build-up of problems such as poverty, unemployment, drug trafficking, poor quality of education and health, deterioration of the environment and deepening of the institutional crisis. All these factors indeed represent serious risks to any investment (Sulmont 1999). Since then, the development of CSR has responded to market demands, donors and international funds' priorities and civil-society pressure (Sanborn 2008). CSR has been promoted mainly by the managers of top companies in the country, while business leaders of medium and small companies were sceptical and saw it as an expenditure rather than as an investment (Sulmont 1999).

According to Sanborn (2008), the second phase of CSR development in Peru corresponds to the 2000s, which were characterised by continued neoliberal economic policy, democracy and an increasing demand for accountability. The relationship between the business and political sectors was unstable, and the government lost its legitimacy to control social conflicts. Furthermore, CSR had gained more promoters, such as non-profit organisations and citizens, and more international allies. CSR was well known, but only in the context of top national or multinational companies based in Peru. CSR activities focused mainly on donations and management of social projects with the community. To take care of that job, some companies created their own foundations or non-profit organisations. Over the years, top companies became concerned about meeting international standards and obtaining certifications validating their responsible practices. In 2006, the Technical Committee of Corporate Social Responsibility ISO 26000 was formed in Peru and allowed local representatives from the for-profit, non-profit and public sectors to take part in the elaboration of the norm. The same year, a new related concept emerged: that of "inclusive business". According to SNV and WBCSD (2010), it refers to

> *entrepreneurial initiatives that are economically profitable and environmentally and socially responsible. Underpinned by a philosophy of creating mutual value, inclusive businesses contribute to improving the quality of life of low-income communities by integrating them in the business value chain in three ways: (1) as suppliers of services and/or raw materials; (2) as distributors of goods and/or services; or (3) as consumers, by offering goods and services to fulfil their essential needs at prices they can afford.*
>
> SNV and WBCSD (2010: 10)

The concept was promoted by the Alliance for Inclusive Business (an organisation comprising the World Business Council for Sustainable Development [WBCSD] and SNV, a Dutch international organisation) with the goal of reducing poverty through the implementation of commercially viable initiatives led by the private sector. Some Peruvian companies with a well-developed sustainability approach integrated the inclusive business proposal in their business practices.

In 2011, Porter and Kramer stressed the concept of "shared value" as a strategy to generate

> *economic value in a way that also produces value for society by addressing its challenges. A shared value approach reconnects company success with social progress. Firms can do this in three distinct ways: by reconceiving products and markets, redefining productivity in the value chain and building supportive industry clusters at the company's locations.*
>
> Porter and Kramer (2011: 6)

Some multinational companies operating in Peru adopted the approach of shared value as their sustainability strategy. However, to date, most medium, small and microenterprises, which represent the majority of enterprises in Peru, remain sceptical and relate those concepts (CSR, inclusive business and shared value) with big companies that have the budget to afford it.

In this context, it is interesting to note that there are 25 companies recognised as B Corps in Peru, and that most of them are medium or small companies (Universidad del Pacífico 2015). B Corps is a certification managed by B Lab in the United States of America. The certification is given to for-profit organisations that get 80 points or more in an evaluation (called "B impact assessment") that considers aspects linked to governance, the community, clients, the environment and the workers. The aim of the certification is to promote companies that are "the best for the world", and not just "the best of the world". In that sense, the certification recognises those for-profit organisations that give the same consideration to social and environmental purposes as to their economic results. So, B Corps incorporate their social and environmental objectives within their business model.

In 2012, a group of Latin Americans inspired by the movement of B Corps and convinced of the importance of disseminating this approach in the economy formed Sistema B. In Peru, it officially started in 2016. The purpose of Sistema B is to achieve an economy in which success is defined by the well-being of people, societies and nature. In order to achieve this vision, Sistema B has a system approach by which they work with investors, public-policy leaders, opinion leaders, academia, B Corps, regular companies and customers to contribute to an ecosystem that is favourable to B Corps and other economic entities that use the power of the market to solve social and environmental problems (Sistema B 2017). Sistema B could be considered as an expression of the current perception that companies could do more for social development, and that CSR is not enough.

2. Social-Enterprise Models and EMES Dimensions in the Peruvian Context

The models of Peruvian SE emerged from the qualitative analysis of a set of selected items from a database on 32 Peruvian organisations that considered themselves as SEs. Answers were analysed based on Kerlin's variables for SE models (2010) and Gordon's tradition-based typology of SE (2015). The database was elaborated on the basis of the international ICSEM survey, a tool developed by the ICSEM Project (see introduction of the book).

2.1. Building Models

The application of Kerlin's (2010) variables to the clustering of data on Peruvian SEs took into account five out of the six variables developed by her study: (1) outcome emphasis, or the immediate goal pursued through the implementation of the SE's activity; (2) programme area focus, or the type of activity that is generally carried out by the SE; (3) common organisational type, or the legal form used by the SE; (4) societal sector, or the immediate sector or environment in which the SE operates; and (5) strategic development base, or the source of funding for the SE. There is a sixth variable proposed by Kerlin (2010), which reflects the existence of a legal framework for SEs, as a group or sector, in a country. However, as in Peru a specific legal framework for SEs does not exist, this variable was removed from the process of modelling, since it did not allow to identify differences among the organisations of the sample. Although Kerlin (2010) used these variables for a comparative analysis at a macro level, with a view to identifying models of SE in seven regions, in the case of Peru, the lack of specific macro-institutional framework led to adopt a *meso-level perspective* (Defourny and Nyssens 2017) in order to adapt Kerlin's (2010) variables to analyse the organisational characteristics of and identify similarities and differences between SEs from the same country.

The approach put forward by Gordon (2015), who distinguishes six types of SE in relation to the "traditions" from which they were born, constituted a second source that contributed to the creation of models. These six types are: the mutual-purpose, community-purpose, altruistic-purpose, ethical-purpose, private-market-purpose and public-statist-purpose types; they explain SEs' different types of production and mission. The mutual-purpose type refers to alternative economic institutions that support their members' mutual interest and benefit. The community-purpose type corresponds to organisations involving collective and cooperative control for community development. The altruistic-purpose type refers to charitable, philanthropic, voluntary or "non-profit" sector organisations seeking to resolve social issues in the fields of health, education, welfare or alleviation of poverty. The ethical-purpose type is linked to entrepreneurship based on ethical values and aiming to achieve radical societal change. The private-market-purpose type encompasses private sector organisations serving individual or group needs through a market- and private-profit-oriented approach. Finally, the public-statist-purpose type refers to the reconfiguration or "externalisation" of public services under the organisational form of social enterprise.

After selecting Kerlin's (2010) variables and Gordon's (2015) types as the analytical lens to be used, specific items of the ICSEM survey were chosen, on the basis of which the clustering of data and analysis were then carried out. Topics that "congregate" these items are shown in table 8.1 (third point). The selected items concern social enterprises' mission and objectives, the products/services they offer, the organisational or legal form under which they operate, their membership of networks or groups and their association with other organisations. In order to build models, answers to the selected items were grouped on the basis of their recurrence.

Table 8.1 Approach used for the definition of Peruvian SE models

1. Kerlin's variables (2010)	2. SE types (Gordon 2015)
Outcome emphasis	Mutual purpose
Programme area focus	Community purpose
Common organisational type	Altruistic purpose
Societal sector	Ethical purpose
Strategic development base	Private-market purpose
	Public-statist purpose

3. Topics analysed on the basis of selected items from the ICSEM survey *(EMES SE dimension[s] analysed through each topic)*	
- Social mission *(social dimension)*	- Legal form *(governance dimension)*
- Main objectives *(social dimension)*	- Description of the SE *(social and governance dimensions)*
- Products/services offered *(economic dimension)*	- Number and type of workers *(economic dimension)*
- Products/services-mission relationship *(social dimension)*	- Type of aid received by the SE *(economic dimension)*
- Degree of formality of the SE *(governance dimension)*	
- Membership in a network or group *(governance dimension)*	

Source: The authors, on the basis of Kerlin (2010), Gordon (2015) and Defourny and Nyssens (2012).

In parallel, with a view to deepening our knowledge of the emergent models, the analysis also included some items that allowed an assessment of the enterprises on the basis of the indicators of the three dimensions of the "ideal type" of SE put forward by the EMES Network (Defourny and Nyssens 2012). These three dimensions of the "ideal-typical" SE are the economic and entrepreneurial dimension; the social dimension; and the participatory governance dimension. Indicators for the first dimension are: (1) a continuous activity producing goods and/or selling services; (2) a significant level of economic risk; and (3) a minimum amount of paid work. Regarding the social dimension, the indicators are: (1) an explicit aim to benefit the community; (2) an initiative launched by a group of citizens or civil-society organisations; and (3) a limited profit distribution. Finally, the governance dimension is analysed though the following indicators: (1) a high degree of autonomy; (2) a decision-making power not based on capital ownership; and (3) a participatory nature, which involves various parties affected by the activity.

Table 8.1 summarises the variables and topics selected among those analysed by the ICSEM survey to build and to describe Peruvian SE models.

As a result of the approach described above, the following four SE models emerged: the non-profit SE; the social cooperative; the social business; and the non-profit/social-business partnership. Table 8.2 synthesises the

Table 8.2 SE models and variables

Variables	SE models	Non-profit SE	Social business	Social cooperative	Non-profit/social-business partnership
Kerlin's variables (2010)	*Outcome emphasis*	Social benefit	Social/economic benefit	Self-sustainability	Social/economic benefit
	Programme area focus	Employment/human services	Employment/human services	Employment/human services	Employment/human services
	Common organisational type	Association	Closed corporation	Cooperative	Association/closed corporation
	Societal sector	Social economy	Market economy	Social economy	Social economy/market economy
	Strategic development base	Market activities/donors	Market activities	Market activities	Market activities/donors
Membership in a network or group		No current membership	No current membership	No current membership	Membership
Type of SE in Gordon's typology (2015)		Community-purpose type	Private-market-purpose type	Mutual-purpose/community-purpose types	Community-purpose/altruistic-purpose/private-market-purpose types

Source: The authors.

results that emerged from the analysis of each variable for each of the four models of SE. A brief description of each model is then presented, and synthesised in table 8.3 at the end of section 2.

2.2. Non-Profit SE Model

This model encompasses SEs operating under the organisational type of association or foundation and which are legally described as non-profit organisations governed by the Civil Code (Legislative Decree No. 295 1984). It may also include some popular organisations, such as formalised soup kitchens (Law No. 25307 1991).

Among Kerlin's (2010) variables, the programme area focus and the strategic development base help to explain how these SEs generate an economic return that supports their social mission. Their strategies focus either on working along with vulnerable people—offering them training and labour integration—and/or on delivering a product or service that contains in itself the social/environmental mission. The programme area focus can involve training, education, workshops, social projects and product sales; non-profit activities include both activities aiming to benefit the human being (social mission) and market activities. The

Table 8.3 Models of SE and EMES indicators

EMES indicators / SE models	Economic and entrepreneurial dimensions of SEs			Social dimensions of SEs			Participatory governance dimensions of SEs		
	PA	ER	PW	BC	LCS	LPD	HAD	DD	PN
Non-profit SE	✓	✓	✓	✓	✓	✓	✓	✓	±
Social cooperative	✓	✓	✓	✓	✓	✓	✓	✓	✓
Social business	✓	✓	✓	✓	±	±	✓	±	±
Non-profit/social-business partnership	✓	✓	✓	✓	±	±	±	±	±

Legend:
✓ = all the organisations belonging to this model comply with the indicator
± = some of the SEs belonging to this model comply with the indicator, others only do so to some extent, and others still do not comply with the indicator
PA = A continuous activity producing goods and/or selling services
ER = A significant level of economic risk
PW = A minimum amount of paid work
BC = An explicit aim to benefit the community
LCS = An initiative launched by a group of citizens or a civil-society organisation
LPD = A limited profit distribution
HAD = A high degree of autonomy
DD = A decision-making power not based on capital ownership
PN = A participatory nature, which involves various parties affected by the activity

commercial activities are not the only source of income; they are complemented by other forms of support, such as donations, subsidies, incubator services and loans, among others.

Regarding Kerlin's societal-sector variable, answers show that organisations belonging to this model tend to adopt a social-oriented approach, benefiting vulnerable communities and populations, but do not exclude market-based activities in order to achieve economic returns to scale up their social mission. As regards the overall SE objective, which corresponds to the "outcome emphasis" variable proposed by Kerlin (2010), non-profit SEs pursue the achievement of social benefits; this is a central element in their statutes. Also worth underlying is the fact that, in our sample, none of the SEs belonging to this model is currently a member of a network or group.

As far Gordon's (2015) tradition-related typology is concerned, answers to the ICSEM survey revealed that over 50% of the SEs belonging to this model were of the community-purpose type. As these SEs' social or environmental purpose is a priority, the community or a group of vulnerable people are their first beneficiaries. Due to their legal form, SEs belonging to this model do not allow the distribution of profits, and any kind of surplus must be reinvested in the organisation. The legal form also dictates that the initiative must originate in the resourcefulness of a group of individuals or a third-sector organisation, with a social mission to benefit a particular community or geographic area.

Organisations belonging to the non-profit SE model thus match all the indicators of the social and economic dimensions of the EMES ideal-typical social enterprise. As far as the governance dimension is concerned, the indicators relating to autonomy and the decision-making power are also met by nearly all organisations in this group. Indeed, almost all the organisations of this model strive for and maintain a high degree of autonomy in their management and direction, despite their dependence on private donations/funds or public subsidies. However, there are mixed situations in terms of the participatory nature of governance. In some organisations, various parties are strongly involved in the decision-making process, while in others, the decision-making power is centralised in the hands of the founding group or of an individual promoter.

An example of SE of the non-profit SE type is APROPO, a non-profit organisation that has been providing free sexual-orientation services (such as family planning and sexual education) to the general public since 1983. APROPO achieves its sustainability through the selling of its own brand of condoms and also receives donations and financial aid. Both operations—the free provision of sexual-orientation services and the commercialisation of condoms—are carried out by the NGO. Due to its legal form, APROPO is authorised to receive external funds from donors or international aid to scale up its social projects.

2.3. Social-Cooperative Model

The social-cooperative model includes SEs operating under the legal form of cooperative, which is regulated by the General Law of Cooperatives (*Ley General de Cooperativas*), enacted in 2011.

The outcome emphasis of SEs belonging to this model is put on providing a social benefit to the SE members and their community, and on achieving self-sustainability through the participation and contribution of the SE's partners. Partners are simultaneously "investors" and beneficiaries of the SE. Therefore, the programme focus of this model is to benefit the partners in different ways such as: (1) possibility for the members to buy and sell products within the cooperative; (2) possibility for the members to act as both providers and receivers of technical training, in a mutual learning process; or (3) possibility for the members to contribute to the SE's governance by occupying governance roles. SEs of the social-cooperative type aim to benefit and develop the community within which they operate and to establish projects launched collectively; they thus correspond to the mutual- and community-purpose types in Gordon's typology.

The strategic development of SEs of this type is supported by the market, but their growth is limited by the financial capacities of the cooperative's members. Indeed, the law provides that cooperatives can only raise funds from their members (Law No. 29683 2011). For example, in the specific case of credit unions, three limitations exist: (1) they can only raise funds from their members; (2) they can only grant credits to their members; and (3) their deposits are not endorsed by the Deposit Insurance Fund (*Fondo de Seguro de Depósitos*) (Law No. 26702 1996). As for Kerlin's societal-sector variable, these organisations fit in the social-economy sector, as cooperatives follow a social-oriented approach, benefiting their members and the community in which they exist through market-based activities. Finally, none of the SEs belonging to this model is a member of a network or group.

As can be observed in table 8.3, regarding the dimensions analysed in the EMES approach, SEs of this type meet all the indicators of each of the three dimensions. Particularly worth noting is the fact that SEs of the social-cooperative type are the only organisations in Peru that explicitly comply with the indicator relative to not having the decision-making power based on capital ownership; this commitment is indeed part of their statutes.

An example of SE belonging to this model is Santa Rosa Savings and Credit Cooperative. A group of citizens, initially motivated by a priest from the area, invested the initial capital to create a cooperative that would give them access to services that the traditional financial system denied them. Each member of Santa Rosa has one vote, regardless of their capital contribution, and strategic decisions are made democratically by the general assembly of members. When there is a surplus, it is distributed to the members in proportion to their transactions with the cooperative. The social goal of the cooperative is to offer credit and financial services to cooperative members. Like it is the case in most savings and credit cooperatives, these services are provided only to the members.

2.4. Social-Business Model

SEs belonging to the social-business model are market-based ventures that pursue social objectives (Yunus 2010). In the Peruvian context, they can operate under three distinct legal forms: as closed corporations (*Sociedad Anónima Cerrada*, or SAC), as open corporations (*Sociedad Anónima Abierta*, or SAA) (Law No. 26887 1997) or as individual limited-liability companies (*Sociedad de Responsabilidad Limitada*, or SRL) (Law No. 21621 1976).

Their strategy development and outcome emphasis are closely connected. The former does not aim at profit maximisation but at the adoption and inclusion of business tools to operate in a competitive market and, at the same time, achieve their social mission. Some SEs of this type have been successful in winning initial funding from incubator services and technical support from private agencies. However, their sustainability depends on the development of initiatives, based on the continuous use of the most effective business methods. As a consequence, their outcome emphasis is on both social and economic results.

The programme area focus of most SEs of the social-business type is the provision of human services through employment and trade activities. The market economy constitutes the immediate environment or societal sector in which these activities are carried out. Production can be central and related to the social/environmental mission but it is not a requirement. In this type of SE, profit distribution is permitted—and even desirable—and it is not formally limited, but it is conditioned by the purpose of creating positive impact in society and the environment. In Gordon's tradition-based typology, these SEs would correspond to the private-market-purpose type of SE. The core value of these initiatives refers to the generation of benefits for their customers and, more broadly, society, while still maintaining a private-profit objective. Finally, none of the SEs belonging to this model is currently a member of a network or group.

In Peru, certified B Corps are an example of this type of SE. One of them is Sustainable Fishery Trade, a closed corporation supporting fair and sustainable trade for artisanal fisheries. The company's supplies come directly from small fishing communities; the fish are then sold to restaurants and retail shops. The corporation develops a shared-value approach. By eliminating intermediaries, Sustainable Fishery Trade helps to ensure improved livelihoods for fishing households. The enterprise also strives to encourage positive conservation practices and to minimise overfishing of marine species by offering training in sustainable harvesting to fishing communities. Beside its trading activity, the SE develops projects to improve the quality of life of fishermen and supports research on marine resources preservation. In order to scale up its operations, the SE has received funds from social investors and research partners.

Concerning the EMES indicators, as table 8.3 shows, SEs of the social-business type meet all the indicators of the economic and entrepreneurial dimension. Regarding the social dimension, it is observed that SEs belonging to this model do pursue an explicit objective to benefit the community; however, as far as the other two indicators of this dimension are concerned, the degree of compliance varies, depending on the founder's choices. Social businesses are not bound to refrain from profit-sharing, but social entrepreneurs from this model aim to ensure that profit distribution does not compromise the organisation's social purpose. And since the existence of the SE is usually linked to strong individual leadership, the indicator about the social enterprise being an initiative launched by a group of citizens or civil society organisations is rarely met. Finally, as regards the participatory governance dimension, organisations belonging to the social-business model fully comply with only one indicator: they have a high degree of autonomy. Compliance with the other two indicators—a decision-making power not based on capital ownership and a participatory nature—is not legally required. As a result, natural or legal persons who chose this organisational form seek to implement a decision-making process based on capital ownership. However, even when such a process is actually implemented, entrepreneurs in SEs belonging to this model use different mechanisms of communication to take stakeholders into account in their decision-making process.

2.5. Non-Profit/Social Business Partnership Model

The last model results from the dynamics at play between at least two organisations that are recognised as being in practice (but not necessarily formally) members of a same network or group. Each organisation of the group adopts a specific legal form that "embodies" its unique organisational dynamics. It can be said that this SE model represents the fusion of the non-profit SE and the social-business models. Such merger can take two forms: (1) a social-business venture can set up a traditional non-profit organisation; or (2) a non-profit organisation can create a social business.

Given the particular nature of enterprises belonging to this model, their outcome emphasis or immediate goals (Kerlin 2010) are both economic and social benefits. The non-profit partner underlines the organisation's foundational social commitment, while the social business implements a strong market-focus strategy in a responsible way. The predominant programme area focus of these SEs corresponds to commercial and employment activities (for the business "side" of the partnership) and to the pursuit of social or environmental benefits (for the non-profit "side"). Therefore, the societal sector in which these SEs operate corresponds both to the market economy and the social economy. As for the SE type according to Gordon tradition-based typology, entrepreneurs of this model consider that their organisations fit with three models: the community-purpose, altruistic-purpose and private-market-purpose types. The ambivalence of this "fusion" model allows a strategic development based both on the market and on donors.

In the specific case of social businesses that create non-profit organisations to develop their social missions/programmes, the fact of adopting the legal form of closed corporation provides them with a framework that allows them to operate with business methods and to generate and distribute profits. Profits generated by the business flow into the non-profit organisation, as this NPO is the social business' main shareholder. Social activities are carried out by non-profit subsidiaries or branches created by the social business. For example, Uma Vida is a closed corporation that sells bottled water under the brand name "Yaqua". Uma Vida created a non-profit organisation, named Bien por Bien, to carry out its social projects. Uma Vida uses the revenues that it generates to finance Bien por Bien—or, in other words, to finance its social mission. To make this partnership relation possible, Uma Vida transferred 99% of its shares to Bien por Bien.

On the other hand, as explained above, there are also non-profits that develop social-business initiatives or provide services or funding to accelerate such initiatives' growth and ensure their success (Gutiérrez and Rafael 2012). These social businesses usually share the social mission of the non-profit founder. In this way, a network is created between two or more ventures, where the grantee is accountable to the one who financed the initiative, and both can have different legal forms. For example, Puriy, a closed corporation, is a social business that sells handmade moccasins with the social objective to help women who have experienced violence. This venture was funded by PADMA, a non-profit organisation that shares Puriy's social mission. As a strategy to achieve self-sustainability, non-profits develop subsidiaries, such as Puriy, to develop a market activity and generate benefits that are then returned to the non-profit. In these cases, the social business can be created under one of the two forms embodied in the Corporation Law, that is either as a closed corporation (SAC) or as an open corporation (SAA).

In terms of the EMES indicators, as can be seen in table 8.3, this model is the one that presents the most complex picture in terms of compliance with the indicators of the social and governance dimensions. All SEs belonging to this model fulfil all the indicators of the economic dimension as well as the social-dimension indicator relating to the explicit aim to benefit the community. Compliance with the other two social indicators—i.e. being an initiative launched by a group of citizens or a civil-society organisation and having a limited profit distribution—and with the three indicators of the governance dimension depends on the type of partnership developed by the social business and the non-profit, as there does not exist any regulatory framework governing this type of initiative.

Conclusions

The emergence of social enterprise in Peru is a product of the hybridisation process undergone by organisations of the third sector that start looking at the market as an ally to survive and to scale up social solutions, and by businesses that believe that their success is interdependent with societal welfare and that they are ethically obliged to be part of a change in the system.

A SE is a private and formal organisation with an entrepreneurial dynamic and market strategies whose aim is to tackle a social or environmental problem and which is economically sustainable, mainly thanks to the sale of a product or service in the market and, to a lesser extent, to the use of other public or private funds. Their profit-distribution policy is coherent with their purpose.

Peru has had a tradition of solidarity practices throughout its history. The country's third sector is made up of organisations based on solidarity and cooperation, such as cooperatives, non-profit organisations and popular organisations. As a result, in Peru, the third sector is considered to be the same as the social and solidarity economy. Nevertheless, the concept of social and solidarity economy has long had only a limited diffusion in the Peruvian society. In recent years, though, external factors, such as the progressive withdrawal of international aid funds, has made non-profit organisations turn to the market as an ally to create welfare.

In parallel, the business sector's social orientation has progressed; this evolution is reflected in the incorporation of social and environmental standards in enterprises' core businesses and in their interest to explore strategic CSR, inclusive businesses and shared-value activities. This situation results in a process of organisational hybridisation which in turn gives rise to initiatives that, in Peru, could be denominated as social enterprise.

One of the challenges for social enterprises in Peru is the lack of a specific legal framework, which leads initiatives to adopt a legal structure (or even two, in some cases) that do(es) not exactly suit their needs. This situation increases the costs incurred by the enterprise and complicates its management.

Four models of social enterprise were found to represent the Peruvian context, namely: the non-profit SE model, the social-business model, the social-cooperative model and the non-profit/social-business model. However, these four types of SE do not necessarily see each other as part of the same group. Consequently, there is a lack of identity among the different types of SE, which might constitute a limitation when it comes to learning from others' good practices. All of these SEs also face challenges for scaling up and for designing and implementing a good governance system.

The social-business model tends to focus more on economic results, while the non-profit SE model tends to concentrate on social outcomes. The challenge for both of them is to find a good balance between these two types of results. The social-cooperative model has a clear communitarian and solidarity spirit, but it lacks legitimacy within a part of society. Finally, it should be mentioned that these three SE models also require donations as an alternative way to generate income and ensure their operation. Therefore, although they generate social transformation and changes in the entrepreneurial ecosystem, greater public and private institutional support is required, at least in the initial phases and for their consolidation.

To conclude, it is also important to note that, although some SEs display a management system based on participatory governance and solidarity, there is no formal concern for these issues in the country. As a result, some EMES indicators of SE were not systematically identified in our analysis of Peruvian SEs: stakeholders' involvement (participatory nature), internal democracy (decision-making power not based on capital ownership), initiatives' leadership (initiative launched by a group of citizens or a civil-society organisation) and solidarity principles (limited profit distribution) are dimensions that are not encountered in all types of Peruvian SE.

Acknowledgements

The authors would like to thank and recognise the exceptional work of Frances Ninahuanca, research assistant at Universidad del Pacífico, who collaborated in the data processing and construction of SE models. His accurate contribution to the final edition of this chapter was also very helpful.

Notes

1 Kerlin (2010) refers to the "organisational type" where, in Peru, the terms "legal form" would be used.
2 Although, originally, the term "NGO" was used to identify a group of non-profit organisations that were created in a context of intense political mobilisation and social change, between 1960 and 1980 (Portocarrero and Sanborn 1998), nowadays the terms "non-profit organisation" and "non-governmental

organisation" are considered as equivalent and used interchangeably in the Peruvian context.

3 "The Glass-of-Milk Programme is a social programme of food assistance managed by provincial municipalities throughout Peru, which consists of the distribution of milk to the population living in poverty, and more specifically to children under 6 and pregnant and lactating mothers, as a first priority, and to children from 7 to 13 years old, the elderly and people with tuberculosis, as a second priority. This programme emerged in the 1980s in a context of crisis, and although it was institutionalised by the mayor of Lima Metropolitan, Alfonso Barrantes, the truth is that the operation and implementation of the programme was entrusted to the women from the local committees" (Cerna 2015: 2). Indeed, women were already in charge of the community kitchens in vulnerable areas, so they quite naturally took responsibility for the promotion and implementation of the Glass-of-Milk Programme in their communities.

References

Alter, K. (2003) *Social enterprise: A typology of the field contextualized in Latin America*, Washington, DC: Inter-American Development Bank. Available HTTP: https://publications.iadb.org/en/social-enterprise-typology-field-con textualized-latin-america (accessed on June 1, 2017).

Ayerbe, L. F. & Dupas, G. (eds) (2005) *América Latina. A comienzos del siglo XXI. Perspectivas económicas, sociales y políticas*, Rosario: Homo Sapiens Ediciones.

Borgaza, C., Galera, G. & Nogales, R. (2008) *Social Enterprise: A New Model for Poverty Reduction and Employment Generation: An Examination of the Concept and Practice in Europe and the Commonwealth of Independent States*, Bratislava: Programme des Nations Unies pour le Développement. Available HTTP: www.emes.net/uploads/media/11.08_EMES_UNDP_publication.pdf (accessed on June 3, 2014).

Caballero, S., Fuchs, R. M. & Prialé, M. A. (2013) "The influence of personality traits on social enterprise start-up: The case of Peruvian social entrepreneurs", 4th EMES International Research Conference on Social Enterprise, Liege.

Caravedo, B. (2010) "Paradigma, ética y gestión (a propoósito de la responsabilidad social)", *Revista de la Facultad de Derecho de la Pontificia Universidad Católica del Perú*, No. 64, pp. 67–82.

Cermeño, R. & De la Cruz, M. (1991) "Inflación y precios industriales: Perú 1980–1990", *Economía*, Vol. 14, No. 27, pp. 171–208.

Cerna, S. (2015) "Mujeres, leche y política: Estudio comparativo del Programa del Vaso de Leche". Available HTTP: http://files.pucp.edu.pe/sistema-ponen cias/wp-content/uploads/2015/01/Mujeres-leche-y-pol%C3%ADtica.-Estu dio-comparativo-del-Programa-del-Vaso-de-Leche.pdf (accessed on July 28, 2018).

Colectivo de ONG Belgas del Perú—COEECI. (2013) "Seis desafíos de la cooperación internacional en Perú: Desafíos, implicancias y recomendaciones". Available HTTP: www.coeeci.org.pe/nueva-publicacion-6-desafios-de-la-coop eracion-internacional-en-el-peru/ (accessed on November 26, 2017).

Confiep. (2017) "Gestión institucional". Available HTTP: www.confiep.org.pe/ articulos/gestion-institucional/educacion (accessed on November 26, 2017).

Conger, L., Inga, P. & Webb, R. (2009) *El árbol de la mostaza: Historia de las microfinanzas en el Perú*, Lima: Universidad de San Martín de Porres. Available HTTP: www.institutodelperu.org.pe/index.php?option=com_content& task=view&id=1187&Itemid=76 (accessed on December 15, 2014).

Congreso. (2003) "Ley No. 28015: Ley de promoción y formalización de la micro y pequeña empresa". Available HTTP: https://alianzapacifico.net/observatorio-regional-pymes/images/ley-28015.pdf (accessed on November 25, 2017).

Congreso. (2013) "Ley No. 30056: Ley que modifica diversas leyes para facilitar la inversión, impulsar el desarrollo productivo y el crecimiento empresarial". Available HTTP: http://www2.congreso.gob.pe/sicr/cendocbib/con4_uibd. nsf/29793AB3817C627505257EF400034156/$FILE/30056.pdf (accessed on November 25, 2017).

Crabtree, J. (2005) *Alan García en el poder: Perú 1985–1990*, Lima: Ediciones Peisa.

De Belaunde, A. (2017) "Proyecto de ley No. 2533–2017/CR". Available HTTP:// www.leyes.congreso.gob.pe/Documentos/2016_2021/Proyectos_de_Ley_y_ de_Resoluciones_Legislativas/PL0253320180308.pdf (accessed on July 29, 2019).

De Belaúnde, J. & Parodi, B. (1998) "Marco legal del sector privado sin fines de lucro en el Perú". Available HTTP: http://revistas.up.edu.pe/index.php/ apuntes/article/view/292/282 (accessed on June 11, 2017).

Dees, G. & Anderson, B. (2006) "Framing a theory of social entrepreneurship: Building on two schools of practice and thought", in Mosher-Williams, R. (ed.) *Research on Social Entrepreneurship: Understanding and Contributing to an Emerging Field*, Indianapolis: ARNOVA, pp. 39–66. Available HTTP: https:// centers.fuqua.duke.edu/case/knowledge_items/framing-a-theory-of-social-entrepreneurship-building-on-two-schools-of-practice-and-thought/ (accessed on October 13, 2016).

Defourny, J. & Nyssens, M. (2012) "El enfoque EMES de la empresa social desde una perspectiva comparada", *CIRIEC- España Revista de la Economía Pública, Social y Cooperativa*, No. 75, pp. 7–34.

Defourny, J. & Nyssens, M. (2017) "Fundamentals for an international typology of social enterprise models", *Voluntas: International Journal of Voluntary and Nonprofit Organizations*, Vol. 28, No. 6, pp. 2469–2497.

Farber, V. A., Caballero, S., Prialé, M. A. & Fuchs, R. M. (2015) "Social enterprises in Lima: Notions and operating models", *Journal of Entrepreneurship and Innovation in Emerging Economies*, Vol. 1, No. 1, pp. 56–78.

Favreau, L., Fréchette, L., Boulianne, M. & Kemenade, S. (2002) "Desarrollo local, economía popular y economía solidaria en América Latina: un itinerario de 30 años en Villa el Salvador, Perú", *CAYAPA Revista Venezolana de Economía Social*, Vol. 2, No. 3, pp. 1–13.

Gestión. (2018) "SBS: En Perú más de 500 cooperativas de ahorro y crédito no tienen supervisión, pero captan depósitos". Available at HTPP: https://ges tion.pe/economia/sbs-peru-500-cooperativas-ahorro-credito-supervision-cap tan-depositos-225999 (accessed on August 2, 2018).

Ghezzi, P. & Gallardo, J. (2013) *¿Qué se puede hacer con el Perú? Ideas para sostener el crecimiento en el largo plazo*, Lima: Universidad del Pacífico y Pontificia Universidad Católica del Perú.

Gordon, M. (2015) "A typology of social enterprise 'Traditions'", *ICSEM Working Papers*, No. 18, Liege: The International Comparative Social Enterprise Models (ICSEM) Project.

Guerra, P. (2010) "La economía solidaria en Latinoamérica", *Papeles de relaciones ecosociales y cambio global*, No. 110, pp. 67–76. Available HTTP: http://base.socioeco.org/docs/la_economia_solidaria_en_latinoamerica_p_guerra.pdf (accessed on June 1, 2017).

Gutiérrez, A. & Rafael, E. (2012) "Incubación empresarial en la Universidad Nacional Mayor de San Marcos: Una estrategia para efectivizar su compromiso con el desarrollo económico y social del país", *Revista de la Facultad de Ciencias Contables*, Vol. 20, No. 37, pp. 131–144.

INEI & PRODUCE (2017) "Perú: Censo Nacional de Cooperativas 2017". Available HTTP: www.fenacrep.org/assets/media/documentos/noticias-docu mentos/resumen-ejecutivo_censo-nacional-de-cooperativas.pdf (accessed on June 11, 2017).

Instituto de Democracia y Derechos Humanos de la Pontificia Universidad Católica del Perú—IDEHPUCP. (2009) *El sistema político durante el proceso de violencia*, Lima: Colección Cuadernos para la Memoria Histórica, No. 5.

Instituto Nacional de Estadística e Informática—INEI. (2013) "Evolución de la pobreza monetaria en el Perú al 2012". Available HTTP: www.inei.gob.pe/media/cifras_de_pobreza/pobreza_exposicionjefe2013.pdf (accessed on February 1, 2014).

Kerlin, J. (2010) "A comparative analysis of the global emergence of social enterprise", *Voluntas*, Vol. 21, pp. 162–179.

La República. (2018) "Las cooperativas de ahorro y crédito se duplicaron en 5 años". Available HTPP: https://larepublica.pe/economia/1248219-cooperati vas-ahorro-credito-duplicaron-5-anos (accessed on August 2, 2018).

Law No. 21621: Ley de la Empresa Individual de Responsabilidad Limitada—E.I.R.L., *Diario Oficial El Peruano*, Lima, September 14, 1976.

Law No. 25307, *Diario Oficial El Peruano*, Lima, January 28, 1991.

Law No. 26702: Ley General del Sistema Financiero y del Sistema de Seguros y Orgánica de la Superintendencia de Banca y Seguros, *Diario Oficial El Peruano*, Lima, December 9, 1996.

Law No. 26887: Ley General de Sociedades, *Diario Oficial El Peruano*, Lima, December 5, 1997.

Law No. 29683: Ley General de Cooperativas, *Diario Oficial El Peruano*, Lima, May 13, 2011.

Legislative Decree No. 295: Código Civil, *Diario Oficial El Peruano*, Lima, July 25, 1984.

Márquez, P. C., Reffico, E. & Berger, G. (2010) *Negocios inclusivos: Iniciativas de mercado con los pobres de Iberoamérica*, Washington, DC: Banco Interamericano de Desarrollo.

Ministerio de Justicia y Derechos Humanos. (2015) "Código Civil". Available HTTP: http://spij.minjus.gob.pe/notificacion/guias/CODIGO-CIVIL.pdf (accessed on June 11, 2017).

Mogrovejo, R., Vanhuynegem, P. & Vásquez, M. (2012) *Visión panorámica del sector cooperativo en Perú: El renacimiento de un modelo*, International Labour Office & ILO Sub-regional Office for the Andean Countries. Available HTTP: www.aciamericas.coop/IMG/pdf/wcms_185026.pdf (accessed on December 3, 2013).

Montoya, L. (2017) *¿Otras economías? Experiencias económico sociales y solidarias en Perú*, Lima: Tarea.

NESST & Digital Divide Data. (2014) *Valor compartido: Haciendo negocios con empresas sociales*, Lima: NESST & Digital Divide Data.

Ortiz, H. (2002) "Economía popular, economía solidaria, fuerza para el desarrollo humano en el Perú y en el sur del mundo". Mimeo. Available HTTP: www.economiasolidaria.org/files/ortiz.pdf (accessed on June 1, 2017).

Peru 2021. (2017) "Nosotros". Available HTTP: http://peru2021.org/nosotros/#3 (accessed on November 25, 2017).

Porter, M. & Kramer, M. (2011) "Creating shared value", *Harvard Business Review*, Vol. 89, No. 1. Available HTTP: https://hbr.org/2011/01/the-big-idea-creating-shared-value (accessed on November 25, 2017).

Portocarrero, F. & Sanborn, C. (1998) "Entre el Estado y el mercado: definiendo al sector sin fines de lucro en el Perú", *Apuntes*, No. 43, pp. 45–80. Available HTTP: http://revistas.up.edu.pe/index.php/apuntes/article/view/477 (accessed on November 25, 2017).

Portocarrero, F., Sanborn, C., Cueva, H. & Millán, A. (2002) "Más allá del individualismo. El tercer sector en el Perú". Available HTTP: http://repositorio.up.edu.pe/handle/11354/199 (accessed on November 25, 2017).

PRODUCE (2009) "Manual para la gestión empresarial de las cooperativas de servicios". Available HTTP: www.apomipe.org.pe/codigo_php/imagenes/download/MANUAL%20DE%20COOPERATIVAS%20DE%20SERVICIOS%20Parte1.pdf (accessed on November 10, 2013).

PRODUCE (2017) "Ministro Pedro Olaechea: En el Perú existen 1.245 cooperativas, de las cuales más del 90% son MYPE". Available HTTP: www.produce.gob.pe/index.php/k2/noticias/item/670-ministro-pedro-olaechea-en-el-peru-existen-1-245-cooperativas-de-las-cuales-mas-del-90-son-mype (accessed on November 25, 2017).

Quijano, A. (1998) *La economía popular y sus caminos en América Latina*, Lima: Mosca Azul Editores, CEIS-CECOSAM.

RPP (2016) "Gobierno publicó nuevo Régimen Mype tributario". Available HTTP: http://rpp.pe/economia/economia/gobierno-publico-nuevo-regimen-mype-tributario-noticia-1017819 (accessed on November 25, 2017).

Sahley, C. & Danziger, J. (1999) *Rising to the Urban Challenge? The Role, Strategies and Performance of NGOs in Lima, Peru*, Oxford: Intrax The International NGO Training and Research Centre. Available HTTP: http://dspace.africaportal.org/jspui/bitstream/123456789/21782/1/Rising%20to%20the%20Urban%20Challenge%20The%20Roles%20Strategies%20and%20Performance%20of%20NGOs%20in%20Lima%20Peru.pdf?1 (accessed on June 11, 2017).

Sanborn, C. (2008) "Del dicho al hecho: Empresarios y responsabilidad social en el Perú". Available HTTP: http://srvnetappseg.up.edu.pe/siswebciup/Files/DD%20-%20Sanborn%20Del%20dico%20al%20hecho.pdf (accessed on November 25, 2017).

Sánchez, A. (2015) "Migraciones internas en el Perú". Available HTTP: www.oimperu.org/sitehome/sites/default/files/Documentos/03-03-2015_Publicacion%20Migraciones%20Internas_OIM.PDF (accessed on July 29, 2018).

Schaller, S. (2007) "Reforma Agraria y productividad: Ensayo sobre las razones de la pobreza rural en el Perú", *Investigaciones Sociales*, Vol. 11, No. 19, pp. 321–343.

Schydlowsky, D. (1989) "La debacle peruana: ¿Dinámica económica o causas políticas?" *Apuntes*, No. 25, pp. 1–25.

Sistema B. (2017) "Quienes somos". Available HTTP: http://sistemab.org/quienes-somos-4/ (accessed on November 25, 2017).

SNV & WBCSD (2010) "Inclusive business: Creating value in Latin America". Available HTTP: www.snv.org/public/cms/sites/default/files/explore/download/wbcsd_snv_inclusive_business_latam.pdf (accessed on November 25, 2017).

Sulmont, D. (1999) "La responsabilidad social en la mirada del empresariado peruano". Available HTTP: http://files.pucp.edu.pe/departamento/economia/LDE-2001-05-15.pdf (accessed on November 25, 2017).

Universidad del Pacífico. (2015) "Las Empresas B se abren paso en el Perú". Available HTTP: www.up.edu.pe/prensa/noticias/las-empresas-b-se-abren-paso-en-el-peru (accessed on November 25, 2017).

Vera, A., Prialé, M. A., Fuchs, R. M., Espinosa, A., Seminario, M. A. & Ninahuanca, E. F. (2016) "Hacia una comprensión del ecosistema emprendedor social peruano: contexto y características del emprendimiento social en Lima", *Ciências Sociais Unisinos*, Vol. 52, No. 3, pp. 343–353.

Yunus, M. (2010) *Building Social Business: Capitalism That Can Serve Humanity's Most Pressing Needs*, New York: Public Affairs.

Part II

Comparative Analysis and Perspectives Across Latin America Countries

9 Social Enterprises in Latin America

Patterns and Historical Relevance

Luiz Inácio Gaiger and
Fernanda Wanderley[1]

Introduction

The main goal of this chapter is to present a brief overview of the set of initiatives that correspond, in the Latin American context, to the ideal-typical[2] concept of *social enterprise* as it has been defined by the EMES Network (Defourny and Nyssens 2011, 2012). As has been explained in the book's introduction and in previous chapters, social enterprises are considered to be those organisations that are guided by a social mission, be it implicit or explicit, and that carry out economic activities in order to attain their social goals. Private appropriation of the surpluses produced by the economic activity of these organisations is prohibited to their members, or else it is restricted; this constraint on the distribution of profits distinguishes social enterprises from the private, profit-seeking companies typical of a capitalist economy. Social enterprises also differ from the public economy, as they are not state-owned and enjoy institutional and managerial autonomy. Finally, being often based on principles of equality and free association, they are usually governed in accordance with democratic standards and in a participatory manner.

In Latin America, organisations that are driven by a social mission preserve or create other types of economic rationalities than the pure capitalist narrow economic rationality. We will emphasise how these economic forms cannot be dissociated from their agents and human surroundings, as they are usually not only socially oriented but also *embedded* (Polanyi 2001: 45–58).

Even though the organisations conceptualised as social enterprises in Latin America operate on the market, their rationality, as will be discussed throughout this chapter, cannot be reduced, in general, to the principle of exchange currently instituted (Polanyi 1957) in the prevailing market economy. Indeed, they also fulfil essential functions of conservation or promotion of hybrid forms of economy, acting as vectors of economic plurality. In some cases, they oppose the capitalist economy and the powers exerted on its behalf; they promote the participation of new actors in politics and in the public sphere and they convey, to a greater or lesser extent, society's demands and calls for change.

DOI: 10.4324/9780429055164-12

Before we examine the panorama of Latin American social enterprises, it is important to introduce some common economic, social and political aspects of Latin America, since the worldviews, interest groups and forms of collective action emerging from these general aspects gave rise to alternative types of economic organisations. Among them, particularly worth highlighting here are the aforementioned socially oriented organisations and other recent innovations that seek to give a new twist to the utilitarian logic of the market, and to create positive social impacts through economic action.

Overall, it can be argued that the initiatives analysed in this book reflect participative and democratic aspirations that have persisted through Latin American history, despite recurrent obstacles and setbacks. The continent has recently undergone a process of political "re-democratisation", following an eruption of military dictatorships in the 1960s and 1970s; such process restored the competitive electoral regime and its associated political rights. However, despite the achievements of the last 40 years, democracy remains a goal that has not yet been fully reached.

One of the causes of Latin American democratic fragility is the perpetuation of high concentrations of wealth in the hands of powerful elites, while a significant portion of the population lives in poverty and destitution. Latin America remains the most unequal region in the world, despite a significant reduction of inequality and income poverty between 2002 and 2014. According to CEPAL (2017), in 2014, the richest 10% of the population owned 71% of the region's wealth, while 168 million people (29.8% of the population) were poor, and 48 million (8.2% of the population) lived in extreme poverty. The positive trend observed between 2002 and 2014 was abruptly reversed from 2015 onward, when 16 million people joined the ranks of those living in poverty (10 million people) or in extreme poverty (6 million people); in 2016, another 8 million poor and 7 million indigents were added to these figures. The lack of substantive democracy in Latin America is also reflected in the exclusion of citizens from the exercise of social rights recognised by the national constitutions. In spite of the expansion of access to education, health, housing, retirement and unemployment insurance, significant differences in coverage and quality of services and public benefits among countries remain.

From the normative standpoint of participatory and deliberative democracy, it can be argued that the Latin American trajectory is still in its early stages, given its irregular, fragmented experiences and incipient institutionalisation. The reduction of democracy to its electoral dimension and the considerable weaknesses rooted in its proper functioning maintain a gap between citizens and their political representatives. These factors also explain the difficulties faced by sectors of organised civil society when trying to implement transparency-enhancing mechanisms in decision-making, and control and follow-up of public policies. As a result, inconsistent and ambiguous legal frameworks, as well as discontinuities in public policy, continue to exist.

In the economic sphere, Latin America has not overcome the colonial legacy of primary-product-exporting economies at the service of global capital accumulation. Despite differences among the region's national productive structures, the growth pattern based on extraction and export of low-value-added natural or agricultural resources still prevails. Besides being highly dependent on the international cycles of high and low prices, the primary production and extractivist growth pattern has been responsible for an accelerated loss of environmental assets, increased social conflicts, violence and human-rights vulnerability. The beginning of the 21st century illustrates Latin America's strong dependence on global dynamics: between 2004 and 2014, the region experienced exponential economic growth, which resulted in social advances, followed by setbacks inseparable from the crises caused by fluctuation in the global demand for raw materials and commodities.

This brief characterisation helps to situate social-enterprise-like initiatives in recent times and, above all, to understand their role in strengthening formal and substantive democracy. A salient feature of many initiatives in the social-enterprise field in Latin America is the predominance of grassroots actors, operating on the margins of capitalist dynamics and excluded from institutionalised systems of solidarity. Their social position has liberated a potent collective energy to transform the asymmetric structures of economic, political and social power in the region. In such cases, the transformational forces that arise from the organisational characteristics of these economic units and from the worldviews of the individuals that promote them are multidimensional. In the economic sphere, the social mission of organisations, the cooperative way in which work is organised within them and the equitable distribution of surpluses among members are powerful channels for subverting the capitalist logic of private accumulation of wealth. In the context of governance, the autonomous collective management implemented by these economic units is a practical exercise and a fundamental institutional learning experience for the strengthening of participatory and deliberative democratic cultures. In the public sphere, the struggle for the legal recognition of the diversity of economic organisations and the leadership assumed by these organisations in proposing appropriate public policies and normative frameworks contribute to building alternative development routes, which take economic plurality into account. In the same way, experiences showing support for issues of general interest have been proliferating—from active participation in the collapse of military dictatorships to resistance against neoliberal globalisation at the dawn of the 21st century.

Having looked at these contextual aspects, we will proceed to share some considerations about the method used to identify the general *patterns* of social enterprise; then, in section 2, an integrated and synthetic view of the models already presented in the chapters on individual countries will be discussed. In the last section of the chapter, we will emphasise some significant features of social enterprise in Latin America, to conclude that their historical relevance, in addition to the aspects highlighted above, resides in the institutionalisation of plural, socially binding forms of economy, based mainly on the principle of reciprocity.

1. Methodological Aspects

As mentioned in the preceding chapters, the concept of social enterprise is unusual, from the institutional and academic points of view, in most Latin American countries. When employed, it usually has connotations restricted to certain social circles or linked to classifications established by the existing legal framework. In studies done at the national level, the concept is usually applied as a heuristic tool, with a view to identifying organisations that have traits notably similar to those that, in the European context, gave rise to the concept. Moreover, given the prevailing absence of comparable empirical cases, the concept of social enterprise has been maintained in the chapters on individual countries as an implicit reference: first, for purposes of demarcating the empirical field to be analysed; secondly, in order to qualify and compare the types of organisation already under consideration, from which the proposed typologies have resulted.

Thus, the national typologies did not emerge, for the most part, from the variation observed, among the empirical types under analysis, in regard to the dimensions and indicators contained in the EMES idealtypical concept. The latter was adopted to qualify and refine the preexisting types, already included in national typologies, in *ex-post* analyses that also made use of other converging theoretical and conceptual frameworks, as illustrated by the chapters on Argentina, Bolivia, Ecuador and Peru. With the exception of Peru, the pre-existing types were not selected based on a national historical evolution that would have been shaped by the concept of social enterprise, nor on any previous classification of these types in an institutional framework: as a rule, such evolution and such frameworks do not exist, even though they may come into being in the future.

As a rule of thumb, the choice of the social fields to be scrutinised in order to identify social enterprises at the national level was guided by the concepts most commonly used in each country, such as the "social and solidarity economy" (Argentina and Chile), the "popular solidarity economy" (Ecuador), the "community economy" (Bolivia) and the "social-impact enterprises" (Brazil). Whereas this chapter aims to propose a synthesis based on the national chapters, it would not be advisable to develop an all-encompassing typology by comparing the various national models and the ideal-typical concept of social enterprise. Indeed, no national model is replicated with a high degree of homogeneity in many countries, despite some similarities in the nomenclature employed; national particularities, in addition to the diversity of theoretical-methodological approaches adopted, makes it rather inappropriate to consider national models as general models for Latin America.

Nevertheless, it is possible and useful to draw some supranational *patterns* so as to produce a panoramic and integrated view of social enterprise in Latin America. This approach should be viewed as an intermediary analytical level—the third among the four levels of analysis presented in this volume:

- Researchers selected pre-existing types, already included in national typologies (first level), which they classified into models (second level). They used the EMES indicators to analyse these models, not to create them.
- In this chapter, we identify some concise "patterns" (third level), using this term in order to avoid any confusion or overlap with the term "model", already used in the chapters on individual countries, and also to point out that this is a third-degree analysis, which uses the results of second-degree constructions (the national models) which, in turn, are based on first-degree typologies, upon which the relevant empirical types in each country are built.
- In the last chapter of the book (chapter 11), on the basis of in-depth information collected from social entreprises on an international scale and of a theoretical framework which identifies a few major SE models (fourth level), the validity of these models at the level of South America will be tested.

In the present chapter, the main criterion used to identify and distinguish the main SE patterns was the identity of the *social agents* that act as the main protagonists and determine the onset and trajectory of the social enterprises included in the national models; these social agents are *collective agents*—a class, a social category, a group of individuals linked to a territory or a certain type of institution that acts and promotes social enterprises to meet needs or respond to common aspirations. Based on our observations, we considered that each kind of social agent corresponds to specific modalities of self-organisation and intervention in society. Under these circumstances, different types of initiatives are born and prosper; their main driving force is the meaning they take on for their leading actors, according to their ways of life and the institutional environment in which they exist.[3]

As far as this aspect goes, the homologies among the countries seem to indicate some important parallel trajectories between the social enterprises in the continent. Still, the methodological choice we have made with a view to defining patterns requires some additional clarification: On the one hand, this analytical perspective differs from institutionally oriented approaches, which are guided primarily by the existing legal frameworks. This choice can be justified by one simple reason: despite some equivalence between national laws, there is usually no congruence between legal normativeness and factual realities, and concrete realities can differ significantly from one country to the other. For example, although all countries have laws on cooperatives, these organisations' behaviour is highly ambiguous in several countries. On the other hand, since the patterns result from a process of reduction by synthesis, the nuances and differences between national realities will not always be mentioned. Finally, regarding the nomenclature of patterns, we thought that it would be better not to adopt terms usually employed, especially by legal frameworks.[4] This is meant to make it clear that the patterns are placed on a higher level of abstraction than the national models, and do not coincide perfectly with any empirical type in particular. Furthermore, it should be emphasised that the existence of a common legal form in national models or in general patterns does not guarantee that the organisations adopting it will be classified as social enterprises. For example, while it is true that the cooperative form constitutes a paradigm for a large number of social enterprises in Latin America, and appears under various models and patterns, in many cases the organisations legally registered as such turn away from cooperative ideals and, *a fortiori*, from the universe of social enterprises.

In addition, inspired by Henry Desroche's lessons (Bouchard 2008), we have adopted a gradualist approach: we did not discard from the list of social enterprises those organisations that do not meet all (or most of) the indicators of the EMES ideal-typical concept of SE, nor did we consider the corresponding empirical type, in its entirety, as *defective* in relation to a given dimension or indicator; instead, we have deemed it more relevant to distinguish the situations of *full* correspondence between the cases and the concept of reference from those of *partial* correspondence, thus identifying some atypical, hybrid situations, located at the border between social enterprises and similar organisations, as will be discussed in section 3.

2. Social-Enterprise Patterns in Latin America

The following patterns do not fit the national models perfectly. Neither are they intended to frame the numerous empirical types of social enterprise mentioned throughout the book. As we contrast patterns and national-level models, situations of partial correspondence and multiple linkages emerge, as a result of the composite state of empirical realities, and of the variety of methods used to construct the typologies in each country.[5] Social enterprises may also shift from one model or one pattern to another. For example, in the last two patterns, as we shall see, while the providers are professionals and volunteers working in the organisation, the beneficiaries are usually an external target audience; however, the dynamics of such organisations lead in some cases to the creation of small businesses, owned and collectively managed by the beneficiaries, as a way of improving their standard of living using market strategies. New collective enterprises then spring up, which have a collective and self-management profile, and rather correspond to another pattern, with these specific characteristics.

2.1. *Ethnic and Community-Based Organisations (COM)*

This pattern comprises the forms of economic and social activity promoted and managed within territorially delimited communities and whose overarching logic depends on individuals and collectives belonging to these communities for ethnic or ancestral reasons. It is characterised by its large extent throughout history and constitutes, for sure, the oldest "source" of organisations comparable to social enterprises in Latin America. Its origins go back to the societies of the native peoples who inhabited the continent before European colonisation. Emblematic cases are to be found in Bolivia and Mexico, although the pattern can also be observed in Chile, Ecuador and Brazil. Moreover, from the 19th century onwards, immigrants who arrived on the continent reproduced, in several regions, social ties of proximity and community dynamics. Subsequently, these patterns of sociability and community organisation moved to urban areas, where they generated similar organisations or promoted new solidarity practices, such as solidarity-finance initiatives.

Although community-based organisations have been systematically labelled by the elites as archaic and relegated to political powerlessness, it is this pattern that explains the historical and current presence of indigenous people, peasants and farmers in the public space. This has sometimes resulted in a high degree of institutionalisation, in which case the ethnic community and its traditions are supported by legal rights granted to the territories and their inhabitants, as is the case with the "traditional peoples" in Brazil. Among the countries surveyed, Bolivia offers the best and most institutionalised example: in this country, the organisations representative of this pattern are based on autonomous ethnic-communitarian structures entrusted with the governance and management of their territories, with respect to common goods (land, water, forests and infrastructure) and economic activities (extractivism, production, marketing, fishing, tourism, etc.). In Chile, indigenous organisations carry out economic activities within the framework of their ethnic and kinship relations. In Ecuador, rural organisations work for the communities' benefit, going beyond their direct members' immediate interest; they engage in environmental issues and fair-trade practices, among others, while being active in the public sphere. In Mexico, the indigenous communities' organisations play a key role in preserving their culture and socio-economic traditions, although they also suffer from neglect by the authorities and a lack of social recognition.

2.2. *Traditional Social-Economy Organisations (SEC)*

This pattern is close to the historical forms of organisation that gave shape to the social economy, mainly in Europe and Canada. It still endures nowadays in several Latin American countries and can be considered as the matrix of a large number of organisations that conduct economic activities, are socially oriented and are conducted by their members on an equal footing. In some countries, the mutualist part of the social economy was very important during the 19th century; this was for example the case in Chile, where mutual organisations' innovative operations extended to a number of fronts, from equal rights for women and men to adult education. Across the continent, associations were created for social-integration purposes and to provide services of common interest. Mutual societies and cooperatives were set up for the most part by European immigrants who developed family farming and based it on community bonds. The main form of organisation was the cooperative, which had its own specific doctrine and was generally identified with the cooperative movement. Over time, cooperatives expanded into several economic sectors—from agriculture to credit—and were gradually promoted by various social, rural and urban categories. In addition, cooperatives "switched" from the universe of workers to the medium-sized-enterprise and business sectors; this was particularly true for (sometimes large) agricultural cooperatives geared to the commodities sector and the international market. Examples of this pattern and its evolution are found in the seven countries studied.

This pattern enjoys a high degree of institutionalisation, including representative bodies and considerable political influence. The cooperative is the most common type of organisation in this pattern, but although relatively homogeneous in their juridical forms, cooperatives often abandon in practice the cooperative principles and established norms. This happens, as has been noted with respect to Chile, especially because of the isomorphic pressure exerted by market logic, which weakens participatory governance in favour of the primacy given to economic efficiency. This results in precedence being given to the members' individual interests, which sometimes end up overriding mutual interests and—in a typically utilitarian fashion—the broader interests of the surrounding community, with which the cooperative doctrine has a historical commitment. Pressures exerted by market logic and corporate interests explain why the cooperative sector in some countries has opposed the growth of other similar organisations and their institutional recognition, as has been underscored in relation to Brazil. In Bolivia, cooperatives are often deficient in terms of transparency, democratic management and compliance with labour rights and conditions. Thus, although they possess a high degree of institutionalisation and relatively well-established communication channels with the state, cooperatives also face legitimacy problems with other comparable social-enterprise organisations.

Although, in practice, many cooperatives are concerned exclusively with their members' interests or even only with their financial interests, it should be noted that such interests acquire a relevant social dimension when the cooperatives belong to and serve social categories coping with unsatisfactory conditions in terms of work, income and well-being (Defourny and Nyssens 2017: 2487). In this case, the cooperatives (and associations that are in a similar situation) fulfil the needs of populations deprived by the economic system and neglected by the government; this often leads these organisations to becoming involved with issues of general interest—as did rural cooperatives for water supply mentioned in the chapter on Chile.

2.3. Organisations Based on the Popular Economy (POP)

This pattern comprises associative and cooperative organisations based on grassroots forms of family and community economy; it can be found in urban peripheries and in areas of family agriculture. It is a section of the broader universe of the popular economy, whose—informal and small-scale—economic activities are integrated into forms of primary sociability, extending over neighbourhoods and supporting community life through a combination of the economic logics of domesticity and reciprocity (Polanyi 2001, 1977; Gaiger 2016). Popular-economy organisations fulfil a social mission by ensuring the survival of social groups overlooked by the market economy, strengthening collective identities and fostering the inclusion of grassroots social actors in local public spaces, even though they usually lack sufficient unity to be effective in their political activities. These organisations tend to reproduce the classic power relations of family life, but they can also, at the same time, raise egalitarian and democratic aspirations within households, thanks in particular to the leading role taken on by women.

The informality that reigns in popular-economy initiatives, their ephemeral nature and the fact that they are primarily dedicated to the subsistence needs of the families involved may raise doubts about the relevance of including them in the field of social enterprise, since their conversion into spaces of cooperation and social solidarity does not constitute a natural development (Wanderley 2017: 17). And yet, perceptions about the popular or the informal economy should overcome the emphasis usually placed on their weaknesses, given the economic environment where they exist, or on their status as organisations operating on the "peripheral fringe" of the economy, since such approaches define them chiefly by their needs and their precariousness. The popular economy—whether that of the peasantry (Wanderley de Nazareth 2014) or of urban sectors (Coraggio 1999)—corresponds to a certain lifestyle and culture, so it is about specific ways of living and working. The economic life of the poor is arduous, but not poor (Abramovay 2004). The popular economy's rationality, based on domestic work units and their internal social ties, has the potential for activating expanded forms of solidarity, triggering cooperation practices and engaging in issues of common interest, precisely because it is not about making viable economic businesses only, but rather about launching and operating ventures that are atypical in the eyes of the market, due to their inherent social dimension. The popular economy may be understood not simply as a palliative and circumscribed response to poverty, but as a source of alternatives to the market logic and its deleterious effects. It can create jobs, promote local economies, strengthen social capital and be a tool for sustainable development (Rusek 2015). Thus, under certain circumstances, it can—indirectly, but effectively—play a role similar to that of social enterprises.

Many organisations that are formally registered as associations or cooperatives are inseparable from the logic and the relational assets typical of the popular economy, so that there are no clear boundaries between these sets of organisations. In Ecuador, for some of the community-based organisations rooted in the popular economy, the priority of economic survival does not rule out getting involved in broader issues of common interest, such as urban improvement, gender equality, access to culture, etc. In Peru, Brazil and Argentina, immigrants who have moved from the countryside to cities have preserved their traditions of cooperation and created mutual-aid groups as collective support against urban poverty. Often led by women, their activities have taken place in a grey zone, insofar as they do not meet all the formalisation requirements imposed by public authorities, but they have been effective in achieving various social improvements, in fields such as housing, urban infrastructure, schools, public transportation and security. In Chile and in Brazil, social projects based on indigenous forms of popular economy have constituted, since the 1990s, one of the most important aspects of the solidarity economy.

2.4. Self-Managed Class-Related Organisations (CLASS)

This pattern features prominently, under different names, in the countries surveyed. As has been highlighted in the case of Peru, social enterprises corresponding to this pattern meet the indicators of each dimension of the ideal-typical EMES concept of SE. Its core protagonists belong to a social class and may be blue-collar workers, artisans, peasants, family farmers, workers in various occupational categories, or even individuals who, due to similar material conditions of life, have common needs. The pattern refers to units of production, service provision or consumption of goods that arise from the association of producers, users and consumers, and which are run according to democratic governance and management principles. Its most salient characteristics are self-management and the tendency to be linked to social movements and other forms of participation in the public sphere, which accentuates its political dimension. In addition to informal groups, associations and cooperatives are also frequently observed in this pattern, in which the mutual interest of members merges with wider, more general demands, and tends to align itself with social-transformation perspectives.

There are emblematic cases of this pattern in Argentina, where the corresponding model predominates and was the only one to prosper during the successive economic and social crises since the military period, producing the phenomenon of "recovered factories" (Ruggeri 2014). In Bolivia, autonomous peasant organisations, based on principles of self-management and rotation of leaders, and registered in most cases as non-profit civil associations, fit this pattern; mention should also be made of artisan organisations, including associations, unions, mutual societies and trade leagues, which have long-standing organisational and representative structures. In Brazil, this pattern is the reference model of the solidarity economy. Chile witnessed the recent emergence of a new wave of cooperatives, based on self-management and on horizontal work practices and decision-making processes. The most salient aspects of these organisations are their collective governance, their consensus-based decision-making and the fact that they create alternatives to the capitalist system, through their links with social movements and their impacts on the social environments in which they operate. In Ecuador, the social enterprises corresponding to this pattern are grouped into a specific model: that of organisations driven by social movements. Their involvement in the public sphere shapes their economic performance and defines their objectives, including commitment to an agenda for transforming society. In Peru, the purpose of these organisations, i.e. to generate benefits for their members and their communities, also stands out, in addition to the fact that they are made viable thanks to the participation and contribution of their members and partners. It should also be noted that such organisations are the only ones in this country that explicitly comply with the requirement not to base their decision-making processes on the shares of capital held by the members.

2.5. *Organisations for Socio-Economic Inclusion (INC)*

Organisations corresponding to this pattern are made up of individuals living in situations of social vulnerability who rely on the support of outside bodies to form collective undertakings in order to meet their needs. This includes individuals with low levels of education, the unemployed, low-income families, people with physical disabilities or psychological disorders and the elderly without assistance. The initiatives are usually based on state policies and social programmes carried out by non-governmental organisations, but are designed with the aim of promoting the beneficiaries' autonomy and of enabling them to conduct the initiatives on an equal footing with the public agencies and civil society bodies that launch or promote them. For this reason, they may evolve into social enterprises corresponding to the previous pattern, whose core principle is self-management.

Economic activity often plays an instrumental role in relation to the social objectives of social assistance and inclusion, as is the case for example for "social cooperatives" in Brazil—a specific legal form that focuses on the field of mental health and whose participative and emancipatory character has been valued as an authentic form (among others) of solidarity-economy initiative. There are also cases where the organisations' main objective is to strengthen the economic dimension of grassroots organisations, as in Ecuador, where state programmes encourage association and networking among households. In general, organisations that fall within this pattern rely heavily on public policies, civil society bodies and sometimes on international cooperation programmes. In such circumstances, ambiguity predominates: the external agents maintain a preponderant weight in managing and guiding the organisations, so that the main social agent springs up from a changeable combination between members of public agencies and civil bodies, on the one hand, and members of vulnerable social categories, on the other.

This ambiguity signals this pattern as an intermediate case in terms of the place and role of the beneficiaries; indeed, in this regard, organisations for socio-economic inclusion are located between the patterns previously described (sections 2.1 to 2.4 included), in which the leading actors and the beneficiaries of social enterprises are (or are intended to be) the same, and the patterns presented hereafter, in which social enterprises are initiated and managed by actors who are external to the beneficiaries, even though these may be the members of the organisation from a formal point of view.

2.6. Philanthropic-Solidarity Organisations (PHIL)

This pattern includes organisations that offer services and benefits to an external target audience through programmes of their own, connected to social demands and related public policies. Their focus is on the basic needs of populations facing poverty and social vulnerability, neglected by the governments and with no prospects for lasting economic integration. This pattern is characterised by high institutional heterogeneity, as it comprises charity associations, foundations and various non-governmental organisations. Its leading social actors are bodies traditionally devoted to charity; more recently, citizens moved by altruism and with links to the third sector have also become significant actors in the field. Organisations corresponding to this pattern are private organisations, and they can enjoy full autonomy or be managed by another organisation, such as a foundation created and maintained by a private company. These organisations' governance exhibits varying degrees of participation by the members, partners and beneficiaries, with the latter being in a relationship of dependence with those in charge of the organisation. The main common feature of these initiatives is their philanthropic and non-profit character, which forbids them from distributing surpluses among their members (in other words, no private appropriation of benefits is permitted), but entitles them to receive donations and public subsidies, besides relying on the voluntary work of members, partners and beneficiaries. These organisations qualify as social enterprises due in particular to their social mission, while the extent to which they meet the indicators related to economic activity and participatory governance varies considerably.

In addition to providing social assistance to vulnerable populations, these organisations' activities include training, education, social projects, art and culture. Commercial activities serve as a source of income for these organisations, but they may also be part of the end-activity; this is for example the case when goods produced by the beneficiaries are sold within the frame of work-integration programmes. This hybrid character can create obstacles to the organisations' viability, as in the case of Mexico, where heavy regulation is imposed on organisations of this type to prevent profit concealment or money laundering. The recent modernisation of the organisations belonging to this pattern in Brazil and Peru is noteworthy; such modernisation is linked in particular to the adoption of new management techniques and the increase of partnerships with multiple sectors and entities. Organisations focusing on environmental causes also stand out, due to their connections with international networks.

From the legal point of view, the organisations corresponding to this pattern are usually defined as "non-profit entities", which differentiates them from market enterprises and gives them a philanthropic and eminently social character, while at the same time including them in a special tax regime, among other peculiarities. This fact should not lead us to confuse them with non-economic organisations: the services they provide are easily measurable in market value, but they are not sold and are not subordinated to the supply-and-demand rule. From this point of view, the distinctive character of these organisations resides in their economic model, which is based on the logics of reciprocity and redistribution, and on the activation of primary (interpersonal, within restricted groups) and secondary (between groups or through organisations) solidarities.

2.7. Social-Purpose Organisations Oriented by Market Logic (MKT)

> Included in this pattern are private companies that, in tandem with their economic activities, seek to generate positive social impacts, either by targeting some specific categories of individuals, territories and communities, or by working in favour of causes of general social interest, such as environmental sustainability. They reflect the emergence of an innovative and socially engaged business ethos. Their management strategies follow the typical model of market companies, but aim to generate positive externalities and provide economic and financial support for their social agenda. They start from the premise that for-profit companies can and should act in a socially responsible manner, and view the efficiency and profitability model characteristic of competitive markets as a suitable basis for sustainable programmes aspiring to achieve social and environmental impact. These initiatives' resources are mainly derived from the market, through the sale of goods and services, but private donations and public subsidies, as well as voluntary work, may also be of prime importance. The audience targeted by the company's social mission is external to it and usually does not take part in strategic decisions about the actions undertaken, except in an advisory capacity. This puts this particular pattern in a low-ranking position as regards the dimensions linked to participatory governance, which are central to the EMES concept of social enterprise.

In Argentina, this pattern is linked to the emergence of social entrepreneurship, that is, initiatives launched by leaders trained in the business world but whose practices are driven by the idea that social problems—such as unemployment, insufficient schooling and a low quality of life—can be overcome or substantially mitigated through innovative, profitable and socially effective initiatives. In this country, as well as in Chile, Mexico and Peru, "B Corps" enterprises also constitute a rising phenomenon; these initiatives' core guideline is to apply their competencies to resolving social and environmental problems. Although these companies are currently few in number, their expansion and their progressive legal recognition in those countries are indisputable. In Brazil, in recent years, a series of initiatives have been developed to generate social impacts through business actions, mainly by expanding the access of vulnerable populations to goods and services; these companies have emerged from the culture of corporate social responsibility, from models previously developed by the country's third-sector organisations and from a new generation of young entrepreneurs, who explore new technologies and concepts such as the creative economy and collaborative economy. In Mexico, the growing wave of "social start-ups" enjoys high cohesion and great popularity in academic, business and public circles.

3. For an Economy Founded on Social Ties

In order to lay down the main characteristics of the seven social-enterprise patterns discussed above, one may compare them from the point of view of their greater or lesser correspondence with each of the three dimensions of the ideal-typical concept of social enterprise such as it is described by the EMES Network. *Ethnic and community-based organisations* (COM) and *self-managed class-related organisations* (CLASS) are the patterns that come closest to fully meeting the various indicators linked to the economic and entrepreneurial dimension, the social dimension and the participatory governance of social enterprises. This explains their central position in figure 9.1, although there are variations in how and to what degree the social enterprises fitting these patterns meet these indicators. *Organisations based on the popular economy* (POP) usually engage in some kind of continuous economic activity, but their social commitment (often tacit) and the levels of participation observable in their governance may be weak. The economic dimension of social enterprises is also present in *traditional social-economy organisations* (SEC) and in *social-purpose organisations oriented by market logic* (MKT), but the former's social ends may be dominated by the primacy given to market logic, while the latter tend to adopt models of governance in which

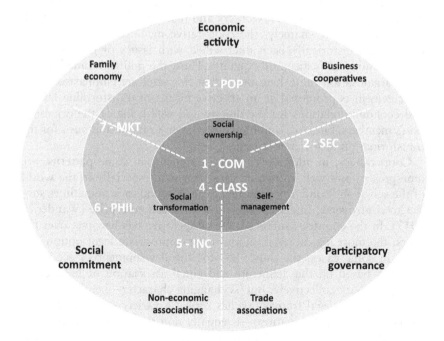

Figure 9.1 General patterns and dimensions of social enterprises

there is no parity between managers and beneficiaries. Regarding this last point, a similar bias characterises *organisations for socio-economic inclusion* (INC) and *philanthropic-solidarity organisations* (PHIL), due respectively to the internal power asymmetry that characterises the former (INC) and to the social distance that separates the latter (PHIL) from their target audiences. By contrast, these two patterns stand out for their deep-rooted social mission; the economic activity only plays an instrumental role in organisations corresponding to these patterns and thus risks being pushed into the background.

It has to be noted that the dividing lines between patterns are permeable and that there are pathways between the patterns, as well as between them and the organisations located along the boundary zones, as exemplified in the outer circle of figure 9.1 by some cases mentioned in the chapters on individual countries.

The shorter the distance to the centre, the greater the degree of internalisation of the characteristics that are close to the ideal-typical concept of social enterprise. The COM and CLASS patterns have practices and orientations that go even further than the three dimensions of the ideal-typical concept in highlighting the collective nature and the social engagement of their organisations: at the internal level, they adopt socially oriented property regimes and self-management systems; at the external level, they commit to an agenda of societal transformation in line with various social movements. They revitalise the worker cooperatives' paradigm, in which owners, workers and managers merge into one and the same category—namely, the cooperative members—whose mutual interest has historically been intertwined with issues of general interest, pertaining to justice and equality. Thus, the political dimension of these organisations and their alternative character are emphasised: self-management is promoted as an effective means of transforming labour and economic relations for the dignity and well-being of the organisation's members, but also, simultaneously, as an example and basis for the transformation of societies at large.

Cooperatives, in addition to their supremacy in some patterns, are omnipresent and well known in Latin America, especially in the world of the social and solidarity economy, whose boundaries, sometimes subject to controversy, intersect with those of social enterprise (Wanderley 2017). In the countries surveyed, the cooperative has become, over the years, the most logical solution and most appropriate legal option—or even, in some cases, the only one—for the development of economic activities based on the deliberate and equal association of individuals willing to work collectively. But its changing character—i.e. the fact that the cooperative legal framework has served a variety of purposes, giving rise to disparate situations—is equally notorious. The role assumed historically by cooperative organisations has been heterogeneous and ambivalent.[6] In Bolivia, there are cases where cooperatives have clearly moved away from the democratic and egalitarian principles of the cooperative doctrine, while in Chile, the recent phenomenon of new cooperatives is seen as promising, thanks to these organisations' horizontal management practices, ethical orientation and connection to the local communities where they operate. But in spite of these differences, the fact that the cooperative is at the same time a society of persons and an economic enterprise confers an inherent social sense to its aims and activities. Cooperatives are intrinsically social: they act in favour of the mutual benefit of individuals, who become associated in a regime of parity and under rules that prohibit the exploitation of each other, unlike what is the case in private companies set up for profit.

In their early days, cooperatives, associations and mutual societies were designed precisely to avoid reproducing ties of dependence and submission between managers and beneficiaries, owners of capital and workers, users or consumers. In this sense, they have historically been driven by emancipatory ideals. The new cooperatives that have been created recently, especially within the scope of the solidarity economy, are fuelled by the same ideals and purposes. The informal enterprises, associations and companies that take this ethical-political stance and do not lose sight of their social mission are also aligned with the cooperative paradigm, whatever their specific modes of regulation. Thus it could be argued that this paradigm is at the heart of the social-enterprise field in Latin America.[7]

Social enterprises are characterised by the use of resources originating not only from the market (through the sale of products and services) or from the state (via subsidies and tax advantages, among others); they blend these resources and combine them to varying degrees with other—monetary or non-monetary—contributions (e.g. donations, volunteering) from their members or third parties. This is evidenced by a large share of social enterprises in Latin America—especially among those corresponding to the last three patterns, whose focus is respectively the socio-economic inclusion of vulnerable populations (INC), the provision of services meeting social needs (PHIL) and the generation of social impact through market-oriented activities (MKT).

On the other hand, ethnic and community-based organisations (COM), those based on the popular economy (POP) and self-managed and class-based organisations (CLASS) also rely on two other types of resources, often crucial: first, resources owned and offered by the members of the organisation themselves, such as land, tools, in-kind support and infrastructure (which makes sense in family-based and community-based enterprises); secondly, additional resources generated through collective cooperation in work and management—a logic that constitutes a productive force *per se*, and is associated, in the chapter on social enterprises in Chile, with the "C factor" (Razeto 2002).

These two types of resources become relevant as other economic principles—distinct from those related to the market (i.e. exchange) and the public economy (i.e. redistribution)—come into play. According to Polanyi's (2001, 1977) substantive approach to the economy, these other economic principles are *domesticity* and *reciprocity*.

Reciprocity refers to a system of mutual benefits among symmetrical units or groups (such as families forming a cooperative or an association of producers, or fair-trade networks linking producers and consumers)[8] whose meaning rests on the will to create or maintain a social bond, generating long-term voluntary commitments, well beyond any contractual obligations. Commitments implying acceptance and trust are achieved, and a community of interests is created that simultaneously produces material values and human values. In modern societies, reciprocity functions and expands mainly through cooperative relationships. It has been identified and recognised in the alternative experiences backed by ties of solidarity (Gaiger and Santos 2017), and throughout this book it has been evoked as a salient feature of social enterprises in Latin America.

The principle of domesticity (or householding) refers to the logic of autarchic groupings (such as households, for example). It operates in environments of primary sociability, designed to ensure the survival and reproduction of life necessary for human groups. It can occur in societies having very different social roots and matrices. In the case of Latin American societies, it is important to note the existence of gender relations based on power and subordination and deeply rooted in the region's patriarchal culture. Relationships of domesticity often reproduce themselves on a larger scale, transplanting their logic into circles of relative proximity, such as working groups and class organisations. Domesticity-based mechanisms of self-organisation favour associative life when they articulate mutual aid, social cooperation and collective mobilisation. In situations where democracy is restricted, domesticity preserves protected spaces where common bonds and values can be cultivated. In the countries of the global South, in particular, it has been the source and underpinning of popular expressions of the social and solidarity economy (Hillenkamp and Laville 2013). It would be a mistake to neglect it and not to consider domesticity's own rationality, since domesticity is the foundation and support of family-owned enterprises, or of ventures anchored in territorially delimited communities which, as we have seen, are at the root of various models of social enterprises.

Figure 9.2 positions the SE patterns according to the relative relevance of the four economic principles in their operation; we take for granted that, in all patterns, all economic principles exert some kind of influence. At the same time, the figure indicates that some factors—such as the predominance of informal companies, participation criteria stemming from the shareholding structure of companies, a marked dependency on the state or the predominance of symmetrical relationships among the members—are specific to a particular pattern. With regard to the issue of symmetrical relations, it is important to give enough attention to the

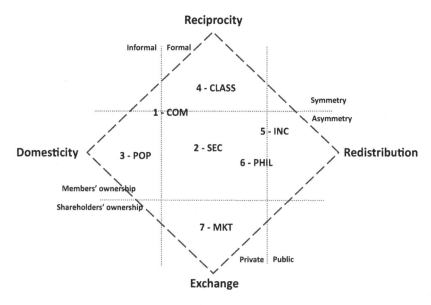

Figure 9.2 Patterns of social enterprise and economic principles

challenges of overcoming the gender inequality that still exists in social enterprises (in all their diversity), if these are to actually fulfil their mission of social transformation.

Moving from domesticity to forms of freely agreed cooperation as well as from the defence of mutual interest to actions of general interest is a crucial condition for the development of social enterprises. It is at this point that reciprocity comes into play: through reciprocity, primary groups succeed in establishing social ties and integrating wider circuits. In other words, social bonds extend to a transitional sphere between primary and secondary sociabilities, and expand in space and time. From this point of view, the economic principle of reciprocity is embedded in a binding social dynamic, which functions as a cornerstone of cooperative relations and related forms of solidarity.

Initiatives rooted in reciprocity have historically shown their capacity to leverage both redistribution and exchange as subordinate methods of generating resources (Polanyi 1968). According to Polanyi, the principle of exchange, which underlies our market economy, is inconsistent with the creation and preservation of stable and persistent social ties; therefore, it is opposed to alliances and lasting agreements based on common interests, instead of self-interest. By contrast, both domesticity and reciprocity tend to create and preserve social bonds, on different scales and with different meanings. They are compatible with forms of economy that are socially embedded, and are prone to enact them—unlike the principle of exchange, whose supremacy leads to a systematic rupture of social ties, which become utilitarian and ephemeral, and gives rise to an opposition between economy and society.

Conclusion

Seen from this angle, the historical singularity of social enterprises and similar initiatives in Latin America is not confined to their hybridity, their combination of resources or of different economic principles. Their uniqueness and relevance also have to do with the fact that they act in favour of new institutions of the economy whose principles of integration, being socially binding, can be guided by plural norms and regulations, including by the desire to promote different types of market. On this point, it is important to clarify that the market, contrary to the usual understanding about it, is not originally one of the Polanyian economic principles, but rather an infrequent and yet varied historical culmination of a particular institution of the economy, based on an unlikely integration performed by the principle of exchange—a process that involves a paraphernalia of values, rules, legislations, entities, authorities and minds (Arensberg *et al.* 1957: xvii). Therefore, redistribution and reciprocity can coexist with exchange, and we do have "reciprocity trade" and "solidarity fairs", in which there is exchange, but not based on a market standard. Broadly speaking, there can be several markets within the market, depending on the level of integration between the economic principles.

A new plural economy is not just a matter of hybridism; creating it is mainly a challenging work of rebuilding our ecosystem, based on a process of institution of the economy (Polanyi 1957), according to other principles. It probably demands a coherent integration between reciprocity, redistribution and domesticity, while the exchange principle may continue to exist as a practical alternative to favour, precisely, the exchange of goods and services, without this principle being given the power to determine the moral sense of human life and the boundaries of our freedom (Hillenkamp and Laville 2013; Gaiger 2016).[9] From this point of view, one interesting question for future research would be: to what extent does the SE field contribute not only to maintaining the economic plurality that is typical of our societies, but also to fostering new hybridisms, in which reciprocity plays a role of integration, instituting by that way other forms of economy?

It could be argued that some patterns of social enterprise discussed above go back in time and give the impression of being out-of-date atavisms. It is because, unlike what happens under the aegis of modernisation, reciprocity does not ask for a constant suppression of the past—on the contrary: it finds in the past know-how matured by the test of time. Nor does reciprocity refuse to go forward. Its renewal nowadays, for the benefit of those organisations that seek to escape the dominant economic logic and the cultural hegemony of the market society, is an important challenge that may confirm Polanyi's (2001) and Mauss's (1990) theses on the restorative virtues of reciprocity and the primordial role of social bonds. In the dark times that Latin America is currently going through, the reciprocity underlying socially oriented models of economy, as well as various demands and mobilisations for rights, justice and freedom, reaffirm the value of human solidarity and lead the way towards a new economic and intercultural democracy.

Notes

1 Translated by Priscilla Kreitlon.
2 As a reminder, according to Max Weber, the ideal type is an analytical construct, neither reality itself nor a reality presumed as authentic or original. "Its primary meaning is that of a purely mental concept against which reality is measured in order to clarify the empirical content of some of its important elements, and to which it is compared" (Weber 1989: 106; authors' own translation). The ideal type combines a set of aspects, relating to a class of phenomena, whose presence is necessary for these phenomena to exist, according to the always partial and unavoidable theoretical assumptions of the investigator. In other words, it is a heuristic tool that seeks the essential, not merely accidental, causal connections of that class of phenomena. Its purpose is to allow comparisons between the analytical construct and individual empirical cases.
3 The presence of external agents and the way in which they interfere in the creation and viability of the initiatives also matter in this process, sometimes decisively.
4 This is in particular the case for the term "cooperative", whose use was avoided even when the social enterprises belonging to a given pattern were mostly cooperatives.
5 In addition, there are hybrid national models, such as Peru's "non-profit/social business partnership model".
6 The same is true of associations, which are less prominent than cooperatives, but equally ubiquitous. The flexibility offered by this legal form favours its adoption for different purposes, and the associative form serves as institutional support for various local initiatives. The artisans of Bolivia demonstrate that associations can operate as small hierarchical enterprises or be participatory and egalitarian, in which case they resemble social enterprises, as documented in several countries.
7 Because this paradigm functions primarily as an archetype, often taken on by cooperative organisations and not always adequately reflected in current legal frameworks, understanding it and differentiating situations requires going beyond an institutional analysis, as we have already noted.
8 These examples were not given by Polanyi himself; they are more up-to-date examples than those provided by Polanyi, which generally referred to archaic societies—although, for this author, it was the dissolution of the social bonds once secured by these two principles that caused a movement of social resistance in the 19th century against the supremacy of exchange and the economy instituted by it, i.e. the market.
9 Polanyi and his team have carried out several huge research works, coming back on history to identify and understand ecosystems in which the prevailing

economic principles were redistribution, reciprocity or both: how have they functioned together, keeping aside the principle of exchange, at least as a major pillar of the instituted economy? The analyses of many different societies led Polanyi to a positive conclusion: so far, our so-called modern civilisation has been the unique one in which the economy and the whole life are integrated by the exchange principle (Polanyi 1968, 1977).

References

Abramovay, R. (ed.) (2004) *Laços financeiros na luta contra a pobreza*, São Paulo: Annablume.

Arensberg, C., Pearson, H. & Polanyi, K. (1957) *Trade and Markets in the Early Empires. Economies in History and Theory*, Glencoe: The Free Press.

Bouchard, M. (ed.) (2008) *Portrait statistique de l'économie sociale de la région de Montréal*, Montréal: Chaire de Recherche du Canada en Économie Sociale.

CEPAL (2017) *Panorama Social de América Latina*, Santiago de Chile: Naciones Unidas.

Coraggio, J. (1999) *Política social y economía del trabajo*, Madrid and Buenos Aires: Miño y Dávila Editores.

Defourny, J. & Nyssens, M. (2011) "Approches européennes et américaines de l'entreprise sociale: une perspective comparative", *Revue Internationale de l'Économie Sociale*, Vol. 319, pp. 18–35.

Defourny, J. & Nyssens, M. (2012) "The EMES approach of social enterprise in a comparative perspective", *EMES Working Paper*, Liege: EMES International Research Network, No. 2012/03.

Defourny, J. & Nyssens, M. (2017) "Fundamentals for an international typology of social enterprise models", *Voluntas*, Vol. 28, No. 6, pp. 2469–2497.

Gaiger, L. I. (2016) *A descoberta dos vínculos sociais. Os fundamentos da solidariedade*, São Leopoldo: Editora Unisinos.

Gaiger, L. I. & Santos, A. (eds) (2017) *Solidariedade e ação coletiva. Trajetórias e experiências*, São Leopoldo: Editora Unisinos.

Hillenkamp, I. & Laville, J-L. (eds) (2013) *Socioéconomie et démocratie. L'actualité de Karl Polanyi*, Toulouse: Ères.

Mauss, M. (1990) *The Gift*, London: Routledge.

Polanyi, K. (1957) "The economy as instituted process", in Arensberg, C., Pearson, H. & Polanyi, K. (eds) *Trade and Markets in the Early Empires: Economies in History and Theory*, Glencoe: The Free Press, pp. 243–270.

Polanyi, K. (1968) *Primitive, Archaic and Modern Economies: Essays of Karl Polanyi* (Edited by George Dalton), New York: Anchor Books.

Polanyi, K. (1977) *The Livelihood of Man* (Edited by Harry W. Pearson), New York: Academic Press.

Polanyi, K. (2001 [1944]) *The Great Transformation: The Political and Economic Origins of Our Time* (3rd ed.), Boston: Beacon Press.

Razeto, L. (2002) *Las empresas alternativas*, Montevideo: Editorial Nordan-Comunidad.

Ruggeri, A. (2014) *¿Qué son las empresas recuperadas? Autogestión de la clase trabajadora*, Buenos Aires: Continente.

Rusek, W. (2015) "The informal economy as a catalyst for sustainability", *Sustainability*, Vol. 7, pp. 23–34.

Wanderley, F. (2017) "Entre el concepto minimalista y el concepto maximalista de economía social y solidaria. Tensiones teóricas y agenda futura de investigación", *Economía*, Vol. 69, No. 109, pp. 13–27.

Wanderley, M. De Nazareth. (2014) "O campesinato brasileiro: uma história de resistência", *Revista de Economia e Sociologia Rural*, Vol. 52, No. 1, pp. 25–44.

Weber, M. (1989) "A 'objetividade' do conhecimento nas Ciências Sociais", in Cohn, G. (ed.) *Weber; sociologia* (4th ed.), São Paulo: Ática, pp. 79–127.

10 Social Enterprise as a Tension Field

A Historical and Theoretical Contribution Based on the Sociology of Absences and Emergences

Jean-Louis Laville, Genauto Carvalho de França Filho, Philippe Eynaud and Luciane Lucas dos Santos

Introduction

The literature about social enterprise mentions many different types of initiatives, using expressions such as "blurred boundaries" to describe how the private, public and community sectors have become intermingled in contemporary societies. This evolution has been discussed by authors such as Teasdale (2010), Simmons (2008) and Lyon *et al.* (2010). Teasdale (2011: 100) claimed that "the construction of social enterprise is ongoing, and fought by a range of actors promoting different languages and practices tied to different political beliefs. That is, social enterprise is politically contested by different actors around competing discourses". The plurality of discourses generates a lot of useful information but also has two obvious limits.

The first limit stems from the number of criteria and categories used, generating a "kaleidoscopic" effect. Moreover, when underlining all possibilities, there is a risk of forgetting how the term has flourished, how it has been framed and reframed in struggles for recognition, and how it is used as a substitute for others like the third sector, the solidarity economy or the "solidary economic entrepreneurship" (*empreendimento economico solidario*). That is why it is relevant to reintegrate a "genealogical perspective" (Foucault 2001) in the analysis.

The second limit is due to the fact that discussion has been dominated by the Anglo-American and European approaches. Consequently, there has been a tendency to analyse all realities through these approaches.

This chapter takes into account these specific methodological biases. It shares the observation made by Gaiger and Wanderley in chapter 9 about the importance of studying social enterprise as embedded economic forms. With a view to doing so, it adopts a historical and theoretical perspective based on the sociology of absences and emergences

DOI: 10.4324/9780429055164-13

promoted by "epistemologies of the South" (Santos 2014). The sociology of absences "consists of an inquiry that aims to explain that what does not exist is in fact actively produced as non-existent, that is, as a not credible alternative to what exists" (Santos 2004: 238). The sociology of emergences "consists of undertaking a symbolic enlargement of knowledge, practices and agents in order to identify therein the tendencies of the future upon which it is possible to intervene so as to maximise the probability of hope *vis-à-vis* the probability of frustration" (Santos 2014: 171–184).

The first part of the chapter shows how the various types of social enterprise have to be relocated in the conflicting history of continental Latin America, and how certain practices were "invisibilised" in the course of this history. It sheds an interesting light on the second part, dedicated to the recent period, which renews popular practices rooted in history. But, today as in the past, these solidarity-based "emergences" tend to become invisible because of the dominant discourses; this phenomenon is described in the third part. The fourth part tries to develop theoretical proposals that do not ignore these emergences and refuse their "invisibilisation". In the wake of a chapter (Coraggio *et al.* 2015) published in several languages by a group of twelve researchers of various continents, it aims to stimulate further debates and argues for a new imaginary in investigations about social enterprise.[1]

1. Beyond the Official History: A Critical Standpoint

During the 19th century, the meaning of solidarity changed with the democratic revolutions and the process of independence that took place on the American continent. Solidarity does not only refer to traditional community ties; it also includes voluntary involvement. It is distinct from both charity and instrumental relationships, and it should be understood as an acknowledged interdependence between people and groups.

According to Polanyi's substantive approach to the economy, based on a large body of anthropological research, human societies rely on various principles beside the market principle: reciprocity, which results from the presence of "symmetrical" groups; redistribution, whereby a central authority organises the allocation of resources; and householding, which specifies the rules for each family closed group, guaranteeing the production and sharing of resources to satisfy the group's members. Following Polanyi's line of thought, it is possible to argue that solidarity reframes the relationships among human beings and between human beings and their natural environment. Among the different types of solidarity, democratic solidarity, which appeared in the 19th century, can be defined as a means to reinforce the political principles of liberty and equality in daily lives; this is linked to associationism, which is a project built on collective actions carried out by free and equal citizens in reference to a common good. Solidarity goes beyond householding to reorganise reciprocity and introduces the idea of egalitarian reciprocity experienced through direct interaction between citizens.

1.1. Democratic Solidarity in Practice

In the 19th century, anti-colonialist social movements developed in Latin America; they succeeded in gaining independence and in establishing national republics, and national independences led to widespread changes in the socio-economic order. The popular economy[2] was very diverse; it could be full of violence, but also of strong solidarities, which is why Coraggio (1999) defined it as a "labour economy", as opposed to a capitalist economy.

The popular economy is a product of places and of historical circumstances at a particular point in time, but it also develops from the everyday behaviour of its actors, and eventually through the political vision they may acquire (Sarria Icaza and Tiriba 2006: 219). What was at stake in the first part of the 19th century was the reduction of situations of dependence and the democratisation of the popular economy. This twofold goal was pursued by applying economic logics to serving social ends, while at the same time giving these social objectives a new democratic coherence. The popular economy could also be a source of dignity, in that it allowed individuals to find collective solutions to their food, housing and health problems. This was the conviction of those who, under the influence of the new democratic political climate, modified large parts of the popular economy. The growing demand for equality which motivated and guided the actions of popular-economy actors transformed them into essential means of resistance against the increasing penetration of capitalism (Mingione 1991). Hoping to emancipate themselves from traditional forms of dependence, they also rejected forms of subordination related to an economic order controlled by capital.

Some experiences were very emblematic, like the *communidades quilombolas* in Brazil—free communes created by escaped black slaves who settled in isolated areas to live in their own way. But a lot of other initiatives were not born from a break with precedent conditions; Latin American associationism combines inherited habits (like *natillera, montepio, minga, convite, ayuda mutual comunitaria, acción comunal*) with a sense of equality among members. What occurred was thus not a break leading to the creation of new institutions but a gradual democratisation of previously existing institutions. In a nutshell, democratic solidarity was based on mutual aid as well as on the expression of demands; it stemmed from both self-organisation and social movement, which presupposed equal rights among people committed to it. On the basis of free access to the public sphere for all citizens, it strived to strengthen political democracy through economic and social democracy.

1.2. The Invisibilisation of Democratic Solidarity Experiences

The newly democratised institutions, however, were marginalised by the rise of capitalism, which in turn resulted from continual efforts on the part of the governments to identify and extend the market-economy sphere; the rise of capitalism was achieved through a series of moves and decisions concerning the definition of economy. This process was based on the presentation of the market economy and capitalist enterprise as the pinnacle of progress. What has been forgotten is that this progress was partly due to the plundering of the economic resources of southern countries, followed by the "annexation" (Lutz 1990) of a popular economy. In Latin America, what prevailed, rather than a free market, was a series of regulations that were designed to benefit an "industry imposed from the top down". Faced with the precarity of their members' living conditions and the emergence of a proletarian class generated by capitalist industries, popular movements became more radical in their stances. The leaders of the mutualist movement and small-farmer (*labradores*) organisations rallied around a modernisation plan which was meant to solve social problems through industrial development. In order to do so, they abandoned the self-organised institutions they had created to devote themselves more exclusively to protest action, demanding state intervention, and to their participation in national negotiations as workers' representatives (Nyssens 1994).

Since Mariategui's seminal work (1979), Western Marxism has been accused of having contributed to a pessimism that led to the demise of the popular economy. Quijano's deconstruction of "coloniality" takes up this criticism, arguing that the productivist ideology underlies both liberalism and historical materialism and, according to him, constitutes "the most Eurocentric version of Marx's heritage", a result of the "combination of his theoretical propositions with evolutionism and positivist dualism along with the Hegelian idea of a historical macro-subject" (Quijano 2007: 160). The consequences were very damaging: the division of social activities was pushed so far that it resulted in the reification of categories such as the economy, society, culture and politics; private ownership and exploitation were absolutised as if they alone embodied oppression. The unicity of the capitalist mode of production was accepted, whereas in reality it rather constituted an "articulation of all other modes of production" (Quijano 2007: 159; see also Quijano 1998). From the moment when the belief in a capitalist system replaced the analysis of a "predominantly capitalist system", to quote Mauss (1997), the popular economy, although present in Latin America, became more and more invisible; this was particularly true of its collective-type components. The denial of their role and history came from a repression by governments and contempt on the part of the colonial oligarchies. Popular-economy organisations were considered as archaic, non-productive or immature attempts, especially because they promoted other principles of economic integration than the market.

Of course, some of these initiatives survived under legal forms such as associations and cooperatives. But three facts influenced very much the trajectories of these organisations.

- First, they lost their connection with other collective actions and became merely social enterprises competing with for-profit private enterprises for the production of goods. Consequently, they were attracted by market patterns. This evolution resulted in the estrangement of these organisations from social movements and their perspectives of social transformations. Some of these movements, like the peasant movement, even accused the big cooperatives of being "agrobusiness" agents.
- Secondly, it appears obvious that the end of the 19th century saw the establishment of a confusion between modern economy and market capitalism. The result was a denial of the importance of a "moral economy"[3] based on notions of common well-being, reciprocal obligations and shared conceptions of rights and obligations. All these notions, grounded in the concrete spaces of intersubjectivity of the popular economy, whether applied to workers or peasants, disappeared behind the performativity of a linear approach to history. This is the trap that Braudel (1985) warned against, that of seeing only the market capitalist economy, of "describing it with such a wealth of detail as to imply an all-pervasive presence, when it is just a piece of a larger whole". As Polanyi (1977) noted, this linear approach to the economy was incorrect, but it was a sign of things to come. Economic reality was created through the development of an economic belief presented as an objective observation. From this perspective, the stage of market capitalism was unavoidable.
- Thirdly, a large negative discrimination against democratic solidarity was articulated with another approach put forward by the elites, namely philanthropic solidarity, which replaced the notion of equality with those of benevolence, solicitude, free-will altruism and donations. It is true that democratic and philanthropic solidarities could be combined, and it is obvious that popular-solidarity arrangements could be supported by non-governmental organisations; but as shown by Pinto (2006) and Lucas dos Santos (2008), such "empirical mixes" served hegemonistic assumptions, invisibilising the specific identities and claims for autonomy of groups that came up with creative solutions to their problems, mobilising redistribution and reciprocity mechanisms themselves.

Finally, isolated from social movements, expelled from the most diffused conceptions of modern economy, and submitted to market isomorphism, traditional associations and cooperatives had very little political strength.

2. A Renewal of Solidarity Initiatives

During the 20th century, philanthropic initiatives showed their insufficiency to "complement" market capitalism. The state gained legitimacy by implementing an industrialisation model and redistributive social policies. A synergy between market and state was thus created, as recommended in Keynes's writings. But some economists opposed to Keynes, such as Friedman and Hayek, turned the Latin American dictatorships of the 1970s and 1980s into laboratories of neoliberalism. As explicitly recommended by these authors, the neoliberal programmes reduced public intervention, and not only state action was at stake. Organised groups—in particular workers' trade unions—were also under pressure; deregulations in labour laws were supposed to reduce their influence in order to give priority to market forces. In the ideology of the "good governance" inspired by neoliberal theorists, civil society organisations were controlled and confined to the residual role of a third sector dedicated to the low-cost provision of services, and they were denied any voice in the public debate.

2.1. The Rediscovery of the Popular Economy

Even though it was often ignored, the popular economy did not disappear. In Latin America, between 1925 and 1950, the urban population grew by 12% and non-agricultural employment increased by 87%. But between 1950 and 1960, the rate of creation of non-agricultural jobs (46%) became lower than the growth rate of the urban population (59%); these rates dropped to 40% and 47% respectively between 1960 and 1970. The dictatorships and authoritarian regimes that interrupted the democratic experiments of the 1950s and 1960s were followed by a debt crisis and social deregulation, and a large sector of the active population was excluded from the formal economy. Once more, this population survived thanks to community-based forms of solidarity. The informal economy served as a refuge for 35% of the active population, according to estimates for Latin America. In this heterogeneous context, many commercial activities were left at the mercy of the outsourcing strategies of capitalist companies, some of which were illegal and used extreme violence. However, another part of the active population formed a popular response to the difficult economic situation. As had happened more than one century earlier, the growth in more associative forms corresponded to an affirmation of solidarity, perpetuating a tradition of cooperation within primary groups. Labour was organised on the basis of collective mobilisation, and the democratic management of projects was inseparably connected to survival.

These popular associations, based on mutual help and shared ownership of the means of production, included manufacturing workshops; organisations of unemployed workers who sought work collectively;

community food groups, such as collective kitchens and vegetable gardens; organisations dedicated to problems of housing, electricity provision and drinking water; pre-cooperative self-building organisations; and associations for the provision of health care and cultural services to the community. Such groups can be observed in Argentina, Bolivia, Brazil, Chile, Ecuador and Peru. Some of them are supported by black and indigenous movements (Alvarez *et al.* 1998: 333); this is for example the case in the countries of the Andes, where the principles of Indian organisation are reactivated to generate original economic models.

If these initiatives have not completely managed to escape their marginal status, at least they are no longer limited to the mere management of extreme poverty. However, it is also true that many questions remain unanswered about the capabilities of the popular economy to get beyond the stage of simply reproducing living conditions to achieve the level of expanded reproduction,[4] or to move from the survival and subsistence level to certain forms of accumulation. There is a tension in the popular economy between technical efficiency and the dynamics of solidarity, and between educating participants (many of whom are illiterate) and respecting the initial values that explain their commitment.

In any case, the perspective that once confused the popular economy with the informal economy has now changed (see the introductory chapter of the present volume). Today, throughout Latin America—from Chile in the 1980s to north-eastern Brazil in the 1990s (Kraychet *et al.* 2000) and Bolivia in the early 21st century, with the notion of communitarian economy—the popular economy is gaining recognition and attention. This new interest results from the legitimisation of these initiatives, and it puts pressure on public authorities to confer full rights upon this economy. In this context, NGOs sensitised to the subject and active in the area are appearing, and university networks have also been set up in some countries, such as Argentina, Brazil or Peru.

The popular economy has thus partly regained a visibility that had been lost. While connections remain tenuous between workers, "recovered enterprises" (*empresas recuperadas*, i.e. enterprises taken over by their workers, usually after industrial bankruptcies), new cooperatives offering services such as cleaning, recycling, artistic production, training, etc., and various churches, unions and university groups today support the popular economy, together with various movements aimed at emancipation and advocacy, such as ecological organisations.

In these expressions of the popular economy, what is at stake is in fact an accentuation of this movement's public dimension. According to Hirschman (1971), in Latin American popular-economy initiatives, the fight for better living conditions is intrinsically linked to the fight for the rights of citizenship. This struggle oscillates between protests and self-resolution of problems, without separating material questions from questions relating to living conditions and coexistence. In the words of Scholnik

(1984: 28), "it is a different way of doing politics". The same point is made by women's groups opposed to the dichotomy between the public and the private, and between production and reproduction—a dichotomy which results in unpaid jobs for women that use up two thirds of their work time, while two thirds of men's work time is remunerated. Historically, women's confinement to a broadly overlooked domestic economy explains their physical and symbolic underrepresentation in the public sphere. A majority of women become involved in popular-economy initiatives because they consider that these collective initiatives might help them identify and contextualise their needs, so that they could express them and bring them into the public sphere. Given the failure of standardised universal measures, these initiatives are a means of consolidating rights and translating them into capacities for action, thanks to the collective dimension, which is a resource for developing self-confidence, relieving the weight of responsibilities assumed in the family sphere and reconciling them with a commitment to social justice. These collective actions aim first and foremost to constitute pragmatic responses to the problems of daily life. However, they also formulate societal and environmental claims, establishing a link with ecological feminism, and opposing a materialist and economicist conception of wealth that assimilates domestic knowledge to "innate" qualities, to "altruism" and to female "obligations".

2.2. The Boom of Citizens' Initiatives

With the restoration of democracy in several Latin American countries, numerous new social movements and collective actions emerged. Two new trends have been distinguished among associations and cooperatives in the national chapters:

- The first trend is formed by voluntary groups trying to act concretely against neoliberalism by encouraging participative decision-making. Social movements—such as feminist, indigenous, anti-authoritarian and ecological ones—enlarged their usual range of protest actions to economic practices in different territories. These socio-economic experiences concern production but also consumption and ways of life. In Latin America, they were grouped by different authors under the generic term of "solidarity economy", defined as a set of activities contributing to the democratisation of the economy through citizens' involvement. Such social innovations are observed in local services, fair trade, solidarity tourism, organic agriculture, critical consumption, short supply chains, renewable energies, recycling and waste valorisation, heritage preservation, microfinance and social currencies, and integration through economic activities.

- The second trend finds its source in the effects of economic policies influenced by the Washington Consensus, signed in 1989. Despite the

democratisation processes that took place in the region, these policies are pursued in different countries, and another trend of the solidarity economy is formed by groups of people seeking to save their
jobs, threatened by the global capitalist restructuration, or to generate decent jobs through an organisation that gives access to rights.
Among these groups are the abovementioned "recovered enterprises", taken over by their workers, with examples like Catende,
in Brazil, which employs over 10,000 workers, or the 368 Argentinian recovered enterprises, which gather around 15,000 workers.
Another example is that of waste-recycling companies. Persons living from waste collection are victims of the intermediaries to whom
they resell, and they also suffer from a form of social contempt that
assimilates them to the rubbish they collect in the street. The creation
of cooperatives in this field of activity, from 1987 onwards, resulted
from a reaction against this ostracism. The founders of these cooperatives aimed to fight their isolation and the direct competition with
intermediaries through the creation of an economic organisation that
would put them in a stronger bargaining position. In addition, these
cooperatives also aimed to combat exclusion. They exist in many
countries; in Colombia, for instance, 300,000 persons live on waste
collection, and cooperative dynamics led to the grouping, in 1991,
at the national level, of 88 waste-recycling cooperatives (out of the
94 cooperatives registered in the country), representing 10% of the
population living on waste collection, within the National Recyclers
Association (*Asociación Nacional de Recicladores*).

Even though the concept of popular economy is important, it is not sufficient by itself to understand all kinds of citizen initiatives. In the Latin
American context, on the outskirts of big cities, citizen groups may be
supported by popular organisations, but self-management practices are
also developed by the actors. In this context, and with a view to overcoming poverty, symbolic autonomy might indeed be even more important
than economic results. And although it is true that these community-
based economic initiatives might not constitute a paragon of market-
oriented performance, it is just as true that they have played a crucial role
in emphasising social links through which scant resources are redistributed by the communities themselves. They thus contribute to local economies' "re-embeddedness", to the extent that they unveil other economic
principles, beside the market principle.

The return to democracy and the boom of citizens' initiatives have to be
differentiated from the above mentioned popular economy (whose roots
are to be found in the informal economy); this boom rather results from
citizens' commitment to find tailor-made solutions to face social inequalities and poverty, in the absence of a welfare state. In Latin America as in
other regions of the word, it is a characteristic of the social and solidarity

economy that minorities collectively organise themselves to create solutions in fields such as access to housing (*mutirão*), redistribution of scant resources (exchange fairs) or popular collective savings (solidarity rotating funds). They initiate non-capitalist forms of organisation and actually adopt participative decision-making processes.

3. Recognition of Emergences or New Production of Absences

Ultimately, new alliances between social movements and the popular economy have emerged, leading to a conception of the solidarity economy as a socio-economic and socio-political phenomenon (Lemaître and Helmsing 2011). Such development has been evidenced by the discussions that took place in the World Social Forum, where the concept of the social and solidarity economy has been mobilised since 2001 by a lot of actors and researchers shaping economic alternatives.

3.1. Recognition of Emergences Mixing the Popular Economy and Social Movements

Pleyers and Capitaine (2016: 8–12, our translation) state that "the distinction established in the 1970s and 1980s between traditional movements, centred on mass organisations and demands for redistribution, and 'new social movements', mobilised around issues of recognition, is no longer relevant". The uprisings of the 2010s are not 'new social movements' anymore. They deeply mix economic, social, political and cultural claims, combined with a strong ethical dimension. Against the instrumentalisation of ethics by neo-capitalism, some civil society actors defend issues concerning day-to-day matters at the local level. They create spaces for experiences and economic activities where they engage in self-transformation and adopt a collective way of living. By doing so, they contribute to "a renewal of solidarity, collective action and democracy".

A significant example of the links that exist between social movements and the popular economy is the Landless Rural Workers' Movement (*Movimento dos Trabalhadores Sem Terra*, or MST), in Brazil, which came into being in 1984. In 2016, according to the data provided by Stédile, one of the movement's leaders, more than 1.3 million families had been settled thanks to MST; they occupied over 88 million hectares of land. MST is Latin America's largest producer of organic rice, and it also organises many schools and crèches.

The MST generates debates. This is due to its syncretism, in which enthusiasm for the agrarian reform and for a "classless society", influenced by liberation theology and the Castro revolution, goes hand in hand with adhesion to traditional values related to land, family and religion. The MST triggers both fascination and distrust as regards ideological "enchantment" and the "canonisation" of collective action. The remarkable mobilisation that it has brought about, amplified through its key role in the international movement "Via Campesina", has been questioned from the point of view of centralised control of its internal debates. Navarro (2002: 232, 289) refers to a "mobilisation without emancipation" from power, to control through financial resources and to a scorn for democracy—to which de Carvalho (2002: 233, 259) retorts that the MST is a movement under construction, and that it is not so much a mass social organisation as a network of marginalised peasants from Latin America. For this author, present practices are explained by the discovery of new cultural codes, through flows of information and symbols, which, despite errors, forge an autonomous social identity. Emancipation is real, he argues, for many actors that were formerly illiterate are now involved in a process of popular education.

More widely, the new wave of popular economy has been the target of controversial analyses. One point of reference is Razeto's (1993) contribution, which stresses the consolidation and democratisation of economic practices—anchored in a community fabric, but effecting the reorganisation of that same fabric—brought about by this new wave of organisations. Quijano (1998) is less optimistic, considering that individualism is imposing itself in grassroots organisations and that action is a result of need rather than solidarity. For this author, there really is a compromise, within those organisations, between the logic of capital and that of reciprocity, which constitutes an undeniable, though insufficient, specificity. For him, these organisations are too dependent for observers to be able to speak, as Coraggio (1999) does, of a labour economy that is opposed to the economy of capital.

The diversity of interpretations proves that the popular economy can no longer be understood as an archaic or temporary phenomenon, doomed to disappear according to the "iron law" of capitalist development. The recognition of the existence of popular economic knowledge becomes unequivocal from the moment when research is launched to understand the internal rationality of the initiatives.

3.2. Social-Business Discourses and Interpretative Controversies

The articulations between social movements and the popular economy are also present in other movements, like the Zapatist Army of National Liberation (*Ejército Zapatista de Liberación Nacional*, or EZLN) in Chiapas, Mexico, or the agroecologist movement in Bolivia, Brazil, Ecuador or Peru. These phenomena, coupled with the important mobilisation of the people concerned, triggered, at the beginning of the 21st century, a huge reaction of the advocates of new capitalism, who introduced what could be referred to as a "second wave of neoliberalism", in which competition is complemented by an explicit social aim. Echoing what had happened in the 19th century, the initiatives linked to this movement combine the personal-interest motive with a form of paternalism, or "moralisation of the poor", to use Thompson's (1963) expression, extending capitalism along philanthropic lines. For example, Yunus (2007: 48–74)—a key proponent of micro-credit—argues that capitalism is a half-developed structure and can worthily be complemented by an "enterprise oriented to a cause rather than to profit". A flood of creativity able to change the world (Yunus 2010) is expected from this innovating entrepreneurship, referred to as "social business". In this perspective, the social entrepreneur is considered as a particular type of actor, acting as a catalyst for social change (a "change agent") and putting forward innovative ideas to tackle social and environmental problems. Such philanthropic capitalism is also supported by donor investors concerned about the impacts of their donations; this is "venture philanthropy", a modernised philanthropy mindful of the social results of its financial contributions. This approach could re-legitimate capitalism, if it manages to nurture innovation with a view to creating economic value and entrepreneurialism, to boosting growth and to solving the related social and environmental problems. Prahalad (2014) agreed with this when he put forward the "bottom-of-the-pyramid" approach, whereby the poorest populations—the 4 billion people living with less than two dollars a day—are engaged either as producers and suppliers in value chains or as consumers of products and services. This requires that the enterprise change its perception of these people's needs so as to meet these needs; this approach, according to its proponents, is a powerful lever, which can be observed in several success stories.

From this point of view, social innovation helps to reconcile capitalism and society; in other words, the social business and the bottom of the pyramid make up a system that is congruent with corporate social responsibility. The "new spirit of capitalism" combines a humanist societal discourse with renewed competitiveness. The aim is to activate the potential for self-regulation and self-correction contained in market relationships and in entrepreneurial action.

Whereas, in democratic solidarity, civil society was taken into account through its public-space dimension, in the philanthropic-solidarity approach, civil society occupies the space of free private initiative, along the lines of the liberal tradition. Proponents of this second approach consider the market as an economic expression of civil society, and they caution against the risks inherent in public interference. This praise of civil society as a defence against public intrusion is reflected in the recommendations of international financial organisations about good governance. Socially oriented private initiatives are expected to work together, as proposed by the social-business, venture-philanthropy and bottom-of-the-pyramid models. With a view to improving their consistency, new tools (such as randomised control trial) are implemented to measure the social impact of their actions.

3.3. Contrasting Two Major Societal Projects

Rather than multiplying the types of social enterprise, adding for instance to the landscape which we have described the social-impact enterprise, B Corps or inclusive business, it seems more appropriate to synthesise our analysis by contrasting two major societal projects.

The first one corresponds to the social- and solidarity-economy approach, with solidarity enterprises feeding into the debate some criteria originating in Latin American realities, as mentioned in the Brazilian and Ecuadorian chapters. The second one is represented by several kinds of social business "bringing a new dimension in the business world and a new feeling of social awareness among business people" (Yunus 2010: 12).

These two projects correspond to completely opposite economic, social and governance-related indicators, as shown in table 10.1.

Most of the patterns identified by Gaiger and Wanderley in chapter 9 are oriented towards the solidarity-enterprise project, with beneficiaries acting as leading actors. Only philanthropic-solidarity organisations and social-purpose organisations seem to be different, but the high heterogeneity of these large patterns is invisibilised by a tendency to reduce this heterogeneity, in discourses, to social business.

Table 10.1 Two models for Latin American social enterprises

Indicators \ Societal projects	Solidarity enterprises	Social businesses
Economic dimension	• Hybridisation of economic principles • Consistency of economic, social and environmental commitment • Valorisation of work via democratic decision-making	• Market orientation • New form of capitalism with social aims • Struggle against poverty
Social dimension	• Objective of transformation and repair • Democratic solidarity • Self-organisation	• Objective of repair • Philanthropic solidarity • Independence, risk taking
Governance-related dimension	• Public dimension • Intermediate public spaces • Institutional entrepreneurship and political embeddedness	• Private action • Diffusion by economic success • Market isomorphism

A paradox can be highlighted here: although social business corresponds only to a small number of entities, it is overemphasised in the prevailing statements by the elites. Behind this paradox lies an epistemological question: why do so few initiatives generate so many discourses? Having in mind the lessons of history, we can put forward the hypothesis that there is a new process of invisibilisation going on.

If the solidarity enterprise has gone beyond governance criteria to integrate clear political indicators, as emphasised in different chapters of this book, the social business rather corresponds to a "depolitisation" of the field and the production of "absences" in the sense given by Santos to this term. Indeed, the social-business approach builds a narrative that progressively replaces the one about the social and solidarity economy. This diversion becomes obvious when researchers also include in this concept initiatives whose stakeholders openly refuse this label: it is for example the case when Limeira (2014) and Comini (2016) refer to Banco Palmas (a community bank deeply involved in the solidarity economy) or to other solidarity-economy initiatives as to social businesses. Without going into detail on the numerous methodological and deontological problems raised by these misappropriations, we can simply say here that they reproduce the mechanisms already used in the past to negate such initiatives, through positive discrimination for philanthropy and negative discrimination against democratic solidarity, and they present efficiency and effectiveness as being the exclusive hallmark of market actors. These misappropriations are expressing power relations and, in this context, it would be very naive to believe in the pacific coexistence of the two narratives; in fact, these two narratives are in conflict. The symbolic invalidation of civil society initiatives is as violent as it was in the 19th century; it is contained in a presentation in which social businesses, which are actually very few in number, are "annexing" solidarity enterprises or reframing them. The fight between a "moral economy", based on self-organisation, and the "moralisation of the poor" is still going on.

At this watershed moment, all researchers, even those who do not admit it, are playing a normative role: Some of them legitimate the social-business approach, accentuating the overemphasis on this approach in the mass medias and in some national policies, like in Argentina or Chile. Others try to work to make visible what is invisibilised by the dominant current. In this perspective, the following section elaborates a proposal for a renewed theoretical framework, based on a North–South dialogue.

4. Theoretical Latin American Contributions Attentive to Emergences

In this last section of our chapter, we first summarise the main elements introduced by Latin American researchers. Then the self-organisation emphasised by these investigations is combined with the commons approach to suggest another way of thinking.

4.1. The Political Dimension of Solidarity-Type Social Enterprises

Latin American academics renew the theoretical discussion about social enterprise by taking into account actors' knowledge and by refusing to adopt an "overhanging" position regarding their practices.

The "economistic fallacy" underscored by Polanyi states that economy is often erroneously reduced to the sole market economy. By proposing the concept of "substantive economy", Polanyi enlarges the scope, including in the analytical framework the redistribution, reciprocity and householding principles. Still, Polanyi mainly characterised modernity as marked by economistic fallacy. The Latin American surveys presented and summarised in two dictionaries (Cattani *et al.* 2009; Coraggio *et al.* 2013) are decisive to understand the extent to which contemporary economies are also plural, even though capitalism clearly dominates the economic landscape. In particular, these surveys provide elements about the genesis of what we called "solidarity enterprises". Resituating social enterprise in the context of the popular economy can allow to gain strength from an economic anthropology that breaks with the evolutionist belief in development by stages. As observed by Meek (1976), the theory of the four stages of development—hunting, pastoralism, agriculture and then market—introduced by Smith (1979) engendered a story of human development that prevented the conceptualisation of multiple types of economy. Indeed, this theory postulates a radical discontinuity between the different stages. The first stage is assimilated to a form of scarcity; the last one, to wealth and abundance. Progress during this last phase is tantamount to growth, and the previous stages are considered as belonging to the past and as having nothing relevant to offer to contemporary society.

Running counter to evolutionism, the popular economy encompasses economic activities and social practices set in motion by groups of people "with a view to guaranteeing, through the use of their own labour and available resources, [the satisfaction of their] basic material and non-material needs" (Sarria Icaza and Tiriba 2006; see also Coraggio 1995; Lisboa 1998; Nuñez 1995; Razeto 1993; Quijano 1998). By detailing the hybridisation between economic principles, authors analysing the popular economy show the mobilisation of reciprocity and householding, as well as the translation that can occur from one principle to another: indeed, householding in the private sphere can be converted in an impulse for equalitarian reciprocity in the public sphere. It is important in this regard to fully rehabilitate the collective power, flowing from equality and reciprocity, which is learned and experienced in collective mobilisations

(Cefaï 2007), and also has an economic potential. The affirmation of the existence of a reciprocity that combines the "spirit of the gift" (Godbout 2000) with a concern for equality is moreover an antidote to philanthropy as embodying the conscience of liberalism and providing the idea of a "gift without reciprocity" (Ranci 1990).

Latin American authors also cross the lines that separate the political and economic spheres; they analyse initiatives to improve daily life via democratic and socio-economic processes which cannot be dissociated. The public spaces needed to implement solid democratic mechanisms in solidarity-type social enterprises refer to these initiatives' internal functioning, but these spaces should not be confined to the perimeter of the organisations. As shown by Nyssens and Petrella (2015), social utility is usually multidimensional, because it refers to a project embedded in organisational practices. Collective benefits are not produced only by economic activities, and democracy cannot be thought of as a positive externality; democracy is explicitly claimed by solidarity-type social enterprises as being at the heart of their project (Laville and Nyssens 2001). If so, democracy must not be considered as an extra component; it is an intrinsic dimension of initiatives. Consequently, public spaces are intricated with solidarity-type social enterprises connecting deliberative spaces. Moreover, these local public spheres have to be complemented by intermediary public spheres, allowing to bring together some local spheres with a view to confronting the dominant rules, to generating a controversial debate about the existing institutional framework and to promoting a process of institutional change.

In such perspective, the solidarity economy is a kind of contextual popular resistance with political meaning, against the weakness of the state and an overvalued capitalist market. Support organisations in the Latin American solidarity economy are committed to stimulating autonomy and self-government with regard to the deliberative decision-making processes; this is one of their outstanding characteristics. But this political dimension is viewable only if we broaden the scope of what can be interpreted and seen as political. In view of what we have said of the Latin American context, "political" should not be understood in its universalised Western sense. As for the supposed collapse of movements, we think that it may be a red herring. What has "collapsed" is representative democracy in Brazil, but social movements and their supporting organisations, despite the lack of funds and support of public policies, continue highlighting the political dimension of solidarity-type social enterprise.

4.2. Linking the Social and Solidarity Economy With the Commons

In the perspective of a sociology of emergences, in-depth monographs on institutional innovations concerning specific connections between social enterprise, the solidarity economy and the commons constitute another possible Latin American contribution to the theoretical debate. The Flok Society (free, libre, open knowledge) project offers a very good illustration of such institutional innovation, mixing elements from social enterprise, the solidarity economy and the commons. This project has created a new ecosystem in Ecuador that is very relevant to rethink social enterprise in the perspective of the creation of transition policies to an open-knowledge society. The Flok platform was initiated in 2011 by a small group of Spanish activists who were part of the anti-austerity movement in Spain, also referred to as the 15-M Movement. This group managed to persuade a minister of the Ecuadorian government to finance a country-wide open-knowledge project. In such an enterprise, the state has a particular role to play. On this subject, the project coordinator, Bauwens, states that the state does not disappear but is transformed, with thoroughly democratised remaining functions based on citizen participation.

The Flok Society project constituted the first attempt to deploy operational proposals throughout an entire country to spark a transition towards a society based on free and open knowledge. It aimed to create the conditions for a simultaneous transformation of civil society, the market and public authorities, based on the paradigm of knowledge commons. The Flok Society project benefited from a remarkable conjunction between the objective expressed by the Ecuadorian people and the potentialities of experiments conducted within the commons. This led indigenous communities to collaborate with groups of hackers to develop shared knowledge. The global hacking culture was indeed seen as a way to bring together Spanish speakers and Quechua-speaking natives.

The assessment of the completed project brings out some strong points. The Flok Society project managed to be simultaneously a scientific research project and a participatory citizen project. It has garnered a certain amount of knowledge that can now be easily modified, adapted and transformed by local communities. In this sense, the knowledge commons that have been created are potential vectors of social change through the emergence of a new kind of social enterprise. Independently of whether these commons will be taken up (or not) by the government, under the form of public policies, or by civil society initiatives in Ecuador, the work of the Flok Society project generated a corpus of proposals and a methodology that gives rise to trials in other contexts, outside of Ecuador, and which can henceforth inspire public policies in other countries.

The Flok Society experiment is of particular value in that it was associated with the creation of a new "social imagination" in Ecuador, connected with the transition towards a more sustainable and more equitable society, while being in synch with the requirements of the 21st century. Bauwens (2016: 13)[5] stated the value of commons:

> *Just as cognitive capitalism depends on the manifold institutional supports supplied by government policy, legislation, free-market*

ideology, and the collective power of firms and the institutions that serve them, a social-knowledge economy depends, to an even greater extent, on appropriate civic and economic institutions, which can support and safeguard the value of commons, of collective benefit, of open and accessible markets, and of social control over capital.

Bauwens (2016: 13) also posits the possible combination between this value of commons and the social and solidarity economy:

These civic institutions are embodied in the structure of democratic enterprises, of peer-to-peer networks, of non-profits and community-service organisations, of mutually supporting small and medium firms, and of civil society and the social economy itself. It is these social and economic structures, based on the principles of reciprocity and service to community, that can best utilise knowledge as commons and safeguard its future as an indispensable resource for the common good and the well-being of humanity as a whole.

In this context, the theoretical perspective of the commons is very useful to experiment and create new kinds of social enterprises. Thus, the Latin American example of the Flok Society project shows that the insistence on self-organisation links the participative dynamic to an "instituting praxis", or "purposeful institution building" (Dardot and Laval 2014: 440). According to Ostrom, the commons are characterised by a long adaptive process of trial and error. This process offers the conditions required to foster public expression and, by doing so, to protect it from individual interests. In the book she co-wrote with Hess, Ostrom describes the knowledge commons (Hess and Ostrom 2006). The authors analyse how free software can be considered as a common. They point out that knowledge commons, unlike natural commons, are non-rival and non-excludable, and that the question of the size of the community is thus expressed differently in this case. Consequently, knowledge commons also require specific collaborative tools.

Beside traditional and knowledge commons, other commons have been identified: cultural commons, medical and health commons, neighbourhood commons, infrastructure commons, global commons and urban commons. Hess proposes to refer to them all as "new commons" (Hess 2008). This label has the advantage of drawing attention to the diversity of the commons and to the necessity of defining them more precisely. According to Hess, the growing number of new commons identified in the literature reflects our societies' high expectations for shaping responses to the challenges raised by globalisation, commodification and privatisation. Bollier (2014) posits that, in order to face these challenges, we need to free ourselves from market-based basic principles, and to promote a new epistemology.

Literature on the new commons emphasises today collective action, voluntary associations, and collaboration in general (Hess and Ruth 2006). Even though property rights and the nature of the goods remain important, literature also goes beyond property rights to address questions of governance, the participatory process, trust and assurance (*ibid.*). In a recent contribution pleading in favour of this convergence between the solidarity economy and the commons, Bauwens (2015) suggests creating global and open cooperatives, based on a new property model and multistakeholder governance. The goal of such cooperatives could be to co-produce commons (Bauwens 2015; Bauwens and Lievens 2016). Citizen initiatives around the commons are designing new solidarity practices (Dardot and Laval 2014). These authors underline the fact that, in order to preserve diversity and to open the dialogue, it is necessary to discover different experiences and to combine them in new ways. As shown by Eynaud and Laville (2017), the new commons help to shift from an aggregative paradigm based on individual preferences to a deliberative paradigm.

The commons are characterised by three main elements: the existence of common-pool resources, a bundle of rights and a large variety of governance forms (Coriat 2015). The theory of the commons is thus well suited to analyse the systems of rules chosen by self-organised communities at the local level. Literature on the commons has also elaborated on governance-related issues, while this is relatively new for the solidarity economy. The introduction of these issues in literature has actually been motivated by the need to better understand how hybrid and multistakeholder organisations work (Borzaga and Depredi 2015). Therefore, the theory of the commons and the solidarity-economy approach can enrich each other; they are two ways going in the same direction.

The solidarity-economy approach offers to the commons a relevant standpoint for rethinking economics and analysing the plurality of public-action and democracy forms. The solidarity-economy conceptual framework is indeed more oriented towards public action, political dimensions and interaction between civil society organisations and public authorities than the theory of the commons. From a pragmatic point of view, the solidarity economy and the new commons both endeavour to enrich institutional diversity by promoting hybrid organisational forms (Nyssens and Petrella 2015). In this sense, the solidarity economy is very close to commons-related initiatives. But at the same time, the solidarity economy has specific features, which make it distinct from the commons:

- The solidarity economy is supported by a mix of resources, including monetary, non-monetary and non-market resources. This allows for many creative strategies in terms of hybridisation of resources.
- The solidarity economy acknowledges the crucial role of public authorities in defending the public interest, and it promotes strategies

in which civil society and public authorities can co-create and co-produce public actions, beyond statism.

Although the Flok Society project is rather linked to the commons (and does thus not acknowledge, to the same extent as solidarity-economy projects, the role of public authorities), Bauwens has shown that this project could not have been developed without the plain support of the Ecuadorian government, whose primary challenge was to establish a social and solidarity economy in the country. We see here the ability of the Ecuadorian project to combine the two perspectives—of the commons and of the solidarity economy. The project had to blaze its own trail to define a plan of action. The project initiators were facing a vast field, which they knew would lead to experimentation, "rhizome-like" development and learning-as-they-go processes. In such context, pluralistic and democratic spaces appear to be necessary. It is not just a matter of promoting large domestic industries or simply limiting imports, but a much more complex task, which entails support to new socio-economic actors. The legitimisation of these initiatives, which has been stifled for too long, sends us back to a new philosophy of the commons, with its roots in *sumak kawsay*, an Aymaran term which has been translated and updated as the "good way of living" (*buen vivir*) and has become the reference put forth in the Ecuadorian Constitution. Article 283 of this Constitution indeed states that the economic system "recognises the human being as a subject and an end (. . .) and its objective is to ensure the production and reproduction of material and immaterial conditions conducive to the good way of living". This *buen vivir* is a way of living in a community which must be achieved throughout history by the Ecuadorian people based on four kinds of balance: the balance of human beings as persons; the balance among humans; the balance between humans and nature; and the balance between communities of human beings. The notion of *buen vivir* aims to replace the blind pursuit of economic growth with the pursuit of the well-being of the Ecuadorian people. In order to facilitate this transition, the *buen vivir* aims to create knowledge commons, open to all. And even though practices still remain far off this target, such approaches pave original ways for social-enterprise theory.

By enriching the political dimension of solidarity-type social enterprises and by linking the social and solidarity economy with the commons, the theoretical Latin American contributions offer a relevant and specific attention to emergences. Thus, they allow social enterprise conceptualisation to be open to plurality, and they argue that imported occidental notions, presented like universal, have to be revisited through the construction of a real "pluriversalism" (Escobar 2014). If it continues to move in this direction, social-enterprise theory will no longer be only a field of tensions; it will also become a field of inventions for global social sciences, far from economicist and managerialist reductionism.

Notes

1 Some ideas presented in this chapter are detailed in a collective book gathering contributions by a group of intercontinental researchers, *Theory of Social Enterprise and Pluralism* (Eynaud *et al*. 2019).
2 The concept of popular economy can be defined as the set of economic activities and social practices developed by subjects who only have their labour force to survive (see Santana Junior 2005).
3 The notion of moral economy was introduced by Thompson in studies of workers and extended to peasants by Scott (1976).
4 Marx distinguishes between "simple reproduction" and "expanded (or enlarged) reproduction". In the former case, no economic growth occurs, while in the latter case, more is produced than is needed to maintain the economy at the given level, making economic growth possible.
5 Bauwens quotes in his text Restakis, expert in cooperatives, research coordinator for Flok's Social Infrastructure and Institutional Innovation investigation and author of "Humanizing the Economy: Cooperatives in the Age of Capital".

References

Alvarez, A., Dagnino, E. & Escobar, A. (eds) (1998) *Culture of Politics, Politics of Culture*, Boulder: West View Press.
Bauwens, M. (2015) "Plan de transition vers les communs: une introduction", in Coriat, B. (ed.) *Le retour des communs: la crise de l'idéologie propriétaire*, Paris: Éditions Les liens qui libèrent.
Bauwens, M. (2016) "A commons transition plan, specific adaptation of the 1st commons transition plan developed for Ecuador's FLOK society project". Available HTTP: http://wiki.commonstransition.org/wiki/Commons_Transition_Plan.
Bauwens, M. & Lievens, J. (2016) *Sauver le monde: Vers une économie post-capitaliste avec le peer-to-peer*, Paris: Éditions Les liens qui libèrent.
Bollier, D. (2014) *Think Like a Commoner: A Short Introduction to the Life of the Commons*, Gabriola Island: New Society Publishers.
Borzaga, C. & Depredi, S. (2015) "Multi-stakeholder governance in civil society organisations: Models and outcomes", in Laville, J.-L., Young, D. & Eynaud, P. (eds) *Civil Society, the Third Sector and Social Enterprise: Governance and Democracy*, London: Routledge.
Braudel, F. (1985) *La dynamique du capitalisme*, Paris: Arthaud.
Cattani, A. D., Laville, J.-L., Gaiger, L. I. & Espanha, P. (2009) *Diccionario internacional de outra economia*, Coimbra and Sao Paulo: Almedina Ediçoes.
Cefaï, D. (2007) *Pourquoi se mobilise-t-on? Les théories de l'action collective*, Paris: La Découverte.
Comini, G. (2016) *Negocios sociais e innovaçao social—um retrato de experiencias brasileiras*, Sao Paolo: Universidade de Sao Paolo.
Coraggio, J. L. (1995) *Desarollo humano, economía popular y educación*, Instituto de Estudios y Acción social, Buenos Aires: Aique Grupo.
Coraggio, J. L. (1999) *Política social y economía de trabajo*, Madrid and Buenos Aires: Minio y Davila Editores.
Coraggio, J. L., Ferrarini, A., França Filho, G. C., Gaiger, L. I., Hillenkamp, I., Laville, J.-L., Lemaître, A., Sadik, Y., Veronese, M. & Wanderlay, F. (2015) "The theory of social enterprise and pluralism: Solidarity-type social enterprise", in Laville, J.-L., Young, D. R. & Eynaud, P. (eds) *Civil Society, the Third*

Sector and Social Enterprise: Governance and Democracy, London and New York: Routledge.

Coraggio, J. L., Laville, J-L. & Cattani, A. D. (eds) (2013) *Diccionario de la otra economía*, Buenos Aires: Universidad Nacional de General Sarmiento.

Coriat, C. (ed.) (2015) *Le retour des communs: la crise de l'idéologie propriétaire*, Paris: Éditions Les liens qui libèrent.

Dardot, P. & Laval, C. (2014) *Commun: essai sur la révolution au XXIe siècle*, Paris: La Découverte.

de Carvalho, A. H. M. (2002) "A emancipação do movimento no movimento de emancipação social continuada", in Santos, B. de S. (ed.) *Produzir para viver. Os caminhos de produção non capitalista*, Rio de Janeiro: Civilisação brasileira.

Escobar, A. (2014) "De la crítica del desarollismo al pensiamento sobre otra economía: pluriverso y pensiamento relacional", in Coraggio, J. L. & Laville, J-L. (eds) *Reinventar la izquierda en el siglo XXI*, Quito: Editorial IAEN.

Eynaud, P. & Laville J-L. (2017) "Joining the commons with social and solidarity economy research: Towards the renewal of critical thinking and emancipation", *Revista de Economia Solidária*, No. 11, ACEESA.

Eynaud, P., Laville, J-L., Lucas dos Santos, L., Banerjee, S., Avelino, F. & Hulgård, L. (2019) *Theory of Social Enterprise and Pluralism: Social Movements, Solidarity Economy, and Global South*, London: Routledge.

Foucault, M. (2001) *Dits et écrits*, tome II, Paris: Gallimard.

Godbout, J-T. (2000) *Le Don, la dette et l'intérêt*, Paris: La Découverte.

Hess, C. (2008) "Mapping the new commons", 12th Biennial Conference of the International Association for the Study of the Commons, Cheltenham: University of Gloucestershire, July 14–18.

Hess, C. & Ostrom, E. (2006) *Understanding Knowledge as a Commons: From Theory to Practice*, Cambridge: The MIT Press.

Hess, C. & Ruth, M. D. (2006) "The name change; or, what happened to the 'P'?", Libraries' and Librarians', Publications Paper 23.

Hirschman, A. O. (1971) *Exit, Voice and Loyalty: Responses to Decline in Firms, Organisations and States*, Cambridge: Harvard University Press.

Kraychet, G., Lara, F. & Costa, B. et al. (eds) (2000) *Economia dos sectores populares. Entre a realidade y a utopia*, Petropolis: Vozes.

Laville, J-L. & Nyssens, M. (2001) *Les services sociaux entre associations, Etat et marché. L'aide aux personnes âgées*, Paris: La Découverte.

Lemaître, A. & Helmsing, B. A. H. J. (2011) "Solidarity economy in Brazil: Movement, discourse and practice. Analysis through a Polanyian understanding of the economy", *Working Paper*, No. 524, The Hague: Institute of Social Studies.

Limeira, T. M. (2014) *Empreendorismo social no Brasil: estado de arte e desafios*, Sao Paolo: Inovaçao em Cidadania empresorial.

Lisboa, A. M. (1998) *Desordem do trabalho, economia popular e exclusao social: algumas consideraoes*, Florianopolis: Dpt. De Ciencias Economicas, UFSC.

Lucas dos Santos, L. (2008) "When the domestic is also political. Redistribution by women from the south: A feminist approach". Available HTTP: https://emes.net/content/uploads/publications/when-the-domestic-is-also-political-reditribution-by-women-from-the-south-a-feminist-approach/Lucas-ECSP-2EMESPolanyi-08.pdf.

Lutz, B. (1990) *Le mirage de la croissance marchande*, Paris: Maison des sciences de l'homme.

Lyon, F., Teasdale, S. & Baldock, R. (2010) "Challenges of measuring the scale of the social enterprise sector: The case of the UK", TSRC Working Paper, Birmingham: University of Birmingham.

Mariategui, J. C. (1979) *Ensayos de interpretación de la realidad peruana*, Caracas: Biblioteca Ayacucho.

Mauss, M. (1997) *Écrits politiques* (textes réunis par M. Fournier), Paris: Fayard.

Meek, R. L. (1976) *Social Science and the Ignoble Savage*, Cambridge: Cambridge University Press.

Mingione, E. (1991) *Fragmented Societies: A Sociology of Economic Life Beyond the Market Paradigm*, Oxford: Basil Blackwell.

Navarro, Z. (2002) "Mobilisação sin emancipação—as lutas sociais dos semterra no Brasil", in Santos, B. de S. (ed.) *Produzir para viver. Os caminhos de produção non capitalista*, Rio de Janeiro: Civilisação brasileira.

Nuñez, O. (1995) *La economía popular, asociativa y autogestionaria*, Managua: CIPRES.

Nyssens, M. (1994) "Quatre essais sur l'économie populaire urbaine. Le cas de Santiago du Chili", *Nouvelle série*, No. 231, Louvain-la-Neuve: Université catholique de Louvain, Faculté des sciences économiques, sociales et politiques.

Nyssens, M. & Petrella, F. (2015) "The social and solidarity economy and Ostrom's approach of common-pool resources: Towards a better understanding of institutional diversity", in Laville, J-L., Young, D. & Eynaud, P. (eds) *Civil Society, the Third Sector and Social Enterprise: Governance and Democracy*, London: Routledge.

Pinto, J. R. L. (2006) *Economia solidaria de volta a arte da associaçao*, Porto Alegre: Editora da Universidad Federal de Rio Grande do Sul.

Pleyers, G. & Capitaine, B. (eds) (2016) *Mouvements sociaux. Quand le sujet devient acteur*, Paris: Éditions de la Maison des sciences de l'homme.

Polanyi, K. (1977) *The Livelihood of Man*, New York: New York Academic Press.

Prahalad, C. K. (2014) *Fortune at the Bottom of the Pyramid: Eradicating Poverty Through Profits*, Upper Saddle River: Wharton School Publishing.

Quijano, A. (1998) *La Economía Popular y sus caminos en América Latina*, Lima: Mosca Azul Editores.

Quijano, A. (2007) "Sistemas alternativas de produccion", in Coraggio, J. L. (ed.) *La economía social desde la periferia. Constituciones latinoamericanas*, Buenos Aires: Altamira.

Ranci, C. (1990) "Doni senza reciprocità: La persistenza dell'altruismo sociale nei sistemi complessi", *Rassegna italiana di sociologia*, Vol. XXXI.

Razeto, L. (1993) *Empresas de trabajadores y economia de mercado*, Santiago de Chile: Ediciones PET.

Santana Junior, G. (2005) "A economia solidaria face a dinamica da acumulaçao capitalista. Da subordinaçao a un novo modo de regulaçao social", thesis for social sciences doctorate, Bahia: Universidad Federal da Bahia.

Santos, B. de S. (2004) "The World Social Forum: Toward a Counter-Hegemonic Globalisation (Part I)", in Sen, J., Anand, A., Escobar, A. & Waterman, P. (eds) The WSF: Challenging Empires, New Delhi: The Viveka Foundation, pp. 235–245. Available HTTP: www.boaventuradesousasantos.pt/media/wsf_JaiSenPart1.pdf.

Santos, B. de S. (2014) Epistemologies of the South, Justice Against Epistemicide, London and Boulder: Paradigm Publishers.

Sarria Icaza, A. M. & Tiriba, L. (2006) "Économie populaire", in Laville, J-L. & Cattani, A. D. (eds) *Dictionnaire de l'autre économie*, Paris: Folio-Gallimard.

Scholnik, M. (1984) "Les organisations économiques populaires et la vie quotidienne", *Nouvelles de l'écodéveloppement*, Vol. 31, supplement to MSH information, December.

Scott, J. C. (1976) *The Moral Economy of the Peasant*, New Haven and London: Yale University Press.

Simmons, R. (2008) "Harnessing social enterprise for local public services: The case of new leisure trusts in the UK. Public policy and administration", in Santos, B. de S. (ed.) (2014) *Epistemologies of the South, Justice Against Epistemicide*, Boulder and London: Paradigm Publishers.

Smith, A. (1979) *An Inquiry into the Nature and Causes of the Wealth of Nations*, Oxford: Clarendon Press.

Teasdale, S. (2010) "Explaining the multifaceted nature of social enterprise: Impression management as (social) entrepreneurial behaviour", *Voluntary Sector Review*, Vol. 1, No. 3, pp. 271–292(22).

Teasdale, S. (2011) "What's in a name? Making sense of social enterprise discourses", *Public Policy and Administration*, Vol. 27, No. 2, pp. 99–119.

Thompson, E. P. (1963) *The Making of the English Working Class*, New-York: Vintage Books.

Yunus, M. (2007) *Creating a World Without Poverty, Social Business and the Future of Capitalism*, New York: Perseus Books.

Yunus, M. (2010) *Building Social Business: The New Kind of Capitalism That Serves Humanity's Most Pressing Needs*, New York: Public Affairs.

11 Latin American Social Enterprise Models in a Worldwide Perspective

Jacques Defourny, Marthe Nyssens and Olivier Brolis

Introduction

The last two or three decades have witnessed a high number of conceptual attempts to define social enterprise (SE). It is rather easy today to identify the criteria or distinctive features that were most debated in such conceptual discussions: the primacy of social aims (Nicholls 2006); the search for market income in non-profit organisations, as developed by Skloot (1983) as early as the 1980s, and then more widely in "mission-driven business" (Austin *et al.* 2006); the specific profile and role of individual social entrepreneurs as described by Dees (1998); the place of innovation, from the Schumpeterian works of Young (1983) through those of Mulgan (2007) on social innovation; and the issue of governance, for a sustainable balance between economic and social objectives, as highlighted by the EMES International Research Network (Defourny and Borzaga 2001).

The concept of social enterprise as such is not widely used in Latin America, even though it has been used in some circles like the Social Enterprise Knowledge Network (Austin and SEKN Team, 2004).[1] When defining social enterprises, Berger and Blugerman (2010), who belong to this network, in their chapter on "social enterprises and inclusive businesses" (*empresas sociales y negocios inclusivos*), consider both non-profit organisations and cooperatives as social enterprises, as they define social enterprises as "private (and formal) organisations that employ market strategies to obtain financial resources, in order to achieve social value for [their] members and/or for groups or communities and which are legally chartered as non-profit or cooperative organisations" (Márquez *et al.* 2010: 97). With respect to the various conceptions of social enterprise in the academic literature, we are here quite close to the "earned-income" school of thought, which defines the field of social enterprises as encompassing all organisations that trade for a social purpose (Defourny and Nyssens 2010). Over the last years, as new networks have started to embrace the concept in Latin America, it has most often been used along the lines of this "earned-income" school of thought or, in other—less

DOI: 10.4324/9780429055164-14

frequent—cases, for very specific types of SE, like in Argentina, where the term "social enterprise" is only used to refer to a particular type of initiative, which aims at the work integration of people with disabilities and mental health problems (see chapter 1 in this book). The various "country chapters" of this book show how other concepts, beside that of social enterprise, such as the "social and solidarity economy", the "popular economy", the "community economy" or the "cooperative economy", are widely rooted in Latin American contexts.

We adopt here the generic concept of social enterprise as defined by the "International Comparative Social Enterprise Models (ICSEM) Project", which encompasses a wide spectrum of organisations that combine an entrepreneurial dynamic to provide services or goods with the primacy of their social aims. As explained in the introduction of this book, this concept has been used in the ICSEM Project as a heuristic tool, with a view to better understanding this type of organisation. Indeed, most researchers today seem to acknowledge the impossibility of a unified definition of social enterprise. A main challenge in this field of research has then become to grasp the diversity of SE types. In such a perspective, many empirical descriptive studies have been carried out in the last decade. Some of them consisted in thorough "case studies", through which various aspects of such diversity could be analysed and even theorised.[2] Beyond such specific issues, however, the comparative analysis of SE types or models still lacks strongly integrated theoretical foundations and, even more, empirical surveys that would allow statistically testing typologies of SE models—all the more so at the international level, as empirical relevance should be sought in this case beyond national borders.

This chapter aims precisely at addressing the lack of a typology of SE models that would combine three key strengths: (1) it would be rooted in sound theoretical grounds, allowing for a wide diversity of SE models within each country and across countries; (2) it would be supported by strong empirical evidence, provided by statistical exploitation of the data resulting from a survey carried out in the same way in many countries; and (3) it would highlight the specificities of Latin America in a worldwide perspective.

In such a threefold ambitious perspective, we first propose—while acknowledging the gaps that characterise existing SE classifications—a theoretical framework to identify a few major SE models, relying on two building blocks: on the one hand, "principles of interest", as key driving forces at work in various parts of the economy and as matrices from which social-enterprise dynamics can emerge; and on the other hand, "resource mixes", as a central dimension of social enterprise, acknowledged by many authors. We then describe the key dimensions to be captured and the methodological choices that were at the heart of a unique survey carried out in 2015 and 2016 on 721 social enterprises in some 40 countries across the world, in the framework of the ICSEM Project (see the introductory chapter of the present volume), and we present statistical work that was carried out on the basis of this dataset—in particular, a hierarchical cluster analysis. Thirdly, we discuss the empirical results obtained, comparing the results at the world level with those obtained at the Latin American level which, as will be shown, provide strong support to our international typology of SE models. Finally, we provide some concluding remarks.

1. Theorising the Diversity of SE Models

What is at stake with SE typologies is not just a wide, although simplified, view of the various types or models of social enterprise; nor is it a "struggle" against too much diversity. It is first and foremost a question of uncovering and acknowledging the fact that today, a wide range of entrepreneurial initiatives, generally private and primarily driven by social aims, actually address social or societal challenges.

Although relying on the sole observation of cases in the US context, Dees argued, as soon as in the late 1990s, that the level of market reliance should be seen as the most relevant criterion to build a classification of SE types. For him, social enterprises can be presented along a single-dimensional continuum between two extremes, corresponding respectively to a "purely philanthropic" pole and a "purely commercial" one (Dees 1996, 1998). However, Dees does not just refer to the market in terms of incomes from sales. Instead, he actually develops market principles (and philanthropic principles at the other extreme) in terms of motives, methods and goals, and he argues that most social enterprises combine commercial and philanthropic elements in a productive balance. The major strength of Dees's social-enterprise spectrum is that his many sources of variations pave the way for an infinite number of operational SE models. It is therefore not surprising that many authors refer to this spectrum (Peattie and Morley 2008), to adapted versions of the latter (Nicholls 2006) or to a critical analysis of it (Seanor and Meaton 2007; Young and Lecy 2014). The other side of the coin is that such multiple variations along a single continuous axis do not really help to define groups or categories of social enterprises. From the point of view of Dees's spectrum, all social enterprises can be seen as "intermediate organisations" and they may all be labelled as "hybrids" (Doherty *et al.* 2014).

Beside some attempts carried out before the early 2010s,[3] only few authors had made attempts, more recently, to delimit, describe and analyse the whole (or a great deal of the) SE field. At the national level, these efforts had mainly taken place in countries that had experienced specific and strong public or private strategies promoting social enterprise and social entrepreneurship. The best example is provided by the United Kingdom, which combines strong third-sector traditions (with mutual and cooperative organisations and charities) with brand new developments in the last fifteen years in terms of SE promotion by public authorities and various other bodies. In such context, Spear *et al.* (2009) identified four types of social enterprise in the United Kingdom, according to their origins and development paths: mutual societies, formed to meet the needs of a particular group of members through trading activities; trading charities, which develop commercial activities to fulfil their primary mission or as a secondary activity to raise funds; public-sector spin-offs, which have taken over the operation of services previously provided by the state; and new social enterprises, set up as new businesses by social entrepreneurs. Much more recently, relying mainly on the US SE landscape, Young *et al.* (2016) proposed the metaphor of a "social enterprise zoo", in which different types of animals seek different things, behave differently and may (or may not) interact with one another in both competitive and complementary ways . . . just like social enterprises, which combine social and market goals in substantially different ways. In the Latin American context, some recent studies were carried out at the national level, like in Brazil, where Gaiger (2013) mapped the solidarity economy, based on data from the National Mapping of the Solidarity Economy, or in Chile, where Gatica Montero (2017), on the basis of a few case studies, highlighted different models of social enterprises (associative, cooperative and business-type SEs).

But when it comes to international comparative works, most of them were hitherto based on conceptualisations and/or policy frameworks shaped by specific national or regional contexts. For instance, Kerlin (2006) and Defourny and Nyssens (2010) mainly focused on comparisons of conceptual approaches of social enterprise in Europe and the United States. At a broad macro level, Kerlin (2013, 2015, 2017) adopted an institutional perspective, developing a macro-institutional framework and identifying key features of macro, meso and micro institutions in various countries to suggest how any set of cultural, socio-economic and regulatory institutions tends to shape a specific major SE model per country (or subregion). But although appealing from a theoretical point of view, Kerlin's approach did not provide foundations to theorise the diversity of SE types within individual countries (or regions).

1.1. Three "Principles of Interest" as a Cornerstone

Considering that social enterprises are often seen as belonging to the "third sector" or are somehow related to the latter (Defourny 2014), we chose to build our analysis upon some of the strongest theoretical frameworks focusing on the very identity of non-profit organisations or the third sector, such as those proposed by Hansmann (1996) and Gui (1991). More precisely, in a seminal contribution on the economic rationale of the third sector, Gui (1991) theorised the coexistence of mutual-benefit organisations and public-benefit organisations within the third sector. In any type of organisation, he first identifies a "dominant category", formed by those who have the residual decision-making power, especially as to the allocation of the "residual income" (profit), and a "beneficiary category", formed by those to whom the residual income is, explicitly or implicitly,[4] distributed. The "residual" character means that these rights are not assigned by contract to other stakeholders than the owners (Hansmann 1996).

To theorise the very nature of third-sector organisations, Gui (1991) states that, in these organisations, unlike what is typically the case in conventional capitalist firms, the allocation of the residual income is not in the hands of investors.[5] Among non-capitalist organisations, he defines the third sector as composed of two major types of entities, i.e. "mutual-benefit organisations" and "public-benefit organisations". "Mutual-benefit organisations" are those in which the dominant category and the beneficiary category are the same group of stakeholders, provided of course the latter are not investors; these stakeholders may be the organisation's workers or the organisation's users (consumers, suppliers, savers and so on). Concretely, the mutual interest pursued here refers to services or goods provided to members under their own control.[6] In other words, mutual-benefit organisations include all traditional types of mutual and cooperative organisations (consumer cooperatives, worker cooperatives, producer cooperatives, savings and credit cooperatives) as well as voluntary associations driven by the interest of their members (such as sport clubs, professional associations, etc.). The second major component of the third sector, namely "public-benefit organisations", corresponds to those organisations in which the beneficiary category is different from the dominant category: they are voluntary organisations oriented to serving other people (beneficiaries) than their members, who control the organisation; more generally, they include all philanthropic and charitable organisations.[7]

The above developments lead us to consider three distinct major drivers or "principles of interest" that can be found in the overall economy: the general interest (GI), the mutual interest (MI) and the capital interest (CI), which we derive directly from the ownership types theorised by Gui. We propose to represent them as the vertices of a triangle in which mixes of principles can also be represented along the sides (see figure 11.1).

Before trying to locate the various SE profiles or types on our graph, let us note that all associations (voluntary organisations) seeking the interest of their members (Gui's mutual benefit) are located in the "mutual-interest" angle—as are all traditional cooperatives. By contrast, associations (voluntary organisations, charities . . .) seeking a public benefit (as the term is referred to by Gui) are located much closer to the general-interest angle, although not in the vertex itself, as their general interest (the community they serve) is usually not as wide (general) as the one served by the state. On the right-hand side of the triangle, shareholder companies mainly

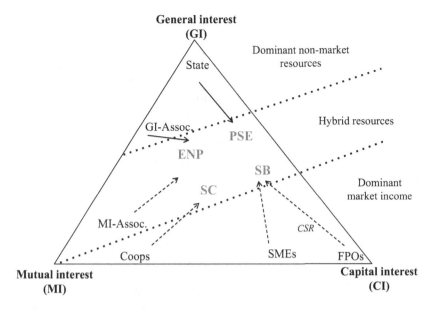

Figure 11.1 Institutional trajectories and resulting SE models
Source: Defourny and Nyssens (2017: 2479).

seeking capital interest sometimes develop CSR strategies through which they tend to express a concern for some issues of general interest, though without calling their main profit motive into question. This may be represented as a limited move upward along this side of the triangle.

The lower side of the figure represents a continuum between the cooperative treatment of profits and the capitalist stance on profits. In a cooperative, the search for profit is instrumental to the productive activity and profits are therefore only distributed as dividends with a cap and/or put into collective reserves with an asset lock; by contrast, distributing profit and increasing the value of their shares are the main goals of shareholding companies. In the case of large listed companies, investors may even consider production activities as instrumental to their quest for the highest short-term returns. By contrast, although capitalist as well, many small and medium-sized enterprises, especially family businesses, may balance in a different way the search for profits and non-financial goals (Zellweger *et al.* 2013).

1.2. Market Reliance and the Resource Mix as Central Issues

A good deal of the literature and discourses on social enterprise underline a significant move towards market activities as a distinctive feature of social enterprise. When it comes to identifying operating social enterprises, many observers look at the proportion of market income and might require that at least 50% of resources come from market sales, like in various surveys carried out in the United Kingdom.

We have shown elsewhere (Defourny and Nyssens 2010) that such a stance is often far from the field reality in many countries, and that it is not shared by all schools of thought. However, we fully acknowledge the fact that the degree of market reliance is a major issue in the debate and we certainly do not want to avoid it.

Therefore, we have drawn two dotted lines across our triangle to take into account the various combinations of resource types (market income, public grants, philanthropic resources), establishing a distinction between situations in which market income dominates, those in which non-market resources (public funding, voluntary resources) dominate and those in which a resource mix (hybrid resources) is preferred with a view to better balancing the social mission and the financial sustainability (see figure 11.1). It should be noted that the lower dotted line also divides the "mutual interest" angle: cooperatives are enterprises operating mainly on the market and they appear below the line, as do all enterprises earning all or the bulk of their income from the market; on the contrary, mutual-interest associations, like sport clubs or other voluntary organisations in the field of leisure, generally rely on a mix of market resources (member fees, sales at a bar or cafeteria) and other resources, such as volunteering and public contributions in the form of sport infrastructures and other indoor or outdoor facilities.

1.3. Institutional Trajectories Generating SE Models

On the basis of our triangle, we represented how various "institutional trajectories" in the whole economy may generate SE models (Defourny and Nyssens 2017).

As shown in figure 11.1, SE models (in grey) emerge from six traditional models through two distinct institutional trajectories:

(1) The first type of logic generating social enterprises can be observed among non-profit or public organisations experiencing a *downward move towards marketisation* (solid-line arrows):

  • **The entrepreneurial non-profit (ENP) model** gathers all non-profit organisations, most often general-interest associations (GI-Assoc.), that are developing any type of earned-income activities in support of their social mission.
  • The **public-sector social-enterprise (PSE) model** results from a movement towards the marketisation of public services which embraces "public-sector spin-offs". These SEs are usually launched

by local public bodies, sometimes in partnership with third-sector organisations, to provide services which are outsourced (such as care services) or new services (such as those offered by work-integration social enterprises—WISEs).

(2) The second type of logic corresponds to an upward move of conventional cooperatives and mutual-interest associations *towards a stronger general-interest orientation* (dotted arrows), and such a move may also be observed through some advanced CSR initiatives launched by the traditional business world:

- **The social-cooperative (SC)**[8] **model** differs from traditional mutual-interest organisations—i.e. cooperatives (Coops) and mutual-interest associations (MI-Assoc.)—in that it combines the pursuit of its members' interests (mutual interest) with the pursuit of the interests of the whole community or of a specific group targeted by the social mission (general interest).
- **The social-business (SB) model** is rooted in a business model driven by shareholders' (capital) interest, but social businesses mix this logic with a "social entrepreneurial" drive aimed at the creation of a "blended value", in an effort to balance and better integrate economic and social purposes.

At first sight, when looking at figure 11.1, the four SE models seem to arise from new dynamics at work in pre-existing organisations. Thus, it may seem that social enterprises cannot be created from scratch. Such an interpretation is clearly misleading as a new (social) enterprise can emerge everywhere in the triangle; its location will depend on its general-interest orientation, and on the way in which the organisation balances social and economic objectives and various types of financial resources.

As suggested above, our typology of SE models is based on some key dimensions, to which we referred as "fundamentals" in Defourny and Nyssens (2017). We do not pretend that it covers all possible SE cases; especially, we are aware of the many types of hybridity and joint ventures that can be observed on the field. However, partnerships can sometimes be related to one of our four models, when a dominant partner can be identified or when the chosen legal status drives partners towards one of the models.

2. Data and Method

2.1. The Unique ICSEM Survey and Database

In the second phase of the ICSEM Project (see the introductory chapter of the present volume), in order to address the lack of reliable data-sets at enterprise level to undertake international comparative analyses, in-depth information was collected about social enterprises on the basis of a common questionnaire. More precisely, ICSEM research partners interviewed the managers of three to five social enterprises[9] that were deemed emblematic of each SE type identified in each country having taken part in the project's first phase.

The questionnaire resulted from several rounds of discussion within the "ICSEM research community"; the goal was to design a questionnaire that would be meaningful and relevant in all world regions.[10] Thanks to the researchers' efforts, detailed data were collected in a rather homogenous way for 721 social enterprises from 43 countries (see table 11.1). Needless to say, such a sample is by no way representative of the SE population across the world. Not only is the distribution across continents particularly uneven, with a quasi-absence of Africa; more fundamentally, the whole SE population is simply unknown, as there is no universal definition of social enterprise. In a few countries where a SE definition does exist, for instance through a law promoting social enterprise, such definition does not generally enable an uncontested mapping and statistical analysis, because such legal approach is often deemed too large or too narrow.

These limitations do not prevent us from arguing that our overall research strategy, which combines a theoretical typology and a quite demanding bottom-up empirical approach, constitutes a major step towards capturing the diversity of SE models. The next step indeed was to exploit the dataset built through the ICSEM survey in order to see whether it provides any empirical support to the above typology of SE models, both at the global level and for Latin America.

Table 11.1 Number of countries and social enterprises covered by the ICSEM survey

	Number of countries	*Number of SEs*
Europe	19	328
Asia	9	100
Latin America	7	162
Argentina		*12*
Bolivia		*4*
Brazil		*31*
Chile		*23*
Ecuador		*20*
Mexico		*40*
Peru		*32*
USA, Canada, Australia and New Zealand	4	45
Middle East (Israel and United Arab Emirates)	2	31
Africa (Rwanda and South Africa)	2	55
Total	43	721

2.2. A Hierarchical Cluster Analysis to Identify Major SE Categories

For the purpose of carrying out a cluster analysis, we extracted quantitative and qualitative (nominal and ordinal) variables from the questionnaire. The ultimate goal was to describe each of the 721 SEs along five major dimensions: (1) general identity (legal form, origin, accreditations); (2) social mission (mission's nature, relation with the SE's main economic activity, price of the goods and services provided, type of innovation); (3) workforce composition (workers and volunteers); (4) financial structure in general and, more precisely, ways in which the SE combines various types of resources; and (5) governance structure and rules regarding the allocation of profits/surplus. Multiple choices and combinations of several choices were possible for many questions, and we defined 141 variables.

Before undertaking a hierarchical cluster analysis (HCA), we had to solve two main issues. First, our database included both quantitative and qualitative variables, while HCA cannot be performed on qualitative variables. Secondly, we wanted each of the five predetermined dimensions to have the same weight, which was not the case since some dimensions were composed by a higher number of variables than others.

In order to overcome these problems, we therefore performed a multiple factorial analysis (MFA) on the 141 defined variables. The goal of MFA is to synthesise the initial information, to the largest possible extent, through a minimum number of factors. We chose to use MFA because it made it possible to simultaneously take into account qualitative and quantitative variables, structured in predetermined groups (our five dimensions). The number of selected factors is the number of factors needed to explain at least 50% of the total variance. Factors are therefore sequentially selected, according to the part of variance they explain. As far as we are concerned, we selected six factors. Using MFA thus solved our two problems: first, it gave the same importance to each of the five predetermined dimensions; secondly, it enabled us to describe each SE through quantitative indicators only (the SE coordinates on each factor).

As a last step, through a hierarchical cluster analysis based on Ward's aggregation method,[11] we classified SEs into different groups that started with each SE being considered as a separate cluster. This means that there were, in this first step, as many groups as there were SEs; the analysis then aggregated the most similar clusters sequentially, thereby reducing, at each step, the number of clusters, until only one group was left.

3. Findings

Our data allowed us to perform a multiple factorial analysis, followed by a cluster analysis, both at the global level, with all 721 observations

(Defourny *et al.* 2019), and, for the purpose of this book, at the level of Latin America, with 162 observations (table 11.1).

At the worldwide level, three of our four theoretical SE models were strongly supported by the empirical analysis: the entrepreneurial non-profit model, the social-cooperative model and the social-business model (Defourny *et al.* 2019). These three models clearly emerged from the examination of the seven clusters resulting from the hierarchical cluster analysis that was carried out on the basis of the full ICSEM sample. Also worth noting is the fact that these three models were found in 39 out of the 43 countries analysed at the global level.

Four clusters are converging towards an entrepreneurial non-profit SE model: two of them gather work-integration social enterprises (WISEs), whereas the other two clusters cover a wider spectrum of social missions. The social-cooperative model[12] embraces two clusters: in the first one, organisations produce a wide diversity of goods and services, which are meant to serve a variety of social objectives; the second cooperative cluster mainly gathers SEs in the field of microfinance. The social-business model is clearly identified through a cluster which gathers small and medium-sized businesses that combine a very strong business orientation and a social mission.

The same statistical treatment was performed for the Latin American sample, thereby allowing to identify clusters and then SE models in this region and to compare them to those described at the worldwide level. On the basis of our Latin American sample, we first identified seven clusters; adding a supplementary cluster did not lead to a significant decrease in intra-cluster variances.[13] Three clusters mainly gathered non-profit organisations; three clusters were dominated by cooperatives; and one cluster was composed mainly by commercial companies. A closer analysis of the features characterising the different clusters within a dominant legal type led us to merge some clusters, when the distinctive traits were not sufficiently important to support an SE model as such. We thus finally decided to keep four clusters: two cooperative-type clusters, an NPO-type cluster and a commercial-type cluster.

3.1. Two Clusters Indicating the Existence of a Cooperative-Type SE Model

At the level of Latin America, as just said, four clusters were identified. A first major result is that the cooperative is the dominant legal form in two clusters (clusters 2 and 3), which gather 71 and 13 organisations respectively (see table 11.2). And whereas, at the worldwide level, the cooperative-type clusters gather 24% of organisations in the whole sample, this share reaches 61% when considering only Latin American countries.[14] The cooperative-type clusters thus clearly dominate the Latin American SE landscape. This is a strong feature, which invites us to look at these two clusters as clearly signalling the existence of a "cooperative-type" SE model.

All the organisations in cluster 3 provide financial and insurance services, mainly under the legal form of cooperative or mutual society, the latter being very close to the cooperative form. This is why we label this cluster "cooperative microfinance SEs", like we did at the international level. Access to financial services has always been a major concern for poor populations and a central issue for an important component of the cooperative movement. Many of these cooperative initiatives were launched well before the "microfinance movement" arrived at the forefront of the public agenda and they are now fully part of it. Results show that these SEs are set up by groups of citizens, third-sector organisations or individuals. In these organisations, the general assembly (GA) holds the ultimate decision-making power. Not surprisingly, users, investors and managers are the stakeholders most often represented in the GAs. These SEs draw almost all their resources from the market (91% from the sales of financial services, especially microfinance, to the users and 6% from investment income). This cluster is very similar to the one emerging at the worldwide level.

Organisations in the other cooperative cluster (cluster 2, by far the largest) produce mainly manufactured goods. Practically all these organisations' productive activities are meant to foster local development: they aim to create jobs, empower poor people, pursue community development, address ecological issues, etc. The social mission and economic activities are clearly interwoven: more than 90% of the organisations making up this cluster perform economic activities that are "mission-centric", according to Alter's influential classification (2007). These organisations rely mainly on market income (which represents, on average, 75% of their total income). The remaining resources are almost equally divided between public grants and membership fees (which are a typical resource for cooperatives).

Most of the SEs belonging to cluster 2 have been launched by workers and citizens, and workers are clearly the dominant group of stakeholders in these SEs' governance: they sit on the board of 70% of these organisations, sometimes alongside some managers but in only a few cases with other stakeholders. These organisations' governance structures display the typical features of cooperatives, with the presence of a GA and a board. Owners do not perceive themselves as shareholders but as members whose main interest most often lies in the creation and sustainability of their jobs. The GA holds the ultimate decision-making power in 83% of organisations.

Regarding the allocation of profits in this cluster, most of them are reinvested in the SE and, when they are distributed, it is among the members (who are, most of the time, the SE's workers). Profits are sometimes equally divided between the members; in other cases, they are returned

Table 11.2 Main features of Latin American SE clusters

SE models	Social-business (SB) model	Social-cooperative (SC) model	Cooperative microfinance SE (3)	Entrepreneurial non-profit (ENP) model
Dominant type in the cluster (cluster no.)	Small and medium-sized SB (1)	Worker-cooperative SE (2)	Cooperative microfinance SE (3)	Entrepreneurial non-profit (4)
No. of observations (share of the sample)*	31 (20%)	71 (53%)	13 (8%)	44 (19%)
Legal form	Mainly sole proprietorship/Ltd companies (51%) Some NPOs (13%)	Mainly cooperatives (63%) Some NPOs (18%)	Mainly cooperatives (69%) Mutuals (8%)	Mainly NPOs (90%)
Goods and services provided	Various	Mainly manufactured goods	Financial and insurance services (100%)	Professional, scientific and technical activities (30%) Education (28%) Health and social-work activities (16%)
Social mission	Various social missions	Various social missions linked to community development	Access to financial services	Various social missions linked to community development
Mission-centric, mission-related or mission-unrelated economic activity	Mission-centric (68%) or mission-related (32%)	Mission-centric (92%)	Mission-centric (67%) or mission-related (54%)	Mission-centric (77%)

Economic models	Dominant market resources			
				Hybrid
Prices applied for the main economic activity and % of SEs applying them	Market: (81%), Investment income: (4%), Subsidies: (5%)	Market: (76%), Subsidies: (11%), Membership fees: (10%)	Market: (91%), Investment income: (6%)	Market: (32%), Subsidies: (16%), Philanthropy: (40%), Membership fees: (7%)
	Market price (42%)	Market price (66%)	Market price (39%) or below (39%)	Free of charge (57%), Market price (16%), Below (20%)
Governance model	Independent or capitalist	Democratic		
Origin	One person (42%), a group of inhabitants/citizens (32%)	Mainly workers (49%), a group of inhabitants/citizens (34%)	Citizens (31%), TSOs (31%), individuals (31%)	Mainly citizens (48%), TSOs (14%), one person (27%)
Ultimate decision-making power	One person (39%) or a board composed mainly by managers, workers or investors	GA/board (composed mainly by workers)	GA/board (composed mainly by users, investors, managers)	GA/board (composed by either workers, volunteers, managers or by a mix of these types)
Rules limiting profit distribution	No (81%)	Yes (59%)	Yes (69%)	Yes (64%)
Actual practice regarding profit distribution	Reinvestment (87%)	Reinvestment (63%), distributed to owners (26%) or workers (30%)	Reinvestment (69%)	Reinvestment (69%)
If the SE terminates, net assets go to . . .	Undetermined (45%)	Members (45%)	Members (44%), Shareholders (31%)	Another SE or NPO (55%)
Paid employees (median)	5	15	69	9
Volunteers (median)	0	0	0	1

Note:
* The total of observations is 159 as 3 Peruvian SEs appear as a-outliers in a separate cluster which was not kept for the final analysis

to the members through rebates proportionate to their transactions with the SE (and not according to their number of shares). One quarter of enterprises do not have predetermined rules about the distribution of net assets in case the activity is terminated, but when such rules exist, they impose that the net assets be shared among the members. The dominant legal form in this cluster is the cooperative (63% of organisations), but 18% operate under the legal form of NPO, which is not surprising: since these SEs do not distribute any profit and are democratically managed, the non-profit legal form also appears as an adequate legal vehicle.

To what extent is it possible to consider the organisations belonging to this cluster as different from conventional cooperatives, in a way which might justify their positioning closer to what we have labelled as the "social-cooperative" model in the above triangle (figure 11.1)? These organisations are clearly mutual-interest organisations, as workers are the dominant category and the beneficiary category at the same time. The pursued mutual interest here refers to the jobs provided to members under their own control. But the workers, who appear to be the main type of stakeholders, are generally poor people, living at the margins of the society,[15] and they are trying to create their own jobs. Therefore, members' mutual interest includes a true social mission from at least three points of view: first, providing workers with a job, and making it stable through these workers' control; secondly, improving members' income and living conditions as well as those of their families; thirdly, in many of these worker-managed initiatives, pursuing a broader goal of empowerment of the poor and economic democracy in the workplace. These worker-cooperative-type organisations have been identified by ICSEM local researchers in their respective countries as "social enterprises".[16]

Coherently, when comparing the worldwide cooperative cluster with this Latin American worker-cooperative cluster, we observe that, in the latter, workers are more present, while other types of stakeholders are less present. These Latin American organisations are also smaller: the median size of the paid workforce is 15 workers, compared to 128 at the world level. Most of these Latin American cooperatives are single-stakeholder social enterprises. By contrast, social cooperatives at the worldwide level which also integrate disadvantaged workers into the labour market more frequently bring together different types of stakeholders in their governing bodies. Indeed, a stronger emphasis on general interest among social cooperatives than in traditional cooperatives could lead to governance structures involving other stakeholders than members looking for their mutual interest. In the case of Latin America, these cooperatives are managed by persons excluded from the labour market and motivated by a dynamic of mutual aid, based on self-help principles, with a view to generating income and improving their own living conditions. This is why these SEs are often single-stakeholder social enterprises and may be qualified as "worker-cooperative-type SEs". However, most of these SEs belong to networks which gather a diversity of actors (social enterprises, NGOs supporting these SEs and sometimes members of public bodies). A multiple-stakeholder nature is therefore observed at the level of second-tier organisations. In turn, these networks are embedded in strong social movements which, as explained in the different chapters, are often shaped by social and political objectives and driven by a quest for an alternative to capitalism.

This analysis leads us to conclude that cooperative values are the crucible from which an important share of Latin American SEs emerge. These cooperative-type models (worker cooperatives and microfinance cooperatives) are strongly driven by community-development goals embedded in broader societal values. In the next section, and with a view to pursuing our goal of documenting the diversity of SE models, we will analyse some of the above features to highlight convergences and divergences between a "cooperative-type" SE model and a "social-business" model.

3.2. One Cluster Indicating the Existence of a Social-Business Model

Comparing the main features of cluster 1 to those of the "worker-cooperative type" (cluster 2), two quite different SE profiles seem to appear.

While "worker-cooperative-type" SEs are set up by a group of citizens or workers, social businesses are more often initiated by one person only (in 42% of cases, while it is only the case for one single SE in cluster 2). However, groups of citizens can also be associated to the launch of the SE (this is the case in 32% of social businesses). These enterprises often adopt the legal form of a limited company or sole proprietorship (51%); in some cases, they register as an NPO (13%).

In 45% of these organisations, there is no GA and no board, and the ultimate decision-making power rests with the owner(s) in 39% of organisations. In cases where these three conditions are met, the ownership and management type can be qualified as "independent". When there is a board, it is composed either of managers, investors or workers, or it includes a mix of these stakeholders. When managers and investors are the dominant stakeholders, the governance might be described as "capital-interest-oriented". This of course contrasts with the "worker-cooperative-type" cluster, whose organisations display democratic governance structures, with a board and a GA composed of their members, most often their workers. Regarding rules and provisions related to profit distribution, it is striking to note that, in 81% of organisations in cluster 1, there is no rule limiting profit distribution. This is not to say, however, that all or most of the profits are usually distributed to owners: the most common practice (which is observed in 87% of organisations in this cluster) is to reinvest at least part of the profits in the social enterprise.

As far as activities and mission are concerned, the economic activity in cluster 1 is more often "mission-related" (32% of organisations) than that of cooperative-type SEs (where a mission-related activity is an exception), which means that they deliver, more often than organisations in the worker-cooperative-type cluster, goods or services to a wider population than the group targeted by the social mission. Another important feature of this cluster is that the median size of the paid workforce is five workers—the lowest figure among the four clusters. This feature is consistent with the already observed key role of an individual entrepreneur as the founder, main owner and dominant decision-maker. These SEs draw the bulk of their resources from the market (81%, and even 85% if income from investment is included).

On the basis of these various features, this cluster indicates the existence of a "social-business" model, generating blended value.[17] This cluster is also very similar to the corresponding cluster emerging at the worldwide level, with a few variations: in the Latin American landscape, beside commercial companies, we also find NPOs (almost absent in the corresponding cluster at the international level), and organisations are even smaller here than in the corresponding world-level cluster.

As this combination of economic and social goals is implemented within less regulated frameworks than those defined by governance rules and structures in "cooperative-type" SEs, the balance between these potentially conflicting goals and its evolution over time raise the question of the social mission's sustainability. For instance, 45% of these SEs have no predetermined rule about the distribution of net assets in case the activity is terminated. In such context, it seems critical to observe enterprises' actual practices more in depth: To what extent do social and/or environmental dimensions actually dominate the profit motive? Are they just mere instruments to better serve the financial interests of the owner(s)? More generally, under which conditions can a social-value-generating economic activity be considered as an expression of social entrepreneurship? Some of these businesses in Latin America adopted the private certification of "B Corporation" (or "B Corps") for environmental and social performance in for-profit firms. This certification does not impose any asset lock nor any cap on the rates of return on investment. It is interesting to contrast this fact with several new legal forms for social enterprise that have been implemented in Europe and reduce the rights of members/shareholders by limiting the distribution of profits in one way or another (Fici 2015). In some Latin America countries (Argentina, Chile, Colombia, Peru), bills are being drafted with the purpose of establishing new legal frameworks for these for-profit organisations that integrate the generation of social and/or environmental benefits in their purpose, but without including any kind of rule regarding profit distribution.

3.3. One Cluster Converging Towards an Entrepreneurial Non-Profit SE Model

The dominant legal form in the last cluster (cluster 4) is the non-profit organisation (90% of organisations in the cluster). These organisations have been launched, in most cases, by a group of citizens, sometimes in partnership with another third-sector organisation. Either the board or the GA holds the ultimate decision-making power, and this body is composed by volunteers, workers and managers. Services provided by organisations in this cluster are mainly "mission-centric". These organisations are small (the median size of the paid workforce is nine workers) and they are active in the fields of professional services, education and health and social-work activities, which are at the core of their social mission. They cover a wide spectrum of social missions.

The organisations belonging to this cluster display a much wider diversity of resources than what is found in the two cooperative-type and the social-business clusters, with only 32% of income coming from the market. The provision of at least some services free of charge or at a price not covering most production costs is a widespread practice among these organisations. In such cases, the organisation also receives donations (40% on the average) and public subsidies or grants (16%) when public authorities consider that the production contributes significantly to the public good.

Such resource mix could be seen as somehow surprising since a usual—although superficial—approach to social enterprise sees it as "a market solution to a social problem". Moreover, when it comes to identifying operating social enterprises at the field level, for some observers, as already mentioned, the proportion of earned income (and more precisely the requirement that at least 50% of resources come from market sales) constitutes the main indicator. For many other scholars, however, among which those belonging to the EMES school of thought (Defourny and Nyssens 2010), the entrepreneurial dimension of social enterprise lies, at least partly, in the fact that the initiative bears a significant level of economic risk, but not necessarily a market risk. This means that the social enterprise's financial viability often constitutes a continuous challenge, and that it depends on the efforts of the members to secure adequate resources to support the enterprise's social mission. This does not involve any requirement that such financial sustainability should be mainly based on market income. In this broader perspective, the resource mix which can best support the social mission is likely to have a hybrid character, as it may combine trading activities with public subsidies and voluntary resources (donations, volunteering . . .).

From an extensive review of literature, Maier *et al.* (2016) identify several dynamics which can characterise "NPOs becoming business-like". Not only can NPOs adopt business-like goals (such as commercialisation or/and conversion from an NPO to a for-profit legal form); they can also adopt business-like core and support processes (entrepreneurial orientation, professionalisation, business-like philanthropy . . .) or develop business-like rhetoric. It is thus not surprising that many NPOs have been identified as social enterprises by local researchers, even though they have far less than 50% of earned income. This cluster may therefore be seen as indicating the existence of a broad "entrepreneurial non-profit" SE model.

At the worldwide level, two major subgroups have been identified within the "entrepreneurial non-profit" SE model: one strongly focusing on work integration and another displaying a diversity of other social missions. The first one is not observed in the Latin American sample. In fact, Latin American organisations that are mainly driven by a mission of employment generation are located in the "worker-cooperative-type" cluster (which, incidentally, also includes NPOs); this tends to indicate that the work-integration movement appears to be mostly driven by the excluded workers themselves in this region. To put it another way, in Latin America, the excluded workers are usually involved in the governance of work-integration SEs, which makes these SEs closer to the cooperative DNA than to the non-profit one. It is also interesting to highlight that public subsidies are lower, on average, in the Latin American non-profit cluster (where they represent around 15% of the organisations' resources) than in entrepreneurial NPOs at the world level (where this figure is around 25%). On the contrary, philanthropic resources are much more important in the non-profit Latin American cluster than in its world-level counterpart. These two differences can probably, at least to some extent, be accounted for by the fact that part of the philanthropic resources of Latin American non-profit SEs are coming from grants allocated through international cooperation channels, which may include both donations and some public resources (not counted in the above 15%).[18]

Conclusion

The objective of this chapter was to test, in the Latin American context, the international typology of SE models that we had put forward (see figure 11.1), and to compare the results for this region with those obtained at the worldwide level (Defourny *et al.* 2019).

Our main finding is that three of our four models are strongly supported by the empirical analysis, as it was also the case at the worldwide level: the existence of a cooperative-type SE model, a social-business model and an entrepreneurial non-profit model is fully confirmed at the Latin American level, as these models clearly emerge from the examination of four clusters resulting from a hierarchical cluster analysis. So, although SEs are influenced by institutional factors at the macro level (which may contribute to shaping some of their organisational features), these results also show that social enterprises stem from all parts of the economy and can be related to different organisational backgrounds—namely, the non-profit, cooperative and traditional business sectors. The three models rooted in these organisational backgrounds have been observed in five of the seven countries surveyed. Not all three models have been observed in the two remaining countries (Argentina and Bolivia), but this is likely due to the small size of the sample in these countries.[19]

The analysis of collected data also suggests the existence of some specific Latin American features.

First, it is striking that the cooperative type—and especially worker cooperatives—constitutes the dominant form of SE in Latin America. Workers are the core of these rather small organisations; their goal is to create their own job and to improve their living conditions. As analysed in various chapters of this book, some Latin American cooperatives have experienced strong isomorphic pressures, which led them, in some cases, to become more similar to capital-interest-driven organisations. As a result hereof, the cooperative legacy sometimes conveys an ambiguous image (see also chapter 9 in this book). However, the importance of this cluster leads us to acknowledge the strong worker-cooperative DNA that characterises the SE field in Latin America. In some way, these worker cooperatives reconnect with the initial roots and values of the cooperative movement.

Secondly, Latin American SEs—be they cooperatives, non-profit organisations or social businesses—are much smaller than their world-level counterparts. This finding echoes the results found by the Latin American SE research network SEKN, which show that, most of the time, social enterprises take the form of "SMEs and small civil society organisations which are agile and open to the internalisation of innovations needed to conduct an inclusive business, particularly in regard to collaborative work" (Comini *et al.* 2012: 390).

Thirdly, the existence of the public or semi-public SE model put forward in our theoretical typology does not appear to be confirmed at the level of Latin America. At the international level, the sample also includes public or semi-public SEs, even though their existence does not appear to be statistically confirmed by the identification of a distinct cluster as such. In fact, at the global level, some SEs involve a governmental agency among their founding members, especially in the field of WISEs. A possible interpretation is that, although they do actively support social enterprises, most public authorities prefer to act as partners—rather than as the main entrepreneur—in the creation and management of WISEs. At the Latin American level, however, we do not observe such an involvement of public authorities in the governance of SEs. It also appears that the resource mix of Latin American SEs includes much fewer public resources than the resource mix of their counterparts at worldwide level.

These features reflect the weakness of state support to the SE field—and, more generally, to the common good—in Latin America.

In the absence of a widely accepted and common definition of social enterprise, we argue that our strategy enabled us to take into account and provide legitimacy to locally embedded approaches, thus resulting in an analysis encompassing a huge diversity of SE. Our data underline the need to go beyond a conception that would view social enterprises simply as "intermediate organisations", if we are to better grasp the diversity of SE landscapes. The identification of major SE models helps to delineate the field on common grounds in Latin America and at the international level. Of course, such an analysis needs to be complemented with qualitative work, so as to gain a deeper understanding of the various models as well as their specificities in each national context. Such qualitative analysis can be found in the national chapters of this book.

To conclude, we would like to adopt a broad societal perspective. We tend to consider as good news the fact that social enterprises actually do stem from all parts of the economy. Societies are facing so many and so complex challenges at all levels, from the local to the global level, that we see the diversity of SE models and their internal variety as a sign of a broadly shared willingness to develop appropriate—even though they are still sometimes embryonic—responses to these challenges, on the basis of innovative economic/business models driven by a social mission. In spite of their weaknesses, social enterprises may be seen as advocates for and vehicles of the general interest across the whole economy. Of course, we cannot avoid the debate about privatisation, deregulation and globalised market competition—all factors that may hinder efforts in the search for the common good. We just note that social enterprises reveal or confirm an overall trend towards new ways of sharing the responsibility for the common good in today's economies and societies.

Notes

1 This network brings together representatives from leading schools of business administration in Latin America (see www.sekn.org/en/publication-en/).
2 See for example case studies carried out by the SEKN network.
3 For instance, Alter (2007) also focuses on the place and role of market logics to put forward a typology based on mission orientation, the nature of target markets and the degree of integration of business activities in social programmes.
4 For example, through the improvement of the service delivered. In an NPO, the beneficiary category is formed by the group of stakeholders at the heart of the social mission.
5 Investors are those who hold shares and are mainly or exclusively interested in the overall return on this capital ownership. Extending such a rationale, an individual owner may also be seen as an investor holding both types of rights.
6 In such case, members consider the production activity as the very *raison d'être* of the organisation. This is also true for members of cooperatives:

although they generally buy one or some capital shares to become members, they are not primarily interested in the return on such capital (which is incidentally quite limited in several ways).

7 In such a perspective, all public (state) organisations and institutions are also typically public-benefit entities, but they form the public sector, not the third sector, as the dominant category is formed by public bodies and not by private entities.

8 The social cooperative concept made its first appearance in the very early 1990s in Europe to qualify new cooperative-like initiatives that were emerging to respond to unmet social needs through the development of economic activities. In some Latin American countries, the "social cooperative" notion has a much narrower meaning, as it designates WISEs targeting mentally disabled persons.

9 In a few countries, like in Bolivia, this number was smaller for various reasons; in particular, it was difficult to collect quantitative data on some organisations located in a "grey zone" between informality and formality.

10 The first version of the questionnaire was submitted to all research partners, discussed, tested and revised in an interactive process before finally reaching a level of quality acknowledged by all involved partners. It was then translated into local languages.

11 The basic algorithm is very simple. First, using Ward's method and applying squared Euclidean Distance, distances are calculated between all initial clusters. Secondly, the two most similar clusters are merged and distances are recalculated. The criterion for merging is that it should produce the smallest possible increase in the sum of intra-cluster variance. Then the second step is repeated until all units are grouped in one cluster.

12 In spite of the narrow meaning of the "social cooperative" notion in Latin America (see note 8), we continue to use it here in its broader meaning, so as to have a coherent conceptual basis to compare SE models in this region and at the world level.

13 The optimal number of clusters (n) corresponds to the number of clusters for which the sum of intra-cluster variances does not decrease significantly when $n + 1$ clusters are considered.

14 From a methodological point of view, an important remark should be underlined: when comparing clusters that emerge from the Latin America sample and those identified on the basis of the global sample, some results may look quite similar, but they should not hide significant differences. For instance, two cooperative-type clusters come out of both the worldwide and the Latin American samples. However, when comparing the "weight" of Latin American cooperative-type SEs at the regional level and at the worldwide level, different pictures appear. At the worldwide level, Latin American SEs belonging to the cooperative-type clusters only represent 37% of Latin American SEs, while the same kind of analysis performed on the sole Latin American sample shows that the cooperative-type clusters cover 61% of the sample. In other words, considering data at the level of Latin America leads to highlight, even more strongly, the importance of cooperative-type SEs in the region. This results from the very nature of statistical methods computing "distances" between observations among and within clusters at all stages of aggregation. Such aggregation process of course generates clusters with different "contents" when carried out on two different samples, with 721 and 162 observations respectively.

15 This may also be underlined for cooperative-type SEs operating in microfinance (cluster 3).

16 A perfect fit between the patterns identified by Gaiger and Wanderley (see chapter 9 in this book) and our models cannot be operated as such, as patterns and models are based on different methodologies. In some countries, like Bolivia, there are only a few quantitative observations, which do not cover all the patterns. However, this cluster displays several characteristics shared by some of the patterns: self-managed class-related organisations, traditional social-economy organisations and, to a lesser extent, ethnic and community-based organisations and organisations based on the popular economy.

17 This cluster appears close to the pattern of "social-purpose organisations oriented by market logic" identified by Gaiger and Wanderley in chapter 9.

18 According to the classification suggested by Gaiger and Wanderley in chapter 9, it can probably be argued that most of these organisations stem from the philanthropic pattern or are "organisations for socio-economic inclusion".

19 Argentina and Bolivia have the smallest number of SEs surveyed (table 11.1). In Bolivia, only four social enterprises were included in the survey, and they were all of the cooperative type.

References

Alter, K. (2007) *Social Enterprise Typology*, Friendswood: Virtue Ventures LLC.

Austin, J. E. & SEKN Team. (2004) *Social Partnering in Latin America*, Cambridge: Harvard University Press.

Austin, J., Stevenson, H. & Wei-Skillern, J. (2006) "Social and commercial entrepreneurship: Same, different, or both?" *Entrepreneurship Theory and Practice*, Vol. 30, No. 1, pp. 1–22.

Berger, G. & Blugerman, L. (2010) "Empresas sociales y negocios inclusivos", in Márquez, P., Reficco, E. & Berger, G. (eds) *Negocios inclusivos: iniciativas de mercado con los pobres de Iberoamérica*, Banco Interamericano de Desarrollo, David Rockefeller Center for Latin American Studies Harvard University, Washington, DC: Editorial Planeta.

Comini, G., Barki, E. & Aguiar, L. (2012) "A three-pronged approach to social business: A Brazilian multi-case analysis", *RevistaADM*, São Paulo [online], Vol. 47, No. 3, pp. 385–397.

Dees, J. G. (1996) *The Social Enterprise Spectrum: Philanthropy to Commerce*, Boston: Harvard Business School, Publishing Division.

Dees, J. G. (1998) *The Meaning of Social Entrepreneurship*, The Social Entrepreneurship Funders Working Group.

Defourny, J. (2014) "From third sector to social enterprise: A European research trajectory", in Defourny, J., Hulgård, L. & Pestoff, V. (eds), *Social Enterprise and the Third Sector*, London: Routledge, pp. 17–41.

Defourny, J. & Borzaga, C. (eds) (2001) *The Emergence of Social Enterprise*, London: Routledge.

Defourny, J. & Nyssens, M. (2010) "Conceptions of social enterprise and social entrepreneurship in Europe and the United States: Convergences and divergences", *Journal of Social Entrepreneurship*, Vol. 1, No. 1, pp. 32–53.

Defourny, J. & Nyssens, M. (2017) "Fundamentals for an international typology of social enterprise models", *Voluntas*, Vol. 24, No. 3.

Defourny, J., Nyssens, M. & Brolis, O. (2019) "Mapping and testing social enterprise models across the world: Evidence from the 'International Comparative

Social Enterprise Models (ICSEM) project'", *ICSEM Working Papers*, Liege: The International Comparative Social Enterprise (ICSEM) Project, No. 50. Available HTTP: www.iap-socent.be/sites/default/files/Typology%20-%20 Defourny%20%26%20Nyssens_0.pdf.

Doherty, B., Haugh, H. & Lyon, F. (2014) "Social enterprises as hybrid organizations: A review and research agenda", *International Journal of Management Reviews*, Vol. 16, No. 4, pp. 417–436.

Fici, A. (2015) "Recognition and legal forms of social enterprise in Europe: A critical analysis from a comparative law perspective", Euricse Working Papers, 82/15.

Gaiger, L. I. (2013) "O Mapeamento Nacional e o Conhecimento da Economia Solidária", *Revista da ABE*, Vol. 12, pp. 7–24.

Gatica Montero, S. (2017) "Delineating, differentiating and understanding social enterprises and their two-way relationship with public policies: The Chilean case over the period 2006–2013", doctoral thesis, London: University College.

Gui, B. (1991) "The economic rationale for the third sector", *Annals of Public and Cooperative Economics*, Vol. 62, No. 4, pp. 551–572.

Hansmann, H. (1996) *The Ownership of Enterprise*, Cambridge: Harvard University Press.

Kerlin, J. A. (2006) "Social enterprise in the United States and Europe: Understanding and learning from the differences", *Voluntas: International Journal of Voluntary and Nonprofit Organizations*, Vol. 17, No. 3, pp. 247–263.

Kerlin, J. A. (2013) "Defining social enterprise across different contexts: A conceptual framework based on institutional factors", *Nonprofit and Voluntary Sector Quarterly*, Vol. 12, No. 1, pp. 84–108.

Kerlin, J. A. (ed.) (2015) "Kerlin's macro-institutional framework", *Social Enterprise Journal*, Special issue, Vol. 11, No. 2.

Kerlin, J. A. (ed.) (2017) *Shaping Social Enterprise: Understanding Institutional Context and Influence*, London: Emerald Publishing Group.

Maier, F., Meyer, M. & Steinbereithner, M. (2016) "Nonprofit organizations becoming business-like: A systematic review", *Nonprofit and Voluntary Sector Quarterly*, Vol. 45, No. 1, pp. 64–86.

Márquez, P., Reficco, E. & Berger, G. (2010) *Socially Inclusive Business, Engaging the Poor Through Market Initiatives in Iberoamerica*, Cambridge and London: Harvard University Press.

Mulgan, G. (2007) *Social Innovation: What It Is, Why It Matters and How It Can Be Accelerated*, London: Young Foundation.

Nicholls, A. (ed.) (2006) *Social Entrepreneurship: New Models of Sustainable Change*, Oxford: Oxford University Press.

Peattie, K. & Morley, A. (2008) *Social Enterprises: Diversity and Dynamics, Contexts and Contributions*, London: Social Enterprise Coalition.

Seanor, P. & Meaton, J. (2007) "Making sense of social enterprise", *Social Enterprise Journal*, Vol. 3, No. 1, pp. 90–100.

Skloot, E. (1983) "Should not-for-profits go into business?" *Harvard Business Review*, Vol. 61, pp. 20–26.

Spear, R., Cornforth, C. & Aiken, M. (2009) "The governance challenges of social enterprises: Evidence from a UK empirical study", *Annals of Public and Cooperative Economics*, Vol. 80, No. 2, pp. 247–273.

Young, D. R. (1983) *If Not for Profit, for What?* Lexington: Lexington Books.

Young, D. R. & Lecy, J. (2014) "Defining the universe of social enterprise: Competing metaphors", *Voluntas*, Vol. 25, No. 5, pp. 1307–1332.

Young, D. R., Searing, E. A. M. & Brewer, C. V. (eds) (2016) *The Social Enterprise Zoo*, Cheltenham: Edward Elgar Publishing.

Zellweger, T. M., Nason, R. S., Nordqvist, M. & Brush, C. G. (2013) "Why do family firms strive for nonfinancial goals? An organizational identity perspective", *Entrepreneurship Theory and Practice*, Vol. 37, No. 2, pp. 229–248.

Index

Printed in the United States
by Baker & Taylor Publisher Services